TWO DEAD WHITE MEN

JAMES CULLINGHAM

Seneca PRESS

TWO DEAD WHITE MEN

DUNCAN CAMPBELL SCOTT

JACQUES SOUSTELLE

AND THE FAILURE OF INDIGENOUS POLICY

JAMES CULLINGHAM

Foreword by **Winona Wheeler**

Afterword by **John S. Milloy**

Two Dead White Men: Duncan Campbell Scott, Jacques Soustelle and the Failure of Indigenous Policy is published by Seneca Press, which supports the distribution of scholarly research from within the Seneca community.

Seneca College, 70 The Pond Road, Toronto, ON M3J 3M6
www.senecacollege.ca

ISBN 978-1-7779410-0-0
Cataloguing available from Library and Archives Canada
Visual content copyright © 2021 by the photographers
Text copyright © 2021 by the author

CONTENTS

Dedication

For my mother,
Mary Ann Cullingham-Kemble, née Bernardo.
And her sisters Carmine and Elsi.

Long may they run!

Indigenous women from Flying Post First Nation, at the 1905 Treaty 9 signing ceremony at Brunswick House, near present day Chapleau, Ontario.

I will refer to present day Indigenous people in Canada as such.

The term "Indian" will be used when required for historical and political accuracy because the place currently known as Canada has an "Indian Act," and Duncan Campbell Scott worked for the "Indian Department."

The term "First Nations" will refer to Indigenous communities recognized under the Indian Act, belonging to the Assembly of First Nations and/or any group that generally self-identities as such.

The term "Métis" with an accent will refer to the Red River people led by Louis Riel and their descendants who self-identify in that manner.

"Metis" without an accent will refer to people of Indigenous and European or other origins who self-identify as such.

"Inuit" will be used rather than "Eskimo" although that term is still used by some Indigenous peoples, particularly in Alaska.

"Aboriginal" and "aboriginal" will be used in a limited way as a general descriptor and particularly in regard to the Constitution Act of Canada 1982, which refers to "aboriginal" peoples and rights.

Words such as "half breed," "native," or "savage" will be used only in historical context and usually with "scare" quotation marks.

I will refer to specific peoples and Indigenous place names whenever possible. I write from Nogojiwanong "place at the foot of the rapids" (Peterborough, Ont.) near the banks of Odonabe "river that bubbles like a beating heart" (Otanabee River) in Michi Saagig territory.

Foreword

Dr. Winona Wheeler
Associate professor, Indigenous Studies, University of Saskatchewan

SITTING ON MY FRONT PORCH wallowing in the gentle breeze of the last days of summer I recall the little bit of time I spent at Osnaburgh House during the filming of *Duncan Campbell Scott: The Poet and the Indians*. This was when I first met James Cullingham. I was a very junior historian in Indigenous Studies, recently returned from my PhD studies at University of California, Berkeley. He flew me up north and conducted the interview at the old Hudson's Bay Company site located among the Mishkeegogamang Anishinaabeg peoples. Listening to the songs of the Snow and Canada geese gathering to journey south, I recall the beautiful landscape, the haunting calls of the loons, and I recall being enthralled to be at this place I had read about. This was more than an HBC post, it was an early stop of the 1905 Treaty Commission led by the notorious Duncan Campbell Scott himself. As a student in Indigenous Studies and History, and the daughter and granddaughter of Indian Residential School survivors, I was familiar with his Indian policies and the impact they had on my family and people. To be honest, I was not much of a poetry buff at the time, but when James told me of his project, I was intrigued to learn more of this side of Scott in the hopes of better understanding him and his motives.

Duncan Campbell Scott: The Poet and the Indians (1995) thoughtfully and poetically probes the contradictory yet complexly woven worlds of a Canadian literary icon who oversaw a series of seemingly heartless and definitely cruel policies against First Nations people during his term as the head of the federal Indian Department. The intent of his policies was to eradicate Indigenous ways of life and assimilate First Nations people into Canadian society. The fact that *Duncan Campbell Scott* the documentary is still being used in classrooms today is a testament to its continued relevance and value.

James Cullingham is an award winning documentary filmmaker, a historian, a journalist, and a scholar. In 1989 he formed Tamarack Productions and produced the earliest national documentary series on Indigenous issues, in 1991. *As The Rivers Flow* is a five part television series that focuses on Indigenous issues in historical and modern times. Since then he has produced more film documentaries about social justice, history and popular culture, in Canada, the USA, Europe, Africa, the Middle East and Pakistan, that have been screened around the world. His latest documentary, *The Cost of Freedom–Refugee Journalists in Canada* (2021), probes the human rights threat to journalists through the stories of three refugees currently living in Toronto. James has published in major newspapers and academic journals, has had a distinguished career in journalism as a producer, an executive producer with the Canadian Broadcasting Corporation, and a Broadcast-Journalism professor and program coordinator at Seneca College in Toronto. He has taught and lectured at a number of Canadian universities and most recently holds positions as an adjunct graduate faculty member in the Canadian Studies and Indigenous Studies graduate program and Canadian Studies PhD graduate program at Trent University in Nogojiwanong–Peterborough, Ontario and a professor in the School of English and Liberal Studies at Seneca College.

Two Dead White Men: Duncan Campbell Scott, Jacques Soustelle, and the Failure of Indigenous Policy, James Cullinghams' first major book publication, is based on his 2014 PhD dissertation in Canadian and

Latin American History (York University), titled "Scars of Empire–A Juxtaposition of Duncan Campbell Scott and Jacques Soustelle." The original manuscript underwent major revisions, resulting in a beautifully presented book made more accessible to a wider-than-academic audience. He begins with a positionality Prelude that provides context, significant influences and experiences that brought him to this work. This is not a dry lacklustre academic prose. Each chapter also includes autobiographical side stories and anecdotal Interludes that give us even more insights on the author and the influences that shaped him personally and professionally.

Indigenous Studies is interdisciplinary and comparative, and so I found the comparison/contrast between the lives, policies, actions, and impacts of Scott and Soustelle instructive and thought provoking. I knew nothing of Jacques Soustelle, but after reading this manuscript, I have a better understanding of why James was fascinated by him. Both Scott and Soustelle received accolades as the best and brightest in their respective times, both also engineered catastrophic Indigenous policies, the long term impacts of which are still felt in communities today. James' overarching question – how could they and their societies they represent, get it so wrong? – does not have an easy answer. Products of their time, yes. But also strong willed men who refused to accept insights or guidance that challenged their views, but which would have alleviated much unnecessary suffering for those they targeted.

Two Dead White Men increases our wider understanding of how colonialism is operationalized, the thinking behind and implementation of colonial policies, and their impacts, through the life histories and times of these two contradictory and complex historical figures. We have come a long way since these times for sure. And there has been a shift in thinking 'from aggressive social engineering aimed at assimilation to apologies and compensation' (p.22). But we can never forgot how we came to be in this position we are in today as we try to rebuild our communities and work towards conciliation.

Winona Wheeler is a member of the Fisher River Cree Nation in Treaty 5 Territory (Manitoba) and her family comes from George Gordon First Nation in Treaty 4 Territory (Saskatchewan). A lifelong student of Indigenous knowledge and history, Winona has been teaching and publishing in Indigenous Studies since 1988. Her areas of research are Indigenous oral histories, Indigenous local histories, land claims and treaty rights, and settler colonialism. She is a mother and grandmother, and lives on a little ranch in the traditional lands of the Willow Cree in Treaty 6 Territory with her horses, dogs, cat, and rabbits.

I HAVE BEEN A TRAVELLER from a very young age. Curiosity, a love of culture and language, and history combined with a certain restlessness have propelled me forward and through this world. As a journalist, a filmmaker, a teacher and a scholar, I realize I have been an explorer of the physical and intellectual world all of my life. During that journey, two men, significant historical figures, Duncan Campbell Scott and more recently Jacques Soustelle have captured my mind and stuck with me in a near incessant manner. I have tried to figure out who they were and why they did...what they did. This a story told by one living white man about two dead white men.

Chaillolet, France *1978*

Early autumn in *les hautes alpes* outside Gap in the valley leading to le Vieux Chaillol, a nearby alpine peak. We've ascended close to 1,500 metres above the valley floor. We are at the tree line. A few *mélèzes* [tamaracks], their needles golden in the autumn light, are the only remaining vegetation. Bernard silently puts his hand on my shoulder. Then he whispers, "*Eh le James, regarde bien là bas,*" pointing to a mountainside perhaps 500 metres in the distance. "*Il bouge,*" says Bernard, "*regarde ça bien.*" Indeed, a marmot is clambering across the stones on the hillside opposite. What would have been invisible to an unaccustomed eye is readily apparent to Bernard, an alpine cheese maker, hunter and shepherd.

The same day as we perch for lunch at a tiny flat spot on an otherwise steep incline, Bernard looks down at the valley below, "*Je n'ai quitté cette vallée qu'une fois dans ma vie.*" "*Quand ça?*" I ask. "*Quand j'ai fait ma service militaire en Algérie,*" responds Bernard.

En route to the Algerian Sahara *April 1979*

I hitchhike from Alger, headed through the mountains of Kabylie towards the plateau of central Algeria and the Sahara desert to the south. As the road winds through oak forests that once provided the French wine industry with corkage, a middle-aged man behind the wheel of a Peugeot 404 tells me the revolution promised much, but things are now worse than under the French occupiers. He claims that Algeria has never seen political corruption like the present.

Winisk, Ontario *1980*

Final day of a canoe trip from Webiquie, an Ojibway village on Lake Winisk north of Pickle Lake, Ontario, to the village of Winisk on the flood plain of the Winisk River where it meets Hudson's Bay. I've led a group of eight along the often surging, sometimes placid, always magnificent course of the Winisk for 21 days.[1]

We spent a night in the village, camped outside a derelict building which, we're told, once housed teachers from the south. Although offered use of the building by the Winisk band manager, we opt to pitch our tents outside because the house is infested with mould; in addition, although the building features some of the community's only indoor plumbing, the facilities are backed up with human faeces and swarming with flies.

During our evening in the village, I sit at a cook fire just outside the tipi of Daniel and Susan Koostachin. They offer me delicious fresh fried pickerel just pulled from the river, along with mugs of sugary, milky tea.

The next morning, we are preparing to paddle across the river to the old airstrip at the abandoned Pine

Indigenous fisherman Andy, on the Albany River near Achapi Lake, Ontario, 1993.

Tree Line airbase across the river to get our DC-3 flight back to Pickle Lake, closer to the Trans-Canada highway in northwestern Ontario. The now decrepit airbase had once been part of the Canadian-USA aerial security system during the Cold War. Just as I prepare to clamber into the stern of my canoe, Daniel Koostachin comes running, carrying a beautiful *tikinigan*, a Cree cradleboard with flowered cloth, soft felt padding inside and caribou hide lacing, framed by a sturdy, expertly wrought tamarack frame. Daniel tells me, "You told us your girlfriend is pregnant. Susie and I want you to have this to carry your kid around in. You take it – we're not going to have any more kids." That *tikinigan* carried our first child Jessica. Her sister Rachel has used it to carry my grandson, Leo.

Albany River, Ontario *June 1993*

My friend and I have been paddling five days down the Albany, approaching Apachi Lake. The Treaty 9 Commission of Duncan Campbell Scott travelled these waters in 1905. As we come out of a winding set of swifts we see a man standing in a canoe where the river widens. As we approach, it becomes clear he is hauling up a net. He smiles a bit as he struggles. After a few more minutes tugging, the large flat head of a fish with long tentacles on its face emerges. As the 60lb sturgeon flops inside his canoe, the man dispatches it with the butt end of a sawed off paddle. Andy introduces himself. He says there's a lot of food in a sturgeon. Andy and his family, camped nearby, have travelled up river from their spring camp.

*Pre-Columbian Mayan
archaeological site, Toniná, Chiapas,
southern Mexico.*

San Juan de Chamula, Chiapas, México *2008*

I've taken a *colectivo*, a packed, lurching communal mini-bus taxi, from San Cristobal de las Casas in Chiapas to a Tzotzil Mayan community nearby. I'm conducting doctoral research into Jacques Soustelle who was here in the 1930s working on his doctoral thesis. The village had been a flashpoint of conflict during the Zapatista rebellion against the Mexican state in the 1990s. San Juan de Chamula, and a few neighbouring villages, now enjoy increased local autonomy as part of an uneasy truce between Zapatista loyalists and the federal government of Mexico.

It's market day. Not only is the town square packed with locals and peasants from more remote mountain villages selling agricultural products, handicrafts and household goods, the elaborate local church is packed with people, many of whom are chanting and swaying while appearing to be in an altered state. I've purchased a pass from the local municipal hall to enter the church – cameras are forbidden in its interior.

As I leave the church, a few middle-aged men invite me to follow them up a flight of stairs to a balcony in the rectory overlooking a courtyard behind. The stairwell is full of men and women playing musical instruments ranging from guitars to fiddles to various drums, to all the brass instruments in a Mexican marching band. By the time we reach the walkway along the balcony the air is thickly clouded with *copal*, a Mayan form of incense. My companions stop just outside a door leading into a small room off the passageway that leads round the courtyard. We pause, enjoying the music and the scent of smouldering copal. Then they beckon me to follow them into the room. Women and men are huddled together – alternately holding, unwrapping and immersing tiny wooden or clay figures of their saints directly in the smoke from small piles of glowing copal. After each figurine has been held for a minute or two directly in the smoke, each is wrapped in a colourful cloth and taken back down the stairs, across the courtyard into the back door of the church. Those in the room, some of whom are very elderly, are speaking as quietly and fervently in the local Tzotzil Mayan dialect. While some of the figurines appear vaguely Christian to me, there are no priests and all blessings are in Tzotzil Mayan. A few people make the sign of the cross.

When all the *santitos* have been cleansed, blessed and returned to the church, I ask my companions the meaning of what we'd witnessed. They explain that once a year, all the saints are removed from the church, cleansed and then returned. They say they were happy for me to see it because I agreed not to take pictures.

---

1. James Cullingham, "Winisk River: Learning about the Land, History and The Human Spirit"
in *More of Canada's Best Canoe Routes*, Alister Thomas, ed., (Erin, ON: Boston Mills Press, 2003)

Pukaskwa National Park, north shore of Lake Superior, Ontario.

Introduction

INQUIETUDES

IN THE SUMMER OF 1992, I was camped with my family near Horseshoe Bay in Pukakswa National Park on the north shore of Lake Superior. At the suggestion of my friend and colleague, the anthropologist, author and filmmaker, Hugh Brody, I took a collection of Duncan Campbell Scott's poems along. In the evenings when the wind calmed down on that great inland sea, I paddled out to the mouth of the Pic River near the Ojibways of the Pic River First Nation and read. Drifting in the prolonged Lake Superior sunset, I discovered that Scott's poetry was more intriguing and perplexing than I had presumed. I had first encountered Scott as an undergraduate student in what was then the Native Studies Department, now known as the Chanie Wenjack School for Indigenous Studies, at Trent University in Nogojiwanong (Peterborough), Ontario, Canada. Chanie Wenjack was an Anishinaabe child who died trying to walk home from a residential school in northern Ontario.

At that time, Scott was regarded, in the academic and activist circles I kept, strictly as the notorious early 20th century bureaucratic mastermind of Canadian Indian policy. Little thought had been given by me nor my academic and activist peers to Scott's artistic pursuits. Paddling in the same waters Scott had visited on a treaty expedition in 1906, I began to realize that his story was far more complex than I had imagined. How did this accomplished artist come to participate in some of Canada's most egregious assaults on human rights? My wrestling with that question led to my 1995 documentary film *Duncan Campbell Scott: The Poet and the Indians.*[1] With control over its own "Indian" policies, a post-Confederation Canada internalized and hardened British imperial systems.[2] Duncan Campbell Scott was as influential as any single person in honing and implementing those policies in the critical post-Confederation era.

This work is also a product of a lifetime's interest in France, French literature and existentialism, particularly the works of Albert Camus and Jean-Paul Sartre. Professor William J. Irvine of York University introduced me to Jacques Soustelle in 2005 when I began work on a paper in his doctoral history seminar about the conflict among French intellectuals over Algeria. I began focusing on Camus and Sartre. Bill said, "Hey, aren't you the guy who made a film about D.C. Scott? You should look into Jacques Soustelle. You'll find him interesting." That's when my doctoral proposal found its focus. Bill died in spring 2021. I owe him a debt of gratitude for setting me off on a fascinating intellectual journey. May that this work meets his high standards.

In his tumultuous career, Jacques Soustelle, although trained as an ethnologist, was also an active politician. Most infamously, Soustelle was the last French governor general of Algeria. He got that post in 1955 because of his familiarity with Indigenous societies. Such knowledge was considered valuable in France's last-ditch effort to reform its relationships with the majority Indigenous population of Algeria.

Soustelle was haunted and inspired by Mexico, a land of ancient civilizations and the site of the western world's first great 20th century revolution. Soustelle believed he could import to Algeria what he had garnered from a particular aspect of post-revolutionary Mexico as a graduate student in the 1930s. His thinking was shaped by the cultural, economic, political and social program known as *indigenismo*, a sweeping and often contradictory set of policies to incorporate the *indio* [Indian] in Mexican society. Soustelle attempted to apply what he deemed valuable from *indigenismo* to relations between Europeans and Muslims in Algeria to salvage France's imperial project in the Maghreb.[3]

By juxtaposing Duncan Campbell Scott and Jacques Soustelle, I am putting Canada, France and Mexico into transnational investigation. These men's shared focus on Indigenous peoples as expressed in ethnology, administration, journalism, literature and politics provides a unifying thread. Their concerns about the place of Indigenousness in what they perceived as liberal democracy are as relevant today as they were in their time. Through an exploration of Scott and Soustelle, I am concerned with legacies of colonialism, imperialism and liberalism. Canada belongs in an international conversation about the domestic colonization of Indigenous peoples.

As I write in the summer of 2021, Canada is in the throes of self-examination. Since spring, hundreds of unmarked graves near residential schools for Indigenous children have been discovered in British Columbia and Saskatchewan. Some non-Indigenous Canadians appear shocked and surprised by the news. Sadly, they could have and should have known decades ago. The revelations of whistleblower Peter Henderson Bryce, various federal inquiries and leading historians foreshadowed these tragic discoveries for decades.[4] Despite the persistent refrain that "Canadians didn't know," in fact leading scholars had done significant investigative work into the matter for decades. At the time of writing, one of these scholars, John S. Milloy draws attention to the mistreatment of Canada's Indigenous "child hostages" in residential schools.[5] It is appalling that Canadian society largely turned a deaf ear to clarion calls for justice. Indigenous voices were decrying conditions in the schools from the beginning. They were rebuffed. In their domestic colonizing zeal, Canadians and their governments were more concerned with the westward advance of their civilization and economic development than Indigenous lives – even the lives of Indigenous children. Right now in this place called Canada, the legacy of the bureaucrat and poet Duncan Campbell Scott weighs heavily on the national conscience. What was ignored by mainstream Canadians for decades is now considered genocidal.

Scott and Soustelle were both among "the best and brightest" of their generations.[6] Journalist David Halberstam coined that phrase in reference to the respected senior bureaucrats and military officers advising American Presidents John F. Kennedy and Lyndon B. Johnson over the Vietnam War. Scott and Soustelle belonged to elites that widely shared convictions, in Scott's case about Canadian Indian policy, and, in Soustelle's, about France's role in Algeria. How could they and the societies they represented get it so wrong? My mission is to look back at their lives while pondering that question.

Scott's legacy

I engage simultaneously with Duncan Campbell Scott the senior bureaucrat and Scott the literary artist and public intellectual. His role in the emergence of Canadian English language literature and his activities as a bureaucrat in the Indian Department under several governments are not contradictory, but rather, consistent expressions of a widely shared Canadian liberal ideology that prevailed for several decades following Canadian Confederation in 1867. Scott's literary defenders have anguished over what appears to some as a contradiction between his art and his bureaucratic endeavours. Canadian cultural theorist Robert L. McDougall expressed the conundrum:

> The gist of the Indian problem is simple. For the first three decades of this century, whether as an accountant responsible for Indian funds or as Deputy Superintendent, Scott administered federal Indian policy relating to the Canadian Indians. Aspects of that policy, questioned in some quarters even in Scott's day, have proved prime targets for attack in the native-rights atmosphere of the sixties and seventies. Because Scott implemented government policy, apparently without seriously questioning it, he has suffered the Nuremberg taint of guilt through compliance with unjust orders.

Particular charges range from duplicity to genocide. And the reputation of the poetry, wrongly, I think, is sometimes brought down with the reputation of the man.[7]

Filmmakers, journalists and his fellow poets have also grappled with Scott's legacy. In 1976, poet John Flood published a collection to evoke Indigenous voices missing from the various accounts of the Treaty 9 expedition, including that of Scott.[8] In 1994, Indigenous poet Armand Garnet Ruffo addressed Scott directly:

> Who is this black coat and tie?
> Christian severity etched in the lines
> he draws from his mouth. Clearly a noble man
> who believes in work and mission.
> See how he rises from the red velvet chair,
> rises out of the boat with the two Union Jacks
> fluttering like birds of prey
>
> See how he rises from the red velvet chair,
> rises out of the boat with the two Union Jacks
> fluttering like birds of prey
> and makes his way towards our tents.
> This man looks as if he could walk on water
> And for our benefit probably would,
> if he could.[9]

In 21st century Canada, Scott's legacy in the Indian Department is widely recognized as part of one of the darkest chapters of Canadian history. In 2015, the Truth and Reconciliation Commission (TRC) reported its findings on an investigation of Canada's residential schools for Indigenous children. The TRC report and senior members of the judiciary and academic communities proclaimed that Canadian policy amounted to attempted cultural genocide. Scott was directly implicated.[10]

In 2008, the government of Conservative Prime Minister Stephen Harper apologized in parliament for the residential school system that Canadian governments – both Conservative and Liberal – had run with Christian churches for almost a century.[11] Scott had senior administrative responsibility over that system for decades. This shift in governmental thinking from aggressive social engineering aimed at assimilation to apologies and in some cases financial compensation to residential school survivors and their families is one of the greatest reversals in social policy in Canadian history.

That shifting paradigm inspired Montreal editor, journalist and poet Mark Abley's *Conversations With A Dead Man*, an experimental work that imagined conversations with Scott's ghost about poetry and the morality of Canadian Indian policy. My 1995 film was among the topics of conversation.[12]

Twenty-first century Canadians experience persistent reminders of unresolved conundrums of Indigenous rights that nag on the national conscience, historical memory and politics. Duncan Campbell Scott, a man widely regarded for decades as Canada's poet laureate, was a prime advocate and implementer of policies that Canadians have come to dread.

Soustelle's legacy

The political and ethical dimensions surrounding Jacques Soustelle's role in Algeria are central to 20th century French colonial history and in the consideration of the role of intellectuals in the debate concerning French rule in Algeria. Accounts of Soustelle's role in the end of French rule are polarized. Some scholars credit Soustelle with the best of intentions upon his arrival in Alger in 1955.[13] Scholars Bernard Droz and Evelyn Lever see his legacy in a relatively positive light:

> *Quelle que soit la sévérité du jugement que l'on porte sur son politique ultérieur, Jacques Soustelle aura eu le rare mérite de rompre avec la bonne conscience compassée de tant de ses prédécesseurs et d'approcher avec humilité les terribles réalités algériennes.*[14]

> Whatever one thinks of his ulterior political views, Jacques Soustelle will have had the rare merit of breaking with the good faith applid rigidly by so many of his predecessors and humbly approaching the terrible realities of Algeria.

Others regard Soustelle as part of a tradition of French brutality in Algeria that began with the 1830 conquest.[15] France's 132-year reign over Algeria began in the final days of the Bourbon restoration. It was maintained by the government of Louis Philippe, then the failed Arab empire of Napoleon III and continued after 1871 in the liberal era with an attempt to transform Algeria into a southern extension of *la métropole*. The enterprise ultimately foundered in 1962 with the signing of the Evian Accords under which Algeria gained its independence. At that moment, France relinquished its Algerian *départements* and control of the Indigenous Algerian population.

Soustelle's *formation* as a doctoral candidate in 1930s Mexico informed the political choices he made as governor general of Algeria in 1955-56. Soustelle's relationship with his doctoral supervisor, and then colleague, Paul Rivet as well as with Germaine Tillion, his peer in ethnological studies and cabinet colleague in Algeria, shaped his thinking.[16]

The shadow of the Algerian-French conflict, in which Soustelle played a central role, is apparent to this day in the French-speaking world. Soustelle and the nature of the conflict over Algeria in the 1950s are under renewed scrutiny. In 2018, author Julian Jackson published *A Certain Idea of France – The Life of Charles de Gaulle*. Soustelle frequently appears as General de Gaulle's foil in the work. As Jackson writes of the 1950s when the general's thinking about Algeria abruptly shifted, leading to Algerian independence and a rupture with Soustelle, his erstwhile resistance colleague and political ally.[17] Author Alain Herbeth published a political study of Soustelle in 2015. Herbeth strived to rehabilitate Soustelle as a champion of a proposed accommodation between France and the Indigenous majority of Algeria who was simply ahead of his time.[18] Herbeth's effort was well received – something that would have likely been inconceivable if he had published the book 20 to 30 years earlier when Soustelle was widely regarded as an outlaw, a gifted intellectual who had strayed.

The colonial context of *l'Algérie française* has also been the recent subject of scrutiny by novelists. For example, Algerian journalist and fiction writer Kamel Daoud won *le Prix Goncourt* in 2015, French literature's most prestigious prize, for *Meursault, contre-enquête*, a work that re-told the story of Albert Camus' *L'Étranger* from the perspective of the brother of the unnamed "Arab" who was murdered on an Algerian beach by a French settler in Camus' novel.[19] Camus, Germaine Tillion and Soustelle were among the handful of French intellectuals who did not support Algeria's independence movement of the 1950s. Daoud's protagonist imagines conversations with both Camus and his fictional creation, the killer Meursault, about the killing and the French occupation of Algeria. The discourse focuses on highly contested matters of colonial history and decolonization that consumed the careers of Camus, Soustelle and Tillion.

Helen Sky at Flying Post, northern Ontario.

This work tackles the failures of Canada and France in the governance of Indigenous peoples. Why has the settler nation Canada failed so miserably to provide justice and economic opportunity for Indigenous Canadians? How could the *indigenismo* of post-revolutionary Mexico inspire Jacques Soustelle in an effort to reform French policy in Algeria? History is not purely a matter of the past. History motivates individuals and animates societies. The concerns and contradictions of Duncan Campbell Scott and Jacques Soustelle are meaningful today. Their preoccupations with Indigenous societies reveal much about Canada and France.

Their beliefs and failures have much to teach us.

Scott in 1913, recently appointed Deputy Superintendent of Indian Affairs.

Chapter One

TWO DEAD WHITE MEN

DUNCAN CAMPBELL SCOTT and JACQUES SOUSTELLE are thorns in the historic memories of their respective nations. In his lifetime as both a literary artist and bureaucrat, Scott was frequently lauded by media and fellow artists. Now, Scott is associated with the worst aspects of Canadian Indian policy. Until the late 1950s, Soustelle was regarded in a positive light by the French as an academic prodigy, a hero of the resistance, and an able politician. After his fateful turn as governor general of Algeria, Soustelle became a notorious, even despicable, figure.

If one combines their output, Scott and Soustelle had a broad geographic impact. They investigated, wrote and administered Indigenous peoples in the Canadian Arctic, across Canada's boreal expanses, prairies and the Pacific coast, the rainforest of Chiapas and the central plains and highlands of Mexico, and the agricultural lands, deserts and mountainous regions of North Africa. Their saga begins in 1879 when John A. Macdonald, Canada's first prime minister, hired Scott to work in the Indian Department. It ends in 1990 when the death of esteemed ethnologist and notorious political maverick Jacques Soustelle was extensively reported in all major French national media.

Duncan Campbell Scott

Scott was the intellectual offspring of a new nation. A parson's son, he grew up in various small towns in Canada east and west before his family settled in a parsonage within walking distance of Parliament Hill. Scott's father William had preached among the Indigenous peoples on Manitoulin Island during his travels.[1] In 1879, William Scott introduced his son to Prime Minister John A. Macdonald who was friendly with the family. Macdonald was happy to help the teenager get a start as a clerk in the Indian Department:

> I shall have great pleasure in helping your son to a position in the public service at an early day. No one deserves more at my hands than a son of yours. Please let me know his age, what his previous pursuits have been and let him send me a specimen of his handwriting.[2]

Reverend William Scott had his own brief stint with the department. In 1883, he wrote a report to the then superintendent general of Indian Affairs about the background to an Indigenous land rights dispute in Oka, Québec, an aspect of a festering conflict that turned bloody more than a century later in the summer of 1990.[3]

Reverend Scott's son, Duncan Campbell Scott, spent his entire civil service career in the Indian Department, from 1879 until 1932 when he retired. He rose from his junior clerical status to become first a treaty commissioner, then head of "Indian" education and ultimately deputy superintendent general of the Indian Department, the department's highest civil service rank. He held this position from 1913-32. As a civil servant, Scott was strategically placed to develop, refine and implement Canadian "Indian" policy. The policy, in its critical late 19th through early 20th century phase, was a direct descendant of a cluster of British colonial policies, which a fledgling Canada inherited from imperial Britain at Confederation in 1867.[4] The new nation would take those imperial policies and harden them in determined pursuit of a national railway, settler colonization and exploitation of natural resources in what King George III had called "the Indian country."[5] Scott was the most influential non-elected official responsible for these policies for a quarter of a century.

Scott's artistic production is sometimes reviled, or simply ignored, by many observers of the Indigenous-Settler relationship in Canada from the latter part of the 20th century until the present day. Scott was in fact an accomplished poet, writer of short stories, essayist, aspiring novelist and musician. In contrast to much of his poetry about Indigenous people, Scott's short stories, an unpublished novel and a deeply expressive letter to his second wife reveal, perhaps, a conflicted and layered approach to the Indian question in Canada. These works, which will be discussed in further depth, perhaps reflect some recognition that during Scott's lifetime Canada inflicted grievous harm on Indigenous peoples – even suggestions that Canadian society itself might be poorer because of the attempted erasure of Indigenous values and ways of life. In sum, Duncan Campbell Scott is a perplexing character to investigate. Author Stan Dragland addressed the conundrum in my 1995 documentary film, *Duncan Campbell Scott – The Poet and the Indians*:

> What is the problem? The problem is that this man who was almost wholly admirable in so many respects… whose poetry I deeply admire… who was in some ways the first truly Indigenous poet of Canada… that's a funny word to use for someone who was responsible for policies that were deeply harmful to Indigenous peoples… but it's true. He wrote some great poems and many of them are about Indian people or the north. This man, who if you could just shave off the Indian Department aspect would be wholly admirable, was also the bureaucrat most responsible for a policy of assimilation.[6]

Some recall that Scott would write poems by pencil as he travelled Canada by canoe and train on Indian Department business. Scott often wrote about Indigenous peoples he administered, about the Canadian frontier, and what he regarded as the necessary struggle to impress the values of British civilization on a sometimes brutish, backward Canada. He wrote convincingly of nature in Canada. Some literary critics claim that he and his friend Archibald Lampman were among the first post-Confederation writers to achieve full poetic realization of the awesome power and beauty of Canadian nature.[7]

Scott's Indian poems can startle and disturb imbued as they often, but not always are, with a transparent ideology rooted in firm convictions about once noble, but now vanishing peoples. *Indian Place Names*, an early poem written before Scott had risen high in the departmental ranks, reveals a conviction that Canadian Indigenous peoples were "doomed races":

> The race has waned and left but tales of ghosts,
> That hover in the world like fading smoke
> About the lodges: gone are the dusky folk
> That once were cunning with the thong and snare
> And mighty with the paddle and the bow;
> They lured the silver salmon from his lair,
> They drove the buffalo in trampling hosts,
> And gambled in the tepees until dawn,
> But now their vaunted prowess is gone,
> Gone like a moose-track in the April snow.[8]

The complex relationship between Scott's bureaucratic career and his artistic production is clear in one respect: Scott the artist mined his "day job" for artistic inspiration. His contemporaries took note of Scott's struggle to balance bureaucratic duty with artistic impulse. Scott's friend Madge Macbeth, an Ottawa society columnist, remembered his approach:

> With a highly-trained, efficient and devoted staff – Indian Affairs was not one of the Government's most exacting departments – Duncan had quite a little leisure during office hours. He did not suppress his artistic impulses at these times, but worked leisurely on his practice piano. It must have startled a new employee to enter his office and find him absorbed not in files or Blue Books, but in working on a soundless keyboard.[9]

Macbeth's observation raises the question: was Scott a well-balanced bureaucrat/artist, or was he derelict in his professional duties? Macbeth was not alone among her contemporaries in noting that for Scott, department business was not top of mind.[10]

The quality of the work and its stature in the development of Canadian literature raise thorny problems for the intellectual historian. Duncan Campbell Scott incarnated the values and aspirations of a new nation. His political values, social mores and artistic predilections reflected the shared aspirations of a post-colonial Canadian elite. In Ottawa, a small capital marked by both the Victorian grandeur of its Parliament Buildings and a tough lumber town edge, Scott and his peers published, played music and entertained in salons and concerts that mimicked elite behaviour in London, New York, Boston and old Québec.[11]

Scott cannot simply be dismissed as a late Victorian racist untethered to Canadian values. He represented and upheld widely shared mores of the Victorian era. As cultural critics have argued, Scott and his peers reflected a set of attitudes about Canada's relationship with Britain, the "mother" country and the obligations of supposedly civilizing a new nation's human inheritance: Indigenous peoples as "savage" wards subservient to a semi-independent Canada.[12] Scott was a central figure in regards to the residential schools' policies suppressing "Indian" dances, languages, political organizations and spirituality. These were policies that Parliament and Canadian voters expected him to enforce.

Scott retired as deputy superintendent general of Indian Affairs in 1932. He spent the remainder of his life writing at his home on Lisgar Avenue near Parliament Hill, travelling with his second wife, the poet Elise Aylen. He also remained in steady contact with Canada's writers, publishers, journalists and visual artists, including Emily Carr, Group of Seven member Lawren Harris and the Québécois painter Clarence Gagnon.[13]

In 1942, on the occasion of his 80th birthday, the venerable poet and champion of Canadian artistic life was saluted in the national press. *Saturday Night* magazine reported:

> On August 2 Duncan Campbell Scott passes his eightieth milestone and walks into the eighty-first year of life as rich in work nobly done as any life ever lived in Canada...
>
> The reputation which he made as an administrator still remains. He brought human and humane understanding to the problems of the Indian wards of the federal government...
>
> It is right that we should salute those among us who share the proud position of a Duncan Campbell Scott. It is right that we should hail them often before we say farewell. It is right that we should honour him to this day and always, because as long as trilliums whiten and maples redden, as long as the crocus empurples the prairie and lupins mirror the sky and dogwood puts forth her stars, many who love Canada and the glories and changing beauty of her lakes, her meadows, her mountains, her skies and her snows, will hold the memory of Duncan Campbell Scott in pride.[14]

When he died in 1947 at the age of 85, many leading newspapers and magazines lamented his demise and even deemed him an unofficial poet laureate.[15]

Scott was also known beyond Canada's borders. Within two months of his death, Britain's poet laureate John Masefield led a memorial service in Scott's honour at St Martin-in-the-Fields church in London.

Chief Cheesequimime posing for a portrait by painter Edmund Morris during 1906 Treaty 9 meetings, Chapleau, Ontario.

Mishkeegogamng First Nation, ON, *August 1994*

My documentary crew and I are driving through Mishkeegogamang First Nation, also called Osnaburgh or "Oz" in north-western Ontario in pitch darkness. We're on our way back to a motel in Pickle Lake in the midst of a film shoot about Duncan Campbell Scott.

He was here on Lake St. Joseph at the headwaters of the Albany River in 1905. A meeting was held. A treaty was signed. Scott wrote poetry and took photographs.

In 1994 Mishkeegogamang is a mess.

The kids burned the school down last winter. The nursing station is abandoned. Windows in the public buildings are covered with thick wire mesh, like one sees in an urban ghetto. That night kids lunge toward our van holding bags of solvents to their faces. As we slow down, a teenage girl bangs on the side of the van. Wendat/Québécois cameraman, René Sioui Labelle, is at the wheel. He rolls down the window and the girl screams in his face, "I want to die!"

Masefield had a long association with Scott. He claimed that an early Scott poem about a haunted ship had encouraged him, then a dockworker in New York, to write poetry. Some four decades before the St Martin's ceremony, Masefield had written a letter of gratitude to Scott:

> I hardly hope that you will remember my name, … Ten years ago, when I was in America, as a factory hand near NY, I read "The Piper of Arll" in the Christmas number of a paper called "Truth." I had never (till that time) cared very much for poetry, but your poem impressed me deeply, and set me on fire.[16]

At the St Martin-in-the-Fields memorial, Masefield returned the favour to Scott as he paid tribute to a man Masefield characterized as a great poet and humanitarian, who understood and sympathized with the lot of Canada's Indigenous peoples. From his British vantage point, Masefield idealized Scott's vision of the Canadian landscape and its presumably primeval occupants:

> When Duncan Campbell Scott began to write, the wish of the younger men was to declare the Canadian scene, with its greatness of mountain, lake, river and forest; its wildness; the fierce and eager dwellers in the wild, whether animal or men, and the exhilaration of being young in a land where poverty did not exist, where a new way of life was beginning, without the follies, the fetters and feuds of Europe.
>
> To be young in such a land at such a time was very Heaven.
>
> He entered the Department of Indian Affairs, in which Service his active life was passed. In this service, he came to know many Indians, to understand them, to see something of what could be done to save them from the evils the white men have brought to them.[17]

As the memorial proceeded, Canadian expatriates read his poetry, primarily from Scott's 'Indian' canon including *Watkwenies*, about an Indian Elder:

> Vengeance was once her nation's lore and law:
> When the tired sentry stooped above the rill,
> Her long knife flashed, and hissed, and drank its fill;
> Dimly below her dripping wrist she saw,
> One wild hand, pale as death and weak as straw,
> Clutch at the ripple in the pool; while shrill
> Sprang through the hamlet on the hill,
> The war-cry of the triumphant Iroquois.[18]

In *Watkwenies*, one of Scott's earliest Indian poems (1898), he reveals a morbid fascination with traits of a "vanishing" race. Scott simultaneously idealizes the "noble savage" while assigning Indigenous people to the past. In this respect, Scott as both bureaucrat and poet expressed commonly held western views regarding the fascinating attributes yet inevitable degeneration of "primitive" and "savage" peoples in the face of progress.[19]

His exaltation of Indigenousness in some of his poems can be seen as an expression of the antimodernism of the late 19th century: a tendency among the North American elite to exalt the wild as an antidote to the chaos of industrial urbanity.[20] Scott's poems do not portray "native" peoples in transition in the sort of positive, material progression that he took for granted for European Canadians. *Watkwenies* also depicts an exchange between an Indigenous woman and an Indian agent (the field representative of the government department where Scott spent his civil service career). The poem might refer to a treaty signing. It may also refer to an annual commemorative treaty day in the bush of northern Ontario or on the Canadian Prairies at which Indigenous people would receive token payments as a symbol of their relationship with Canada. Scott had first-hand experience as commissioner for Treaty 9 in 1905-06, which took him on long trips between Lake Superior and the coast of James Bay in northern Ontario. Scott believed such transactions were fulcrum points in the taming of "savage Indians" into civilized Canadians.[21]

The Forsaken, a poem about a woman left abandoned to die in a snowstorm by her starving companions, was also proffered to those assembled in the venerable British church. Perhaps it seemed a fitting choice to Masefield because of its exotic portrayal of harsh Canadian conditions and its poetic empathy for a woman with an ill infant:

> Once in the winter
> Out on a lake
> In the heart of the north-land
> Far from the Fort
> And far from the hunters,
> A Chippewa woman
> With her sick baby,
> Crouched in the last hours
> Of a great storm. Frozen and hungry,
> She fished through the ice
> With a line of the twisted
> Bark of the cedar,
> And a rabbit-bone hook
> Polished and barbed;
> Fished with the bare hook
> All through the wild day,
> Fished and caught nothing;
> While the young chieftain
> Tugged at her breasts,
> Or slept in the lacings of the warm tikinagann[22]

Scott encountered children in *tikinaganns*, the distinctive Ojibwe and Cree cradleboards of the boreal region, in his lengthy treaty voyages of 1905-06. *The Forsaken* was a particularly dramatic choice by Masefield. At its conclusion, the Indigenous woman, weakened and incapable of travelling on, is left to die by her starving people during a great snowstorm. Scott's poem drew attention to what he considered "barbaric" Indigenous practices, the presumed remedy for which was a Canadian civilization administered by the Indian Department. This was deemed a lofty and humane goal in the eyes of Scott, Masefield and the audience gathered at St Martin's.

In a letter written to Scott's second wife, the young poet and playwright Elise Aylen (who did not attend the London ceremony), Masefield wrote about "a service for your husband in a church famous here for the keeping of memories of great men… Miss Robinson who is, I think, the best living speaker of verse, made *The Forsaken* a living experience… nothing more beautiful has been done here…"[23] At the service, Masefield also read from a message from Canada's Prime Minister William Lyon Mackenzie King, "Much of his work we believe will find an enduring place in the vaster field of English literature. For all who love nature, he has mirrored the Canadian scene in its varying aspects of tender loveliness and rugged beauty."[24]

*Queen Elizabeth II leaving the
2010 St. James Cathedral service,
Toronto.*

Toronto, Ontario, *2010*

On July 4, American Independence Day, Queen Elizabeth attended a Sunday morning service at St. James Cathedral in downtown Toronto. Four days after Canada Day, the visit was a reminder of the living presence of history.

This was apparent in Queen Elizabeth's personal decision to present two peals of hand bells to the Chapels Royal of the Mohawks. Representatives from Mohawk communities at Oshwegen and Tyendinaga received her gift.

In his homily, Cathedral Rector Douglas Stoute re-minded listeners that the Queen honoured a relationship that pre-dates the existence of Canada by more than 150 years.

The event was scrupulously scripted and choreographed but 21st century realities of the Indigenous-Settler relationship could not be entirely effaced.

A group of police officers kept a small group of residential school survivor activists out of the Queen's sight. The protesters expressed a rising tide of outrage over the residential school legacy of Canadian governments that Duncan Campbell Scott had served.[28]

As the recently widowed Aylen Scott made her way through Ceylon to India where she would eventually settle, she granted a newspaper an interview about her husband. In its tribute to Scott, *The Times of Ceylon* called him "the uncrowned poet laureate of Canada" and stated that he was "…one of the few Canadians to receive international recognition in the field of literature."[25] In both England and India, Scott's stature as a stalwart of Canadian literature was affirmed at the time of his death. In the contemporaneous press, there is no concern expressed about the merits of Canadian Indian policy. Scott was seen as a noble example of an artist and servant of both the Canadian government and British Empire.

At his British memorial, the last selection read was from Scott's *Fragment Of An Ode To Canada*. The poem from 1911, when Scott was achieving high ranking in the Canadian civil service, evokes Canadian nationalism imbued with attachment to Britain:

> THIS is the land!
> It lies outstretched a vision of delight,
> Bent like a shield between the silver seas
> It flashes back the hauteur of the sun…
>
> And Thou, O Power, that 'stablishest the Nation,
> Give wisdom in the midst of our elation;
> Who are so free that we forget we are–
>
> That freedom brings the deepest obligation:
> Grant us this presage for a guiding star,
> To lead the van of Peace, not with a craven spirit,
> But with the consciousness that we inherit
> What built the Empire out of blood and fire,
> And can smite, too, in passion and with ire.
> Purge us of Pride, who are so quick in vaunting[26]

Fragment Of An Ode To Canada is one of several of Scott's overt tributes to the Empire. Before a British audience just two years after the Second World War, its selection underscored the close ties between Canada and its "mother" country. Like many of his contemporaries in the Canadian elite, Scott was an enthusiastic defender of the British connection. He was commissioned to write poems for Royal visits in 1901 and 1939. On the latter occasion, a poem for the departing Royal couple was read on the national radio service of the Canadian Broadcasting Corporation.[27]

In the final stages of his life and at his death in 1947, Scott was venerated by the literary and journalistic elites who were familiar with his artistic output and civil service career. Ottawa columnist Macbeth remembered Scott tenderly:

> He was a gentle man, a sensitive man, a man with deep fondness for his friends. Never aggressive or assuming a superior pose, he was humble, and yet did not like to be ignored…
> In a certain mood, he was a wonderful mimic. I remember, for example, his imitation of a circus barker. As soon as he began his spiel in the manner of a red-faced, harsh-throated barrel-bodied man, the room fell away and we were choking in the dust of the Mid-way, our ears tortured by the whine of the distant calliope; and we were surrounded by a crowd of corn-gnawing, corn-licking, goggle-eyed rustics doing the fair.[29]

For several decades following his death, Canadian literary critics and anthologists routinely lionized Scott's role in the development of a national literature. They often pointed to his Indian Department experience as a positive source of inspiration for Scott. Such critics overlooked the many negative impacts of the policies that Scott championed. In 1985, poet Raymond Souster paid tribute to Scott's contribution in an introduction to a collection of Scott's poems:

> Nature was for him not merely as it was for Lampman – a friendly refuge from the meanness of man and the growing encroachments of a vulgar new mechanization of life, but a stage on which human demands were enacted in all their nobleness and ignominious failure. His years in the Department of Indian Affairs, where he was able to get to know the character of the Canadian Indian more intimately than any other poet before or since, stood him in good stead and led to the creation of a handful of unforgettable poems.[30]

Douglas Lochead, Souster's partner on the 1985 edition of Scott's poems, credited Scott with articulating an appreciation of the Canadian landscape that Lochead felt made Scott a proto-environmentalist, "For me these poems represent the way we look at our Canadian environment now, and Duncan Campbell Scott saw it first. In this, he was poet as visionary."[31] Lochead and Scott's contemporary enthusiasts appreciated the poet's depiction of wild nature even if it came along with an infantilizing, dismissive portrait of Indigenous peoples. In this respect, Canadian artists like Scott in the early post-Confederation period projected upon Indigenous people, and wilderness, contradictory impulses of admiration and domination. Such tensions are consistent with the antimodernism depicted by the historian and theorist T.J. Jackson Lears.[32]

Regardless of Scott's literary merit or lack thereof, he often appears to us in our time as an agent of assimilation and Canadian genocide. It is important to historicize Scott and reflect on what he means as both Canadian artist and bureaucrat. In my 1995 film, which strives to situate and understand Scott as both writer and bureaucrat, historian Winona Wheeler (then Stevenson) reminded viewers that Scott reflected mainstream Canadian values about race and nation:

> He was a Victorian man. He was very stoic. I would say he was anal retentive. I think he really tried to, if not become a role model, at least live up to his perceived ideals of western civilization.
>
> He was pivotal in that he took the initiative and actually ran with it. He imposed the policies. I guess a lot of us can look back in retrospect, in presentist terms, and see him as an evil force. We can blame him. We can call him the devil, but he was a man of his time. He represented an era. His ideology was the ideology of the day.[33]

Jacques Soustelle

Scott exemplified the ideals of a new nation, while Jacques Soustelle, born in 1912 just as Scott reached the heights of Canada's civil service, represented the highest intellectual traditions of France's Third Republic. Soustelle was the quintessential expression of *la mission civilisatrice*, an ideology that underpinned French colonial rule in the modern era. He was a scion of an imperial and revolutionary tradition that kept France at the forefront of Western art, literature and science.

Like Scott, Soustelle had humble beginnings; his rise was made possible by the educational opportunities of the Third Republic. The son of a lower middle class family, Soustelle was a prodigy. He earned a national reputation as a student and writer before he was 25.

Soustelle was born in southwestern France of Protestant stock, which set him apart from his Catholic peers who were in the majority. His birth father abandoned the family when Soustelle was a young boy. His mother re-married a middle class man in Lyon with whom Soustelle got along well. He excelled in France's rigid system of national academic testing. He was one of a handful of *lycéens* of his cohort in Lyon to aspire to France's *grandes écoles*, a set of prestigious universities aimed at producing France's future leaders.

At 17, he was accepted to France's pre-eminent training college for post-secondary educators, *l'École Normale Supérieure* in Paris, located on the left bank in the shadow of the Pantheon.[34] There he began graduate studies in philosophy as a teenager. His professors included Marcel Mauss, a pioneer of French sociology, and Paul Rivet, a physician who became an archeologist and linguist after leading an expedition of cartographers and earth scientists through Peru prior to the First World War. Among his classmates were his wife Georgette Soustelle (birth name Georgette Fagot) who also became an ethnologist of Mexico, and the ethnologist Germaine Tillion, whose doctoral research took her to Algeria. In Rivet, Soustelle would find a *maître* who would serve as doctoral supervisor and his employer at *le Musée de l'Homme*. He also discovered a kindred soul in the struggle to combat the rise of European fascism in the 1930s, and a comrade in French resistance to Nazism after the military defeat of France to Germany in June 1940.

Rivet convinced Soustelle and Georgette to make Mexico the subject of their graduate research.[35] Soustelle first visited Mexico in 1932 when he was 20. As Soustelle continued his doctoral research in Mexico, he chronicled the experience in a non-academic work published in 1936. Soustelle's literary élan and contrarian attitude were already on display:

> Comme tout le monde, j'ai détesté Veracruz.
> On arrive imbu de cette marque européene, et nord-américaine, qui mesure la civilization à la hauteur des maisons et au bas degré de la temperature. Or à Veracruz les maisons sont basses et la temperature élevée. C'est un « pays chaud ». Je songe au froidement du tête qui accompagne, dans notre petit-bourgeoisie française, ces phrases: « Il est allé dans les pays chauds… Il a fait les colonies… » Car il n'y a que la France et les colonies. Cela vous classe un homme.[36]

> Like everyone, I detested Veracruz.
> One arrives imbued with the European and North American attitude of measuring civilization by the height of the houses and by a low degree of temperature. But in Veracruz the houses are low and the temperatures are high. It's a "hot country." I can imagine the cold gaze of our middle class French saying , "Oh he's gone to the hot countries… he's doing his colonial tour." Because in that way of thinking there is only France and its colonies. That makes a man.

It was the beginning of a love affair with the country that would inspire Soustelle to write works of ethnology and histories of civilization, some of which are published to this day.[37]

As a young scholar, Soustelle was particularly marked by his encounter with proponents of Mexican *indigenismo*, an attempt to redeem Mexican Indians by helping them join a *mestizo*, modern Mexico. Often in the company of Manuel Gamio, one of post-revolutionary Mexico's great theorists and a leading *indigenista* of his time, Soustelle toured the rural schools and cultural missions in Hidalgo, Oaxaca and Chiapas.[38] In his popular account *Mexique terre indienne*, Soustelle recounted a visit to a village near Querétaro in traditionally Otomí territory north of Mexico City:

> En accord avec la mission culturelle (qui vient de s'installer à 50 kilomètres plus loin à Ixmilquilpan), on a assaini le village, trace deux petits jardins publics, donné des représentations théatrales. On

introduit chez les Indiens des notions d'hygiène, on lutte contre l'alcoolisme produit par la pulque. Un peu plus loin, les terrains communaux, l'ejido s'organisent sous la direction d'un ingénieur. Oui, malgré tout, c'est une vie nouvelle qui commence; l'indien soulève peu à peu cette Pierre tombale qui l'écrase: le fanatisme prêché par la clergé, qui le maintient dans sa misère. … mon première contact direct avec l'éducation rurale.[39]

With the agreement of the cultural mission (that was recently established about 50 kilometres further on at Ixmilquilpan), they had cleaned the village, created two small public gardens and put on theatrical shows. They are introducing concepts of hygiene to the Indians and are struggling with alcoholism brought on by pulque. A little further on, there are communal agricultural plots, the ejido (communal farm) is organized under the direction of an engineer. Yes, despite all, a new life is beginning, the Indian lifts bit by bit the tombstone that crushes him: the fanaticism preached by the clergy that keeps him in poverty… this was my first contact with rural education.

Even as he became embroiled in the resistance against Nazism and later in the bloody tragedy of Algeria, Soustelle returned literally and intellectually to Mexico. Mexico's Indigenous present and past was the wellspring of his worldview. In 1941, following working with General Charles de Gaulle in London, Soustelle returned to Mexico to continue his resistance efforts of diplomacy and propaganda on behalf of *France Libre* (the French resistance movement against Nazi occupation):

Lorsque dans le nuit, le train franchit le pont international sur le Rio Bravo, entre la ville américaine de Laredo (Texas) et la ville mexicaine de Nuevo Laredo (Tamaulipas) et je vis dans l'aube tiède, les contours quadrangulaires des maisons d'adobe, je me retrouvai avec joie sur le sol de le Mexique qui était devenu, depuis dix ans, comme ma seconde patrie. J'avais appris à l'aimer, à aimer ses montagnes, ses steppes crevassées, ses forêts mystérieusement vibrantes, à aimer son peuple si riche de traditions millénaires et d'élan rénovateur. Déjà le général Cardenas président de la République, m'avait généreusement accordé la qualité de réfugié politique que la constitution Mexicaine, la plus humaine et la plus progressiste du monde, reconnaît à tous les persécutés.[40]

During the night, the train crossed the international bridge over the Rio Grande between the American city of Laredo, Texas and the Mexican city of Nuevo Laredo, Tamaulipas and I saw in the mild dawn the square contours of adobe houses, I found myself joyfully on Mexican soil that had become for ten years my second homeland. I had learned to love it, to love its mountains, its steep crevices its vibrant mysterious forests and to love its people so rich in ancient tradition and renewing energy. Already General Cardenas president of the republic had generously offered me the status of political refugee that the Mexican constitution, the most humane and progressive on earth, recognizes for the persecuted.

In 1955, having just published his most widely read and highly respected work about Mexico, *La vie quotidienne des Aztèques*, Soustelle would strive to import his understanding of *indigenista* policies to French Algeria in a doomed effort to integrate Arab and Berber populations with Europeans.

Soustelle's work in Mexico between 1932 and 1936 began among the Otomí and Pame Indians in then remote mountain areas around Mexico City. As was required of him by French doctoral academic standards, Soustelle also undertook a secondary, comparative study of the Lacandón Mayans in southern Mexico.[41] The Lacandón Mayans reside primarily in the rainforests of Chiapas. In the 1930s, Soustelle visited a group of approximately 400 pre-industrial holdouts. The Lacandóns of the Chiapas rainforest had resisted the lure of Spanish colonizers, as well as the promoters of 19th century Mexican independence, the modernizing dictatorship of Porfirio Díaz and even the *indigenista* prescriptions of 20th century revolutionary Mexico.

In addition to his academic research, the youthful Soustelle fired off articles under a pseudonym to leftist publications in Paris. The articles condemned the Mexican Catholic church and the behaviour of landowners and foreign corporations plundering Mexico's natural resources at the expense of Indigenous rural peoples.[42] Soustelle opposed what he considered unbalanced, sensationalistic accounts in the mainstream French press about the persecution of the Mexican Catholic church by the Mexican revolutionary left.

Despite his enduring achievements in Mexican ethnology, Soustelle is by no means known exclusively as a social scientist. He is better known for his work in Algeria. The ethnologist and resistance hero Soustelle, once associate director of *le Musée de l'Homme*, was selected across party lines by then French minister of the interior François Mitterrand in 1955 to become France's last governor of Algeria. Just as a vicious war of independence entered its decisive phase. On February 1, 1955, Abdelmadjid Ourabah, an Algerian member from Constantine, rose in France's *Assemblée Nationale* to read a ringing endorsement of the rights of Mexico's Indigenous peoples from Soustelle's work. Ourabah then posed a question which would haunt Soustelle and those who try to understand him for decades to follow:

> La place que M. Soustelle revendiquait pour le peuple indien dans la nation mexicaine, comment pourrait-il la refuser aujourd'hui au peuple algérien dans la nation française?[43]
>
> Given the place that Mr. Soustelle claimed for the Indian people in the Mexican nation, how can he refuse it today to the Algerian people in the French nation?

Just days later Soustelle arrived in Algeria heady with an ambitious reform program informed by his knowledge of Mexican land reform and *indigenismo*. He recruited some of the most progressive social scientists that France could proffer, including his former colleague at *Le Musée de l'Homme*, Germaine Tillion.

Tillion is renowned for her theory of *clochardisation* in which she detailed the poverty of the Algerian masses that resulted from settler colonialism coupled with a population explosion made possible through the introduction of antibiotics and mass vaccination.[44] She and Soustelle had a remarkable relationship. They were both students of Mauss and Rivet; they joined their colleagues at *Le Musée de l'Homme* in resistance against Nazism (Tillion was arrested and survived incarceration in a Nazi concentration camp); and in 1955, she and Soustelle would introduce their ambitious reform program of education and community organization based on Soustelle's understanding of the *indigenista* policies. The reform program known as *le plan Soustelle* crashed against the reality of an expanding military conflict between the French army and Algerian militants bent on national independence. Within six months, Soustelle, while still espousing reform, was determined to win a war against what he regarded as barbarous opponents, while Tillion quit Soustelle's cabinet but remained on as a civil servant.[45]

By the time Algerian independence was declared in 1962, Soustelle was a fugitive from France suspected by many for plotting assassination attempts against Charles de Gaulle, the man he had served in the resistance but had broken with over French policies in Algeria.[46] While on the run from French authorities, Soustelle continued to write about Mexico including *Les quatre soleils*, a contemplation of civilizations and the role of ethnology, in which Soustelle considered the Mayan and Aztec civilizations alongside great European and Asian cultures.[47] In his valorization of ancient Mexico, Soustelle was echoing the political ideology started during the rule of Mexican President Porfirio Díaz; as well as Mexican archaeology and anthropology of the late 19th and early 20th centuries that sought to establish Mexico as a cultural peer of Europe by drawing

A Lacandón Maya family, photographed by Jacques Soustelle c.1934.

attention to achievements of the Aztecs, Mayans, Olmecs and Toltecs.[48]

Soustelle returned from self-exile to France in 1968 following an amnesty for opponents of Algerian independence and just prior to the death of his erstwhile mentor Charles de Gaulle. He re-claimed his seat in the *Assemblée Nationale*, was named to prestigious academic posts and continued writing books and documentary film scripts about Mexico. In 1984, the former exile was named to *L'Académie française*. At the induction, French anthropologist Claude Levi-Strauss hailed Soustelle's early academic works as masterpieces.[49]

His death in August 1990 provoked a litany of contradictory assessments. Some treated Soustelle as an unrepentant fascist supporter of anti-independence movements in Africa. Others remembered his service in the resistance. Most agreed that as an ethnologist he had been one of France's great 20th century intellectuals. As the leftist daily *Libération* expressed it, the French struggled to reconcile the divergent aspects of Soustelle's *mouvementé* career:

> *Jacques Soustelle laisse, au choix, le souvenir d'un intellectuel "gauchiste" des années trente, d'un animateur de la France libre, d'un gaulliste convaincu, d'un membre du CNR-OAS ou d'un connaisseur hors pair des civilisations aztèque, toltèque ou maya. Plus qu'une carrière politique sinueuse, ses livres sur le lointain passé de l'Amérique centrale lui survivront.*[50]

> Jacques Soustelle leaves us to choose between the memory of a leftist intellectual of the 1930s, a resistance organizer, a convinced Gaullist, a member of CNR-OAS or an incomparable expert on the Aztec, Toltec or Mayan civilizations. More than his complicated political career, it is his books about the distant past of central America that will survive him.

France's most respected newspaper *Le Monde* eulogized Soustelle on its front page. Like its rival *Libération*, the paper chose, above all, to recognize Soustelle's ethnological work:

> *Plus que la longue fidélité à de Gaulle, rien que sa fidélité plus longue encore à une Algérie française qu'avec acharnement il avait cru pouvoir maintenir en la transformant, ce sont ces « Indiens aux yeux d'obsidienne » des temps précolombiens qui auront marqué, sans déception, le long itinéraire d'un intellectuel dont la guerre avait fait un homme d'action.*[51]

> More than his long loyalty to de Gaulle, more than his even longer faithfulness to a French Algeria that he stubbornly believed he could maintain through transformation, it is those "Indians with obsidian eyes" of pre-columbian times that marked, without disappointment, the long itinerary of an intellectual whom war made into a man of action.

An accompanying article praised Soustelle's singular contribution to the world's understanding of Mesoamerica:

> *Le sens de sa mission s'impose alors à Jacques Soustelle : son œuvre montrera que ces Indiens, héritiers d'une tradition millénaire, sont dépositaires d'une véritable culture et qu'ils doivent être respectés comme tels. Dans toute son oeuvre, Jacques Soustelle s'est attaché à mettre en évidence le continuum historique entre la préhistoire, les hautes civilisations et la culture des Indiens actuels.*[52]

> Jacques Soustelle was imbued with a sense of mission: his work shows that Indians, inheritors of a millennial tradition, are the carriers of a veritable culture and should be respected as such. In all his work, Jacques Soustelle applied himself to bring to light the historic continuity between pre-history, classic civilizations and the Indians of today.

The French Communist Party daily *L'Humanité* condemned Soustelle as a murderer of Algerian citizens, a failed assassin and apologist for right-wing regimes from Asunción to Pretoria.[53] Finally, the centre right *Quotidien de Paris* surveyed Soustelle's life in tragic terms:

> *…la grande faiblesse de Jacques Soustelle fut précisément de ne pas se comporter en homme politique mais en homme de passion, de croire à ce qu'il croyait et de se battre pour des idées qui furent des siennes toute sa vie durant. Soustelle restera un cas à part, un homme de courage et de fidélité douloureuse.*[54]

> …the great weakness of Jacques Soustelle was precisely that he did not behave as a man of politics but as a man of passion, to believe what he believed and to fight for his ideas throughout his life. Soustelle will remain a singular case, a courageous man of painful loyalties.

Five years after his death, an international group of anthropologists and archaeologists held a conference in Soustelle's honour. One of his Mexican peers, Eduardo Matos Moctezuma, then director of *el Templo Mayor*, the ruins and museum at the site of the Aztec city of Tenochtitlan now in the centre of Mexico City, wrote an introduction to the conference's collected papers. First, Matos Moctezuma saluted the *savant* of Mesoamerica who had inspired a Mexican student:

> The first time that I heard the name of Jacques Soustelle was in Mexico's National School of Anthropology. It was in 1960 and I was a second year anthropology student. I eagerly read a book that fascinated me: *The Daily Life of the Aztecs*. Its contents led me to one of the Mesoamerican societies and for the need to read both historical and archeological sources… Soustelle's book opened the door to Mesoamerican societies.[55]

Moctezuma did not shy from what might be the central contradiction in Soustelle's life: his steadfast support of *l'Algérie Française*. He evoked a time in the late 1960s and 1970s when the mention of Soustelle's name among Mexican social scientists would trigger a denunciation of Soustelle's position on Algeria. Even Moctezuma, a friend of Soustelle's to the end, confessed he was unimpressed with Soustelle's stance:

> I was never convinced by what he wrote about his decision to break relations with General de Gaulle with whom he had been a close collaborator during the Second World War.[56]

The elder Soustelle was astonishingly impolitic for a man who spent a great deal of his life in politics. He cultivated a reputation as something of a crank among French intellectuals, taking positions in defence of Israel and some Latin American right-wing leaders such as Alfredo Stroessner of Paraguay. And most provocatively for the time, the government of South Africa, as it muddled murderously towards the end of apartheid. Soustelle was almost singular in his public refusal to embrace causes like Palestinian nationalism or the liberation struggle of the African National Congress. Soustelle aired his decidedly untrendy, contrarian views about the apartheid regime (and the United States of America) in prestigious publications such as *Le Monde*:

> *Je peux affirmer, par expérience personnelle qu'il y a quelques années on voyait encore au Texas ou Louisiane plus de traces d'apartheid qu'en n'en voit aujourd'hui à Johannesburg.*[57]

> I can affirm from personal experience that a few years ago one still saw more signs of apartheid in Texas or Louisiana than one sees today in Johannesburg.

DUNCAN CAMPBELL SCOTT and JACQUES SOUSTELLE once appeared to be shining examples of their society's best values and traditions. Since their deaths they have been characterized as unsavoury reminders of shameful pasts. Scott's comeuppance came well after his 1947 death. Soustelle was demeaned and demonized in his lifetime, beginning with his rupture with de Gaulle over Algeria. He became an exile during the prime of his life. In our time, the work and the values both embraced has been cast into a dark light. Both are now tarnished by their association with aspects of their countries' most infamous deeds. Soustelle was one of France's greatest 20th century intellectuals. Was he also a neo-fascist who planned murder? Scott wrote some accomplished poems and short stories; he campaigned for a lifetime on behalf of Canadian writers and painters. What individual responsibility must be ascribed to Scott for a comprehensive assault on the human rights and dignity of Indigenous peoples in Canada that is now deemed to be cultural genocide, or even genocide *tout court*?[58]

For Scott, this conundrum has resulted in a fundamental re-thinking by Canadian literary critics of the relationship between his "day job" at the Indian Department and his poetry. The great Canadian literary and cultural theorist Northrop Frye grappled with the Scott enigma on several occasions. Frye was a cultural theorist and literary scholar. He did not investigate Scott, the bureaucrat. Yet, Frye's take is definitive and almost prophetic of Scott's reputational demise. Equally attracted by the skill of Scott's best work, and repelled by the colonized and colonizing ideology at times present in the poetry, Frye recognized Scott as a fundamentally important early Canadian artist. Frye pointed to the tension between Scott's exaltation of the wild and his fear and denigration of Indigenous peoples.[59] Frye's most celebrated student, Margaret Atwood, deals parenthetically with Scott's Indian Department legacy while acknowledging the fundamental contribution that he and fellow civil servant Archibald Lampman of the Canadian Post Office made to the development of Canadian letters:

> Part of the delight of reading Canadian poetry chronologically is watching the gradual emergence
> of a language appropriate to its objects. I'd say it first began to happen in poets such as Lampman
> and Duncan Campbell Scott.[60]

In 1986, Atwood included "Les Desjardins," a Scott short story in a collection of Canadian short stories that she co-edited.[61] Atwood was not the first to include Scott in such a compilation. In 1928, the literary critic Raymond Knister released his compilation *Canadian Short Stories*. In the forward he wrote, "and a perfect flowering of art is embodied in one volume, *In The Village of Viger* by Duncan Campbell Scott. It is work which has had an unobtrusive influence, but it stands out after 30 years as the most satisfying individual contribution to the Canadian short story."[62] It is perhaps a sign of Scott's diminished stature in Canadian letters, due to increased knowledge of his Indian Department role, that he is omitted from a 21st century collection of Canadian short stories.[63]

Gradually Canadian literary theorists began to fold Scott's Indian Department work more directly into their considerations. In 1980, critic Robert McDougall submitted a biography of Scott for a new encyclopedia:

> ...his literary reputation has never been in doubt. He has been well represented in virtually all
> major anthologies of Canadian poetry published since 1900. His "Indian" poems, in which he drew
> on his experiences in the field, have been widely recognized and valued. There is some conflict here
> between Scott's views as an administrator committed to an assimilation policy, and his sensibilities
> as a poet saddened by the waning of an ancient culture. Precise in imagery, intense yet disciplined,
> flexible in metre and form, Scott's poems weathered well the transition from traditional to modern
> poetry in Canada.[64]

In 2000, literary critic Stan Dragland offered perhaps the most trenchant re-evaluation. Dragland confesses to being "torn apart"[65] by his conflicted view about Scott, but he wisely underscores Scott's enduring yet shifting place in Canadian intellectualism:

> As a benign or sinister spirit, Scott continues to haunt us. Many of his essays show him consciously constructing Canada, still a work-in-progress fifty years after his death. By introducing his contributions to nation-making into the light of newer thinking about empire and race, we hope to enlist him for a further phase of the process.[66]

Scott's reputation has been churned by shifts in the Canadian national agenda. The 1982 entrenchment of "existing Aboriginal and treaty rights of the Aboriginal peoples of Canada" in the Canadian constitution, disputes over Indigenous land rights and debates over the Meech Lake and Charlottetown constitutional initiatives of the government of Prime Minister Brian Mulroney, brought a sharper focus to Indigenous-Settler relations. Some confrontations became violent including the Kahnawake (Oka) crisis in Québec, Gustafson Lake in British Columbia and the unlawful death at the hands of Ontario policy of Indigenous activist Dudley George. Each situation provoked a saturation of media coverage and a wide range of legal, military and political responses. The Kahnawake conflict led directly to the Royal Commission on Aboriginal Peoples by the Mulroney government. Indigenous activists and scholars transformed the persona of Scott, the foundational poet, into Scott, the sinister ideologue at the wheel of monstrous national policy.

Scott may have become *persona non grata* by the 1990s, but the reconsideration of the history of Indigenous-Settler relations gained momentum earlier. By the 1970s and 1980s, Canada's Indigenous rights movement gained an audience schooled by the American civil rights and anti-Vietnam War movements. In the aftermath of the failed White Paper on Indian Policy presented by the government of Pierre Trudeau in 1968, a policy which would have resoundingly capped the assimilation policies under Scott's watch, "Indian" leaders sparked a national reconsideration of the assimilation project.[67] If Trudeau and his Indian Affairs Minister Jean Chrétien insisted that Francophone Canadians had a right to their identity throughout the Dominion, surely Indigenous peoples warranted some special recognition of their rights and identities under Canadian sovereignty. As a CBC journalist, I spoke with Chrétien about the matter in 1984 when he ran for the leadership of the Liberal Party of Canada, following the resignation of Prime Minister Pierre Trudeau. A self-congratulatory Chrétien made no apologies for his role as minister of Indian Affairs:

> I think that a lot of people say that when you read the White Paper again and you read what is happening that we have moved very much in that direction. You know you have to go back to the situation when I took over the department. At that time the department was a very paternalistic department. There was a white superintendent on every reserve, there was virtually no local government, you know the band councils did not exist in many places. There was no Indian association at all or virtually none. They had no money from the government. I started to finance these associations to give them the possibility. In fact, I made the Georges Erasmus and Harold Cardinals in some ways in helping them to emerge. If we had not given them money, they would not have been in a position to express their grievances.[68]

As "Indian" policy became a frequent subject of national discourse during this period, Canadian historians began focusing on Scott's role at the Indian Department. Unlike earlier scholars who had been primarily, if not exclusively, interested in his poetry and prose, E. Brian Titley expressly rejected consideration of Scott's literary output, while insisting that the real stuff of inquiry about the man lay in his civil service career. The Scott that emerged in Titley's groundbreaking 1986 work *A Narrow Vision: Duncan Campbell Scott and the Administration of Indian Affairs in Canada* was a portrait from the dark side of the Canadian psyche.[69] Officious, conniving, Victorian to his marrow in his absolute certainty regarding British superiority, Titley's Duncan Campbell Scott was the determinedly effective *bête noir* to Indigenous aspiration in Canada. In Titley's view, post-Confederation Canada had primordial national business in seizing "Indian" lands and resources and in snuffing out systems of spiritual belief, language, customs and political organization deemed inconsistent with rapid "civilization." In this quest, in Titley's view, Canada had a willing champion in Duncan Campbell Scott.

Clearly, Scott, in the minds of many observers, was no longer a sensitive artist with a trying bureaucratic job in which he acquitted himself admirably. Some scholars regarded Scott through the lens of post-colonial theory and looked at the Indian Department's activities as the lynchpin of Canada's assertion of national sovereignty and domestic colonization of Indigenous peoples.[70] This perspective was illuminated by historian Ian McKay in a series of influential works about Canada's "liberal order framework." McKay casts the first 75 years of Canada's history as a nation state as an on-going revolution led by, and for the benefit of, a liberal elite often at the exclusion of minorities and with particular malevolence in regard to policies concerning Indigenous peoples.[71]

Similarly, Soustelle, the academic prodigy, heroic *résistant* and grand interpreter of Mexican civilizations, was replaced by the end of the 1960s with the image of a self-serving, ultra-conservative stalwart of indefensible causes. After Soustelle's death, the British spy novelist Robert Stillman, then embroiled in a legal dispute over Soustelle's alleged ties to anti-Algerian independence terrorists known as *Organisation armée secrète* or OAS, called him "a pathetic, bronchitic old man, who really had nothing to say… at the end of the day, (he) was a *pauvre type, pauvre con* [a pathetic figure, an idiot]."[72] Soustelle's final days were marked by conflict with publishers and his political opponents. As correspondence with his lawyer reveals, Soustelle felt wrongly accused of association with leaders such as Paraguay's dictator, Stroessner, even while at the same time being attacked by Stroessner's loyalists:

> …*des amis français résidant au Paraguay m'écrivent que la clique fasciste au pouvoir se vante de me faire arrêter par Interpol ! N'y a-t-il pas moyen de bloquer cette persécution?*[73]

> French friends who live in Paraguay write to me that the fascist clique in power is bragging about having me arrested by Interpol! Is there no way to stop this persecution?

Just a month before his death, Soustelle pleaded with his lawyer to resolve a rights dispute between French publishers over his works:

> *Votre lettre fait apparaître que je suis amené à m'engager dans un labyrinthe sans fin.*
> *Je n'ai ni le temps, ni le goût, ni les moyens de partir à la chasse de documents, lettres, etc. vieux de plusieurs années.*[74]

> Your letter shows that I am being led to engage in a never-ending labyrinth.
> I have neither the time, the willingness nor the means to undertake a hunt for documents, letters, etc. of many years past.

The contrarian, feisty and prolific Soustelle was embattled still in his declining years. It was a lifelong stance. Biographer Bernard Ullmann fittingly dubbed Soustelle *le mal aimé*, or black sheep.[75]

After his death, Soustelle was replaced in the *Académie Française* by Jean-Francois Deniau, one of the architects of the European Union. Deniau was a diplomat, a politician, a great sailor, a journalist and a novelist. As convention has it, it was Deniau's duty at his induction to offer an "*éloge*" of the man he replaced "*sous la Coupole*":

> Je n'ai pas essayé d'analyser une œuvre. Il y a parmi vous bien plus compétent que moi, les plus hautes autorités en ethnologies, mais aussi en sciences, en philosophie, en littérature… Non, j'ai seulement cherché à approcher un homme pour le comprendre un peu mieux que ce que les notices peuvent nous apprendre. A l'approcher avec prudence et, plus j'avançais, émotion. En sachant qu'il restera un mystère Soustelle. Et en trouvant cela bien. Parce qu'il n'y a pas, sans cette ombre portée du mystère, de véritable stature humaine; et que l'incompréhensible, l'inexplicable sont les derniers remparts de notre liberté.[76]

> I have not tried to analyze a body of work. There are among you many who are more qualified than I, the highest authorities in ethnology, but also in sciences, in philosophy, in literature… No I searched only to get close to a man, to understand him a little better than the obituaries can teach us. To approach with prudence, and the further along I got, with emotion. In knowing that there will always be a Soustelle mystery. And finding that to be a good thing. Because there is not without this shadow carried by mystery, real human stature; and that the incomprehensible, the inexplicable are the final ramparts of our liberty.

Deniau also revealed for the first time that Soustelle had tipped off French intelligence about a planned assassination attempt on Charles de Gaulle. Clearly, Soustelle who was then hidden "*quelque part en Europe*" (the "somewhere in Europe" phrase he added to the by-line he used in his anti-de Gaulle screeds to French newspapers) was in contact with the plotters. On this occasion, rather than joining the conspiracy, Soustelle chose mercy for his old comrade in arms.[77]

Soustelle's work as a social scientist and politician places him at the centre of French debates about its imperial past and its future in a post-colonial world. His formative academic associations with his teachers, Marcel Mauss and Paul Rivet, and his colleague, Germaine Tillion, make Soustelle a foundational figure in the emergence of French ethnology and anthropology. His ambitious but doomed tenure as governor general of Algeria, plus his intellectual jousting with leading French writers about post-colonialism such as Raymond Aron, Albert Camus and Jean-Paul Sartre, make Soustelle an inescapable and compelling character in France's end-of-empire reckoning.

Canada is often seen, and certainly Canadians enjoy seeing themselves, as a beacon of light in international human rights. However, Canada was part of a larger story of rapacious settlement colonization rooted in firm convictions of the racial superiority of the "Anglo-Saxon races." The life and times of Scott, contrasted with Soustelle's, demonstrate that Canada was part of a global struggle to "develop" natural resources, settle colonists and "civilize" Indigenous peoples with often brutal methods. Such methods were largely accepted by non-Indigenous Canadians throughout Scott's career.

Sierra Gorda Biosphere Reserve, Querétaro, north-central Mexico.

Chapter Two

THEIR VOYAGE IN

SCOTT and SOUSTELLE undertook formative voyages early in their careers. These voyages inspired some of their most profound and revealing writing. The enduring impressions and crystalline moments of focus from these voyages contributed essentially to the making of each of these men.

Scott was a treaty commissioner for the government of Canada in the summers of 1905 and 1906. He made two extensive journeys through the lands of the Anishinaabe and Cree peoples living in a large area from Abitibi Lake near present day Timmins, north to the west coast of James Bay at Fort Albany and south again to the shore of Lake Superior at the mouth of the Pic River near present day Marathon, Ontario.

Soustelle conducted field research in Mexico for a doctorate in ethnology from 1932-34. His journeys were twofold: firstly, in central Mexico in an arc extending just southeast of Mexico City, north and west through the states of Hidalgo, Mexico and San Luis Potosí.

Soustelle conducted a secondary trip in Chiapas in southern Mexico through the Lacandón rainforest that lies approximately between Palenque near the Gulf of Mexico to Ocosingo, a town about 70 kilometres east of the city of San Cristóbal de Las Casas, in the highlands of Chiapas.

Soustelle and Scott were transformed by these expeditions. The journeys involved wilderness travel and encounters with Indigenous peoples in then remote territories of northern Canada and central and southern Mexico. They met people and had experiences that affected their judgement and their work for the rest of their lives.

Scott's extended exposure to Indigenous communities crystallized an ideology that underpinned his ambitious and determined career in the Canadian Indian Department. As an artist, the treaty expeditions of 1905 and 1906 provided the inspiration for many poems and short stories. Mexico of the 1930s provided Soustelle with a second home. The mountains, jungles, plains and deserts of Mexico remained a sanctuary, a solace and an inspiration for him until his death in 1990. His love affair with Mexico began in the summer of 1932 when the then 20-year-old Soustelle disembarked in Vera Cruz. His observation of the attempts to alleviate the poverty and suffering of Indigenous peoples in the social and educational policies of the Mexican revolution informed the fateful policies of *le plan Soustelle*, which he attempted to introduce in war-torn Algeria in 1955 after he was named governor general.

The literature on travel as rite of passage, a coming of age and a moment of personal transformation for a wide range of 19th and 20th century writers, intellectuals and explorers is diverse and rich. Such literature exposes different ways of evaluating the imperial gaze. Although such works by no means deal exclusively with Mexico, Canada, France or Algeria, they share powerful insights about the transformative power of travel in regions shaped by European imperialism.[1]

Both Scott and Soustelle were informed by particular national experiences of travel and exploration essential to their heritage and motivation. In Canada, the early European explorers including Samuel de Champlain, Samuel Hearne and David Thompson were among the earliest expressions of a Euro-Canadian literary tradition of which Scott became part.[2] Growing up in France, Soustelle was very much aware of the extraordinary 18th century Latin American travels of Alexander Humboldt, particularly his accounts of New Spain or Mexico. As a young boy, Soustelle was transfixed by accounts of explorers and devoured books about

France's African and Asian territories.[3] As an emerging scholar, he was emboldened by the accounts of the cartography and archaeological expeditions undertaken by his supervisor Paul Rivet in South America. As a young French traveller and explorer among Mexico's Indigenous people, Soustelle was also following in the footsteps of people such as Désiré Charnay, the enterprising 19th century photographer of Mayan temples of the Yucatan and Chiapas.[4]

Both Scott and Soustelle travelled through some rough terrain making extensive use of forms of transportation such as canoes, mules and horses. Each of them relied on Indigenous guides to make their way. They wrote extensively about these journeys and each took photographs. Soustelle also made audio recordings.

In the spring of 1905, Scott was rising through Canada's Indian Department when he was named treaty commissioner for Treaty 9. Scott was then 35 years old, a married father of one daughter. He was an established literary figure in Canada with publishers in Toronto, Ottawa, New York and Boston. As a journalist and cultural commentator, he was known to the readers of such publications as the *Toronto Globe* through the column "At the Mermaid's Inn" that he produced with fellow poets Archibald Lampman and Wilfred Campbell. His short stories and poetry had appeared in American magazines such as *Scribner's Magazine* and *Muncey's*.

His career at the Indian Department was progressing smartly. He had risen from the post of clerk, for which he was hired in 1879, to become the department's chief accountant. The poet showed a surprising facility with numbers and his handwriting – which was often obscure at best in the archive of his poetry and correspondence – was clear and precise in the department's records. As a functionary of the department, Scott had already taken journeys into Indigenous communities and territories. His visit to the areas along the northern shore of Georgian Bay in 1898 introduced him to a boreal expanse and a world of the imagination that the surroundings of Ottawa only hinted at. That trip would begin a poetic meditation that would inspire Scott's most evocative, accomplished and troubling Indigenous poems when coupled with his more extensive journeys into Indigenous communities and territories in the summers of 1905 and 1906. He was accompanied by fellow bureaucrats, members of the Royal Canadian Mounted Police and, in 1906, by a few select friends who were educators, writers and painters. The Treaty 9 trips bolstered Scott's career. Within a few years, he received a significant promotion as the department's director of education. By 1913, he would become deputy superintendent general, the top official in Indian Affairs. He held that post for the rest of his civil service career.[5]

Soustelle was a graduate student in 1932 when he first visited Mexico. He travelled with his wife Georgette, also a graduate student of French physician and social scientist Paul Rivet. The couple had met at *l'Institut d'ethnologie* in Paris where Rivet taught them. Soustelle, then 20 years of age, was an academic prodigy. After excelling in national examinations, he was selected from his *lycée* in Lyon at age 17 to study at *l'École normale supérieure* in Paris, a graduate school for those who would become France's leading academics. Rivet profoundly influenced and impressed the young Soustelle and would continue to play a mentoring role for the remainder of his life.[6]

The teaching of Rivet inspired emerging scholars such as Jacques and Georgette Soustelle to select Mexico for a place of study.[7] Rivet championed fieldwork and face-to-face interaction with ethnological subjects and had made a name for himself as a cartographer and anthropologist undertaking exotic and dangerous journeys in Ecuador, Peru and Colombia. At *l'École normale supérieure*, Soustelle was exposed to two gifted teachers with vastly different approaches: Rivet and Marcel Mauss. Mauss had pioneered modern sociology along with Émile Durkheim. Mauss had also charted a path from sociology to ethnology when he evinced a fascination with comparative social studies. His essay on giving, which compares various Indigenous societies, including "Eskimos" and tribal groups of the Canadian northwest, in their attitudes about property, is a classic comparative study.[8] Mauss had whetted the young Soustelle's interest in foreign lands and encouraged a multidisciplinary approach to academic work that Soustelle found appealing. He also provided Soustelle with one of his first professional academic assignments: writing an entry on shamanism for a French encyclopedia.[9] However, it was the diminutive "*doctorcito*" Rivet of the legendary Latin American expeditions, a man of action who served France as a physician in the First World War, who fired the imagination and commanded the unswerving loyalty of the young Jacques Soustelle.

Rivet introduced a more active approach to social science. He encouraged his students to understand the living reality of Indigenous people. This emphasis on the present day was an important distinction for youthful scholars seeking the adventure of fieldwork in exotic locales. Late in life, Soustelle reflected that he, his wife and their peers found inspiration in Rivet's insistence that Indigenous peoples survived colonialism and could not merely be seen as relics of the past.[10] Distinguishing themselves from the "armchair" theories of sociologists such as Mauss, Soustelle and his peers ventured out into remote parts of the world seeking the linguistic and cultural vestiges of ancient civilizations and Indigenous peoples.

For Jacques and Georgette Soustelle, this sense of mission meant Mexico. Meanwhile, their young colleague at *L'Institut d'Ethnologie*, Germaine Tillion, who had also studied with Rivet and Mauss, went deep into the remote Aurès mountains of Algeria to conduct a study of Berber tribal peoples. Soustelle and Tillion joined forces 20 years later in Algeria after Soustelle was named governor general. As Soustelle's thinking about Mexico and larger questions of civilization developed over the course of his life, he would emphasize the fundamental importance to him as a thinker in seeing things first hand by living among Indigenous peoples.[11] As a scholar formed in the French elite tradition, he respected classic traditions of intellectual inquiry, but his taste for action and his sense of adventure found an outlet in the emerging field of ethnology.

Such an approach also appealed to Soustelle's commitment to social justice. He supported anti-fascist movements in which Rivet was also extremely active in movements in France, Spain (as the Spanish Civil War raged), and in Italy as Mussolini consolidated power and Hitler began to emerge as a threat to all of Europe. Soustelle went to Mexico imbued with social democratic principles. The 20-year-old Soustelle was an admirer and thoughtful critic of the Mexican revolution, an advocate for Indigenous rights and an acerbic critic of the Mexican church, large landowners and the American capitalists that dominated Mexico's economy and coveted its rich natural resources. These ideas resonate in his first book and in the journalism that he penned from Mexico under the pseudonym of Jean Duriez, published in French leftist newspapers between 1932-35.[12]

Conversely, Scott travelled with a sense of privilege and superiority bestowed by the Canadian government. A man on the rise, a writer already confident in his abilities, in 1905-06 Scott undertook matters of fundamental importance to a still fledgling state. As a treaty commissioner, Scott represented the Crown. In post-Confederation Canada, Scott's role was vital to maintaining the tricky balance between federal power in Ottawa, with its responsibility for Indians, and provinces which jealously guarded their jurisdiction over abundant natural resources in hinterlands.

The border area between the forests of northwestern Ontario and the prairies had been fraught with conflict for Canada since the earliest days of Confederation when Louis Riel and the Red River Métis challenged Canadian authority in what would become Manitoba in 1871. Scott and his fellow commissioners were bringing a treaty with terms pre-determined by the governments of Canada and Ontario. The treaty applied to an area that encompassed some of the lands to which the British commander Garnet Wolseley had led a force of 2,000 British regular soldiers and southern Ontario volunteers in the summer of 1870 in hot pursuit of Riel. With border questions resolved and with the completion of one transcontinental railway and the building of a second line to the north, the unceded Indigenous lands north of Lake Superior became a region of vital national interest.[13] The official Treaty Report co-signed by Scott, Samuel Stewart and Ontario Commissioner D.G. MacMartin tersely expressed the Canadian state's desires:

> Increasing settlement activity in mining and railway construction in that large section of the province of Ontario north of the height of land and south of the Albany River rendered it advisable to extinguish the Indian title.[14]

The use of the word "extinguish" is worth noting.[15] As the official account goes on to say, the commissioners repeatedly told recalcitrant Indigenous people in places like Osnaburgh, now called Mishkeegogamang, that they would continue to enjoy their hunting, fishing, gathering and trapping activities throughout their territories in exchange for settling on defined reserves. The construction of railways and highways, mineral exploration, hydro-electric development and timber cutting encroached on traditional pursuits. The presence of an Ontario commissioner indicated what was really at stake given that the province held constitutional jurisdiction over natural resources – an authority which would soon trump Ottawa's responsibilities for its "Indian" wards.

In addition to the official report, Scott also wrote a journalistic account of the trips which appeared in 1906 in the prominent American magazine *Scribner's Magazine*. In often paternalistic terms, Scott describes his duty on the part of Canada of bringing the treaty to Indians along the Albany River. In his introduction, Scott refers to Canada's longstanding tradition of "puerile negotiations" between representatives of the British crown and the troubled, marginalized vestiges of what Scott deemed to be a once proud race foundering on the edge of irrelevance, if not outright extinction.[16] His account for his American readers contains significant omissions from a man working at a high level on Canadian Indian policy. In the article, Scott did not mention the historic contribution that Indigenous peoples made in the creation and maintenance of the very nation state he represented. Many historians agree that Britain required the support of its Indigenous allies after the fall of New France.[17] This was the initial strategic context for the terms protecting "Indian country" in King George III's Proclamation of 1763. The strategic value of the proclamation was proven during the War of 1812 when Britain relied heavily on its Indigenous allies to protect British North America by fighting to a stalemate with the burgeoning power to the south. The proclamation laid down the legal rules for the signing of treaties that prevailed in the Canada of Scott's day and which are now enshrined in the provisions concerning Aboriginal rights in the Canadian Constitution.[18] In his *Scribner's Magazine* article, Scott indulged in a sensationalistic portrayal of frontier Canada:

> In the early days the Indians were a real menace to the colonization of Canada. At that time there was a league between the Indians east and west of the River St. Clair, and a concerted movement upon the new settlements would have obliterated them as easily as a child wipes pictures from his slate. The Indian nature now seems like a fire that is waning, that is smouldering and dying away in ashes, then it was full of force and heat. It was ready to break out at any moment in savage dances, in wild and desperate orgies in which superstitions were involved with European ideas but dimly

U.S.A.

Gulf of Mexico

Mexico

San Luis
Potosí

Querétaro

Mexico City

Oaxaca

Toniná

Chiapas Lacondón
rainforest

Pacific Ocean

As a graduate student at l'Institut d'ethnologie in Paris, from 1932-34, Soustelle conducted doctoral research in rural Mexico.

understood and intensified by cunning imaginations inflamed with rum. So all the Indian diplomacy of that day was exercised to keep the tomahawk on the wall and the scalping knife in the belt.[19]

Scott's view of the "early days" of Indigenous-Settler relations in "The Last of The Indian Treaties" is his-
torically flawed. Its analysis flowed from a mid-19th century historiography that glorified European military
commanders and either romanticized or demonized the roles played by Indigenous peoples.[20] Perhaps he was
pandering to his American audience, but Scott, who could not afford to attend university, was dependent on
a Victorian-era schoolboy's understanding of Indigenous-Settler relations and yet he was handed senior responsibilities over Canadian Indian policy. Scott made clear that he was patient with his Indigenous charges:

> The simpler facts had to be stated, and the parental idea developed that the King is a great father of
> the Indians, watchful over their interests, and ever compassionate.[21]

Scott grandly entitled his article "The Last of The Indian Treaties." Subsequent events would demonstrate
that he was grossly inaccurate in his inflated view of the undertakings. In the course of the 20th century,
Canada would engage in major treaties with terms vastly different and more generous from those of Treaty 9.
Treaties such as those with the Cree of James Bay in northern Québec (1975), with the Inuvialuit in the western Arctic (1984) and with the Nisga'a of northwestern British Columbia (1998). Further by 1982, Canada
changed its constitution to acknowledge the existing Aboriginal and treaty rights of Indigenous peoples in
Canada. On paper at least, the amendments to the constitution represent a significant departure from a policy of "extinguishment." Canada has further disavowed the policy of extinguishment in recent years. In 2019,
the governments of Canada, British Columbia and the First Nations Summit co-developed the "Recognition
and Reconciliation of Rights Policy for Treaty Negotiations in British Columbia," stating that extinguishment
of Aboriginal rights would not be a model in future settlements. The position was reiterated by Dr. Carolyn
Bennet, Minister of Crown–Indigenous Relations, at a parliamentary committee in 2020.[22]

Scott's treaty expedition required a large crew to make its way across the north. In 1905 and 1906, the
treaty expedition team would sometimes consist of 24 men. The commission held a feast of tea, bannock and
bacon at each major community. Scott and his fellow commissioners were paddled by their "native" guides in
a 32-foot birch bark canoe which carried up to 2,500 pounds of provisions, camp equipment, and a treasure
chest containing $30,000 in small notes for treaty payments of $8 per adult. The crew was accompanied by
two officers of the Royal Canadian Mounted Police (RCMP).[23] Scott was convinced the RCMP officers were
of no small significance in establishing his team's credibility along the Albany River:

> I am bound to say that the latter outshone the members of the Commission itself in the observance
> of the Indians. The glory of their uniforms and the wholesome fear of the white man's law which
> they inspired spread down the river in advance of the Commission and reached James Bay before
> the Commission. I presume they were used as a bogey by the Indian mothers, for no children
> appeared anywhere until the novelty had somewhat decreased and opinion weakened that the mag-
> nificent proportions and manly vigour of our protectors were nourished upon a diet of babies.[24]

Scott's journalism in the *Scribner's Magazine* article was riddled with inconsistencies and contradictions. Scott proclaimed that Indigenous signatories were ignorant while at the same time describing in
some detail the pointed questions directed at the commissioners in places like Osnaburgh, now known as
Mishkeegogamang First Nation.[25]

Scott, his fellow commissioners and the RCMP officers were guided by a team of Indigenous guides.[26] The large, windswept lakes, fast moving rivers and sometimes tortuous *nastawagan*, Anishinaabe and Cree trails, that linked waters of the Canadian Shield in the treaty territory, made for arduous travel. Indigenous guides portaged the elaborate camp equipage in order to keep the distinguished commission comfortable on the trip. This meant long and repeated carries over the narrow, rocky, muddy, mosquito-infested trails.

Scott was photographed at the end of one such portage. He appears urbane and out of place, mosquito netting pulled back from his face while sporting argyle socks pulled up over his trouser legs. As Stan Dragland recounted in his literary analysis of the Treaty 9 expedition, that single image crystallizes the complicated role of Scott, a poet/bureaucrat from Ottawa, simultaneously pursuing Canada's political ends and his own artistic fulfilment in Anishinaabe and Cree Territory of northern Ontario in 1905-06.[27]

Interlocuteurs Valables: Guides for Scott and Soustelle[28]

On these formative journeys both Scott and Soustelle displayed fascination and even empathy with certain interlocutors they met along the way. Scott, on the one hand, was responsible for convincing the Indigenous peoples to agree to treaty terms that were at best reductive and in some respects, duplicitous. However, some of his best writing was inspired by the Treaty 9 experience. Some of that work demonstrates an affection for the peoples of the north and an appreciation for the lands and waters he travelled across.

Likewise, in central Mexico, Soustelle encountered impoverished Mazahua, Otomí and Pame Indigenous peoples whose religious festivals, agricultural practices, music and resilience to a harsh life inspired him. In southern Mexico, Soustelle met families of Lacandóns in Chiapas for whom he developed an abiding respect. In particular, Soustelle spent extended periods in the rainforests of Chiapas in the company of a Lacandón hunter and shaman Tchank'in or "*anacleto*" who would figure prominently in Soustelle's youthful account of his journey in *Mexique terre indienne* in 1936:

> *C'était un homme grave et plein de dignité que cet "anacleto," grand causeur mais sobre de gestes, sa tunique d'une blancheur immaculée, ses cheveux noirs semblables à la perruque d'un seigneur à la cour du Roi-Soleil. Je ne peux raconter toutes les attentions qu'il montrait pours ses hôtes; tantôt il apportait des régimes des bananas, tantôt il roulait avec soin entre ses paumes des feuilles de tabac pour me confectionner des cigares.*[29]

> He was a serious, dignified man that "anacleto," a great talker but of understated gestures, his tunic of impeccable whiteness, his black hair similar to the wig of an aristocrat in the court of the Sun King. I cannot recount all the kindnesses he showed his guests; sometimes he supplied a diet of bananas, sometimes he carefully rolled tobacco leaves in his palms to make me cigars.

Soustelle wrote extensively about his friendship with this Mayan Elder in his first book. Soustelle lauded and claimed to have befriended Tchank'in, but the relationship was consistent with ethnographic field practice. Thirty years later in 1967, while on the lam « *quelque part en Europe* » from French intelligence and international police who were investigating his links to anti-de Gaulle terrorists, he paid tribute to Tchank'in again in the *Les Quatre Soleils*.[30] This work is a contemplation of the apogee of civilizations and their decline. As Soustelle meditated in *Les quatre soleils* from his Cold War-era vantage point, he would often refer to the Mayan legend recounted to him by Tchank'in and others about worlds ending in a storm of fire and a plague of human-devouring jaguars:[31]

Nous le savons maintenant: tout soleil est condamné à s'éteindre. Une civilisation peut succomber sous l'assaut des barbares – les jaguars du premier univers; elle peut sombrer dans l'impuissance et la futilité – les hommes sont transformés en singes; ou bien s'effondrer sous les coups des forces naturelles – déluge, tremblement de terre; ou enfin explorer dans ultime conflagration – la pluie de feu qui n'est plus, à notre époque, une simple image légendaire. Le mythe mexicain, expression d'une sagesse antique, rejoint l'inquiétude d'aujourd'hui.[32]

Now we know: every sun is condemned to extinguishment. A civilization can succumb to an assault of barbarians – the jaguars of a first universe; it can fall apart in impotence and futility – men transformed into monkeys; or could just as well collapse under the blows of natural forces – flood, earthquake; or finally explode in terminal conflagration – the rain of fire that is no longer, in our age, merely an image from legend. The Mexican myth, an expression of ancient wisdom, connects with the anxieties of today.

Through his contemplation of Tchank'in, Soustelle pondered the gap between western civilization and the bush existence of Indigenous people he encountered deep in the jungles of southern Mexico in 1933-34. In his first book, Soustelle distanced himself from any affiliation with a romantic notion of the "noble savage." His admiration for the Lacandóns was tempered by realism and a rather grim view of human society:

Je ne crois pas avoir embelli à plaisir les conditions de vie des Lacandóns, ni leur caractère. Leur liberté est un des biens qui coutent cher à conserver. Cracher sur la civilisation matérielle est commode, lorsqu'on en jouit. Je crois l'apprécier mieux que jamais, depuis que j'ai vu ce que signifie réellement, de labeur écrasant et d'insécurité constante, la vie primitive. Vivre en sauvage, ce n'est pas vivre insouciant et heureux; il n'y a pas d'hommes heureux sur la terre.[33]

I do not believe that I have gratuitously embellished the living conditions of the Lacandóns, nor their character. They pay dearly for their liberty. It is fashionable to spit on material wealth when you have it. I think I appreciate it more than ever, since I have truly witnessed the crushing labour and constant insecurity of primitive life. To live in the wild is not to live carefree and happy; there are no happy people on earth.

In his journalism and more obliquely in his poetry and prose, Scott profiled several Indigenous individuals who impressed him favourably in the summers of 1905 and 1906. He extolled the physical strength and bush wisdom of the paddlers. Names of some of the guides would later crop up as fictional characters in Scott's short stories and poems. Jimmy Swaine, a Métis guide and fiddler, made the strongest impression on Scott.[34] Swaine led the team that paddled, poled, carried and cooked as Scott made his way across the north in 1905. Scott heartily commended Swain to his American readers:

He is a fine type of the old half-breed race of packers and voyageurs which is fast disappearing; loyal and disinterested, cautious but fearless, full of the joy of life which consists in doing and possessed by that other joy of life which dwells in retrospect, in the telling of old tales, the playing of old tunes, and the footing of dance steps. Jimmy was enjoying a mighty old age after a mighty youth. He had been able to carry 600 pounds over a portage nearly a quarter of a mile long. He had run on snow-shoes with the mail from Moose Factory to Michipicoten, a distance of 500 miles, in six days, carrying only one blanket, a little hardtack, and a handful of tea. Now in his sixty-seventh year he was the equal of the best of the young fellows.[35]

Scott's admiration for Swaine's apparent manliness reflects a common yearning among early 20th century Anglo-North American men to sample and extol more rugged lifestyles as a temporary alternative to ur-

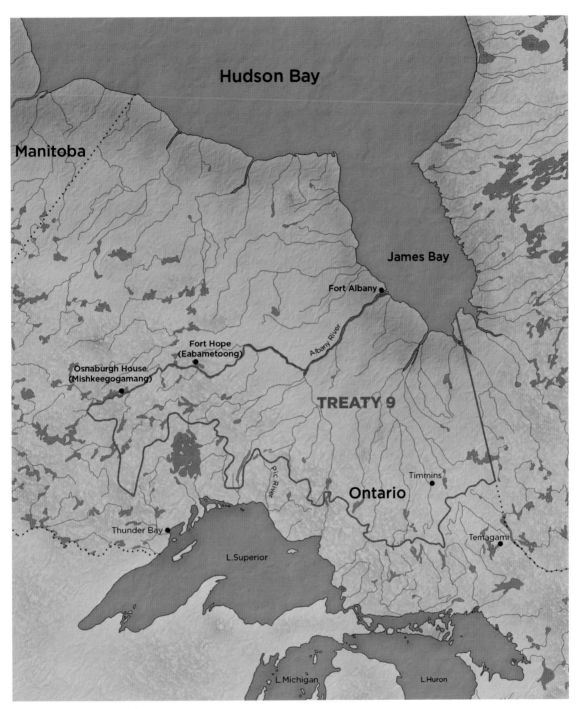

Treaty 9 stretches south from the Albany River to below present day Timmins, and west from James Bay almost to the Manitoba border, covering more than 233,000 km².

banity and industrialization.[36] This attitude was Scott's generation's adoption of myths of "the noble savage." While canoeing the Gatineau with Archibald Lampman or on summer treaty expeditions, Scott could experience and poeticize wilderness and some of its Indigenous inhabitants such as Jimmy Swaine. It was his own form of salvage ethnology.[37] In addition to running a wilderness crew and carrying, in bare feet, the heavy portage loads of a man in his 20s, Swaine's musical abilities held special appeal to the artist cum treaty commissioner. Jimmy Swaine was an accomplished fiddler. Scott writes fondly of evenings by the campfire hearing Swaine play and later at night in his tent listening to the Métis fiddler play tunes on his beat-up, but adequate instrument:

> He had scraped the belly and rubbed it with castor oil, and the G string had two knots in it. But what matter! When Jimmy closed the flap of his tent and drew it forth out of its blue pine box, I doubt whether any artist in the world had ever enjoyed a sweeter pang of affection and desire.[38]

Although Scott, an accomplished pianist who was then married to the American violinist Belle Botsford, recognized the humanity in fellow musician Jimmy Swaine, that did not deter his steadfast determination to execute the Crown's colonizing purpose of clearing the way for Canadian dominance of the north and its Indigenous peoples. Scott imprisoned people like Swaine in the past. Their virtues might be reflected in his journalism or poetry but the reality of their culture and their contributions to Canada were bound to be effaced in the emerging nation imagined by Scott.

Musiciens, Poetes, Adorateurs

Jacques Soustelle had a keen ethnological interest in music. His mentor Paul Rivet had instructed his students that music was a bridge between contemporary Indigenous folkways and ancient civilizations. In 1932, Soustelle brought a rudimentary wax cylinder recording device to Mexico.[39] He recorded the very high-pitched, choral keening of Mazahua women accompanied by drums, among other instruments. Field audio recording was widely practiced by students of Paul Rivet. Germaine Tillion recorded Berber musicians in the Algerian mountains, while the Soustelles were making recordings in Mexico.[40]

Soustelle wrote at some length about his audio recording. Often, he was accompanied by the expatriate German engineer and amateur ethnologist Roberto Weitlaner who worked for a mining company in Mexico City. In Soustelle's popular account of his early days in Mexico, he wrote that sometimes the enterprising audio engineers provided alcohol to encourage the performances of recalcitrant singers, « *Le seul problème consistait à verser assez pour les faire chanter et assez peu pour ne pas les assommer complètement... Il est vrai que cette limite paraissait difficile à atteindre.* »[41] [Trans: "The only problem consisted in providing enough (alcohol) to get them singing, but little enough so as to not get them plastered... It's true that this limit seemed difficult to achieve."]. Soustelle well knew that *pulque*, the fermented juice of the maguey cactus, was a staple of many festivals and rituals in the Mazahua, Otomi and Pame villages he frequented in central Mexico.

Soustelle devoted an extensive chapter of his *Mexique terre indienne* to the music, dance and rituals of Indigenous peoples he encountered. Soustelle described a moonlit night of music in an Otomí village in 1933. An occasion on which Soustelle, wife Georgette and Robert Weitlaner were taken to an impromptu outdoor concert in a mountain valley of central Mexico:

Tchank'in, a Lacondón hunter and shaman, photographed by Soustelle c.1934.

Jimmy Swain (also spelled Jimmie Swaine, Suain or Suaine), a guide of the 1905 expedition.

Soustelle (standing, left) with
expedition colleagues and
Lacondón Mayans, Chiapas,
Mexico c.1934.

*Parfois un indigène du cercle élevait brusquement la voix et chantait trios ou quatre vers sur un ton
aigu d'incantation, sans que personne parût l'entendre. En fait, personne ne semblait rien entendre ni
faire attention à rien, nous étions tous comme pétrifiés, laissant aller nos pensées emportées par le vent
au gré des deux musiciens. Si j'en juge par moi, ces pensées étaient chargées d'une tristesse sereine ou
plutôt d'une indifférence heureuse, comme si nous étions devenus des oiseaux entrainés sans savoir où
par quelque grande tempête... J'ai encore ce chant-là dans les oreilles quand j'écris, ou quand je pense
à Jiliapan. Il se lie pour moi à la vision d'une vallée verte au creux des montagnes hostiles, et d'une
groupe compact d'hommes, à peau brune où l'on est absorbé, retenu, un des leurs.*[42]

Occasionally one of the Indians in the circle raised his voice and sang three or four verses in an
acute tone of incantation without anyone understanding. In fact, no one seemed to understand
or to pay particular attention, allowing our thoughts to soar with the wind and the will of the

musicians. In my case, these thoughts were full of serene sadness or moreover a happy indifference, as if we were birds carried away by a great storm… I still have that song in my ears when I think of Jiliapan. It's linked with a vision of a green valley in the heart of hostile mountains, and a small group of men, of brown skin where one is absorbed, and held onto as one of theirs.

Soustelle also participated in the preparation of a yearly festival in San Bartolo del Llano in 1933. He accompanied musicians on a tortoise shell guitar after he and his wife Georgette were instructed in ritualistic dance steps by the *jefe* of a *cofradía*, brotherhood, that had a troupe of dancers and musicians in the festival. As he recalled in *Mexique terre indienne*, Soustelle sported a skirt made of tiny strips of metal fashioned and illustrated for him by the *jefe*. He wrote:

> *Un autre motif piqua ma curiosité. C'était un petit bonhomme, de face, deux paillettes rondes figurant les yeux, et il tenait dans la main droite un objet carré. A ma demande le capitaine éclata de ce rire violent qui lui était particulier, et m'expliqua non sans satisfaction que ce bonhomme, c'était moi-même. Et l'objet carré? Eh bien c'était l'appareil photographique; je trainais toujours et partout, c'était devenu évidemment mon caractère distinctif aux yeux des Indiens de San Bartolo del Llano.*[44]

> Another motif piqued my curiosity. It was a fine little fellow with two little objects for eyes, and he was holding a small square object in his right hand. When I asked, the chief broke into the raucous laughter that was uniquely his, and explained to me not without satisfaction that the little fellow depicted was me. And the square object? Well that was the camera that I was forever carrying, that became part of my distinctive character in the eyes of the Indians of San Bartolo del Llano.

Soustelle's dance costume was topped off by a crown of feathers. To the amusement of his Mexican *confrères* Soustelle donned the costume, « *Avec l'aide du chef qui ne se lassait pas d'admirer son œuvre, je revêtis le costume et me plaçai la couronne sur la tête. Chacun s'émerveillait de voir un étranger si brave sous ce vêtement. Ce fut un instant glorieux.* »[45] [Trans: "With the help of the chief who could not stop admiring his work, I put on the costume and he placed the crown on my head. Everyone marvelled at the sight of a foreigner who looked so brave in that clothing. It was a glorious moment."]. The incident contradicts the received perception of the middle-aged Soustelle in his native France where he gained a persona as a dour intellectual and politician in the years after the Second World War. Clearly, the youthful, public exuberance of Jacques Soustelle graduate student was subsumed over time by a poker-faced, humourless public presentation. The skirt and the feathered hat from the *cofradía* are to be found now in the archives of *le Musée du quai Branly* in Paris.[46]

Unlike Scott, who tended to see signs of *métissage* as unequivocal symptoms of Aboriginal demise, Soustelle sometimes expressed his admiration for the Indigenous Mexican genius for cultural absorption and survival. On other occasions, he bemoaned the toll Indigenous languages and folkways suffered under the official Mexican federal government ideology of *indigenismo* that purported to embrace a "cosmic race" of mixed race peoples with Indigenous and European origins.[47] Soustelle's writings reveal, in turns, admiration, skepticism or confusion over Mexican *indigenismo*, the cluster of policy and ideology designed for the incorporation of the Indian in Mexico that was a hallmark of the post-revolutionary era in Mexico. Soustelle was welcomed to Mexico by Manuel Gamio, an ethnologist, archaeologist and government mandarin.[48] Gamio was a leader of an activist ethnology and assertive *indigenismo* of the 1930s that sought to redeem and valorize Mexico's Indigenous past in the building of a *mestizo* nation.[49]

Her fierce soul hates her breath

Duncan Campbell Scott's travels with the fiddling guide Jimmy Swaine in 1905 inspired a plethora of works by Scott in which culture and ethnicity intersect. Scott expressed admiration for the Métis Jimmy Swaine. That stands in contradiction to much of his literary output which generally privileges the European and predicts doom for what he considered the darker, disturbed, infantile Indigenous element. In his Indian poems, Scott sometimes exalts the prowess of a "weird and waning" race while simultaneously predicting its demise.[50] A number of Scott's pivotal poems that brush on the subjects of miscegenation and trans-cultural lives, "The Onondaga Madonna," "Indian Place Names," "A Scene at Lake Manitou" and "The Halfbreed Girl" among them, express no sympathy nor reveal little understanding of how Indigenousness might be woven into and preserved in a "civilized" Canada. Such poems suggest that the Métis imagined by Scott suffer from what scholar Brenda Macdougall has called "damaging cultural ambivalence."[51] These poems argue that Aboriginality, whether noble or "savage," must stand down to allow the Canadian nation to progress. Macdougall:

> Over time, the idea that race not only existed but was meaningful came to be regarded as natural and immutable in western European thought. Within such a system of classification, there was little room for those who did not easily fit. When these discrete categories mixed – when miscegenation occurred between races rather than between subcategories of the same race – these systems became problematic.[52]

In the fall of 1906, immediately following the second treaty expedition, Scott published *Via Borealis* in a handsome edition featuring reproductions of wood engravings by the Canadian artist Alfred Howard.[53] The publicity notice for the work proclaimed:

> "Via Borealis," slender though its contents, will surely enhance the poetic reputation of Mr. Duncan Campbell Scott. His art here is to be seen in its fullest perfection, and will be a revelation to many readers already familiar with his work. This little book will take flight on the wings of Christmas and will settle in many homes beyond the sea.
>
> The seven poems it contains were written this summer during an extensive canoe trip which the author made through the wilderness of new Ontario.[54]

The publicity material does not state the actual purpose of Scott's "canoe trip." A reader unaware of his civil service duties might have well imagined the intrepid poet finding his inspiration by campfires he had lit himself on evenings following arduous days of paddling. While Scott and his friend Pelham Edgar, the expedition secretary, did paddle together in evenings in a small birch bark canoe and occasionally joined in the paddling from their positions in the freighter canoe, generally they were seated without paddles along with other treaty officials.[55]

Via Borealis included a poem entitled "The Half-Breed Girl." The poem almost certainly owes its inspiration to the treaty expedition. It is likely among the poems that Scott began to compose en route. Edgar made several references to Scott's poetic output on the 1906 journey in both his journalistic account and in his memoirs. "Duncan caught a poem as we were going through Island Lake and is still reeling it in. I have not seen it yet. This morning he read two splendid stories to me that he has written lately."[56] Edgar also refers to Scott's preoccupation with the camera.[57]

"The Half-Breed Girl" reflects Scott's broodings about the north, miscegenation and the merits of "civilization" and perceived Indigenous "savagery." Its protagonist is caught between worlds. Like Jimmy Swaine, Scott's imagined Métis female is to be admired for her adaptability to western norms while maintaining traces of Indigenousness. As a woman, she is regarded by Scott as an agent of change via intermarriage. The conflict within Scott's mind is apparent in his poetic lament for the romanticized "savage" past that he believes haunts her being:

The Half-Breed Girl

She is free of the trap and the paddle,
    The portage and the trail,
But something behind her savage life
    Shines like a fragile veil...

The reek of rock-built cities,
    Where her fathers dwelt of yore,
The gleam of loch and shealing,
    The mist on the moor...

She wakes in the stifling wigwam,
    Where the air is heavy and wild,
She fears for something or nothing
    With the heart of a frightened child...

She covers her face with her blanket,
    Her fierce soul hates her breath,
As it cries with a sudden passion
    For life or death.[58]

The poem has attracted the attention of some of the leading critics of Scott's poetry.[59] It puts into opposition the "civilized" traits the girl has from her Scottish side with the "savage" elements of her Indigenous forebears. Scott's illusory race theory reflects thinking about Métis peoples that was common in his era.[60] The structuring assumption of the poem is that a "half-breed" girl's soul can only be the site of racial conflict. Her Scottish ancestry echoes in her soul bespeaking a civilized world that conflicts with her Indigenous background and lifestyle of netting fish and living in bush camps. Scott refers to the "frail traces of kindred kindness" that haunt her as she awakes in a "stifling wigwam."

According to Scott, her mixed ancestry leads to confusion and despair, "she cannot learn the meaning – of the shadows in her soul." Late at night with stars peering through the tent flap "like the eyes of dead souls," the girl is poetically forsaken by Scott, abandoned to a state trapped between worlds, "her fierce soul hates her breath,…" When one considers this poem alongside Scott's admiration for Swaine, a fundamental contradiction arises: Scott sees merit in the male, musically inclined guide who literally charts a course between societies. However, in this particular poem, and others, Scott seems incapable of evoking the same successful possibility for his female protagonist who must, in Scott's view, suffer a dual identity.

The poem reflects Scott's primary concern with Indigenous peoples: their inevitable disappearance via an absorption into Canadian life. In "The Last of the Indian Treaties" Scott reported to his American readers on a process that he believed he was witnessing firsthand along the Albany River in 1905. Although he was impressed by the religiosity of some of his guides, he did not believe they would integrate Christianity so much as be inexorably overwhelmed by it:

The crew that took the commission from Moose Factory to Abitibi were constant in their vespers and every evening recited a litany, sang a hymn and made a prayer. There was something primitive and touching in their devotion, and it marks an advance, but these Indians are capable of leaving a party of travellers suddenly, returning to Moose Factory in dudgeon if anything displeases them, and the leader of the prayers got very much the better of one of the parties in an affair of peltries. But any forecast of Indian civilization which looks for final results in a generation or two is doomed to disappointment. Final results may be attained in, say, in four centuries by the merging of the Indian race with the whites, and all these four things – treaties, teachers, missionaries, and traders – with whatever benefits or injuries they bring in their train, aid in making an end.[61]

Scott's predication of "an end" for Indigenous peoples changed according to his audience. In 1921 as deputy superintendent general of Indian Affairs, Scott delivered an extensive briefing before the Parliamentary Committee on Indian Affairs. At that session, Scott declared that he wanted to end "the Indian problem" and that the policies of the government he served would ensure that there were no more Indians in the "body politic" within 50 years. Scott predicted that the toughening of rules regarding compulsory attendance at residential schools and the loss of status under the Indian Act for Indians who left the reserve under certain circumstances or for the children of women who married whites, would speed the assimilation project.[62]

In Scott's day, he and fellow adherents of the assimilation creed believed that Christian religion and government policy would dovetail to achieve "civilization." As historian John S. Milloy has demonstrated, the Canadian government inherited colonial policy that featured as, "Its central mechanism, the partnership of Christianity and civilization – represented by the joint presence and activity of departmental agents and missionaries on Canadian reserves."[63] As a principal architect of such policies, Scott's own religiosity is a conundrum. Although Scott himself was the son of a Methodist missionary, he was not an active Christian. He never claimed that he was driven to his "day job" out of a sense of Christian duty. His poetry contains only infrequent overtly Christian sentiments. However, there are recurrent evocations of spirit, of soul and ghostly presences as in "The Piper of Arll."

In 1893, two years after his father's death, Scott published "In The Country Courtyard – To the memory of my Father."[64] The poem is a meditation on death and loss set in a rural church cemetery in the evening. Although the poet allows that "God's own weeds are fair in God's own way," Scott does not use the occasion to celebrate, share or take comfort in his father's Christian faith. His poetic contemplation is remarkable for its absence of Christian religious sentiment:

> And now I leave the dead with you, O night;
>> You wear the semblance of their fathomless state,
>> For you we long when the day's fire is great,
> And when the stern life is cruelest in his might,
>> Of death we dream;
> A country of dim plain and shadowy height,
>> Crowned in strange stars and silences supreme.

Given what appears to be an almost agnostic approach to life, it is striking that Scott, the bureaucrat, always privileged strict Christianity as a lever in Indian policy. In his prose, Scott repeatedly invokes the fundamental place of Christianity in Indian policy.[65] In his poetry, Scott often dealt with the contest between Christianity and "savagery" in the Indian heart. This is tellingly expressed in a poem written following an

1898 departmental journey that Scott took near the shores of northern Georgian Bay and the northeast corner of Lake Superior in northern Ontario, an area just south of the Treaty 9 territory he visited in 1905-06. "Night Hymns on Lake Nipigon" describes a moonlit paddle of a canoe brigade in which singing takes on a tone of syncretism:

> Sing we the ancient hymns of the churches,
> Chanted first in old-world nooks of the desert,
> While in the wild, pellucid Nipigon reaches
> > Hunted the savage.
>
> Now have the ages met in the Northern midnight,
> And in the lonely, loon-haunted Nipigon reaches
> Rises the hymn of triumph and courage and comfort,
> > Adeste Fideles.
>
> Tones that were fashioned when the faith brooded in darkness,
> Joined with the sonorous vowels in the noble Latin
> Now are married with the long-drawn Ojibwa,
> Uncouth and mournful.[66]

The scene of paddling Lake Nipigon at midnight rings with poetic and practical truth. It is often best to paddle large lakes late at night or just before sunrise – the wind is generally light. Lake Nipigon is a huge, infamously treacherous body of water for an open canoe. Also, singing can pace the exertion required in hours of paddling, particularly on a lake. "Night Hymns on Lake Nipigon" is a truthful, evocative poem about canoeing that endures. It found new life in the 1980s when filmmakers wed it to paintings by Anishinaabe artist Norval Morrisseau in a video.[67]

Scott's denigration of Anishnaabemowin (the Ojibwa language) as "uncouth and mournful" in *Night Hymns* contradicts Scott's own *At Gull Lake, August 1810*, also published in 1935, about the beautiful Keejigo, an Anishinaabe (Saulteaux) woman:

> As Earth abandons herself
> To the sun and the thrust of the lightning.
> Quiet were all the leaves of the poplars,
> Breathless the air under their shadow,
> As Keejigo spoke of these things to her heart
> In the beautiful speech of the Saulteaux.[68]

Scott's poetic output is replete with such contradictions.

As a young scholar travelling in Mexico, Jacques Soustelle reflected at length on the religiosity of Mexican Indigenous peoples. Soustelle took a very negative view of the Catholic church's responsibility in the subjugation of Mexican Indigenous peoples:

> *Ainsi l'introduction du christianisme au Mexique n'a nullement signifié, contrairement à ce que l'on entend répéter sans cesse, une élévation de la culture des Indiens. Avec souplesse et diplomatie, le clergé a su conquérir sur ceux-ci une énorme influence, et cette conquête a été son seul but.[69]*
>
> So the introduction of Christianity to Mexico in no way means, contrary to what one hears repeatedly, an elevation of Indian culture. With skill and diplomacy, the clergy knew how to win an enormous influence over the Indians, and that conquest was its only goal.

Soustelle was also very skeptical about the "conversions" that the church claimed. In his ethnological work, he repeatedly discovered vestiges of Aztec and Otomí religious practices in the fiestas, songs and in the visual representations in *oratorios*, small private chapels throughout central Mexico. He detected the traces of pre-Colombian beliefs as he studied the Otomí language by establishing links in the music and poetry he observed first-hand in the 1930s with the foundational texts of Mexican people recorded by Friar Bernardino de Sahagún and his peers in the decades following the 16th century Spanish conquest of Mexico.[70] He observed that descriptions of natural events in Otomí were often related to the deity who was thought by the pre-Hispanic Otomí to control such events:

> *La phrase: "Il y a eu une éclipse du lune" se traduit par "L'Honorable Dame Lune est morte." On comprendra pourquoi de demeure sceptique sur la profondeur de l'évangélisation chez les indigènes du Mexique.*[71]

> The sentence: "There is an eclipse of the moon" is translated as "The Honourable Lady Moon is dead." We will understand why we remain sceptical about the depth of evangelization of Indians in Mexico.

He also carefully observed and documented the non-Christian practices of the Lacandón Maya in the rainforests of Chiapas in southern Mexico. The contrast between Scott and Soustelle on this matter, between Canadian Indian policy and emergent values of French ethnology infused with *indigenismo*, is stark. In the left-wing publications *MASSES* and *Spartacus*, Soustelle opposed the French political right and the French Catholic church who bemoaned the anti-clerical aspects of the Mexican revolution. Soustelle insisted on the fundamental legitimacy of the revolution:

> *Et tel Français moyen, ne sachant rien de la révolution mexicaine ni de son dernier chef, le général Calles, a pourtant appris son nom comme celui d'un tyran et d'un Néron moderne. Pas une voix ne s'est élevée pour remettre les choses en places pour étudier et exposer clairement dans ses origines comme dans son développement présent le "conflit religieux."*[72]

> And the average French person, knowing nothing of the Mexican revolution or of its last leader General Calles, has however learned his name as a tyrant and sort of modern Nero. Not a voice is raised to put things in proper context and to clearly expose in its origins the present development of the "religious conflict."

Soustelle implored his readers to appreciate the tenacity and adaptive genius of Indigenous religions in Mexico. Soustelle perceived the limitations of Catholic hegemony among Mexican Indians:

> *Tous les Indiens du Mexique, à l'exception de quelques tribus inaccessibles dans les forêts et les montagnes comme les Lacandóns, sont nominalement catholiques et se considèrent comme tels… Mais ce « christianisme » mérite examen. Avant la conquête, les indigènes du Mexique possédaient des religions hautement élaborées au point de vue théologique et rituel et solidement ancrés dans leur vie quotidienne. Les missionnaires se rendirent bientôt compte de la difficulté de les supplanter entièrement: ils trouvèrent préférable, avec la souplesse de la clergé de fabriquer une sorte de « mixte » en adaptant les dogmes catholiques aux croyances indigènes, et vice-versa.*[73]

> All the Indians of Mexico, with the exception of some inaccessible tribes in the forests and mountains such as the Lacandóns, are nominally Catholic and consider themselves as such… But this "Christianity" merits examination. Before the conquest, the Indigenous peoples of Mexico possessed highly elaborated religions from the theological point of view and ritual solidly anchored

Soustelle and wife Georgette c.1934
in rural Chiapas, Mexico during his
doctoral research travels.

> in daily life. Missionaries soon realized the difficulty in supplanting this entirely: they found it
> preferable, with the suppleness of the clergy to create a sort of mixture in adapting Catholic dogma
> to Indigenous beliefs, and vice versa.

Soustelle of the 1930s, while a man of the left and an anti-fascist, was not a Marxist.[74] While he was not religious himself, he insisted that religious freedom should be a right of citizenship in a modern state. As a young man, he was adamant in his support of religious diversity in Mexico; as a middle-aged politician he argued for respect for Islam and the religious rights of Christian and Jewish minorities in *l'Algérie française*.

Scott in his early Indian poems and in statements on behalf of the Indian Department sometimes observed the tensions in mixing of Indigenous and Euro Canadian world views. These inklings surfaced in some of Scott's final poems and short stories in which Indigenous characters are featured. From time to time, the up-and-coming functionary of the 1905-06 treaty commission perceived something more admirable at work in Indigenous culture. One occasionally detects empathy in Scott's writing, for the difficult transition that Anishinaabe people were undergoing at that time. "The Last of the Indian Treaties" concludes with Scott's recounting of a meeting with an Indigenous man who had ventured from the deep bush to meet the commissioners:

> The James Bay Treaty will always be associated in my mind with the figure of an Indian who came
> in from Attawapiskat to Albany just as we were ready to leave. The pay-lists and the cash had been

securely packed for an early start next morning, when this wild fellow drifted into camp. Père Fafard, he said, thought we might have some money for him. He did not ask for anything, he stood, smiling slightly. He seemed about twenty years of age, with a face of great beauty and intelligence, and eyes that were wild with a sort of surprise – shy at his novel position and proud that he was of some importance. His name was Charles Wabinoo. We found it on the list and gave him his eight dollars. When he felt the new crisp notes he took a crucifix from his breast, kissed it swiftly, and made a fugitive sign of the cross. "From my heart I thank you," he said. There was the Indian at the best point of a transitional state, still wild as a lynx, with all the lore and instinct of his race undimmed, and possessed by the simplest rule of the Christian life, as yet unspoiled by the arts of sly lying, paltry cunning, and the lower vices which come from contact with such of our debased manners and customs as come to him in the wilderness.[75]

In his official capacity, Scott insisted that the "transitional state" for Indigenous peoples must lead to absolute incorporation into Canadian society. As a mature poet and writer of short stories, more nuanced and complex narratives emerged.[76] The short stories, "Expiation," "Spirit River," "Vengeance is Mine," "Labrie's Wife" and "Vain Shadows" all revolve around relations between fur traders and Indigenous peoples.[77] "Expiation" is the tale of a trader who ostracizes himself for cruelly mistreating a loyal Indigenous servant and contributing to his death. This tragic and well-wrought story is one of the very few occasions in which Scott's fictional work deals with white guilt. "Spirit River" is set in a fictional village on the shore of Lake Superior where a multicultural cast of Indigenous peoples, Métis and southern European immigrants interact. The fictional "Spirit River" is a believable imagined turn-of-the-century version of towns like Schreiber, Marathon and Jackfish on Lake Superior's northern shore. There is perhaps a link between these artistic renderings and Scott's concluding vignette in "The Last of the Indian Treaties." Scott's muted admiration for Charles Wabinoo of Attawapiskat is bound up in a sense of Victorian imperial superiority tempered by artistic curiosity and a humanism that Scott often squelched in his governmental pursuits.

That humanism and artistic force emerged in some of the later Indian poems. "A Scene At Lake Manitou," published in 1935, is a depiction of the grief of an Indigenous mother over her dead son – a grief that Scott could fully appreciate having lost his 12 year-old daughter in 1907; the aforementioned "At Gull Lake: August, 1810" tells of the heartbreak and eventual murder of Keesigo, a beautiful Anishinaabe (Saulteaux) woman in love with a trader from the Orkneys; and finally, "Lines in Memory of Edmund Morris" published in 1916 pays tribute to the painter who briefly accompanied the treaty commission near Chapleau and Biscotasing, Ontario in the summer of 1906. Edmund Morris drowned in 1913.[78] In his poem, Scott compared his deceased friend to Akoose, a great prairie chieftain.[79]

"Lines in Memory of Edmund Morris" encapsulates the Scott conundrum. In the poem, Scott memorializes a deceased friend by evoking the prowess of a great plains hunter. As author Edward W. Said argued, artists of empire more often than not reflect imperial values, but that does not mean they cannot produce accomplished work. As Said wrote about one great artist of the British Raj, "What a sobering and inspiring thing it is therefore not to just read one's own side as it were, but also grasp how a great artist like Kipling (few more imperialist and reactionary than he) rendered India with such skill."[80] Duncan Campbell Scott was an artist in the employ of a fledgling nation state imbued with British imperial values. "Lines in Memory of Edmund Morris" in its way is respectful of Indigenous ways. Nevertheless, the attributes of Akoose are of the past, the splendid, primeval, Aboriginal, mythic past of Scott's imagination. Confronted with the real, breathing fully human Charles Wabinoo in 1905, Scott sees vestiges of Indigenous nobility, "still wild as a lynx," but

*In 1977 author Cullingham was
a child care worker with the
Kenora Children's Aid Society in
Kenora, Ontario.*

Kenora, Ontario, 1977

As I dress in my basement room, two pairs of running shoes dart by my window. Quickly I finish dressing and head up the basement stairs and out the back door making as little noise as possible. As I peer around the corner of the house in the -35c morning light off Black Sturgeon Lake, I see two kids dressed in T-shirts, denim jackets, jeans and Adidas shoes. One is holding a clear plastic sandwich bag to his face and then hands it to the other. I intercede. They giggle and stagger, snot dripping from their noses and saliva gathered at the corner of their mouths. They drop the plastic bag and a tube of model airplane construction glue, their intoxicant of choice.

I'm a worker for the Kenora Children's Aid Society (CAS) at the Birchcliff Group Home. It houses "wards of the crown" who are primarily Ojibway children from reserves like Grassy Narrows, Whitedog and others in the Kenora District. The economic and social life of such reserves have been disrupted by timber and mining devel-opment, by road and railway construction and especially by the poisoning of the English Wabigoon River system with mercury from the Reed Paper Company's mill downstream in Dryden, Ontario. Reed is a conglomerate ultimately controlled by interests in then apartheid-era South Africa. Reed and its timber cutting associates in the bush of north-western Ontario enjoy favourable concessions from the province, which claims jurisdiction over natural resources.

I'm a childcare worker at Birchcliff with a special em-phasis on outdoor education because of my cross-country skiing and canoeing background. My suggestion of having parents from neighbouring reserves visit the group home to teach Ojibway language and culture is rejected. I am told that the children are "culturally deprived" and must be removed from Aboriginal influences in order to facilitate their transition to regular schools in Kenora. According to CAS, that is the most effective means to combat the children's "acculturation."

Scott with an unidentified
Indigenous woman.

has forebodings of how such character will be diminished in a process of cultural transition. Scott's ideology dictated that the man in transition must surrender. Akoose, however, will live forever in Scott's poetry.[81]

Scott had a formative encounter of a more psychologically unsettling nature during the treaty voyage of 1905. After he and his companions left the rail line at Dinorwic, Ontario, they began an arduous canoe journey upstream to the headwaters of the Albany River. En route, the treaty commissioners decided to stop at the Lac Seul post. Given that federal representatives of the rank of Scott and Samuel made infrequent trips to remote Indian country, Scott also decided to pay a visit to the local Treaty 3 reserve. Treaty 3 had been signed in 1873. It covered the Northwest Angle near the present-day Ontario-Manitoba border. Like Treaty 9, the earlier treaty had been formulated to ease westward Canadian expansion – in this instance the passage of the Canadian Pacific Railway to the west.[82] He learned from a trader located at the post there that Indians camped elsewhere on the lake were holding a Whitedog Feast. Anishinaabe people held such feasts for various reasons. Ethnologists and First Nations Elders recount that hopes of curing sickness and seeking success in warfare were among the motivations.[83] On July 6, 1905, members of the Lac Seul band were feasting likely in hopes of warding off illness. One of the Dominion police officers with the commission, Joseph L. Vanasse submitted an account of the proceedings to a magazine a few years after the event. He described signs of ill health at Lac Seul:

> Here was a centenarian couple sitting on the ground under their tent; there was a four-year-old boy
> stretched on the ground, the poor little fellow was dying of consumption.[84]

Under such circumstances, goods and money would be collected as payment for the medicine person holding the feast. The Anishinaabe of the Treaty 9 region also practice shaking tent ceremonies in which medicine people would seek visions inside a wigwam or tent. During such ceremonies, the structure often begins to shake violently as the fasting medicine person received visions. Sweats in different tents, in which water is poured on rocks inside a tightly sealed tent or wigwam to produce steam and vapour to cleanse the body and purify the spirit, sometimes accompany these ceremonies. Sweats were designed to open the mind for the reception of an enhanced perception of life and the cosmos. Such ceremonies are practiced by Anishinaabe to this day.[85]

The events of July 6, 1905 profoundly affected Scott. There are three written accounts of the day's events: those of Scott himself, that of co-commissioner Samuel Stewart and that of police officer Vanasse. There appears to be no record, written or oral, of how the day's events were perceived by the Anishinaabe participants. Approximately 20 years later these events inspired Scott's most disturbing Indian poem, "Powassan's Drum," published in 1926. That poem expresses Scott's anxiety over "native" spirituality. It is difficult to ascertain exactly how Scott arrived at the name Powassan, but a Chief Powassan of Shoal Lake near the present-day Ontario-Manitoba border had run afoul of Indian Department restrictions on the use of the *mitigwakik* (water drum) in ceremonies.[86]

In 1905, an Indian agent recommended he be arrested for unlawful spiritual practices. As Anishinaabe historian Brittany Luby has investigated the controversy over *mitigwakik* use in Treaty 3 Lake of The Woods territory and imagines Chief Powassan holding a drum ceremony in a poetic invocation in her work of Indigenous environmental history.[87] In 1921, in the period between his Treaty 9 trips and the publication of "Powassan's Drum," Scott sent a circular to Indian agents in the Kenora region suggesting a crackdown on Indigenous dancing.[88]

The official report of the treaty commission, co-signed by Scott, Stewart and D.G. MacMartin makes scant mention of the encounter that inspired Scott's poem, "The afternoon of the 6th was spent in a visit to the Lac Seul Reserve in an attempt to discourage the dances and medicine feast which were being held upon the reserve."[89] In 1905, many Indigenous religious rites were illegal in Canada. Scott and his fellow commissioner Stewart extended the intent of a law directed primarily at the west coast "potlatch" and the sun dance of the prairie peoples to sacred activities of the Anishinaabe in the woodlands.[90] The other accounts are more capacious than the official record. In his personal journal, Samuel Stewart produced a detailed report, one of the longest entries in the personal journal that Stewart kept through the Treaty 9 voyages during summers of 1905 and 1906:

> Before arriving at the post, we had heard the sound of a drum some distance up the Lake, and we now learned that that was a medicine drum that was being used at a "Dog Feast" which was being held on the reserve about eight miles distant.
>
> As certain of the proceedings connected with the feast are contrary to law, we decided to go to the reserve and endeavour to put a stop to them. Henry Kau-agee, Chief of the Lac Seul Band, who had come to meet us, informed us that he had used his influence to the upmost to prevent the feast from being held but that the majority of the band was against him in regard to this matter. Accompanied by the Chief and Mr. Mackenzie we left about noon for the reserve and arrived there about 1pm. Our approach to the reserve created not little excitement among the Indians who were assembled on a hill overlooking the lake. This excitement was to a great extent occasioned by seeing the two policemen in uniform in the canoe, and also from the fact that we formed a

rather large party evidently intent upon important business. On landing Mr. Scott speaking for the Commissioners demanded to see the Conjuror. For a time, the Indians professed ignorance as to the whereabouts of this important personage but the Chief at last located him for us. The man was a short, stout-built Indian and it was soon very evident that he had all the Indians under his control. He was very diplomatic in his answers to the questions asked of him and would not commit himself by a promise to discontinue the practice of conjuring. We learned that his name was Nistonaqueb, and that he was considered to have great skill in driving out the evil spirits from those afflicted with any kind of disease. We heard that Nistonaqueb made a good living by his conjuring, but he professed to be giving his services for free and out of compassion for those who were suffering from various ailments. The goods and money received by him were used to appease the evil spirits that were tormenting those for whom his services were called into requisition. He also said that he was acting under instructions from Pow-wassang the head Conjuror of the district who would visit him with diverse pains and penalties if he neglected to hold these Dog Feasts. Nistonaqueb showed great diplomacy in the manner in which he conducted his case. We could not but be surprised at the wisdom shown by him in the replies given to certain questions and the manner in which he avoided to answer others. We gave the Indian a lecture on the folly of their actions conduct and told them that their actions for the future would be carefully watched. Afterwards we invited them all to come to the post in the evening where a good meal would be given them. We arrived back at the Post at 4pm and found that Mrs. Mackenzie had an excellent dinner ready for us. We were sorry that Mr. Scott was not able to partake of the good things provided which included a roast of caribou as he was somewhat indisposed. Miss Mitchell, Mrs. Mackenzie's niece, assisted in entertaining us and we were well looked after.[91]

Like Scott in "The Last of the Indian Treaties," Stewart believed that the Indians were impressed, even fearful, of the presence of the two Canadian policemen. A photograph taken from a high vantage point on shore shows the treaty flotilla crossing a lake, canoes aligned side-by-side and with flag raised. This panorama was afforded the feasting Indians of Lac Seul who looked out as the commission approached and landed on shore. Police officer Joseph L. Vanasse recreated the scene in his account:

This being the third day of the White Dog Feast, as practiced by the Ojibway Indians at Lac Seul, it was consequently the most interesting. As we approached, we could hear easily in the distance the beating of the drums at the camp. We had been seen coming, for the natives were all standing on the brow of the hill, lining the shore. They were quite amazed by our presence among them, as they did not expect that we would go to them. In order to impress them all the more, I picked up the Union Jack which was waving over our canoe and carried it up the hill, to the camp, marching in the footsteps of the Commissioners.[92]

Returning to Stewart's account above, it is clear that the Indians were not the only impressed parties. Stewart used the upper case every time he wrote the word "Conjuror," and he states that the commissioners "could not but be surprised at the wisdom" Nistonaqueb displayed. The commissioners encountered a self-possessed, confident man who was nothing like the projections of childish "natives" in their pre-conceived ideas. Nistonaqueb and "Pow-wassing the head Conjuror" were clearly different from the grateful, proto-Christian Charles Wabinoo. These medicine men had perhaps more in common with the fictional Akoose than the "Indians in transition" along the Albany River that summer. In Stewart's account, we also learn that Scott, who had "demanded to see the Conjuror" fell ill after returning to the Lac Seul trading post and did not join in the entertainment provided that night. Perhaps Scott's health was disturbed by the powerful and confident Indigenous man he encountered earlier in the day.

The final account of July 6 is Scott's, a hand-written journal kept during the treaty expedition. The entries were written in truncated phrases, really nothing more than a series of bullet points. Scott was familiar with point form written communication as he often carried on important departmental business by telegram. In his treaty voyage journals, Scott appears to have been keeping a sparse factual record to aid in the writing of the official report back in Ottawa. Apparently, he spent more time on the treaty trips writing poetry, as the rapid publication of *Via Borealis* in autumn 1906 and the accounts of the academic Pelham Edgar who accompanied the commission in 1906 would attest.[93] Scott's journal scribbled in the bush and water-damaged in places, makes for laborious, sometimes, inconclusive reading.[94] The entry for July 6, 1905 is almost entirely legible:

> Broke camp at 6:45. Up at 5 bath in lake. Lovely morning. Reached Lac Seul Post at Very few Ind. Had breakfast with the Mackenzies in charge of the Post. Lunched whitefish. Learned that the Inds were having a dance and making medicine on the Res. About 7 miles away. Went down in canoe. Mac-rae and his party. Long argument with old medicine man – cunning old gent with a swollen jaw. Powassan the head medicine man had sent them word to [indecipherable] the medicine. Conference with Mackenzie about this. Warned Ind. Not to dance. He promised to do what he could to stop it. But we must speak to Powassan. Returned about 4 taken ill[95]

Scott's firsthand account resurfaced years later in his poem "Powassan's Drum." Scott's encounter with "the old medicine man – cunning old gent with a swollen jaw" clearly made a strong impression. Although the local trader and de-facto Indian Department agent Mackenzie "promised to do what he could do to stop it," Duncan Campbell Scott decidedly did not win the day with Nistonaqueb. Scott left the encounter puzzled and troubled by the "old gent" and by the apparent eminence of his master Powassan. Scott described Nistonaqueb in grotesque terms, specifying his "swollen jaw." By day's end, Scott was taken ill. The question arises, was he cursed by Nistonaqueb? Certainly, ethnological evidence of curses in Anishinaabe culture abounds.[96] One can only speculate as to what truly occurred as a result of the argument with Nistonaqueb that day. What is certain is what remains – "Powassan's Drum," a foundational work of Canadian literature that raises unsettling questions about Scott and the collective Canadian psyche.

"Powassan's Drum" is a long nightmarish poem. Selected stanzas follow that illustrate Scott's bewilderment and apprehension over what he witnessed in July 1905. The poem was completed in 1922 and published in 1926. In April 1925, it was read by playwright and producer Bertram Forsyth at Victoria College Chapel at the University of Toronto. In addition to Forsyth's performance, Scott read his own poetry at the Victoria College event.[97] He read the first lines of "Powassan's Drum," "Throb-throb-throb-throb/Is this throbbing a sound?/Or an ache in the air?," evoke the only mention that Scott made of Indian drumming in "The Last of The Indian Treaties":

> In our journey we had been borne by the waters of the Albany through a country where essential solitude prevails. Occasionally the sound of a conjurer's drum far away pervaded the day like an aërial pulse;…[98]

The suggestion that "solitude prevails" betrays a widely shared misapprehension of the Canadian north as profound as the miscomprehension of "native" spirituality in the poem "Powassan's Drum" itself. To the Anishinaabe, their homelands were not a solitary place. Humans, animals, plants, the winds, stars, sun and moon made the territory a homeland for the people who lived along the Albany. In 1906, Scott was burdened with reductive perceptions of what civil society and civilization might contain. By 1922, Scott inflated his unpleasant brush with shamanism on the treaty commission into nightmarish poetry. He transmuted Nistonaqueb, the "cunning old gent with a swollen jaw" into a satanic figure:

> He crouches in his dwarf wigwam
> Wizened with fasting,
> Fierce with thirst,
> Making great medicine
> In memory of hated things dead
> Or in menace of hated things to come,
> And the universe listens
> Headless and impotent in power.
> The canoe stealthy as death
> Drifts to the throbbing of Powassan's Drum.
>
> To the throb – throb – throb – throb –
> Throbbing of Powassan's Drum.
> Is it a memory of hated things dead
> That he beats – famished –
> Or a menace of hated things to come
> That he beats – parched with anger
> And famished with hatred –[99]

Scott interprets the drum as a signal of hatred. However, in Anishinaabe culture, drumming is frequently associated with healing and the benevolence of the world's creator.[100] As the poem gathers in intensity, frequent allusions to the sounds of wind, water and thundering skies are added to the steady throbbing of Powassan's drum-sound is prevalent in the work of Scott an accomplished musician.[101] As a raging storm gathers strength, Scott introduces a nightmare of Aboriginal potency:

> Then from the reeds stealing,
> A shadow noiseless
> A canoe moves noiseless as sleep,
> Noiseless as the trance of deep sleep
> And an Indian still as a statue
> Molded out of deep sleep,
> Headless, still as a headless statue
> Molded out of deep sleep,
> Sits modelled in full power,
> Haughty in manful power,
> The Indian fixed like bronze
> Trails his severed head
> Through the dead water
> Holding it by the hair,
> By the plaits of hair,
> Wound with sweet grass and tags of silver.

The terror of "Powassan's Drum" harkens perhaps to Scott's subjective feeling as he departed ill from his confrontation with Nisconequeb on July 6, 1905. What is clear is that on that day, Scott encountered something imponderably non-Christian, something utterly at odds and resistant to the ideology that he was expected to advance as a representative of the Canadian government. The episode fixed the adversary in Scott's mind. He emerged understanding, intellectually and viscerally, that the Aboriginal world contained forces beyond his control. That realization fueled both his art and his determination to further policies aimed at creating a Canadian identity more palatable to his own understanding and beliefs about liberal progress and modernity. The episode steeled him for the hardening of Indian policies of which he would become a principal advocate as he climbed up the ladder at the Indian Department.[102]

Scott's revulsion is also contradictory, even hypocritical. Scott dabbled in the supernatural himself. He practiced various aspects of theosophy and divination that were prevalent in Ottawa of the 1920s and 1930s.[103] Scott's second wife, the poet Elise Aylen, was a noted theosophist and spiritual seeker who left Canada permanently after Scott's death in 1947 to live out her days in an ashram in India.[104] On one occasion, as Scott courted the young Aylen in the latter part of his career at the Indian Department, he wrote of his frustrations in attempting to get to the "other side" from a Halifax hotel room where he was on departmental business, "I tried divination this morning with the Gideons Bible but did not get much out of it."[105]

Ceux d'en bas

Scott's unwillingness to abide aspects of Anishinaabe spirituality along the Albany River reflects the ideological predisposition of a post-Victorian representative of the Canadian state. The young ethnologist Jacques Soustelle, however, was keenly fascinated in the spiritual ways of Mexican Indigenous peoples. In the remote villages in the states of Hidalgo, Mexico, San Luis Potosí and Oaxaca, Soustelle carefully observed festivals and religious rites and wrote extensively in both his popular works and his academic papers about vestiges of ancient spiritual ways.[106]

Between 1932 and 1934, Jacques and Georgette Soustelle often lived among Mexican Indians. In a chapter of *Mexique terre indienne* entitled "*Ceux d'en bas*" (literally "those from below," best translated to English as the "underdogs"), Soustelle denounced the racism that Mexican Indigenous peoples faced particularly in rural areas. Soustelle borrowed his chapter's title from the eponymous novel by Mariano Azuela, a frank depiction of the suffering of ordinary people during the revolution – a work that Soustelle admired greatly:[107]

> *… les notabilités,…, n'ont pas assez de mots pour exprimer leur intime sentiment de supériorité sur les "Inditos" assez bêtes pour tomber dans les panneaux qu'on leur tend. J'ai rarement vu poussée à un haut degrés que chez ces gens la morgue de « la gente de razón » selon le titre que se donnent à eux-mêmes les créoles et les métis par opposition aux indigènes. Chez les propriétaires de la maison où nos quartiers étaient installés, notamment, cette morgue insupportable me repugnait; ce n'étaient, en s'adressant aux Indiens, que cris violents: Andale!: vas-y! Cours! Comme si tout indigène était un domestique né.*[108]

The wealthy do not have enough words to express their profound sense of superiority over the "little Indians" who (they believe) are stupid enough to be duped. I only saw this attitude displayed by the so-called "people of reason" which is the title the creoles and mixed-race people give themselves in opposition to Indigenous folk. The owners of the house where we were lodged disgusted me with their insufferable arrogance when speaking to Indians with violent cries of "Fetch! Go! Run!" As if every Indigenous person was a born domestic.

Querétaro, Mexico, *July, 2016*

Jacques Soustelle is remembered still in Mexico at the regional museum of Querétaro, a colonial city where Mexican emperor Maxmiliano was executed in June 1867, a month prior to Canadian confederation. The Hapsburg prince was named to the post by France's second emperor Napoleon III. The museum of Querétaro has a display of Otomí artefacts and culture; the Otomí people are Indigenous to the plains and mountains immediately north of Mexico City. The display includes reproductions of some of his sketches, and a citation from a song transcribed by Soustelle on his first visit to Otomí villages as he embarked on his doctoral research with his wife Georgette.

A colourful sketch (detail) that Georgette Soustelle made of a painting from inside one of the Otomí oratorios in San Bartolo del Llano, Ixtlahuaca, during Jacques Soustelle's Mexican doctoral research (Museum of Man, 1933).

The Soustelles travelled widely through central Mexico and also ventured to the Lacandón rainforest of Chiapas in 1934. For months at a time, the Soustelles lived in small villages or in the forest in homes and camps of Otomí, Mazahua or the Lacandón Mayan people. Jacques Soustelle became sufficiently conversant in both Otomí and the Mayan dialect of the Lacandóns to pursue research in the local languages.[109] In his written work, Soustelle exhibited an open mindedness and lack of moral judgement about the practices he observed.

The Lacandóns numbered less than 400 in 1934. Most of them did not speak Spanish. None among the group that the Soustelles encountered had converted to Christianity. They lived without electricity, running water or internal combustible engines in family groups numbering between 20 and 50 people. Lacandóns hunted animals and cultivated small plots that they hacked out from under the rainforest canopy. In the early 20th century social scientists began investigating them.[110] As a doctoral student, Soustelle was aware of American anthropologist Alfred M. Tozzer's 1904 doctoral thesis from Harvard University; Soustelle was also familiar with the disparate works of the German explorer and photographer Teoberto Maler and of the French photographer Désiré Charnay, who travelled through Mayan territory, including the Lacandón rainforest, in the late 19th century.[111] In addition to academic requirements, his sense of adventure was piqued by the Lacandón Mayan. He first accompanied some American and German amateur explorers to the region in 1933 in an ill-advised misadventure led by a German pilot from Mexico City.[112]

Although that group did make contact with the Lacandón Mayan, Soustelle was embarrassed when its members falsely reported to the Mexican and French press they had discovered abandoned treasure in the rainforest. Soustelle enlisted Paul Rivet in Paris to clear his name of the sensational story.[113] He decided to return to the Lacandón rainforest with a more scientific approach and in January 1934, Soustelle lived for four months among the Lacandóns. In occasional letters to his supervisor, Soustelle kept Rivet abreast of his itinerary:

> … d'abord, avec l'avion, nous avons survolé le fleuve Jatalé et les régions voisines pour aller atterrir au lieu dit San-Quentin, où nous avons fait préparer un champ d'atterrissage; de là nous avons rejoint à pied l'unique « Caribel » de la région, qui est habité par 5 familles de Lacondóns… avec qui nous sommes très bien entendus – Ils nous ont servi de guides et d'informateurs jusqu'à notre retour à El Real, l'hacienda qui nous servait de base.[114]

> … first with the plane we flew over the Jatalé River and the surrounding region to land at a place called Saint Quentin, where we had prepared a landing strip; from there we walked to the only "Caribel" of the region inhabited by five Lacandón families… we got along with them very well… They served as our guides and informants until our return to El Real, the hacienda that was our base camp.

It was there Soustelle met the redoubtable hunter and shaman Tchank'in. With Tchank'in as their interlocutor, the Soustelles trekked from their base camp among the Lacandón Mayan to Metsaboc Lake, a spiritual site for the Lacandón Maya, located in the heart of the Lacandón rainforest an area in southern Chiapas just north of Guatemala and west of the Yucatan peninsula. There they were shown a number of caves and petroglyphs that Soustelle argued linked these people to the people who lived in the same region before the Spanish conquest.[115] Proof to Soustelle of the validity of Rivet's teachings: traces of ancient Indigenous ways persist among their living descendants.

Soustelle, like Tozzer before him, pondered the link between these rainforest people and the great civilizations that had built magnificent temples and monuments at nearby Yaxichilan, Bonampak and Palenque. The Lacandóns' reverence for the vestiges of those great civilizations and the evident link of language convinced Soustelle and ethnologists that these people were descendants of the Mayan classic period. During the same period, the Mexican revolutionary state government was busy unearthing and curating official archaeological sites where Mexico's glorious imperial civilizations could be held up as shining remnants like ancient Greece and Rome.[116] Although Soustelle was interested in such archaeological projects, his academic focus in Mexico and his primary concern as a political figure decades later in Algeria was on the lot of living Indigenous people.

Soustelle considered Tchank'in a wise man and, as he did in the Otomi-Pame-Mazahua villages in central Mexico, he absorbed as much as he could of Lacandón religious practices. He was invited by Tchank'in to observe an invocation which required the careful building of a special structure and the laborious preparation of an intoxicating beverage made from forest plants. The piety and rigorous spiritual practices of the Lacandóns impressed him:

> *Au total, la religion, dans la vie quotidienne d'un Lacandón, pèse lourdement… Or il bâtit encore un temple, souvent plus spacieux et mieux agencé que sa propre case, avec sa table – autel ou ses étagères; il façonne avec soin ses encensoirs, modèle les figurines qui représentent les dieux, utilise le roucou, le noir de fumée la craie pour les décorer; il va récolter dans la forêt la gomme aromatique du copal et les baies odorantes; il bat dans la foret l'écorce dont on fait les bandeaux rituels, creuse un tronc d'arbre pour la fabrication du baltché, érige un abri sous le quel on prépare le k'ayem, entreprend de longs et fatigants pélerinages à Yaxchilán: bref, lui qui a déjà tant de mal pour se procurer ce qui lui est indispensable, pour lui-même et pour le siens, s'astreint en outre à un travail presque équivalent pour les services de ses dieux.[117]*

> In sum religion weighs heavily on a Lacandón's daily life… For he builds a temple that is often more spacious and better appointed than his own dwelling, on a table, an alter and shelves he carefully arranges the censers modelled on figures of the Gods, using roucou, the black substance used as a crayon for decorating; he goes out to collect the aromatic gum of copal and odorous berries; he takes from the forest bark that is used for ritual headbands, digs into a tree trunk to make baltché, erects a shelter to prepare k'ayem, undertakes long and exhausting pilgrimages to Yaxchilán: so he who has so much difficulty that which is indispensable, also compels himself to undertake almost as much work in service of his Gods.

Among the Lacandón Mayan, Soustelle began to ruminate about questions that would concern him for the rest of his career. He became deeply aware of the role of religion in people's lives across cultures. The fate of the Lacandón – their link to the great ancient Mayan civilizations – gave rise to a life-long concern in Soustelle about the destinies of civilizations. In contemplating such matters in his writings, his point of reference was the demise of classic Mayan civilization and the rise and fall of the Aztecs who had tamed most of Mexico in a few centuries but fell to the Spanish in the course of two years. His highly regarded *Les quatre soleils* of 1967, a mature work which complements his first, *Mexique terre indienne*, uses the ancient Mexican account of a succession of worlds that end in destruction as his leitmotif of human progress and decay. Soustelle believed this way of looking at human history and the cosmos was imbued in the daily lives of the Lacandóns. He experienced this way of looking at the world himself one day as he and his companions paused to eat during a long day's journey through the rainforest:

Pour manger, ils s'accroupissaient sur le sol, tiraient de leurs filets de portages des calebasses graves où ils mélangeaient avec l'eau le mais qu'ils avaient pris comme provision. Avant de porter la nourriture à leur bouche, ils plongaient le bout des doigts dans la bouillie, et en jetaient des gouttes aux quatre points cardinaux en psaodiant une courte formule sur des tons montants et descendants.

« Si nous faisions pas cela, il y aurait des orages, et puis des tigres viendraient, et nous dévoreraient, » disait Tchambor.[118]

To eat, they crouched on the soil, taking from their carrying bags deep gourds in which they mixed corn they brought with water. Before bringing the food to their mouth, they plunged their fingers into the mixture, and then through droplets to the four directions while murmuring a short chant with rising and falling tones.

"If we don't do that, there will be storms, and then tigers will come and devour us," said Tchambor.

Soustelle believed that civilizations could and would terminate. By the 1960s, he came to consider France's abandonment of Algeria as the sign of a French civilization in decay. Questions about the place of religion in everyday life, the fate of civilizations and the observation of politics were among the preoccupations that the young Jacques Soustelle took from Mexico in 1932-34. The comparative status of peoples and the risk of degeneration within a civilization was part of the bedrock of French social science of the late 19th century.[119] It would have been part of the formation of a scholar such as Soustelle born in 1912.

Soustelle was alternatively an advocate and a skeptic about the Mexican revolution. With the archaeologist and educator Manuel Gamio and other *indigenistas* as his guides, Soustelle visited several rural schools where Indigenous peoples were expected to benefit from the revolution's social progress. In a letter to Paul Rivet, Soustelle mentioned the first such visit:

Beaucoup de choses se sont passé depuis la dernière fois que je vous ai écrit, et en somme cette période pourrait se résumer sous le titre de « chasse aux Otomis.» La première expédition a été à Actopan, où nous sommes allés avec Gamio. Nous avons logé dans l'École normale rurale, très bien accueillis naturellement.[120]

Many things have happened since the last time I wrote to you, and in sum this period could be summarized under the title "hunt for Otomis." The first expedition was to Actopan where we went with Gamio. We were accommodated at the country normal school where we were very well received naturally.

In Canada, as Deputy Superintendent General of Indian Affairs, Duncan Campbell Scott led an effort of "aggressive civilization" in which policies of compulsory education, often in residential schools, and enforced assimilation through a variety of means was designed to terminate Indian identity.[121] Jacques Soustelle came to Mexico as the Mexican revolution's very different approach to Indian redemption and integration was shifting.[122] The *Secretaría de Educación Pública* (SEP) had begun to dedicate itself to the establishment of local-run rural schools and cultural missions throughout Mexico. The intent was still assimilation, an effort to eventually forge a *Mestizo raza cósmica* as the social bedrock of a unified Mexican nation.[123] In general terms, one can say that *indigenismo* aspired to enlist Mexican Indigenous peoples in the project of institutionalized social revolution. Overall, it was a government initiative with which Soustelle found favour and one that he thought courageously challenged the past predations against Indian people by the Catholic church and the long dictatorship of Porfirio Díaz (1876-80 and 1884-1911) that preceded the revolution:

Enfin ceux des Indiens qui sont déjà en marche, par l'agrarisme et par la diffusion de l'éducation, vers une autre destine que celles de leurs pères, de leurs aïeux et de cent générations dont l'incessant labeur est resté cache derrière le brillant décor du Mexique colonial, républicain et porfiriste. J'ai déjà rendu hommage plusieurs fois, dans ce souvenirs, aux maîtres ruraux. Je les tiens pour le vrai ferment du Mexique d'aujourd'hui eux dont la peine et quelquefois le sang fondent peu à peu un people nouveau avec sept millions de paysans à peau brune opprimés et méprisés. Qu'on feuillette les rapports des missions culturelles et des écoles rurales publiées par le Secrétariat de l'Éducation; on y verra les marches épuisantes à travers les montagnes, l'hostilité des caciques et des prêtres, les rebuffades et les mauvais traitements. Dans un village du Querétaro, l'instituteur se voit boycotté par les pauvres ignorants; à force d'insistance, il finit par en connaître la cause: « Le curé nous a dit que vous veniez élever nos enfants dans la religion protestante et qu'ils iraient tous en enfer. »[124]

Finally, these Indians are progressing, by agrarianism and the spread of education, towards an alternate destiny from that of their fathers, their ancestors and a hundred generations of those whose constant labour was hidden behind the brilliant décor of colonial Mexico, republican and Porfirian. I have already paid homage many times, in these memories, to rural teachers. I take them to be the real ferment of today's Mexico whose pain and sometimes blood is gradually forming bit by bit a new people with seven million oppressed and despised peasants of brown skin. One only has to look through the pages of the reports from the cultural missions and rural schools published by the Secretary of Education; you will see there the exhausting walks across mountains, the hostility of local leaders and priests, the rejections and the nasty treatment. In a village in Querétaro, the instructor found he was boycotted by the poor ignorant locals; after insisting, he learned the cause: "The priest told us you would raise our children in the Protestant faith and that they would all go to hell."

In 1936, with the publication of his first book, it was already clear that Soustelle felt the initiative was an essential plank for social justice in Mexico.

In his first book, he also registered concern about the cultural flattening that the *indigenismo* project could entail. His Mexico, it would appear, needed to display its Indigenous characteristics with pride:

Dans l'accomplissaient de leur tâche, pourtant, ne risquent-ils pas de dépasser le but, en poussant les Indiens à abandonner leurs particularités ethniques ou plutôt nationales pour se fonder dans la masse indistincte des métis?[125]

In the accomplishment of their task, however, do they not risk overstepping the mark, in pushing Indians to abandon their ethnic or even national particularities to place themselves in the indistinct Mestizo mass?

Ethnology student Jacques Soustelle under the pseudonym Jean Duriez registered his harshest critique of the Mexican revolution in the political realm.

Perhaps it was because he was a rising scholar in receipt of French scholarships from the French government who did not want his real name associated with left-wing journals such as *MASSES* and *Spartacus*; perhaps as a guest of the Mexican government he was worried that "Jacques Soustelle" might wear his welcome out in Mexico if its embassy in Paris took note of his dispatches. In neither his incomplete memoirs, nor in a long interview with an oral historian published after his death did Soustelle speak to the mystery.[126]

In these articles, Soustelle displayed the contrarian streak which earned him the *sobriquet,* or nickname, *le Mal Aimé*, the French equivalent of "the black sheep," from his biographer Bernard Ullmann.[127] He called

Diego Rivera *"un farceur pseudo révolutionnaire."*[128] Some analysts suggest that Soustelle developed an overly positive outlook on the post-revolutionary Mexico he observed as a young man.[129] However, a review of his journalism from Mexico reveal tendencies that haunt, or distinguish, his political career after the war. His loyalty lay not with the official revolutionary party, then led by Plutarco Elías Calles, but with the peasants. He made common cause with the subjects of his ethnological research, the agrarian Indians of Central Mexico and the oppressed of Chiapas.[130] He attacked the Catholic church in a long series of articles about religion in Mexico.[131] He also was extremely dubious about the socialist qualifications of the incoming president Cárdenas:

> Mais plus dangereux encore que le fascisme bruyant à chemises de couleur et à saluts romains, est le fascisme larvé, le fascisme méconnu qui se présente sous le nom même du socialisme: telle est justement la tendance du gouvernement actuel du Mexique. A la suite des dernières élections, en effet, général Cárdenas, doit entrer en décembre à la Présidence, et consacrer sa période de gouvernement à la réalisation du Plan de Six Ans.
>
> Comme l'écrit Salazar Mallén, fasciste notoire et grand admirateur de Mussolini, la caractéristique du fascisme est justement de planifier l'économie tout en conservant le régime d'exploitation capitaliste. Le Plan comporte surtout une offensive raisonné contre les organisations ouvrières: tous les syndicats « minoritaires » c'est-à-dire révolutionnaires devront disparaître au profit des syndicats unique contrôlés par les leaders corrompus à la solde du Parti officiel. S'ajoutant aux mesures déjà existantes (Tribunaux du travail, etc…), cette unification des syndicats tiendra la classe ouvrière mexicaine prisonnière d'un système corporatif destiné à perpétuer la collaborations des classes, c'est-à-dire l'exploitation d'une classe par l'autre. C'est ce qu'on appelle, dans les discours officiels le « socialisme mexicain ».[132]

But even more dangerous than the noisy fascism of coloured shirts and Roman salutes, is fascism in its larva form, unrecognized fascism that presents itself under the very name of socialism: this is precisely the tendency of the current government of Mexico. Following the last elections, in effect, general Cárdenas, will assume power in December, and will dedicate his period in government to the realization of a Six Year Plan.

As the notorious fascist and admirer of Mussolini, Salazar Mallén writes the characteristic of fascism is exactly in planning the economy while preserving exploitative capitalism. The Plan features above all a reasoned assault on labour organizations: all "minority" unions that is to say revolutionary ones must disappear for the benefit of unions under the control of corrupt officials under the control of the official Party. Adding to existing measures (Workers' Tribunes, etc.) this unification of unions will hold the Mexican working class prisoner to a corporate system destined to perpetuate the collaboration of classes, that's to say the exploitation of one class by another. That's what they call according to the official discourse "Mexican socialism."

Soustelle was convinced that the revolutionary elite of Mexico City, along with its bevy of international leftist and bohemian artistic followers, did not truly understand rural Mexico. Soustelle admired the courage and tenacity of rural teachers who worked directly with villagers, but he had little faith in the grandiose plans of the official Mexican revolutionary party in power:

> Ce que veulent, ce qu'ont toujours voulu les éducateurs révolutionnaires mexicains, c'est suivre le sens de l'évolution qui depuis les temps de la Conquête et surtout de l'Indépendance, brasse les races et fait que le nombre des métis tende à en former la base humaine du pays. Ils veulent créer une culture métis, où les éléments indigènes tiendront leur place et seront revêtus d'une éminente dignité, mais sans refouler les éléments européens. C'est quelque chose d'infiniment plus délicat et plus difficile que

d'exalter systématiquement tout ce qui est Indien ou que l'on croit tel; …

La réalité n'est pas si belle. La réforme agraire est privée de toute signification socialiste par le fractionnement des terres communales, qui est en train de créer au Mexique une petite propriété individuelle aussi arriérée et aussi lourde pour le progrès social qui constitue la base des certains pays d'Europe.[133]

What they want, that which revolutionary Mexican educators have always wanted, is to follow the path of evolution that since the times of the Conquest and above all since Independence, is to mix races and therefore to the Mestizos the human base of the country. They want to create a Mestizo culture, where Indigenous elements maintain their place and will be accorded eminent dignity, but without rejecting European elements. This is something infinitely more difficult than to systematically exalt all that is Indian or what one believes to be such.

Reality is not so beautiful. Agrarian reform is deprived of all socialist meaning by the breaking up of communal lands, that is part of a process of creating in Mexico of small individual properties that is as backward and burdensome for social progress such as the basic system in certain European countries.

In the 1930s, Soustelle evinced a skepticism of left leaning intellectual elites that would resurface in his lone wolf approach to the Algerian question. In the 1950s, he insisted that the *Front de Libération Nationale* (FLN), the leading Algerian revolutionary party, did not represent a majority of rural Algerians. As we shall see, Soustelle would famously claim that he understood the plight of the *fellaghs*, the Algerian peasants, in a way that FLN intellectuals and his *boulevardiste* opponents on the Parisian left of the 1950s did not.[134] Soustelle believed that the FLN and its supporters were removed from everyday Algerian reality, just as he believed the advisors surrounding Lázaro Cárdenas could not reconcile their *indigenista* policies with the harsh truths of Mexican rural existence.[135]

The Mexican education of the 20-something Jacques Soustelle is summed up in a letter to his mentor Paul Rivet written after he and his wife had completed the first phase of their research in Central Mexico. The letter begins with Soustelle's scientific interests. He speaks of the pottery that he collected at archeological sites; expresses mild annoyance that some of his would-be subjects have become *Mestizos*; but confidently proclaims that he has found "*survivants*" in Otomi, Pame or Mazahua villages scattered through the mountains.[136]

What is most intriguing about the letter is how Soustelle shifts to political concerns. He mentions the change of power in Mexico and the ongoing violence of the Cristero revolt in parts of Mexico. In an article on the anti-fascist movement in Mexico, Soustelle made specific mention of the atrocities, including mutilation and rape, committed by the Cristero side.[137] The Cristeros were right-wing Catholics sometimes with fascist tendencies that opposed the revolution and wished to restore the Catholic church's primacy in Mexican life. The Cristeros were reacting to the harsh anti-clericalism of the revolution in some areas, particularly Sonora in northern Mexico:

Vous savez peut-être qu'en ce moment le pays n'est pas très tranquille. Le général Calles a dû se retirer aux Etats-Unis, remplacé par Cárdenas, autour duquel s'est formé une sorte de front commun groupant le Parti National Révolutionnaire, les syndicats et les communistes. Mais, surtout ces derniers temps, une attaque très vive s'est déclenchée contre les communistes, tendant à les mettre au ban des activités officielles. Il y a environ 10 jours, sur le Zócalo de México, au moment des manifestations ouvrières en honneur de l'anniversaire de la Révolution, les fascistes « Chemises Dorées » ont chargé à cheval la foule; des centaines de coups de feu ont étés tirés, il y a plusieurs morts et des quantités de blessés. De leur côté, les catholiques font preuve d'une activité très inquiétante. Ces sont soulevés en

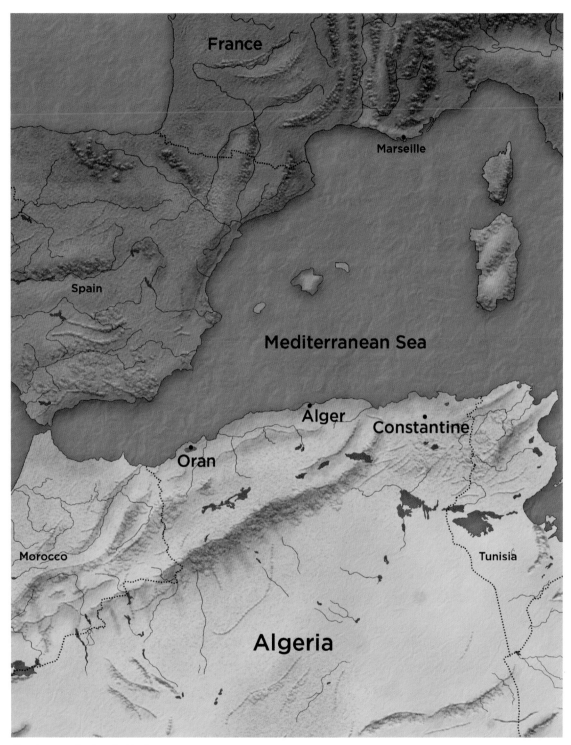

Algeria, a predominantly Muslim country, was ruled by France from 1830–1962.

armes dans Jalisco et Sonora, et dans plusieurs régions d'Aguascalientes, Puebla, Morelos, Michoacán. Ils se consacrent principalement à brûler les écoles, tuant les maîtres ou les mutilant. Il est arrivé récemment à Mexico deux institutrices à qui les bandits « cristeros » avaient coupé les oreilles, après les avoir violés.[138]

Perhaps you are aware that this country is not very calm at the moment. General Calles had to retire to the United States, replaced by Cárdenas, around whom has formed a sort of common front grouping the National Revolutionary Party, the unions and the communists. But most significantly, recently a very vigorous attack was unleashed against the communists, tending to exclude them from official activities. About 10 days ago, in the main plaza of Mexico City, at the moment of workers' demonstrations in honour of the anniversary of the Revolution, fascist "Golden Shirts" charged the crowd on horseback; hundreds of shots were fired, there were several deaths and a large number of wounded. For their part, Catholics are demonstrating some troubling activity. Some have raised weapons in Jalisco and Sonora, and in many parts of Aguascalientes, Puebla, Morelos, Michoacán. Very recently two female teachers had their ears cut off by "cristero" bandits after they had been raped.

Continuing in a political vein, the letter begs Rivet for information on the political scene in France where leftist supporters of the Popular Front were struggling with the right and worried about the rise of fascism in Spain, Italy and Germany.

On his return to France in 1934, Soustelle quickly finished his thesis and published *Mexique terre indienne*.[139] Rivet immediately enlisted him in the creation of *Le Musée de l'Homme* in Paris and named Soustelle, at the age of 25, assistant director.[140] However, from a promising career at the highest reaches of French social science as the designated successor to Rivet as director of *Le Musée*, Soustelle's life and career was changed irrevocably by the Second World War. As a resistance leader, Gaullist politician and controversial advocate of *l'Algérie française*, Soustelle would swerve dramatically from an exclusively academic career. However, Mexico would remain a fundamental source of his intellectualism as both a social scientist and political activist.

The Treaty 9 Commission of 1905-06 was a step up the ladder for the promising Indian Department bureaucrat Duncan Campbell Scott. He demonstrated to his superiors in Ottawa that he was capable of senior responsibilities. He, along with Samuel Stewart, was able to bring the Indians under treaty in a geographically critical area with the acquiescence of Ontario without major difficulty. Scott witnessed firsthand the ground on which the department's civilization campaign would be waged. The Treaty 9 Commission enhanced his understanding of the reserve system and the pattern of growth in schools and departmental management that would be required as settlement proceeded west. In Scott's mind, his Treaty 9 Commission experience re-affirmed the merit of the designation as "wards of the state" accorded to Indian peoples under Canada's Indian Act. He emerged more convinced than ever that the civilization program must continue. In future years, particularly after he became deputy superintendent general in 1913, he actively pursued toughening the policy in areas such as mandatory school attendance, the removal of Indian status, the suppression of Indian political organization, the outlawing of land claims research and enforcing existing prohibitions on Indian spiritual activities such as the potlatch and sun dance.[141] As he wrote in "The Last of the Indian Treaties," Scott the senior bureaucrat was convinced such steps were necessary in "making an end" of Indigenousness in Canada. Scott as bureaucrat was an inflexible defender of a system rooted in the traditions of British colonialism. Scott resided uneasily between polarities of brutal assimilation and humane accommodation that has afflicted Canadian policy concerning Indigenous peoples since the creation of the Canadian state in 1867. Although he seldom referred to his Indian Department career following his retirement in 1932, it is clear that Scott viewed the Treaty 9 Commission as a watershed in his civil service career. A year before his death, he re-published "The Last of The Indian Treaties" his 1906 essay for *Scribner's Magazine* in his final book.[142]

As an artist, the Treaty 9 Commission of 1905-06 was equally important to Scott. The publication of *Via Borealis* immediately following the commission enhanced Scott's stature as one of Canada's premier poets. The commission also provided a vein of inspiration that Scott would mine for years. As we have seen, "Powassan's Drum" emerged in 1922 following the encounter on Lac Seul with Nistonaqueb in July 1905. Later chapters explore other major poems including "The Height of Land," published in 1916, and short stories such as "Expiation," published in 1923 that reveal additional aspects of Scott's world view that flowed from the experience of the treaty commission. Also, Scott's friendships with the scholar Pelham Edgar and the artist Edmund Morris were affirmed by their joining the commission in 1906. In that way, the treaty commission played a part in consolidating the network of Canadian artists and intellectuals of which Scott was a charter member.

For Jacques Soustelle, the Mexico he first encountered in the 1930s would inspire and comfort him for the rest of his turbulent life. The understanding of Mexico that he garnered in that initial voyage would echo in his academic writings and even political speeches. To this day, Soustelle is a respected authority on Mexican ethnology.[143] Admirers of Soustelle's trenchant works on Mexican Indians are faced with a singular conundrum: why was he incapable of exhibiting a similar empathy for those beaten down by 125 years of French domination of Algeria? Like Scott, Soustelle was the inheritor of a refined colonial system. As we shall see, Soustelle's ideas, actions and dilemmas in Algeria are part of a French intellectual tradition concerning matters of colonialism and imperialism that run throughout the thoughts of Alexis de Tocqueville in the 1830s to Albert Camus, Franz Fanon and Jean-Paul Sartre in the 1950s and 1960s.

This giant imaginary creature [*alebrije gigantesco*] greeted visitors to a Mexico City park in 2018.

Chapter Three

LIBERAL IMPERIALISM

SCOTT and SOUSTELLE represented their respective nation's imperial ideals at critical junctures. Each man was an exponent of an elaborate imperial tradition.

Soustelle incarnated the contradictory impulses surrounding imperialism in post-Revolutionary France. Since 1789, France has been both aggressively imperialistic and eloquently anti-imperialistic, often simultaneously. In 1955, as a man of politics and the academy, Soustelle represented a tradition that uneasily encompassed both the colonial leaders who savagely quelled "native" revolts in the French empire and the likes of the *pied noir* writer Albert Camus and French Caribbean apostles of de-colonization such as Aimée Césaire and Franz Fanon.[1]

When Soustelle was named governor general of Algeria in 1955, France had been in Algeria for 125 years. At the time, almost no one in either France or Algeria was predicting that the French would be gone seven years later.[2] Since 1830, a succession of governments including a restored Bourbon monarchy, the constitutional monarchy of King Louis-Philippe, the "liberal empire" of Napoleon III, the second, third and fourth republics, and the Vichy regime, supported *l'Algérie française*.[3] Until the late 1950s, socialists and communists also joined in the general enthusiasm for France's *mission civilisatrice* in Algeria. Most French people, across a broad ideological spectrum, championed metropolitan control over Algeria which was regarded as an extension of France, separated merely from *la patrie* by the Mediterranean.

Duncan Campbell Scott came of age as Canada was in its infancy as a nation-state and as such he was also a leading technician of a particular imperial system. Scott began his career in 1879, only three years after the passage of Canada's Indian Act, which consolidated various colonial laws particularly from Canada West (later Ontario) and Canada East (later Québec) which the fledgling state inherited from its British parent.[4] Indian policy was a matter of fundamental importance to the new country. Scott was a central figure in the process of adapting Indian policies inherited from British North America to serve Canadian national purposes. In 1879, the Canadian Pacific Railway had not even reached the Canadian prairies, let alone the Pacific Ocean in distant British Columbia. The political leadership and emerging civil service of the nascent state had to "civilize" the Indigenous peoples residing between zones of settlement in Ontario and the new province of British Columbia. That responsibility fell to the Indian Department, then part of the Ministry of the Interior.

As we have seen, in 1905-06, Scott represented Canada in treaty negotiations in the north. As a functionary of the Canadian Indian Department, Scott was part of a tradition of Indian policy, including the making of treaties, that had its origins in the Royal Proclamation of 1763, which established guidelines for British policies towards Indigenous peoples following the conquest of New France.[5] Throughout his career at the department, Scott honed policies and administrative procedures rooted in British imperial practice. In the three or four decades leading to Canadian Confederation in 1867, British imperial theorists, colonial administrators, and politicians debated settler colonialism and policy regarding Indigenous peoples in Australia, Canada, the Cape colonies in southern Africa and New Zealand.[6]

I shall focus on select foundational texts that situate Scott as a political actor for a Canadian Indian Department spawned directly from British imperialism. From the 1830s to the 1860s, British academic and colonial administrator Herman Merivale wrote and lectured about "native" policy in the empire.[7] Following Confederation, the Canadian Indian Department soon found itself enmeshed in the dilemmas and contradictions that Merivale had foreshadowed. In 1879, the year Scott was hired, the Canadian government asked journalist and politician Nicholas Flood Davin to study American "industrial schools" for Indians. The "Davin Report" gave rise to Canada's own system of residential schools for Indian children. Merivale and Davin's texts define the spectrum of Canadian imperial policy, from an approach tempered by Christian humanism that respected some aspects of Indian culture, on the one hand, and aggressive civilization on the other which proposed a rapid transitional phase to outright assimilation into a presumed Canadian mainstream. Canadian Indian policy has uneasily resided between these poles since Confederation. It suffered its most contradictory and lethal phase during the tenure of Scott in the Indian Department. As Canadian historian Keith Smith has argued, when the new Canadian state asserted its hegemony westward, an aggressive Indian policy steeped in imperial tradition was a foundational tool:

> While imperialism and colonialism are never the same in any two situations, Euro-Canadians
> imposed themselves on the territory and First Nations of western Canada in many ways parallel
> to British interventions elsewhere. They brought with them generally British cultural understand-
> ings, legal and political structures, social and gender hierarchies and capitalist economy. They were
> just as prepared as Britons in Africa or India to promote and protect their economic interests and
> cultural values, with force, if necessary.[8]

Whether in the treaty-making territories of Ontario and the prairies or in the unceded territories of British Columbia, Canada's Indian Department during the career of Scott waged a comprehensive assault on the lands, resources and intricate life ways of Indigenous peoples. The new Dominion of Canada developed and projected an identity as a modern nation that acknowledged its English-French duality institutionally, but was determinedly British, monarchist, white and male in its essential character and mores.

The imperial legacies that informed Scott and Soustelle both depended on what Uday Singh Mehta, a political theorist, has called "liberal strategies of exclusion."[9] The British and French systems, as well as the Canadian system of internal colonialism, demanded that "natives," be they Arab, Berber, Indian, Métis or Inuit, be excluded from supposedly universal liberal norms of democratic inclusion. The ironies and contradictions in the policies that these "best and brightest" men implemented are illuminated by examining in some detail the machinery of such exclusionary strategies in French Algeria and post-Confederation Canada. Scott as a representative of a new dominion and Soustelle as representative of French republicanism were pledged to uphold what they saw as the ideals of western democracy. Yet, both men violated those ideals in the pursuit of policies they deemed to be essential to the growth of a mitigated democracy in Canada and a severely limited form of representative government in French Algeria. This disconnect is less contradictory than it first appears. Mehta and other scholars argue that historic actors like Scott and Soustelle, rather than being exceptions from liberalism, acted in a manner thoroughly consistent with the intellectual bedrock of British and French liberalism.[10] Political theorist Patrick Deneen has augmented these considerations by demonstrating that liberalism has depended on elites that do not reflect the culture of the polity they claim to represent. Deneen further argues that thinkers such as John Stuart Mill at the bedrock of the liberal English-speaking world had very illiberal ideas about "uncivilized" peoples.[11] The careers of Scott and Soustelle underscore the fundamental inability of the liberal regimes to engage effectively and humanely with Indigenous peoples.

As 19th century nation-states emerged, whether in concert with or in opposition to imperial powers, they simultaneously developed mitigated forms of democracy (women and those without property were more often than not excluded from the franchise) and barred specific groups from participating in aspects of political and economic practice.[12] Sets of conditions about matters including notions of property, the accumulation of individual wealth, the treatment of women and adherence to Christian faiths were employed to bar Indigenous peoples and others from full admittance to the circle of civilized men who could rightly expect democratic and human rights. Uday Singh Mehta observes that liberal appraisals of human capacity lead logically to a sort of "private members only" club. The requisite conditions for membership preclude the very universality the ideology pretends to uphold:

> …what is concealed behind the endorsement of these universal capacities are the specific cultural
> and psychological conditions woven in as preconditions for the actualization of these capacities.
> Liberal exclusion works by modulating the distance between the interstices of human capacities
> and the conditions for their political effectivity. It is the content between the interstices that settles
> boundaries between who is included and who is not.[13]

The tendency to exclude was apparent in the founding moments of the Canadian state. Conferences in 1864 Charlottetown and Québec City led to the promulgation of the British North America Act (BNA Act) and limited Canadian independence from Great Britain in 1867. Conference delegations were made up exclusively of Caucasian men who represented the political and economic elites of the British colonies which would unite to form Canada. There were no representatives of the various Indigenous groups residing in these colonies. The liberalism that informed the limited democracy envisaged by these men excluded not only Indigenous people but women and anyone without private property as well.

The division of powers in the federal system outlined in the BNA Act entrenched the exclusion of Indigenous peoples in the very machinery of the new state. "Indians, and lands reserved for Indians" became a federal responsibility.[14] Public lands and timber resources were placed under provincial jurisdiction at the time of Confederation. Then as Canada expanded westward and new provinces were created, legal precedent and political talks confirmed that oil, gas and mineral resources within provinces were eventually under provincial control as well.[15] The core of Canadian-style apartheid resides in the country's constitution which created a jurisdictional separation from Indigenous peoples and the lands and waters on which their cultures and livelihood depend. As the signatories of Treaty 9, and as many other Indigenous peoples who signed treaties with the Canadian government, learned in the course of the 20th century, this division of powers placed rural-based Indigenous peoples whose economic lives depended on harvesting natural resources in a tenuous economic and constitutional position. As Canadian historian Robin Jarvis Brownlie and other scholars have shown, provincial management of natural resources outside the strict boundaries of the federal lands "reserved" for Indigenous peoples under the numbered treaties undermined economies based on fishing, hunting, trapping and sustainable forestry practices.[16] In the "liberal strategy of exclusion" developed in Canada, the Indigenous wards of the federal state often became targets of jealous provincial jurisdiction over natural resources.

In July 1905 when Scott and the Treaty 9 Commission arrived at Osnaburgh at the headwaters of the Albany River these matters were central to what became a protracted debate over treaty terms. In his *Scribner's Magazine* account, Scott described the scene that welcomed him and the treaty commission at 2 p.m. on July 11, 1905:

But even the dogs of Osnaburgh gave no sound. The Indians stood in line outside the palisades, the old blind Chief, Missabay, with his son and a few of the chief men in the centre, the young fellows on the outskirts, and women by themselves, separated as they are always. A solemn hand-shaking ensued; never once did the stoicism of the race betray any interest in the preparations as we pitched our tents and displayed a camp equipage simple enough, but to them of the highest novelty; and all our negotiations were conducted under like conditions – intense alertness and curiosity with no outward manifestation of the slightest interest.[17]

To the surprise of the treaty commissioners the "stoicism of the race" meant skepticism of the treaty terms which had been agreed upon in advance by the federal government in Ottawa and the province of Ontario. The blind Chief Missabay stated that his people were prepared to accept the promised benefits of education and economic development provided that the treaty would allow tribal members to hunt, fish, trap and gather wild rice in traditional territories, activities which were the economic and cultural mainstays for the people of Osnaburgh. As the official treaty report under the signature of the commissioners' recounts:

Missabay, the recognized chief of the band, then spoke, expressing the fears of the Indians that, if they signed the treaty, they would be compelled to reside upon the reserve to be set apart from them, and would be deprived of the fishing and hunting privileges which they now enjoy.

On being informed that their fears in regard to both these matters were groundless, as their present manner of making their livelihood would in no way be interfered with, the Indians talked the matter over among themselves, and then asked to be given to the following day to prepare their reply.[18]

Both the official treaty report as well as Scott's account in *Scribner's Magazine* state that after a night's deliberation, Chief Missabay and his council decided they were satisfied by the reassurances and agreed to sign the treaty. However, this questions the mutual understanding that was achieved in such negotiations and in the case of Treaty 9 whether the commissioners simply lied about the true intent of the terms.[19] Scott's journalistic account of the proceedings at Osnaburgh lends credence to the view that the Indigenous peoples along the Albany River were assured of the economic rights under the treaty:

"Well for all this," replied Missabay, "we will have to give up our hunting and live on the land you give us, and how can we live without hunting?" So they were assured that they were not expected to give up their hunting-grounds, that they might hunt and fish throughout all the country just as they had done in the past, but they were to be good subjects of the King, their great father, whose messengers we were. That was satisfying, and we always thought that the idea of a reserve became pleasant to them when they learned that so far as that piece of land was concerned they were the masters of the white man, could say to him "You have no right here; take your traps, pull down your shanty and begone."[20]

The procedure at Osnaburgh sheds light on the peculiar give and take of Canadian Indian policy in the early post-Confederation period. The Treaty 9 process was consistent with the provisions of the Royal Proclamation of 1763. The proclamation set out in some detail the means by which the new Indian allies of the Crown should be treated. The proclamation dictated that Indians "should not be molested or disturbed in the possession of such parts of our dominions and territories as, not having been ceded to or purchased by us, are reserved to them. Or any of them, as their hunting grounds…" The proclamation also stated explicitly the formal process by which Indian title could be surrendered:

And whereas great Frauds and Abuses have been committed in purchasing Lands of the Indians, to the great Prejudice of our Interests. and to the great Dissatisfaction of the said Indians: In order, therefore, to prevent such Irregularities for the future, and to the end that the Indians may be convinced of our Justice and determined Resolution to remove all reasonable Cause of Discontent, We do. with the Advice of our Privy Council strictly enjoin and require. that no private Person do presume to make any purchase from the said Indians of any Lands reserved to the said Indians, within those parts of our Colonies where, We have thought proper to allow Settlement: but that. if at any Time any of the Said Indians should be inclined to dispose of the said Lands, the same shall be Purchased only for Us, in our Name, at some public Meeting or Assembly of the said Indians, to be held for that Purpose by the Governor or Commander in Chief of our Colony respectively within which they shall lie.[21]

Proceeding in a manner outlined in the Royal Proclamation, Scott and his fellow commissioners were the selected representatives of the Crown "in the right of Canada" during the Treaty 9 Commission. The commission held public meetings at each of the villages where formal treaty signings took place. The commissioners' conspicuous display of the British flag, the RCMP officers in full uniform and the holding of feasts of tea, bannock sweetened with raisins, and bacon provided by the treaty commission in the Osnaburgh palisade symbolized the venerable 18th century pledge. In these ways, the Treaty 9 signing marked a limited inclusion for the people of Osnaburgh. They were formally accepted in the Canadian federal constitutional system with the status of wards of the federal government in Ottawa. Their eventual "civilization" and ability to participate in Canadian democracy depended on the successful outcome of their tutelage. This process of civilization rested on compulsion – the social engineering of the federal government and Christian churches via residential schools and the corralling onto reserves cut off from natural resources coveted by provincial governments and industry.

With the imposition of the reserve system, the development of residential schools and crackdowns on Indigenous spirituality and political organization, Canada evolved a labyrinth of inherently contradictory strategies to, on the one hand, marginalize Indians, and, on the other, aggressively "civilize" them.[22] Canadian historian Ian McKay dissected these moves in an influential article which he developed further in a book on liberal order in Canada inspired by his original essay.[23] Mackay encourages his peers to examine Canada's liberal traditions in new ways that would, among other things, demand a re-examination of Canadian "Indian" policy:

It would mean a re-evaluation of Ottawa's handling of the "Indian question" as not just a series of misunderstandings premised on a distanced misreading of native societies, but rather as a fulfill-ment of liberal norms, which required the subordination of alternatives. Canadian imperialism in the High Arctic and in the West was not incidentally related to the Canadian values articulated by the 'Ottawa men' of the nineteenth and early 20th centuries. From Joseph Howe and John A. Macdonald down to the 1940s, there was a consistency of approach to Amerindian issues which invites theorization within a liberal-order research program. It was perhaps in the residential school system that the full utopianism of a vanguard liberalism came to the fore, for within these Christian/liberal manufactories of individuals, pre-eminent laboratories of liberalism, First Nations children were 'forced to be free,' in the very particular liberal sense of 'free,' even at the cost of their lives.[24]

Their status would also be defined by their exclusion from voting in federal elections – a prohibition that

Canada maintained for Indian people residing on reserves until 1960 with the passage of the Bill of Rights by the government of John Diefenbaker.[25] This potent "exclusion" had immediate political consequences as Canada added territory and granted provincial status to its western territories. For example, as Manitoba entered Confederation the majority of the population in the final boundaries of the province was Indigenous, either Métis or Indian.[26] Yet Indians living on reserves were denied the right to vote and the Canadian state-imposed itself on Indigenous peoples as late 19th century Winnipeg enjoyed an unprecedented real estate boom and the rich agricultural lands of southern Manitoba were flooded with settlers.[27] Similarly, approximately 70 per cent of the population of British Columbia was Indigenous at the moment the province joined Canada in 1871.[28] As Indian wards of the federal Canadian state, these people had no voting rights. In addition, provincial governments denied Indians in British Columbia the sort of public meetings and treaty negotiations that the Royal Proclamation guaranteed. With the exception of a few treaties on Vancouver Island, negotiated by colonial governor James Douglas prior to Confederation, the federal and provincial governments negotiated no treaties until the end of the 20th century in British Columbia. The situation prevailed until the Nisga'a of the spectacular, resource-rich Nass Valley in northwestern British Columbia began tripartite talks with the provincial government in Victoria and its federal counterpart in Ottawa in the 1990s.[29] Determined resistance by Indigenous peoples in the province supported by increasing numbers of non-Indigenous Canadians, coupled with the need for clarity for resource extraction companies around the title issue put increasing pressure on both the provincial and federal government.[30] It became clearer to more people that the liberal project of Canadian Confederation was profoundly illiberal as the country grew, property was divided, settlers arrived and natural resources in Indigenous territories were tapped.

In Canada, the transition from colony to nation meant a hardening of Indian policy. In this regard, Canada must be seen in the international context of nation-state formation in the 19th century. As national borders replaced the mutable boundaries between spheres of imperial influence, nascent nation-states asserted their own system of land entitlement and resource management. The result for a fledgling Canada and elsewhere in the Americas, as historians Jeremy Adelman and Stephen Aron demonstrated in a pivotal borderlands essay, meant a loss of prestige and power for Indian allies. These groups had been influential military allies, guides and had provided invaluable expertise on nutrition, weather and other matters in pre-industrial colonial conditions for French, Spanish and English dominions.[31]

Indigenous intellectuals such as Glenn Sean Coulthard and Leanne Betasamosake Simpson have grappled incisively with Canadian liberalism and the state's often contradictory web of policies concerning Indigenous peoples. They raise many of the inquietudes around liberalism explored by political theorists Patrick Deneen, Jennifer Pitts and Uday Singh Mehta but through a Canadian prism rather than via places such as French Algeria, colonial India or the United States.[32] In the Canadian context, they have augmented and further challenged the contribution of historian Ian McKay. Both see liberalism as part of the problem. Canada's "politics of recognition" of Aboriginal peoples in the form of official apologies and commissions of inquiry does not ultimately challenge Canadian assumptions about individual rather than collective rights, private property and the merit of resource extraction. Intriguingly for the purposes of this inquiry, Coulthard is influenced by Franz Fanon, a psychiatrist, political writer and thinker, who was marked deeply by his Algerian experience. Coulthard acknowledges his intellectual debt to Fanon in his *Red Skins, White Masks* – rejecting the colonial politics of recognition. One of Fanon's most influential works is entitled *Peau noire, masques blancs* [Black skin, white masks] from 1952 which explores the psychological tensions of dark-skinned peoples in a decolonizing world. Fanon, although originally from the French Caribbean, honed his revolutionary theories working as a psychiatrist in *l'Algérie française*.

Political writer Leanne Betasamosake Simpson brings an idiosyncratic blend of humour, poetry, satire, social science, song and wit to the fore in her cross-disciplinary, genre-crossing *oeuvre*. She illuminates some of the uncomfortable divisions between Indigenous activists and self-described Canadian liberals. In this passage she comments on the experience of working with her non-Indigenous neighbours in Peterborough Ontario, a place Simpson calls Nogogjiwanong:

> We know how to do this so they'll be into it. Listen to their paternalistic bullshit and feedback. Let them have influence. Let them bask in the plight of the native people so they can feel self-righteous. Make them feel better and when reconciliation comes up at the next dinner party, they can hold us up as the solution and brag to their real friends about our plight.[33]

Policies concerning Indigenous peoples and their lands have been a primary focus for liberal exclusion in Canada since Confederation. In constitutional terms, political history and relationships between communities over time, the disconnect between the project of liberal expansion in Canada and Indigenous rights is fundamentally Canadian and ongoing. In our era of official reconciliation following the release of the Truth and Reconciliation Report of 2015, Canadians have turned their attention, at least temporarily, to these issues. Change will be a complicated, grudging and slow matter particularly regarding the extraction of natural resources on lands on which Indigenous and settler interests conflict. Coulthard, Russell Diabo, McKay, Pamela Palmater, Betasamosake Simpson, Tanya Talaga and Chelsea Vowel are among the public intellectuals grappling with the underlying historical and social issues in play.[34]

Canada has moved from policies of aggressive civilization to a clutch of reconciliation measures in less than half a century. As recently as 1969, Canadian Prime Minister Pierre Trudeau (father of Canada's current leader Justin Trudeau) denounced the concept of Aboriginal rights in Canada:

> One of the things the Indian bands talk about is their Aboriginal rights. This really means saying, 'We were here before you, you came and you took the land from us and perhaps you cheated us by giving us some worthless things in return for vast expanses of land and we want to re-open this question. And our answer, and it may not be one that is accepted, our answer is 'No.' We can't recognize Aboriginal rights because no society can be built on historical might-have-beens.[35]

Prior to entering politics, Trudeau's antipathy to Québec nationalism led him to attack his separatist opposition by accusing them in an essay of suffering from a "wigwam complex." The language of the future prime minister's assault makes for uncomfortable reading in our day:

> *La verité, c'est que la contre-révolution séparatiste est le fait d'une minorité petit-bourgeoise impuissante, qui craint d'être laissé pour compte par la révolution du vingtième siècle. Plutôt que de s'y tailler une place à force d'excellence. Elle veut obliger toute la tribu à rentrer sous les wigwams, en déclarant l'indépendance.*[36]

> The truth is that the separatists counter-revolution is the work of a powerless petit-bourgeoisie minority afraid of being left behind by the 20th century revolution. Rather than carving themselves out a place in it by ability, they want to make the whole tribe return to the wigwams by declaring independence.

By 1982, Prime Minister Trudeau made a remarkable about face when he agreed to the recognition and affirmation of existing Aboriginal and treaty rights in the Canadian constitution. However, in 1969, the intellectual turned politician could not reconcile Aboriginal rights with his conception of a society rooted in classical liberalism. Trudeau's argument to "forget many things" echoed that of French liberal Ernest Renan in a lecture made at the Sorbonne in March 1882:

> L'oubli, et je dirai même l'erreur historique, sont un facteur essentiel de la création d'une nation, et c'est ainsi que le progrès des études historiques est souvent pour la nationalité un danger. L'investigation historique, en effet, remet en lumière les faits de violences qui se sont passés à l'origine de toutes les formations politiques, même de celles dont les conséquences ont été le plus bienfaisantes.[37]

> Forgetfulness, and I would even say historical error, are an essential factor in the creation of a nation, and that is why historical studies often endanger nationalism. Historical investigation, in effect, illuminates facts of violence that are at the origin of all political formations, even those that have been the most worthy.

In his *Qu'est-ce qu'une Nation?* Renan insisted on the necessity of forgetfulness, a deliberate act of exclusion, as a prime condition for national sentiment. Renan who ranks with Toqueville among the most influential 19th century French liberal theorists, insisted that a nation required a coming together that transcended religion, race, ethnicity, and even memory. So too it was for Pierre Trudeau, the great hope of Canadian liberalism circa 1969. The fact that his son, the current Prime Minister, at least rhetorically represents an entirely different vision for Indigenousness within Canadian society is a testament to the profound change and challenge that Canadians face in addressing the issue.

Liberal exclusions in French Algeria: Republican universalism versus settler colonialism

In the autumn of 1954, François Mitterrand, then France's minister of the interior, turned to his opposition in the national assembly to name the Gaullist deputy and respected academic Jacques Soustelle governor general of Algeria. After a fractious political process that would see one government fall, due in no small part to right-wing opposition to that nomination, Soustelle was re-nominated by a centrist coalition that succeeded the government of Pierre Mendès-France in which Mitterrand had served. In January 1955, Soustelle climbed aboard an aircraft bound for Algiers.[38] Before landing, he donned a fine suit and was then greeted at the airport outside the colonial capital by a group of French Algerian politicians. At that very moment, Soustelle stepped into a role in which he assumed executive responsibility for a cluster of liberal policies that formed a labyrinth of "strategies of exclusion." France had conquered Algeria in 1830. Every French government from that time on was convinced that economic opportunity and *la mission civilisatrice* demanded that France remain.

It is very difficult to overstate the magnitude of the Algerian question to French identity politics, culture and intellectual life during the 132 years of French rule there. Raymond Aron, Pierre Bourdieu, Albert Camus, Franz Fanon, Jules Ferry, Gustave Flaubert, André Gide, Guy de Maupassant, Auguste Renoir, Camille Saint-Saens, Jean-Paul Sartre and Alexis de Tocqueville are some of the internationally prominent French cultural and political figures whose careers and thinking were significantly shaped by Algeria.[39]

The stakes were very high indeed when Soustelle was named to the governorship of Algeria. Earlier in

1954, the French were defeated by Vietnamese revolutionaries in French Indochina. In November, an armed revolt erupted in *l'Algérie française*. France's post Second World War standing in the world was suddenly at risk. Although the situation across the Mediterranean was troublesome, no one seemed aware that the final chapter in France's history as ruler of Algeria was approaching a calamitous, bloody end. François Mitterrand, future *Président de la République*, turned to Soustelle at a pivotal moment. It was a "Hail Mary" nomination in which political foes suggested they could set aside their differences for the greater national good and to enhance the nation's standing in the world. There was bipartisan hope that Soustelle's understanding of Mexican Indigenous cultures could be applied to enhance understanding between Algerian Muslims and European settlers.[40]

The history of the process of French de-colonization following the Second World War is complex and inherently contradictory. These are the broad outlines of the situation in which Soustelle was thrust.[41] On November 2, 1954, just weeks prior to Mitterrand's surprising announcement, France had suffered a shocking and humiliating wakeup call in Algeria. On *le Tout Saint*, All Saints' Day, Algerian rebels mounted a multi-pronged attack on French settlers, military and police installations in many parts of Algeria. A mysterious organization known as *le Front de Libération National* (FLN) claimed credit. Suddenly what French generals and politicians had hitherto described as merely a few out-of-touch "bandits" lurking in the mountains representing almost no one emerged suddenly as a threat to be reckoned with.[42]

The timing of the attack was calculated for maximum psychological effect. *Le Tout Saint* came hard on the heels of a greater humiliation for France: Dien Bien Phu. In the spring of 1954, on the other side of the world in French Indochina, the post Second World War era of de-colonization began in earnest for the French when Vietnamese nationalist forces under the political leadership of Ho Chi Minh and the military stewardship of General Vo Nguyen Giap, who had both been trained at the finest French educational institutions, destroyed a French military base at Dien Bien Phu. It was a French defeat that echoed around the world – a well-trained, peasant army of small, brown-skinned men defeated a European army in a fixed battle with big guns.[43] Historians of French foreign policy identify the battle for Dien Bien Phu as a key moment for the decolonization process that would accelerate in the coming decades.[44]

By the autumn of 1954, the social democratic French Prime Minister Pierre Mendès-France made the fateful decision to make peace with the Vietnamese nationalists.[45] Vietnam was divided between a communist north controlled by Ho Chi Minh's government and a wobbly pro-western south. Thus, the stage for American involvement in defending south Vietnam was set and the imperial wheel took another fateful turn. In France, the loss of Indochina led to political recrimination and national soul searching. The military and political right bemoaned Mendès-France's position. The left generally approved of Mendès-France and saw in him the prospects of a post-imperial, humanistic, de-colonizing republicanism. Much of the respectable media, leading intellectuals and politicians of the centre and the left hoped France's withdrawal from *l'Indochine* would make France a moral leader in the west's approach to nations that would have to emerge from the enduring colonialisms and mandates of the mid-20th century.[46] To that hope was appended a firm belief: Algeria would remain French. After all, in the perception of many, it was not a colony, it was part of France.[47]

In terms of French administration, Algeria was in fact actually not a colony. It was an extension of France divided into large *départements* around the principal cities of Alger, Constantine and Oran in its northern littoral zones and an expansive, exotic Saharan territory to the south. That is why it fell to Mitterrand, minister of the interior, to name Soustelle governor general.

However, even though French governments declared Algeria part of France, it was an administrative fiction that was belied by cultural, economic and political facts on the ground. The government in Paris and a small group of local politicians and business people of European descent were in control. Full political rights were available only to those of European background, approximately 10 per cent of the population.[48]

The settler population largely of French, Spanish, Italian and Maltese descent had grown to about two million people by 1955, out of a total population of approximately ten million. Despite the intentions of the leftist Popular Front government of Léon Blum prior to the Second World War, as well as vague commitments made by General Charles de Gaulle following liberation, the French had not made good on promises to gradually extend the franchise on an equal basis to the overwhelming majority of Algerians of Muslim descent.[49] A small number of highly educated Algerian Muslims could vote in French elections; most were limited to voting in a second college of Muslim members that had limited impact on government policies.[50]

The humiliation of Dien Bien Phu stiffened French resolve to hold on to Algeria.[51] After the bloodletting of *le Tout Saint*, the government immediately made clear that Algeria would never be abandoned. Soustelle was brought in to hasten long-promised reforms. France had only recently faced the humiliation of Nazi occupation. With liberation came the realization that "old Europe" had been supplanted in global influence by the United States and the Soviet Union. Also, as the French imperial historian Raoul Girardet points out, Dien Bien Phu was compared to another French defeat – this one of 18th century in Canada:

> *Durant plusieurs générations, les jeunes Français avaient appris, sur les bancs de l'école publique, à considérer comme l'un des pires épisodes du « malheureux règne de Louis XV » la signature du « honteux traité » de Paris, qui avait livré aux anglais le Canada et l'Inde. En fait devant la désagrégation de l'Union française, c'est tout le système des valeurs élaboré par le civisme républicain et considéré, jusqu'aux lendemains de la seconde guerre mondiale comme constituant le fondement même de la conscience nationale qui est apparu aux yeux de beaucoup, comme brusquement et totalement remis en cause. Et c'est aussi dans la fidélité à ce système de valeurs que beaucoup ont trouvé la justification passionnée de leur attitude.*[52]

> Over several generations, French youth had learned, on the benches of public schools, to consider one of the worst episodes of the "unhappy reign of Louis XV" the signing of the "shameful treaty" of Paris, that handed Canada and India over to the English. In fact with the disaggregation of the French union, the entire value system of civic republicanism that was considered, until the aftermath of the Second World War, to constitute the very foundation of national consciousness that appeared in the eyes of many to be suddenly and totally undermined. And it's also in faithfulness to that set of values that many found passionate justification for their attitude.

Initially, criticism of Soustelle's unexpected appointment came from the political right in Paris and the hard-line settler faction in Algeria itself. As the prospect was debated by the press and politicians in Paris, some hard-line settlers in Algiers went so far as to suggest that Soustelle was an Arabic Jew coming to dispossess the European population.[53] More moderate opponents merely worried whether Soustelle, the academic who specialized in Mexican Indians, would effectively engage with political and economic reforms to which most previous governors general had paid lip service.[54] As it turned out, Soustelle would indeed undertake a broad range of ill-fated reforms during his short and eventful tenure as governor general in 1955-56. In the late fall of 1955, speculation about his plans for Algeria was front-page news. After consulting with his wartime mentor de Gaulle by telephone, Soustelle agreed to take the job even though it was proffered by an anti-Gaullist government.[55]

The Algerian whirlwind that Soustelle entered in 1955 dominated his career for the next decade. The experience transformed and tarnished his standing among French intellectuals and politicians. However, it must be said that the ideas that he advanced as governor general in 1955-56 were consistent with the ideology held by France's intellectual elite since the late 19th century. Algeria was the centrepiece of France's self-styled *mission civilisatrice*, a vast laboratory for the dreams of economic development, agricultural progress and social experimentation that was designed to enhance national stature as France's influence spread in Africa and beyond. According to French military historian Jacques Frémeaux, in times of national self-doubt, *l'Algérie Française* served as a medium of national affirmation. These crises included the transition from the Bourbon Restoration to the proto-liberal democracy of the July Monarchy that immediately followed the 1830 conquest of an Algeria under the Ottomans, or as in 1954-56 on the heels of stinging defeat in Indochina:

> *…le discours sur la nécessité de l'Algérie pour la grandeur de la France revient comme un appel des formules utilisées au moment de la conquête.*
>
> *Faut-il s'étonner de cette convergence ? En 1956 comme en 1830, le sentiment du danger de dégradation des positions internationales de la France est très présent… Ainsi, des régimes séparés par plus d'un siècle, et par l'abime des idées et des événements, se trouvent d'accord pour penser que, « on ne renonce pas à l'Algérie ! Ce n'est pas ni honorable, ni possible ! »*[56]

> …the discourse about the necessity of Algeria for the grandeur of France came back like a well-known formula used at the moment of the original conquest.
>
> Must one be surprised by this convergence? In 1956 just as in 1830, the feeling about the degradation of France's international stature is very present… Thus regimes separated by a century and by the abyss of ideas of ideas and events, find themselves in agreement in thinking, "one does not give up Algeria! That's not honourable, nor possible!"

Soustelle's allegiance to *l'Algérie française* was consistent with a long tradition of French liberalism rooted in secularism, religious freedom, the sanctity of private property and public education. Soustelle's imperial formation can be linked to the liberalism of the 19th century philosopher and politician Alexis de Tocqueville. Tocqueville, renowned for his works on the United States and his revisionist views of the French revolution, spent much of his career as a thinker and man of action concerned with Algeria. Tocqueville was an unrepentant advocate of the French conquest and occupation of Algeria that began in 1830. Further, despite his critique of American treatment of its Indigenous population, Tocqueville's views on how best to deal with Algerian Indigenous peoples were often brutal.[57]

Tocqueville visited Algeria twice. He led a parliamentary board of inquiry into settlement there. He wrote widely on the matter of French expansion in Algeria as both an active politician and political theorist. In correspondence with his friend, the British liberal political theorist John Stuart Mill, Tocqueville promoted the French presence in Algeria and expressed admiration of what he perceived as British success in India.[58] Like his friend and peer Mill, who tolerated violations of human rights in India that he would otherwise deem universal for civilized male human beings, Tocqueville was often unsparing in his militancy towards any Indigenous intransigence to France's *mission civilisatrice* in Algeria:

> *…j'ai souvent entendu en France des hommes que je respecte, mais que je n'approuve pas, trouver mauvais qu'on brûlât les moissons, qu'on vidât les silos et enfin qu'on s'emparât des hommes sans armes, des femmes et des enfants.*
>
> *Ce sont là, suivant moi, des nécessités fâcheuses, mais auxquelles tout people qui vaudra faire la guerre aux Arabes sera obligé de sa soumettre.*[59]

I have often heard in France from men that I respect, but of whom I do not approve, that they find it bad to burn harvests, or to empty silos and finally that we take over unarmed men, women and children.

These are, in my estimation, unfortunate necessities, but of which any people which wants to make war on Arabs will be forced to undertake.

Tocqueville shared a common French misconception. In fact there were relatively few "Arabs" among the native population of Algeria. Most of the non-European population descended from various Berber tribes that inhabited the coastal regions and mountains of the Aurès and Kabylian regions. Romans, Islamic armies from the Persian Gulf and Ottomans had mixed with the local population for centuries prior to the French conquest of 1830. By that point, most of that population was Islamic but distinctly non-Arab. In the mountainous regions that would prove to be a breeding ground for young men in 1956 taking up arms against the French, many people spoke languages other than Arabic and many practised local religions.[60]

In tactical matters, Tocqueville espoused a two-pronged approach to "civilizing" Algerians:

> Il y a deux moyens, d'amener chez les Arabes le schisme dont nous devons profiter :
> On peut gagner quelques-uns des principaux par des promesses ou des largesses.
> On peut dégoûter et lasser les tribus par la guerre.
> Je n'hésite pas à dire que ces deux moyens peuvent et doivent être employés simultanément et que le moment d'y renoncer n'est pas venu.[61]

> There are two means to create the schism among Arabs of which we must take advantage:
> We can win over some leaders by promises and largesse.
> We can disgust and weary tribes by warfare.
> I do not hesitate to say that these two means can and should be employed simultaneously and that the moment to abandon them has not yet come.

The liberal Tocqueville transparently advocated a dual strategy of political manipulation and armed repression that was applied by many subsequent French leaders in Algeria, including Soustelle.

Within a few months of his arrival, with *l'Algérie française* veering toward a full-out civil war, Soustelle demanded more troops and advocated ramping up the military campaign against the Algerian National Liberation Front (FLN). Simultaneously, Soustelle engaged in soft, personal diplomacy. Soustelle began regularly meeting local political and religious leaders in the urban slums and remote villages of Algeria as soon as he arrived in Algiers. To his dying day, Soustelle would argue that it was in such meetings he was hearing there the real voice of Algeria which, according to him, was suffocated by FLN firepower and terror.[62] In 1973, he bitterly denounced the "benefits" of decolonization for Algeria in an "open letter to the victims of decolonization":

> L'Algérie ayant été « décolonisée » je désire savoir si l'Algérien « moyen », l'homme de la rue à la ville, le fellah dans le bled, a gagné en bien-être, en dignité, en liberté, en culture, en sécurité depuis qu'il a été soustrait au joug du colonialisme.[63]

> Algeria having been 'decolonized,' I beg to know if the average Algerian on a city street, or the peasant of the village, has benefited in well-being, in dignity, in liberty, in culture, in security since he was subtracted from the yoke of colonialism.

As in many facets of his Algerian tenure, Soustelle's consultative approach, whatever its inspiration, was contradicted by other aspects of French policy. Soustelle also oversaw the establishment of euphemistically named *camps d'hébergement* [detention centres] designed to separate those Algerians advocating revolt from the general population.[64] In other circumstances, the likes of Soustelle would call such installations concentration centres. We will return to the question of these centres.

Soustelle's determination to keep Algeria as a place to re-assert French prestige and restore tarnished national dignity echoes Tocqueville who viewed French Algerian colonialism as an antidote to national political decadence. Tocqueville was unsure whether post-revolutionary France could ever build the sustainable liberal, democratic institutions that he believed were rooted in British and American political culture. Intellectual historian Jennifer Pitts argues that Tocqueville saw the agricultural and eventual industrial development and human settlement of Algeria as the sort of grand project that could unify the French and help reclaim national prestige after decades of post-revolutionary chaos and political intrigue:

> To build a cohesive, stable, and liberal domestic political order after the collapse of the ancient régime, revolutionary upheaval, and continuing political turmoil was Tocqueville's appointed task as a political thinker and actor. The notion of a proud French presence in Algeria, a vibrant and glorious new America filled with prosperous farms and engaged settler-civilians, played an important if too often overlooked part in Tocqueville's nation-building project.[65]

Tzvetan Todorov, a political theorist and historian, argues that for Tocqueville the conquest of Algeria was a national imperative born out of economic and strategic interests even if it meant compromising liberal values:

> *La politique n'est pas la morale: c'est la leçon qu'on peut tirer de la juxtapositions des divers écrits de Tocqueville. La morale doit être universelle; la politique ne saurait l'etre.*[66]

> Politics is not morality: that's the lesson one can derive for the juxtapositions in the various writings of Tocqueville. Morality must be universal; politics cannot.

Unlike Pitts and Mehta, Todorov believes that Tocqueville's recommended path of action in Algeria contradicts his philosophy. Pitts and Mehta would agree that Tocqueville was never sincerely universalist, and that his political ideology depends on a hierarchy in which full democratic and human rights are reserved for a self-appointed group of "civilized" men.[67] Todorov argues that Tocqueville's politics trumped his universalist liberal theory on the ground in Algeria. Simply put, in his writings about America and the French Revolution, Tocqueville was a universal humanist; as a politician concerned with French prestige in Algeria, he was a nationalist. In the 1830s, France was in a state of protracted political upheaval since the Revolution; Tocqueville imagined Algeria as an antidote to quell what he regarded as France's predilection for political disunity through national focus on the great task of settling and civilizing Algeria.[68]

In the 1950s, France was adjusting clumsily to a changed world. Having suffered an ignominious defeat at the hands of German Nazis in 1940, France was liberated as a crippled middle power at best, finding itself bracketed by two superpowers – an expanding Soviet bloc to the east and a triumphant America across the Atlantic. Losing Algeria, particularly following the defeat at Dien Bien Phu in Indochina, was unthinkable.[69] This impulse was similar to French politics concerning Algeria in Tocqueville's day. As we have seen above, following the collapse of Bonapartism in the early 19th century and subsequent political convulsions, Algeria offered the prospect of renewal to many French thinkers across a broad political spectrum. Historians such as Pitts assert that the policies of 19th century French Algeria are fundamental to an understanding of French liberal intellectualism. For Tocqueville and other 19th century liberals, Algeria was a proving ground for the French nation, just as it was for those of Soustelle's generation. As Pitts explains:

> This rather desperate grasp at imperialism at a crucial moment of nation-building left its mark not only on the French nation – whose subsequent century and more of colonial rule and fight against decolonization would be more violent than Britain's – but on French liberalism as well. The dominant strand of liberalism that was forged during this period was to be exclusionary and nationalist; and it would sit uneasily with the Revolution's apparent legacy of universal human equality and liberty.[70]

For a century, French liberals were unified in the belief that France could advance the democratic values of its revolution and colonize at the same time. As the historian of French intellectualism James Le Sueur has argued, this surprising unity stemmed from the belief that French ideals enshrined in the Declaration of the Rights of Man could and should be exported:

> … one idea in which many French intellectuals continued to believe explicitly or implicitly was French universalism. The notion of French universalism also formed the bedrock of French colonial policy, especially in Algeria. It was this universalism (a product of the French Revolution and the Enlightenment), ironically, that, according to historians, allowed many intellectuals to waver uncomfortably on the Algerian question because French colonialism in Algeria simultaneously contradicted and affirmed universalist intentions and ideas.[71]

This enthusiasm for *l'Algérie française* was seized upon by a coalition of advocates of expansionism abroad often referred to as "*le parti coloniale*," a broad grouping of academics, business people, journalists, politicians and others, who forced the issue to build a consensus that began to splinter following Dien Bien Phu and the outbreak of war in Algeria. Le Sueur describes the high stakes of this sudden fracture in a consensus around colonialism:

> For over a hundred years French colonial theorists had applied enormous pressure on the national community to affirm the civilizing mission and to ensure that colonialism and universalism would be the measure of French national eminence. This, of course, would have grave consequences during the era of decolonization.[72]

Arguments over decolonization would end friendships, sully careers and engage virtually the entire cast of French intellectuals of the 1950s – Raymond Aron, Simone de Beauvoir and Jean-Paul Sartre were among the prominent intellectuals that rallied to the FLN cause.[73] As the war in Algeria grew bloodier and more frightening and as newspapers such as *Le Monde* and magazines like *L'Express* and *Combat* began to reveal the brutality of French military actions, many intellectuals shifted towards the FLN which was suddenly deemed by many elements of the social-democratic left as the spearhead of decolonization. This shift represented a fundamental rupture of a consensus that had largely prevailed for 125 years. From a belief that revolutionary ideals and colonization could co-exist, the general trend of French intellectualism after 1955 was to insist on decolonization and the empowerment of independence movements in Algeria and elsewhere that were often in conflict with French settler populations and the military. As Le Sueur has observed, this placed Soustelle at the centre of a virulent debate with grave personal consequences for many:

> While French and Algerian intellectuals rethought the question of national and personal identity,

tried to comprehend the loss of French universalism, and attempted to understand the national significance of the demise of French power overseas, the French-Algerian war also presented them with a unique opportunity to re-assert intellectual legitimacy... Violence, identity and the question of intellectual legitimacy, … forced intellectuals during the war to make a choice: either situate their privileged status as intellectuals within the new France, the post-colonial France, or attach their status as intellectuals to an empire in peril. Very few intellectuals (Jacques Soustelle is among the important exceptions) opted for the latter.[74]

Soustelle was certainly among the most important exceptions, but he was not alone. Soustelle's assessment, at least until approximately 1958, was actually not entirely removed from that of French Algerian writer Albert Camus who never reconciled himself to Algerian independence.[75] Soustelle was also backed by his mentor Paul Rivet who opposed Algerian independence until his death.[76] Germaine Tillion, an ethnologist and former member of Soustelle's Algerian cabinet, only accepted the inevitability of Algerian independence near the war's end.

Imperial humanism versus aggressive civilization

Soustelle carried the baggage of French policies and ideology with him to Algiers in January 1955. Similarly, Scott was not a rogue exponent of a mean-spirited policy of his own device. Scott was an effective and loyal civil servant implementing policies that sprang from British imperial roots. He hardened and honed such policies with determination as an early enforcer of the Indian policy of a newfound settler state. Certain foundational works illustrate the ideological sources and intellectual discourse surrounding Scott's beliefs about Indigenous people in Canada.

In 1837, Herman Merivale was named professor of political economy at Oxford University. Over the next five years, Merivale delivered a series of lectures on Britain's colonial possessions. A number of leading historians on Indigenous-Settler relations in Canada identify Merivale's lectures as critical underpinnings to the "native" policy that Canada would inherit in 1867.[77] Merivale was a proponent of civilization, the term used for a cluster of educational and missionary policies that would as the thinking went, after a considerable passage of time, lead Indigenous people to take on full responsibilities as British subjects. He rejected the widely held belief that "natives" in places like Canada were simply doomed to extinction. He challenged Britain's leaders to make the effort and spend the money to protect Indigenous populations and to ease their passage to civilized status. Merivale argued that foresight and proper colonial management of the "native question" could obviate widespread wrongs:

> The history of the European settlements in America, Africa and Australia, presents everywhere the same general features – a wide and sweeping destruction of native races by the uncontrolled violence of individuals, if not of colonial authorities, followed by tardy attempts to repair the acknowledged crime.[78]

Merivale was also a proponent of the removal of Indigenous peoples from the path of settler colonization. His writings reveal the tension between removal and civilization that bedevilled Canadian Indian policy for the century following the publication of his lectures in 1861. Generally, he championed a moving reserve system at the edge of a transitory frontier that would allow Indigenous people to gradually adjust to European progress while preserving aspects of their lifeways the state could identify as being of use in a modern nation.

However, in the case of Canada, a place he visited on one occasion, Merivale believed Indigenous peoples would make difficult subjects for such a program:

> The North American Indians are well known to us by description; the favourite study alike of philosophy and romance for these two centuries, their character fixed in our minds as almost the type of that of man in a savage condition; yet they have many peculiar features. They seem possessed of higher moral elevation than any other uncivilized race of mankind, with less natural readiness and ingenuity than some but greater depth and force of character; more native generosity of spirit, and manliness of disposition; more of the religious element; and yet, on the other hand, if not with less capacity for improvement, certainly less readiness to receive it; a more thorough wildness of temperament; less curiosity; inferior excitability; greater reluctance to associate with civilized men; a more ungovernable impatience of control. And their primitive condition of hunters, and aversion from every other, greatly increases the difficulty of including them in the arrangements of regular community.[79]

In Merivale's assessment, it was not merely the "primitive condition" of Aboriginal people in British North America that would slow the pace of civilization. Merivale took a dim view of the activities of colonial authorities responsible for Indigenous affairs. He was very skeptical of the conduct of those in Upper Canada (now Ontario) who were more determined to promote settlement and clearing of land than protecting Aboriginal interests.[80] That approach reached its apogee from 1835-56 under the administration of Governor Frances Bond Head who recommended the mass migration of Indians in the Great Lakes region of Upper Canada to Manitoulin Island.[81] That policy was ultimately rejected by the Colonial Office in London. Head's policy is seen by some scholars as a failed attempt at a "homelands" policy utilized by British colonists in the Queen Adelaide Province area of the Cape Colony, which would become known as *Ciskei* under an apartheid regime in 20th century South Africa.[82] As Merivale compared colonial administrations in New Zealand, the Cape, Australia and British North America, he found particularly worrisome conditions in the latter where Head's legacy and other wrong-footed tactics had complicated matters:

> In Canada, there is a considerable and expensive department, with superintendents, secretaries, and interpreters; but the mismanagement of the affairs of that colony, as regards the natives, seems to have rendered them of little service, except to superintend the mischievous practice of the annual delivery of presents.[83]

In the view of Merivale, who would become under secretary of state for colonies in 1847, it was Britain's imperial moral responsibility to safeguard Aboriginal interests in places like Canada where colonial governments were primarily interested in rapid settlement, the expansion of frontiers and the development of natural resources. Following the conquest of New France, Britain established the office of the Deputy Superintendent General of Indian Affairs for Québec and Acadia, which would become the Indian Department after 1867.[84] Merivale believed that the department was tainted by a familiar colonial problem: settler governments tended to run rough-shod over the intent of the Royal Proclamation of 1763 which codified King George III's policy effort to achieve harmony between settlers and Indian peoples. Humanistic imperial measures were overwhelmed by local settler interests expressed through proto-democratic political systems under the influence of land developers and railway promoters. As Merivale saw the situation:

> When men superior in intelligence and in power are brought into contact with their feebler brethren, when they are turned loose among them without the possibility of a complete, efficient, and

above all, a disinterested control, to expect that will not grossly abuse their power, is to imagine that the evil principle of human nature will be rendered harmless by diminishing restraints and an extended sphere of action.[85]

Merivale articulated a humanist strain of British imperial theory. In the tradition of philosopher Adam Smith, who was skeptical of imperialism, Merivale believed that British colonial policy created conditions of abuse; in a discussion of Smith's cautionary imperial analysis, Merivale claimed, "he (Smith) can only be shown to have been wrong where he hesitated to push his views far enough…"[86] That is not to suggest that Merivale was opposed to all forms of settler colonialism. He believed that Christian ideals must be brought to bear in colonial settings to gradually "amalgamate" Indigenous peoples into the colonial population:

> We must view, in the occupation of their country by the Whites, not the necessary cause of their destruction, but the only possible means of rescuing them from it. We are not then their predestined murderers, but called to assume the station of their preservers. If we neglect the call, we do so in defiance of the express and intelligible indications afforded us by Providence.[87]

Pitted against men of "superior intelligence," Indigenous populations had to be protected and nurtured to a point of "amalgamation… the only possible euthanasia of savage communities."[88] Despite his generalized concerns about the culture of North American Indians, Merivale went on to prescribe a process in which Indigenous peoples of Canada could be protected in the short-to-medium term on lands reserved for them at the edge of settlement. He suggested that such reserves could be moved along with the frontier until economic opportunity, inter-marriage and the migration of some fitting individuals to settled areas would achieve the ultimate goal of Merivale's sought-after "amalgamation."[89] In general terms, these would remain planks of Canada's Indian policy for the first century of its national existence.

Merivale's "amalgamation" imagined gradual assimilation. Post-Confederation Canada upped the ante: impatient and land hungry federal governments ramped up to a variant of Indigenous administration known as "aggressive civilization," a draconian set of policies developed in the United States during the administration of President Ulysses S. Grant, the famed civil war military leader and renowned "Indian fighter."[90] One of the principal Canadian proponents of aggressive civilization was the journalist and politician Nicholas Flood Davin. Its primary bureaucratic advocate in the critical period of 1913 to 1932 was Duncan Campbell Scott.

Davin emigrated from Ireland to Canada in 1872. He was an active supporter of Prime Minister John A. Macdonald. In 1879, Macdonald sent Davin on a fact-finding mission to the United States to investigate the "industrial schools" for Indians, which the administration of President Grant had established. As the struggle for the American west closed in 1869, the Grant administration tackled the matter of education for newly conquered "tribes." Davin reported:

> The experience of the United States is the same as our own as far as the adult Indian is concerned. Little can be done with him. He can be taught to do a little at farming, and at stock-raising, and to dress in a more civilized manner, but that is all. The child again, who goes to a day school learns little, and what little he learns is soon forgotten, while his tastes are fashioned at home, and his inherited aversion to toil is in no way combated.[91]

The desire of the American government to hasten the process of "aggressive civilization" resulted in the establishment of industrial schools in the American west as well as in places like New Carlisle, Pennsylvania, where Indian children from the west were subjected to rigorous tutelage.

Davin derived a few fundamental convictions from his tour. He agreed with the educational pioneers of American Indian education that separating children from their parents was crucial. Day schools should be supplanted by industrial boarding schools "because the influence of the wigwam was stronger than the influence of the school."[92] Davin was particularly impressed by his meetings at the Indian Department in Washington with representatives of schools in the American west where Indigenous peoples who had been removed from the southeast were achieving success. As Davin understood things, the "civilized" members of the Creek, Cherokee, Chickasaw, Choctaw and Seminole nations whose children experienced industrial schooling in the "Indian Territory" of present-day Oklahoma, made an effective case:

> All the members of the civilized tribes declared their belief that the chief thing to do in dealing with the less civilized or wholly barbarous tribes, was to separate the children from the parents. As I have said, the Indian Department in Washington, have not much hope in regard to the adult Indians. But sanguine anticipations are cherished respecting the children. The five nations are themselves a proof there's a certain degree of civilization within the reach of the red man while illustrating his deficiencies.[93]

He overlooked the harsh experience these Indigenous nations had faced just decades earlier when they were removed from the eastern United States during the 1830s Trail of Tears.

Davin was also convinced that Christian churches had vital roles to play in Indian education:

> The importance of denominational schools at the outset for Indians must be obvious… A civilized skeptic, breathing though he does, an atmosphere charged with Christian ideas, and getting strength unconsciously there from, is nevertheless, unless in the instance of rare intellectual vigour, apt to be a man without ethical backbone. But a savage skeptic would be open to civilizing influences and moral conduct only through the control of desires, which, in the midst of enlightenment, constantly break out into the worst features of barbarism.[94]

Davin also analyzed the challenges confronting the government of Canada in the northwest. He travelled to Winnipeg where he met with religious leaders concerned with Indian education. Davin conducted his research following the first uprising led by Métis Louis Riel in Red River in 1869-70. He reflected on the aftermath of rebellion:

> Among the Indians there is some discontent, but as a rule it amounts to no more than the chronic querulousness of the Indian character, and his uneasiness about food at this time of year will unfortunately leave no trace in his improvident mind when spring opens and fish are plentiful. The exceptions are furnished by one or two chiefs whose bands are starving, that is in the Indian sense of the word, without a certain prospect of food in the future… No race of men can be suddenly turned from one set of pursuits to another set of a wholly different nature without great attendant distress. But, suddenly, to make men long accustomed to a wild unsettled life, with its freedom from restraint, its excitement and charm, take to the colourless monotony of daily toil, the reward of which is prospective, is impossible.[95]

Even though Davin regarded education as a vital component of the national imperative to settle and pacify the west, he expressed concern that Canada had unwisely raised expectations in its early prairie Indian treaties. While he regarded education for Indigenous people as a "sacred duty," he felt the government was mistaken in making specific treaty promises in this regard. Having done so, the government was inviting, according to Davin, a surfeit of Indian participation in the process:

> It might have been easily realized, (it is at least thinkable), that one of the results would be to make
> the Chiefs believe they had some right to a voice regarding the character and management of the
> schools, as well as regarding an initiatory step of their establishment.[96]

Davin recommended a more coercive, accelerated approach to the education of Indian children. The Davin Report on Industrial Schools was a blueprint for the exclusion of Canadian Indian parents from the development of educational programs and schools for their own children. The report was submitted in 1879, the same year that Scott was hired by the Indian Department. Davin recommended the opening of industrial schools, which came to be known in the 20th century as Indian residential schools. His advice regarding the involvement of the Christian churches was implemented: Anglicans, Catholics and Methodists were prominently involved in the running of schools.[97] Canadian historians have emphasized the ideological and tactical weight of Davin's report in the development of the department's educational policy.[98]

By 1909, Scott was the senior civil servant in charge of Indian education. In 1913, Scott was promoted to the position of deputy superintendent general of Indian affairs.[99] Throughout his career, Scott championed Indian education as a means to achieve the rapid assimilation of Indian children. On this file, Scott was not a mere implementer of the received policy. He became an activist. In the 1920s, Scott argued to members of parliament that the department needed enhanced powers to coerce Indian parents to send their children to residential schools and keep them there.[100] Related policies such as the suppression of Indigenous languages, spiritual practices involving dancing and drumming, ceremonies of Indigenous peoples in British Columbia known as the potlatch and the systemic demeaning of Indian parenthood, which were hallmarks of the ideology of American "aggressive civilization" as observed by Davin, were adopted and honed by the Canadian state under the supervision of Scott.[101]

Canadian Indian policy in the immediate post-Confederation period can be considered on a spectrum. At one end, there existed a humanist, civilizing approach, as expressed in the writings of Herman Merivale. This approach was imbued with Christian obligation and underpinned by an imprecise, yet relatively positive, appreciation of Indigenous ways of life. At the other end of the spectrum resided a sterner settler ideology more contemptuous of Indigenous culture and complicated by the belief that Aboriginal people were doomed to die off or be entirely absorbed by an expanding settler civilization. Colonial governors such as Francis Bond Head and post-Confederation senior administrators of Indian policy such as Scott were principal exponents of that point of view.[102]

Jacques Soustelle and the burden of empire

The central argument among "civilizers" in Canadian Indian policy, in the crucial transitory hand-off from British colonial to federal Canadian rule, was between advocates of an aggressive approach seeking to swiftly terminate Indian identity within the new nation by means of coercion and those that saw the reserve system and education as a means to facilitate a gradual Indian absorption or integration into Canadian life. Similarly, French intellectual history of imperialism and colonial policy can be usefully analyzed by interrogating the spaces between a humanistic approach wary of betraying the ideals of republicanism stemming from the French Revolution and an activist, muscular liberal imperialism in the tradition of Alexis de Tocqueville. The *encyclopédiste* Denis Diderot and the post-revolutionary political philosopher Benjamin Constant argued that the spirit of 1789 meant Republican France should be a non-imperial power.[103] This impulse was shredded by Napoléon's armies and tattered further at the end of the Bourbon restoration with the conquest of Algeria in 1830.

An intellectual virage from unrepentant settler colonialism in Algeria under metropolitan control occurred during Louis-Napoléon's régime in the Second Empire, from 1852-70. Louis-Napoléon spoke of an "Arab Kingdom" in an idealized vision of Indigenous-Franco cooperation in Algeria.[104] Louis-Napoléon was prepared, in theory at least, to countenance Indigenous collective property and agricultural practices that flew in the face of liberal beliefs regarding private property. He was opposed by settler interests in Algeria and the policies were never activated in a meaningful way.[105]

Leading scholars of *l'Algérie française* such as Charles-Robert Ageron, have observed that following the establishment of the Third Republic in 1870, a liberal consensus, built on the ideology of men like Alexis de Tocqueville, emerged in which France's revolutionary, republican legacy demanded a *mission civilisatrice* as French political influence, military and economic interests extended into parts of Africa and Asia:

> *Aux incertitudes des régimes précédents concernant le destin de l'Algérie succéda sous la IIIe République une politique continue fermement appliqué, qui donne tout son sens à la période proprement coloniale de l'histoire de l'Algérie française. Par cette assimilation administrative et politique qui intégrait définitivement le pays au sein de la République une et indivisible, on entendait rejeter toute éventualité du retour en arrière, toute possibilité du « Royaume Arabe », de protectorat ou de comptoirs coloniaux.*[106]

> Following the uncertainties of previous regimes concerning the destiny of Algeria the Third Republic firmly applied a continuous policy which gave form to the actual period of colonial history of French Algeria. With the administrative and political assimilation that integrated the country into the heart of the unified and indivisible Republic, one understood the rejection of any backsliding, any possibility of an "Arab Kingdom," of a protectorate or of mere trading posts.

As an authority on Mexican civilizations, Soustelle wrote extensively about the development and eclipse of empires. Immediately prior to his departure for Algeria in the winter of 1955, Soustelle completed *La Vie quotidienne des aztèques* [The Daily Life of the Aztecs]. In this work, Soustelle situated Aztec civilization in the context of the history of empires:

> *Sans doute il n'est pas inexacte d'interpréter l'histoire de Tenochtitlan depuis 1325 jusqu'à 1519 comme celle d'un état impérialiste qui poursuit sans répit son expansion par la conquête.*[107]

> There is no question that it is not inaccurate to interpret the history of Tenochtitlan from 1325 until 1519 as that of an imperial state that unceasingly pursued expansion by conquest.

One of Soustelle's principal works, *La vie quotidienne des Aztèques*, is a dense, thickly researched, but eminently readable examination of what Soustelle unhesitatingly identified as one of humanity's greatest accomplishments, the short-lived Aztec empire with its great capital Tenochtitlan, the site of present-day Mexico City:

> *Mexico était la jeune capitale d'une société en pleine mutation, d'une civilisation en plein essor, d'un empire encore en formation. Les Aztèques n'avaient pas atteint leur zénith : c'est a peine si leur astre avait franchi les premiers degrés de sa course. Il ne faut jamais oublier que cette ville était détruite par l'étranger avant d'avoir atteint son deuxième centenaire, et qu'en réalité son ascension datait du temps d'Itzcoatl, moins d'un siècle avant l'invasion.*[108]

Mexico was the young capital of a changing society, of a soaring civilization, of an empire that was still forming. The Aztecs did not reach their zenith: it's questionable if their star even got past the first stages of its course. One must never forget that the city was destroyed by foreigners before it even reached its second century, and in reality its ascension dated from the time of Itzcoatl, less than a century before the invasion.

Soustelle's understanding of imperial behaviour and devoir was influenced by his study of ancient Mexican civilizations. Soustelle's thinking about imperial systems was rooted intellectually in a classic liberal formation at one of Europe's elite universities and his own profound archaeological, ethnological, historical and linguistic study of Mexico. Crucial to his analysis of the Aztec ascendancy was that empire's ability to absorb and adapt to new cultures as the Aztec empire extended its military and trading power in Mesoamerica. As Soustelle understood it, the Aztecs absorbed and integrated, rather than annihilated, their enemies. As the Aztecs expanded their influence to the south and west of their capital Tenochtitlan, short military campaigns were followed by the establishment of integrating networks of commerce and religion. Aztec religion was mutable – each region under its influence proffered gods and religious customs that were incorporated into Aztec cosmology. In Soustelle's understanding, the Aztecs were different than their European conquerors in their willingness to integrate. However, that same tendency contributed tragically to their demise at the hands of the Spaniards:

> *Telle fut la base du grand malentendu qui opposa les Mexicains aux Espagnols: les uns, adorateurs de dieux multiples, et prêts a recevoir parmi les leurs ceux que les nouveaux venus apportaient; les autres, sectateurs d'une religion exclusive qui ne pouvait élever ses églises que sur les ruines des temples anciens.*[109]

> This was the basis of the great misunderstanding that pitted the Mexicans against the Spaniards: the former, worshippers of multiple gods, and ready to receive among their own those brought by the newcomers; the latter, cultists of an exclusive religion that could only raise its churches on the ruins of ancient temples.

Soustelle would not forget what he learned about the Aztec empire. On his arrival in Algeria as governor general, Soustelle immediately spoke of his plan for Algeria as one of "integration." He demanded urgency in a comprehensive effort to integrate Algeria and its Muslim majority into French society and politics. Seemingly ignoring the scars of more than a century of settler brutality and the systemic abrogation of liberal universalism that had defined French rule for over a century, Soustelle argued that Muslims must soon join a single legislative body and that massive investments from *la métropole* in education, health and social services would lead to an integration of Arabs, Berbers and European Algerians. His plan called for equal respect for Christian, Jewish and Muslim faiths. In his mind, integration did not mean assimilation.[110] These ideas flowed logically from Soustelle's understanding of the world as an authority of both ancient and revolutionary Mexico. Soustelle regarded the Aztecs as mentors in his understanding of *intégration*.

As governor general of Algeria, Soustelle hoped to convince a sceptical *pied noir* population that its future lay in melding with a majority Muslim society.[111] In the long run, Soustelle imagined a Euro-Arab population in which French Algerians of all faiths would fully participate in French republicanism.[112] But Soustelle arrived at a moment when 125 years of French rule left scorched earth rather than fertile ground for such an accommodation. He failed to adequately factor in the legacy of French brutality in Algeria. In this regard,

Soustelle revealed a naïve idealistic streak that perhaps betrayed his academic, theoretical background rather than emphasizing the political arts he must have observed as a cabinet minister and political activist in Paris. He arrived in Algeria at the very moment the FLN had revealed itself an implacable foe of French *rule tout court*. As he soon discovered, his responsibilities as governor general grew more militaristic in nature with every passing week of his doomed administration.

In early 1956, Soustelle left Algeria as governor general following yet another change of government in Paris. He wrote immediately of his experience in a memoir entitled *Aimée et souffrante Algérie*.[113] Over the next three years, Soustelle was in and out of government, but always actively pursued a vision of integration to save France's great national project in Algeria. In 1958, he was one of a handful of political and military operatives who brought General Charles de Gaulle out of retirement to resume leadership of France in what was effectively a bloodless *coup d'état*.[114] Soustelle believed that he had received a personal guarantee from de Gaulle that he would win the war and then save *l'Algérie française* through social and political reforms. Soustelle's hopes were dashed two years later when de Gaulle fired him and then announced to the nation that he would abandon Algeria.[115]

Soustelle viewed the abandonment of *l'Algérie française* as a fundamental failure of imperial will. In *Aimée et souffrante Algérie* and in a quick succession of polemical works in the 1960s, Soustelle insisted on the moral obligation of France to all Algerians and on what he regarded as the basic rectitude of *la mission civilisatrice*.[116] In these works, Soustelle often reached back in history to compare what he considered de Gaulle's abandonment of *l'Algérie française* with ignominious moments in French imperial history, including the fall of New France after the defeat of General Montcalm on the Plains of Abraham outside the citadel of Québec City in 1759:

> *Quand la monarchie déjà chancelante dut abandonner ce qu'on appelait les quelques arpents de neige » du Canada – expression qui rappelle « cette Algérie si cher » – encore nos armées avaient-elles subi trop de revers pour pouvoir poursuivre une guerre aussi lointaine… Pour abandonner l'Algérie, il a fallu déployer dix fois plus d'efforts que pour la sauver; il a fallu, obstinément, vouloir la défaite. Le Pouvoir a fabriqué de toutes pièces le Dien-Bien-Phu diplomatique d'Evian, « bâti » lui-même la F.L.N. comme seul interlocuteur valable et comme gouvernement de l'Algérie.*[117]

> When the already teetering monarchy had to abandon what one called "a few acres of snow" in Canada – an expression that recalls "this Algeria so dear"– our armies had already experienced too many reversals to pursue such a faraway war… To abandon Algeria required ten times the effort of saving it; one had to want defeat. The Power fabricated from whole cloth a diplomatic Dien-Bien-Phu of Evian, erecting on its own the FLN as the only useful interlocutor and government of Algeria.

Soustelle also drew on his understanding of Mexican empires to caution the West about the risk of decay and regression in the 20th century as he furthered his scholarly output about Mexico under extreme personal circumstances. As he travelled clandestinely between Italy, Belgium, Switzerland and perhaps, the United States, during his self-exile from France between 1962 and 1968, Soustelle composed one of his greatest works as a Mexican specialist. Between the highly polemical rages of the pen aimed at de Gaulle, Soustelle worked on *Les quatre soleils*, the book that Soustelle's biographer, political journalist Bernard Ullmann considered his masterpiece.[118] *Les quatre soleils* is a contemplation of the meaning of the rise and fall of civilizations which employs Aztec and Mayan civilizations as templates in a consideration that draws on many thinkers including Karl Marx, Friedrich Engels, Herbert Spencer, Arnold J. Toynbee and Arthur Kroeber.[119] Interweaving his recollections of touring Otomí and Mayan Lacandón territories in the 1930s with an interdisciplinary analysis of a broad sweep of human civilizations around the globe, Soustelle wondered about the meaning of the decline of Mayan civilization. As a linguist and ethnographer, he, like other Lacandón specialists, was convinced that the "primitive" 20th century forest dwellers of southern Mexican *selva* [rainforest] were the descendants of the very Maya who had created an elaborate, monumental civilization in Mesoamerica. That led Soustelle to pose the question: what had happened?

> *Si les Lacandóns nous apparaissent, pour l'essentiel, comme des Maya, lointains petits-neveux de ceux dont le cerveau et la main nous ont laissé en témoignage de leurs temps d'incomparables merveilles, alors une conclusion s'impose : il ne sont pas des primitifs, mais des décadents. Vestiges d'une humanité qui, fut capable, pendant sept siècles, de s'élever très haut au-dessus d'elle-même, ils sont retombés au plus bas. Leur histoire nous présente un cas exemplaire de ces processus de régression dont nos esprits se tiennent pas assez compte, obsédés qu'ils sont par le mythe du progrès uniforme et continu. Et j'incline à croire que beaucoup de prétendus « primitifs », loin de représenter les débuts tâtonnants du notre espèce, figés par quel miracle ? – dans un passé immobile et toujours semblable à lui-même, sont les témoins d'une histoire qui les a entraînés tout au long d'une courbe déclinante, les épaves d'un naufrage lointain.*[120]

> If the Lacandóns appear to us in their essence to be like the Maya, distant little cousins of those whose brains and hands left us witness of their time of incomparable marvels, then a conclusion imposes itself: they are not primitives, they are decadents. Vestiges of a human group that was capable over seven centuries, to reach far above itself, they have now fallen to the bottom. Their history presents to us a formidable example of regression that our minds does not usually acknowledge, obsessed as we are with the myth of universal continuous progress. And I am inclined to think that many whom we believe to be "primitive", far from representing the struggling preliminaries of our existence – frozen in time by what miracle? – in an immutable past always similar to itself, are the witness of a history that swept them along a downward path, the residue of a far off shipwreck.

Soustelle conflated his despair over the loss of *l'Algérie française* and his aspirations for *la mission civilisatrice* with the conviction that de Gaulle's decision to leave Algeria signified the decay of French civilization.[121]

Like Alexis de Tocqueville, Soustelle was a French nationalist. Even in a highly sophisticated and cultured *oeuvre* such as *Les quatre soleils*, one detects the influence of Soustelle's brooding about what he perceived to be France's defeat in Algeria through Soustelle's insistence on the impermanence and decadence that lurks in every human civilization. In the nuclear age, Soustelle reminded his readers of Mayan and Aztec predictions of civilizations ending in cataclysms of fire. In ancient Mexican cosmology stories of "the four suns" are constant reminders of human fragility in the face of mercurial and sometimes disdainful gods.[122] Soustelle did not believe that the western civilization of the 20th century was more likely than any other to survive. He believed that empires had to impose their rule, establish normative relations with their satellites, and resist aggression from barbarous forces to prevent decay. In this regard, he believed that he identified the fatal flaw of Aztec civilization: the very willingness to absorb and accommodate its neighbours helped make the Aztecs quick victims of a Spanish civilization that was forged on conquest and cultural annihilation following the *reconquista* that defeated the Moors in the Iberian Peninsula prior to the conquest of Mexico.[123]

Soustelle was imbued with a sense of imperial obligation. Like many French intellectuals of his generation, Sosustelle believed that France possessed both the authority and the duty to lead by example in the developing world. As far as Soustelle was concerned, this necessary tutelage was disrupted in Algeria by the

FLN at the expense of both the Muslim majority and the multi-denominational European minority. For Soustelle, the most infuriating aspect of this failure was the complicity of most of his peers – the intellectual leaders of metropolitan France.[124] He perceived a massive *trahison de clercs* – a betrayal that in Soustelle's view led logically to the victimization of Algerian minorities and the subjugation of its majority in a terrorist, semi-theocratic state led by an anti-democratic post-colonial elite.

Duncan Campbell Scott and the British connection

Scott was a principal exponent of an Indian policy that rested on British foundations. The policy was aimed at swiftly "civilizing" Indians while sheltering them from the ills of rapid industrialization by keeping them on reserves throughout a hazily defined transitory phase. When Scott became superintendent general of Indian Affairs in 1913, he made several efforts to hasten the civilization process by proposing changes to the Indian Act that would further restrict political and religious freedoms and by toughening educational policies based on the suppression of Indian languages and the separation of children from their parents.[125]

Queen Victoria died at the dawning of the 20th century on January 21, 1901. Her son was crowned King Edward VII. Victoria's grandson George was named Duke of Cornwall. Following three months of official mourning for the Queen, the newly minted Duke was sent out on a grand tour of the empire. In the autumn of 1901, the Duke and Duchess were on an extensive Canadian tour travelling largely on the Grand Trunk Railway. Readers of *The Montreal Star* received a colourful commemorative insert in September 1901 that featured photographs of His and Her Highness, the royal coat of arms, the British flag, maple leaves and a poem by Duncan Campbell Scott:

> The Ophir climbs the shoulder of the world,
>   Leaving the sultry seas with isles empearled,
>   Where India smoulders in the torrid light,
>   Australia and her welded destinies;
> She crashes through the crests on Cartier's track,
>   Where bold Lasalle dreamed of the Western Seas,
>   And Wolfe victorious lion-crowned the height.
>
> Old England federate of her utmost isles,
> One from the lone lodge where the trapper piles
>   His beaver skins, to where in nervous power,
>   London lies triumphing in her trampled mart.[126]

However clumsy the poem may appear to 21st century readers, Scott, ever the loyal Canadian civil servant, knew well how to express a vision of a global empire on which the sun never set and how to poetically evoke Canada's place within it. From the poetic nod to the founding peoples of "two tongues;" to the regional acknowledgements of the maritimes and the far northwest; to the evocation of far off Australia and India; to the naming of great explorers and of the heroic, yet doomed, Wolfe; and finally to the exaltation of the nordicity and wildness that distinguishes an iconic Canada, Scott played on the imperial sentimentality that was no doubt vibrant for many readers of *The Star*.

The commission by *The Montreal Star* was fitting given the poet's stature. By 1901, Scott was 39 years old and already a 20-year veteran of the Canadian civil service. His day job in the Indian Department may have helped lend him sufficient gravitas in the eyes of *The Star's* publishers for this particular job. While the poem groaningly lacks the subtleties and refinement of his best work, it reflects Scott's own commitment to empire. As his essay about the Treaty 9 negotiations, "The Last of the Indian Treaties," demonstrated, Scott unabashedly prescribed British monarchism and parliamentary tradition as a basis for the development of Canadian nationhood, and as the civilized standard Canada's Indians could perhaps meet in the distant future. Literary scholar Northrop Frye argued that a Canadian is "someone who doesn't want to be an American." Since Confederation Canadian nationalists like Scott emphasize the British connection to underscore the point. As a public intellectual in a young nation, Scott viewed the British connection as a means to distinguish Canada from its southern neighbour. Late in his life, he reflected, in a letter to a critic and editor, on how fundamentally different relationships with the British empire contributed to cultural differences between Canada and the United States:

> If colonialism is the right word for our deadness, well and good; it requires a definition… The States had defeated Colonialism and their literature came from a spring of fresh independent feeling. Our foundations are not built on rebellion and a frontier period of political experiment but on acceptance of tradition and a determination to perpetuate it.[127]

In 1939, Scott was called on to herald an extraordinary royal visit. While members of the Royal family had been coming to Canada with some regularity since 1867, King George VI was the first reigning British monarch to set foot in Canada. Archival radio broadcasts reveal the patriotic fervor of large crowds (and the unbridled enthusiasm of the Canadian public broadcasting service) that gathered to greet the King upon his arrival in Québec City and a week later on his tour of Manitoba in May 1939.[128] In June, the royal couple departed from Halifax. Scott, by then a dignified icon of Canadian letters in retirement in Ottawa, was commissioned to write a poem (excerped in part below) that was read by an actor as part of a live radio broadcast on June 15, 1939:

A Farewell To Their Majesties
Master of life whose Power is never sleeping
    In the dark void or in the hearts of men,
Hold them our King and Queen, safe in Thy keeping
And bring them to their western Realm again.

And for their Canada be watchful ever,
    Grant us this boon, if there be one alone,
To do their part in high and pure endeavour
    To build a peaceful Empire round the Throne.[129]

As a bureaucrat in the Canadian Indian Department, Scott upheld and refined policies that his new nation had inherited from England. That inheritance was part of a global network of "native" policies at play in related, but regionally specific ways, in Australia, the Cape Colony, Canada, India and New Zealand. As an artist, Scott's poetry and prose was also imbued with loyalty to the perceived ideals of the British empire. Jacques Soustelle was a lifelong adherent to the ideology of France's *mission civilisatrice*. In the tradition of French liberal imperialists such as Alexis de Tocqueville and Jules Ferry, Soustelle stubbornly held to the view that France had rights and responsibilities for tutelage in the "developing" world, even in a decolonizing modern world following the Second World War.

In 1959, Jacques Soustelle was featured on the cover of TIME newsmagazine.

Chapter Four

ARTS and SCIENCE

IN ADDITION TO THEIR GOVERNMENT DUTIES, Scott and Soustelle performed intricate and foundational roles in literature, social science, journalism, photography and broadcasting during their careers. These activities mirror their ideological concerns and underscore their importance as prominent participants in their cultures.

Scott was involved in the creation of a national literature; he identified emerging Canadian talent in the visual arts; he was active in both music and theatre in Ottawa; late in life he contributed regularly to the radio service of Canada's fledgling national broadcasting network.

Soustelle was among the academics who engineered a fundamental shift in French social sciences as archaeology and anthropology accommodated a more socially active and present-day concern with Indigenous societies in the field of ethnology.[1] He contributed to newspapers and magazines throughout his adult life. Beginning with his first experiences in Mexico, he penned journalism and launched publications to advance his political views. As a graduate student, he contributed to leftist French weeklies; in the Second World War, he ran a propagandistic news agency for France Libre, the anti-Nazi resistance movement, out of Mexico City; as a frustrated politician, he ran a bi-monthly anti-Gaullist magazine that tried to argue for the maintenance of *l'Algérie française*. In the later part of his life, he contributed articles about Mexico, the Middle East and southern Africa to French newspapers. While Soustelle will long be remembered for his voluminous writings in the social sciences, journalism and for his political tracts on the Algerian question and Gaullism, he also produced an edition on Indigenous Mexican art and contributed essays to artistic collections of prominent photographers about Mexican archeology and anthropology.[2]

Scott emerged nationally from his civil service cocoon in Ottawa as a cultural columnist with *The Globe* newspaper from 1892-93.[3] He was already well known among literary circles in Canada, as a poet and writer of short stories from about 1890. Soustelle first came to prominence as a prodigiously brilliant student and chronicler of all things Mexican in the French press at *le Musée de l'Homme* and in his first highly journalistic book *Mexique terre indienne* in the 1930s.[4] Unlike Scott, Soustelle's career flourished at the beginning of the age of mass media, and he lived through the first three decades of the television age. As a French politician and as governor general of Algeria, Soustelle made frequent, calculated use of radio; he produced a 33rpm vinyl recording of political speeches charting what he viewed as the betrayal of Gaullism by de Gaulle himself over the Algerian question; he acted as curator of a United Nations Educational, Scientific and Cultural Organization sponsored vinyl LP collection of modern renditions of ancient Mexican music; and worked as a narrator, producer and writer for television documentaries about his cherished Mexico.[5]

Scott and Soustelle were public intellectuals, political actors and artists. In addition to his foundational role in the emergence of a national Canadian literary movement, Scott was also an accomplished musician, a knowledgeable champion of Canadian painting and on the Treaty 9 Commission 1905-06 a photographer with an ethnological eye. Scott travelled throughout northern Ontario in the summers of 1905 and 1906 with a Brownie camera, the camera that first introduced personal photography to the world. In photographs of Scott, that camera is sometimes seen hanging around his neck.[6] Like Scott, Soustelle was a competent photographer; his photos from the 1930s illustrate two of his most convincing works on Mexico.[7] Each sometimes included his photographs to illustrate articles, books and reports. The choice of subjects, framing and means of publication reflect each man's intellectual concerns and political aims, as well as their aesthetics. Soustelle's included shocking photos of torture victims of the *Front de libération nationale* (FLN) in his memoir on serving as governor general of Algeria.[8]

As Scott was involved with the emergence of a literary movement in Canada, Soustelle was a key player in a process in which French ethnology and archaeology emerged from its transparently imperialist roots and evolved generally into a more accessible, empathetic and interactive model.[9]

Soustelle was part of a French scientific tradition concerning Mexico that began in the mid-19th century. Photographers and amateur ethnologists such as Désiré Charnay and Augustus and Alice de Plongeon documented peoples and archaeological sites in central Mexico, the Yucatán and Chiapas from 1857 until the early part of the 20th century. These adventurers had carefully studied the itineraries of the Prussian naturalist Alexander van Humboldt and the French missionary and proto-ethnologist l'Abbé Brasseur de Bourbourg who preceded them.[10] In an unpublished memoir, Soustelle recalled his childhood fascination with adventure books and accounts of North American Indians in the novels of James Fenimore Cooper.[11] As a student prodigy with an interest in Mexico, Soustelle would certainly have been aware of geographer Alexander von Humboldt's accounts before he set foot in Mexico in 1932.

Scholars who have looked carefully at the transformative nature of travel on the lives of intellectuals have often focused on how the exotic allure of Mexico with its clash and convergence of European imperial and Mesoamerican cultures, its dramatic landscape, its astounding archaeological sites and its array of Indigenous societies inspired the curiosity and imaginations of 18th and 19th century travellers, explorers, amateur artefact collectors, military personnel and missionaries.[12] The young Soustelle followed that path. He was 20 years old when he first arrived in Veracruz. Although the nature of the quest that Soustelle and his wife Georgette undertook in the 1930s had its innovative aspects, he was walking in the footsteps of established French tradition.

Modern French social scientific involvement in Mexico began in earnest with the French Intervention of 1862-67 and the establishment of the doomed Mexican Empire of Maximilian. Half a century earlier, the famous Egyptian campaign of Napoléon Bonaparte established a marker for revitalized French imperialism. Historian Paul N. Edison has observed that the Egyptian campaign became "an influential model for state directed scientific conquest" that French governments employed in both Mexico and Algeria. Bonaparte ultimately failed militarily in Egypt, but his foray succeeded as a scientific and ethnographic enterprise. Adopting that social scientific methodology, Napoléon III, Bonaparte's nephew, commanded his appointed Mexican emperor Maximilian to undertake a thorough agricultural, archaeological, botanical, ethnological, geographic and geologic survey of what Napoléon III imagined to be his new Mesoamerican empire.[13]

In Mexico, Napoléon III's scientific commission was an attempt to underscore both French imperial stature and to enlist the support of Mexican intellectuals who wished to project their interpretation of a Mexican classical past of Aztec and Mayan empires that, in their minds, rivaled those of Greece and Rome. The quest for modernity and the desire to establish a positive image for Mexico abroad by linking it to a glorious classical Indigenous past, is a point of connection between 19th century liberals of *la Reforma Juarista* (the liberal reform period led by Benito Juárez), the *científicos*, a clutch of economists and sociologists who advised the dictator Porfirio Díaz, and the *indegenista* social engineers of the 20th century's first great revolution which erupted in 1910 in Mexico.[14] Such Mexicans believed that the exploration and cataloguing of Mexico's archaeological treasures in partnership with foreign partners would contribute to Mexico's international prestige. Most critically of all in considering the development of Soustelle's thinking was the shared belief that affirming the Indigenous past of Mexico could aid in integrating its descendants to build a modern Mexican nation.[15]

The proto-ethnology of Spanish missionaries to New Spain of the 16th century such as Bernardino de Sahagún and Toribio de Benevente Motolinía connects to the work of foreign social scientists like Soustelle. European observation and knowledge exchange began during the colonial period, long before the stirrings of Mexican independence from imperial Spain. The modernizing impulse that encompassed archaeology and policies toward the Indigenous peoples of Mexico also served the purpose in forging links with established scientific communities in Europe and the United States and in asserting Mexican national identity.[16]

Soustelle arrived in Mexico at a critical stage of evolution for the French social sciences. Paul Rivet, Soustelle's doctoral supervisor and eventual patron as director of *le Musée de l'Homme*, began his archaeological career with excavations in Peru and Ecuador.[17] Rivet enjoyed international respect for most of his career as an advocate for a humanist, accessible ethnology and as a socialist champion of human rights and resistance to Nazism. He began his career in the field as a collector of artefacts that could be sent to French museums. The field conduct of the early European archaeologists and anthropologists in the Americas raises ethical concerns for their 21st century counterparts. Rivet and his ilk routinely plundered Indigenous gravesites in search of skulls and other artefacts.[18]

In the tradition of founding French anthropologist Paul Broca, Rivet was initially concerned with craniology and linguistics. Broca insisted on the value of craniology as a means to analyze the differences between peoples of the world and their respective evolutionary status.[19] In Ecuador and Peru, prior to the First World War, Rivet was eager to exhume and collect the skulls and bones of Indigenous people in burial sites. In collecting skulls, Rivet was part of a western movement that adopted thoroughly dubious ethical and scientific standards:

> The leaders of craniometry were not conscious political ideologues. They regarded themselves as servants of their numbers, apostles of objectivity. And they confirmed all the common prejudices of comfortable white males – that blacks, women and poor people occupy their subordinate roles by the harsh dictates of nature.[20]

In 2008, the remaining collections at the then foundering *Musée de l'Homme* in Paris prominently featured a massive display of skulls from around the world collected in significant part by Rivet's generation as they explored those regions of the world that appeared to be remote and exotic to European sensibilities of the early modern era.

As Rivet's biographer Christine Lauriére has noted, at no time at this stage of his career, or later in fact, did Rivet deplore the activities of the *guaqueros*, the grave robbers who were often employed by early archaeologists in their explorations. For Lauriére, the contradictions of Rivet's activities in Ecuador and Peru are acute:

> *Cela lui est possible parc qu'il ne considère pas l'humanité des Colorados de la même façon que l'humanité blanche, européenne. Ces Indiens ne sont plus les sujets de leur histoire, ils ne choisissent plus leur destinée, ils sont devenues des représentants de l'humanité à un stade primitif.[21]*

> This was possible for him because he did not take into account the humanity of the Colorados in the same way as that of white European humanity. These Indians were no longer authors of their

own history, they were not choosing their own destiny, they had just become representatives of primitive humanity.

There may be intellectual continuities between the traditions of the early French anthropologists with their predilection for collecting artifacts of "doomed" peoples before their time ran out and the attitudes that Soustelle carried with him to Algeria. Soustelle assumed that he and a *cadre* of French social scientists, including Germaine Tillion, possessed a formula to assist in building a bridge between Indigenous groups in Algeria and the modern world. He arrogated a role as go between with Indigenous Algeria and European modernity, whether Algerians wanted it or not.

That cavalier approach to the dignity of living Indigenous peoples, which Lauriére condemns, places Rivet in a French and pan-European tradition that went relatively unexamined until after the First World War. The few opponents of such practices and beliefs among western academics and journalists were swimming against the tide of a new sort of imperialism embedded in a bogus science of race and a fundamentally pessimistic outlook on the prospects for Indigenousness in an industrializing world. Such social scientists frequently met with skepticism or outright resistance from their Indigenous subjects. Many researchers, including Rivet, believed they were engaged in a "salvage" operation to preserve the traces of "doomed" races for emerging nations and all of humanity; in this light, their behaviour can be seen, at best, as a misguided humanism, at worst as imperialism buttressed by conventional academic wisdom.[22] As Michel Leiris, one of Soustelle's ethnological peers saw it, this emphasis on salvaging what one might from doomed cultures depended in part on a belief that Indigenous cultures were somehow "*figée*," that is to say frozen or stuck in time.[23] Leiris argued that ethnology remained bound up in imperialism even in a post-colonial or "decolonizing" world; ethnologists, after all, no matter what their particular political views, derived their funding from governments and museums in Europe that maintained colonizing relationships with countries in the developing world. Further, the national academies and museums of Europe, Leiris maintained, which could afford to send researchers to the developing world, had enriched themselves and built their reputations and collections during an earlier age of plunder. Soustelle's academic research and work commissioned by the Canadian Indian department in Scott's day raise similar questions about the ethics and politics of such undertaking. Historians of anthropology have observed and commented extensively on the tensions between collecting, research and Indigenous rights.[24] Historians of western Canada's Indian Department used bogus social science to inform its agricultural policies for Indigenous peoples who were considered backward and therefore have to be brought slowly along in adapting modern farming methods.[25]

By the late 20th century, activism and concerns about "native" rights began to inform the behaviour of social scientists in the field; in some cases, social scientists from the developed world find common cause with their subjects. Soustelle was present at the germinating stage of this move in the French archaeology, anthropology and ethnology. It began with ethnologists Paul Rivet, Marcel Mauss and Lucien Lévy-Bruhl and the creation of *l'Institut d'Ethnologie* at the University of Paris in 1926, where 17-year-old Soustelle began to study in 1929.[26] Some of these scholars were active in anti-fascist movements in France; their politics were generally left-of-centre. In the 1930s, they and their students sought to align their domestic politics with their scientific endeavours and concerns. Late in his own life, Soustelle paid homage to his mentor Rivet in a Peruvian journal, as he recounted the shift the new ethnology institute represented for French letters in the late 1920s and 1930s:

Governor General Soustelle (right) meets with Algerian representatives.

Este Instituto daba una enseñaza que se calificaría ahora de "pluridisciplinaria": etnografía, antropología física, lingüística, prehistoria, se combinaban y se asociaban allí estrechamente. Pues era en eso precisamente que se afirmaban la sorprendente maestría de Paul Rivet, su extraordinaria lucidez y su talento pedagógico. Ahora bien, Paul Rivet, médico de formación, convertido en etnógrafo y arqueólogo "en el terreno" en Ecuador, ha resultado ser el hombre de la síntesis.

This institute provided instruction that would now be deemed "interdisciplinary": ethnography, physical anthropology, linguistics, pre-history, were all combined and rigorously associated there. This was precisely affirmed in the surprising mastery of Paul Rivet, his extraordinary lucidity and pedagogical talent. Paul Rivet, a medical doctor by training, converted into an ethnographer and 'on the ground' archaeologist in Ecuador and became a man of synthesis.[27]

The new institute marked a significant parting of ways with salvage anthropology. Salvage anthropology rested in part on notions of imperial supremacy and in the belief that the remnants and memory of supposedly doomed peoples would be preserved best in European museums on display to the public with the rarest, most precious exhibits worried over by privileged academics and their students. Intellectual historian Jacob W. Gruber examined the assumptions that many of these earlier social scientists shared:

The sense of salvage with its concern with loss and extinction, stressed the disorganization in a social system at the expense of the sense of community; it stressed the pathology of cultural loss in the absence of any real experience with the normally operating small community.[28]

Historian Mary Louise Pratt furthered understanding of the "imperial gaze" in archaeology, anthropology, ethnology and travel writing. Her analysis raises fundamental questions for social scientists at work in impoverished parts of world with rich Indigenous pasts. She raises fundamentally important issues about the conduct and belief of the academic tradition which was beginning to change as a student like Soustelle set out on the formative Mexican expeditions of his ethnological career. Pratt asserts:

> The European imagination produces archaeological subjects by splitting contemporary non-European peoples off from their pre-colonial, and even their colonial, pasts. To revive Indigenous history and culture as archaeology is to revive them as dead. The gesture simultaneously rescues them from European forgetfulness and reassigns them to a departed age.[29]

Soustelle aspired to transcend earlier European and French social scientific tradition, which objectified Indigenous peoples. When Soustelle arrived for the first time in Mexico in 1932, he set out to find living communities. His ethnographic and linguistic studies of the Otomí and Lacandón peoples were rooted in a fascination with the continuity of Indigenous cultures in the modern world.[30] As an anti-fascist activist and admiring student of Rivet who was an active supporter of the Popular Front – the French socialist government before the Second World War – the young Soustelle's ethnological works and journalism from Mexico emphasized the living presence of Indigenous peoples in Mexico and the urgent necessity of government to assist them in integrating into modern Mexico with their identities and languages intact.[31] In this respect, Soustelle's fervent embrace of *indigenismo* was the polar opposite of the brutally assimilationist policies advanced by Scott and the Canadian Indian Department.

The Soustelles' research enterprise was not without contradiction in this regard. Despite the emphasis on living cultures, Soustelle gathered a sizeable collection of artefacts that he and his wife, Georgette, brought back to France from their early trips. The couple gathered hundreds of objects such as masks, ceramic bowls, looms, bows, arrows, statues, musical instruments, toys and a fabulous feathered headdress from an Otomí *confradía*, a unit of musicians and dancers gathered for fiestas and religious ceremonies.[32]

In the 1930s as a doctoral student in Mexico and in the 1950s, as a colonial leader in Algeria, Soustelle was wedged between imperial superiority and an emerging ethics of ethnology and politics imbued with acceptance and fascination with Indigenous peoples acting in the present day. Soustelle's enduring dilemma is captured in his first book when he recounts meeting a grieving Lacandón woman whose child was murdered:

> *J'ai encore présent à la mémoire le visage ravage, rongé par le chagrin, de la vieille femme. Je dus discuter avec elle assez longtemps pour acquérir un splendide métier a tisser qu'elle possédait, chargé d'une belle jupe à des raies violettes, jaunes et blanches, inachevée, sans doute depuis la catastrophe. Du seuil de la case où elle demeurait accroupie à longueur de journée, elle levait sur moi ses yeux rouges; sa voix était un soufflé. Tout en elle montrait une lassitude écrasante, l'hébétude où est plongé un être après le coup le plus rude qu'il puisse supporter sans mourir. La journaliste parisienne qui me demandait un jour à Mexico: "Mais enfin, Monsieur, vos Indiens, est-ce qu'ils pensent?" aurait dû voir cette femme; elle se serait rendu compte qu'au moins ils sont capables de souffrir.*[33]

I still hold in my memory the ravaged face, gnawed by despair, of the old woman. I had to chat with her for a long time to obtain the beautiful loom she possessed, that held a beautiful skirt with violet, yellow and white stripes, still incomplete no doubt because of the catastrophe. From the doorstep of her little house where she sat crouched all day, she raised reddened eyes; her voice was a whisper. Everything about her showed a crushing weariness, the lethargy into which she had fallen after the hardest blow one can suffer without dying. The female Parisian journalist who asked me one day, "But really sir, your Indians, do they think?" should have seen that woman; she would have at least realized that they can suffer.

Soustelle may have been empathetic to her lot, but he also obtained her loom to bring it back to Paris. Soustelle began his career at the forefront of a movement toward a humanist, participatory and democratic ethnography and yet as his collecting habits in Mexico attest, he did not entirely transcend earlier traditions. As with his political activities following the Second World War, Soustelle, the social scientist, incarnated in stark relief the contradictions of his day.

Duncan Campbell Scott and the foundations of Canadian culture

Scott is a foundational figure in Canadian literature. He was at the vanguard of a new national literature, that while steadfastly British in orientation, also sought to carve out an identity that would be distinct from contemporary British and American works. As a poet, Scott and his friend and associate Archibald Lampman, a civil servant with the Canadian post office, are among the very first writers in Canada to articulate an appreciation and wonder about the Canadian natural world, particularly the rugged boreal zone that they could see across the Ottawa River from their office buildings. When Scott died, a contemporary critic wrote the following appreciation in a popular Canadian magazine:

> Is it too much to suggest that in these quietly powerful poems, seldom brilliant but always competent in style and solid in substance, we catch an authentic glimpse of the Canadian spirit at its finest?[34]

Canada's new capital, the Ottawa of Scott's youth, was not far removed from its pre-Confederation state as a swampy, lumber town from which it had been wrested by the government of Queen Victoria when she selected it as the new nation's capital. Its location along the Ontario-Québec border made it a convenient solution to the squabbling of ambitious English- and French-speaking colonial politicians from competing candidate cities Toronto, Kingston and Montreal. With significant English- and French-speaking populations, the capital grew along the Ottawa River and Rideau Canal. The city featured magnificent parliamentary buildings built on a promise of nationhood, which rose on a bluff looking out over the rapids of the Ottawa River and beyond to the Gatineau Hills of Québec.[35] It was an inspiring setting for young poets. As a boy at his father's Ottawa parsonage and again later as an adult with a home on Lisgar Avenue and an office next to Parliament, Scott could walk up Metcalfe Street to the Hill. Scott loved Ottawa. Although he occasionally expresssed frustration with his civil service career, he managed to find solace in the cultural life Ottawa could support and was forever comforted by the city's natural setting, as he indicated in an essay from the 1920s:

> In 1883 the population was about 30,000 and the place had the appearance and the social life of a large town. There was not a great necessity for a streetcar system, although a single line existed, and the country was almost part of the town. All that is changed now, but the spirit of the city, the almost breathing personality that pervades certain places, is unchangeable. The variety of the landscape, the vigour of the rivers, and the comradeship the city has through them with the wild

country of their sources, and then the vision of the city itself seen from all quarters of the environs as something exalted, an ideal as an inspiration, these remain; the wilderness is a little pushed back, more remote, but the beauty of the situation can never be destroyed.[36]

Some of Scott's peers felt he was out of place. The British poet Rupert Brooke visited in 1913:

The only poet in Canada was very nice to me in Ottawa – Duncan Campbell Scott, age 50, married, an authority on Indians. Poor devil he's so lonely and dried there: no one to talk to. They had a child – daughter – who died in 1908 or so. And it knocked them out. Canada's a bloody place for a sensitive – in a way 2nd rate – real, slight poet like that to live all his life. Nobody cares if he writes or doesn't. He took me out to a Club in the country near, and we drank whisky and soda and he said 'Well, here's to your youth!' and drank its health and I nearly burst into tears.[37]

Scott's poetic isolation increased when his friend Archibald Lampman died of heart disease in 1899 when he was only 38. Scott, who had been encouraged to write poetry by Lampman, spent the rest of his life preserving the artistic legacy of his friend in supervising the publication of collections of Lampman's works and through essays, speeches and memorials. Scott turned his attention to Lampman's legacy despite his senior responsibilities for the Indian Department. Late in his civil service career, he described the effort of publishing a Lampman collection as a "labour of love."[38] The two met in 1884, the year after Lampman had begun working as a clerk in the post office. They formed a friendship that was based on poetry, hiking and canoeing in the wilds. Scott recalled first meeting Lampman and their forays into the forests and waterways of the Gatineau Hills:

Archibald's room had a window that looked to the west, a sunset window with a view of the old tower of the Parliament House and within sound of the bell told the hours. During the next summer, as we were both fond of the fields and woods, we began those walking tours and canoe trips which took us near and far over the country. Much of what was seen and experienced went into his lines, and I might even now localize and identify the references, the point of view, the itinerary.[39]

Canadian literature scholars tend to agree that Lampman and Scott represent a watershed in the emergence of a national English language literature. At their best, Lampman and Scott evoke a landscape that is distinctly non-European. Canadian cultural theorist and literary scholar Northrop Frye declared that Scott was, "…one of the ancestral voices of the Canadian imagination."[40] He saw Scott as an expression of a Canadian type, deeply moved by and yet simultaneously terrified of the natural world. Frye appreciated the extent to which Scott internalized the two realities in which he lived – as a rising civil servant in the post-colonial Canadian administration and the artist who sought refuge and inspiration in the woods. Like poet John Masefield's eulogy of Scott at St Martin-in-the-Fields church in January 1948, Frye made specific mention of *The Forsaken*, Scott's morbid work about a starving Indian left abandoned by her "tribe." Frye juxtaposed that poem with another, *On The Death Of Claude Debussy*, one of several Scott poems with specific mention to composers:

Whatever one thinks of the total merit of Scott's very uneven output, he achieved the type of imaginative balance that is characteristic of so much of the best of Canadian culture down to the present generation,… On one side he had the world of urbane and civilized values, on the other, the Québec forest with its Indians and lonely trappers. He could write a poem on Debussy and a poem on a squaw feeding her child with her own flesh; he was at once primitive and pre-Raphaelite, a recluse of the study and a recluse of the forest. Not since Anglo-Saxon times it seems to me has there been the same uneasy conflict between elemental bleakness and the hectic flush of a late and weary civilization that there has been in Canadian poetry and painting of the period from Confederation to the depression. It had to go as the country became more urbanized, and we may regret its passing only if nothing new comes along to replace it.[41]

In his own scholarly manner, Frye situates Scott within the antimodernist tradition described so powerfully by historian Jackson Lears.[42] Scott imagined Indigenous peoples as an antidote to the very modernity he claimed they could not join.

As an aging poet, Scott was vaguely aware of Frye. During the Second World War, Scott was sufficiently intrigued by the new contributor to *The Canadian Forum* to make inquiries to a critic friend:

Do you get *The Forum*? If so you will have read the article in the Dec. No on Canadian Poetry. If not I will send you one; let me have your comments sometime. I suppose Northrop Frye is a nom de plume; if so who is he?[43]

The elderly Scott was unaware of Frye, the then emerging maven of Canadian letters. For Northrop Frye, however, Scott became a continuing subject in a contemplation of Canadian poetry and prose.[44]

For poetic inspiration, no experience in Scott's lifetime rivaled the Treaty 9 expeditions of 1905-06, which were ostensibly about terminating Indian title to large swaths of northern Ontario. These trips separated Scott from the other early Canadian poets because they gave Scott an exposure to the north and to Indian communities which was infinitely more profound than the experience he had shared with Lampman in the Gatineau. Like some of the earlier European ethnographers in Mesoamerica, Scott, the poet, assumed that Indian people were doomed. Yet, some of the aspects of the culture he witnessed survive in his poetry such as *The Forsaken* and *The Height of Land*, works that speak directly to Scott's northern voyages.

The Indian Department bureaucrat put the treaty expeditions of 1905-06 to the service of his poetry. Following the 1905 expedition in difficult areas such as the remote Albany River flowing north to James Bay, in 1906 Scott invited his friend Pelham Edgar, principal of Victoria University in Toronto, to act as the expedition's secretary. The 1906 voyage visited communities close to rail lines around Longlac; in the Chapleau District north of Sudbury. It reached the shores of Lake Superior near the present-day mining town of Marathon and Pukaskwa National Park close to the mouth of the Pic, Pukaskwa and White Rivers on the Superior shore. South of Superior, in Biscotasing and Chapleau, the expedition was joined by the painter Edmund Morris. Morris made sketches that were the basis of some of the portraits of Indigenous leaders that are displayed in the Royal Ontario Museum to the present day. After his death by drowning, Morris became the subject of what Pelham Edgar considered Scott's greatest poem, "Lines in Memory of Edmund Morris."[45] The team also paddled the beautiful Lady Evelyn River en route to Lake Temagami and the Teme-Agama Anishnabai village at Bear Island, before returning to Ottawa by train via Temiscaming, Québec.

In a memoir of his own career, Edgar relied on his personal Treaty 9 journal and "home letters" to reconstruct his 1906 experience with Scott, in a chapter entitled "Travelling with a Poet." The excerpt below is from a journal entry of June 1, 1906, written in the Temagami region:

When we are near the shore the birds are very vocal and Duncan knows them well… We have the Oxford Book Of Poetry always handy, and when I paddle Duncan often reads. Then I take a wild respite, and make myself comfortable with a pull at a pipe and a short peep at a book. A hard life is it not?[46]

Author Cullingham in 2013 on
the Red Squirrel River near
Camp Wanapitei, n'Daki Menan,
Temagami.

In May 1977, I climbed into my Ford 'Econoline' van outside the group home north of Kenora where I was employed as a childcare worker and outdoor activity animator with Indigenous children. I drove for close to 20 hours around the north shore of Lake Superior and then south on the Trans-Canada Highway to a spot just north of Temagami village about 90 kilometres north of North Bay, Ontario.

I then followed instructions to drive across 30 kilometres of the barely passable Red Squirrel Road to a spot at the top of a portage trail leading to the edge of the Red Squirrel River.

As my instructions indicated, there was a canoe waiting for me and my gear. I paddled a few kilometres downriver to the camp's canoe docks at the mouth of the river at the north end of Lake Temagami.

That began a relationship with Wanapitei, N'daki Menan – the homeland of the Teme Agama Anishinaabe and with friends and mentors like then Teme Agama Anishinaabe Chief Gary Potts and then Wanapitei director and historian Bruce Hodgins and his wife Carol, a physiotherapist and canoe trip provisioner.

As an academic, canoeist, filmmaker and journalist, the lessons I learned in Temagami have guided and informed me ever since.

At that time, Scott was working on the romantic poem *Spring on Mattagami*, a work modelled on the work of British poet George Meredith. Scott wrote about its inspiration in a letter to E.K. Brown, a Canadian literary critic:

> A note on Spring on Mattagami: The provenance of this piece was my having taken a copy of the Oxford book with me on that Indian trip; Pelham and I sitting side by side in our thirty foot canoe had been reading 'Love in a Valley'. I said to myself (or out loud) I will write a love poem in the same form in these surroundings; I did not think to rival it and I added the technical problem by using an additional rhyme; and so I did it in three days. I think and hope the passion is sincere but you will have to count the lady as imaginary, the lady of the city and the garden and the Lido; the Venice stanza was written last as I felt some change in colour would be a relief and add to the drama.[47]

Brown collaborated with Scott on a Lampman collection and edited a Scott poem a few years after the poet's death.[48] A Canadian academic who taught for many years in the United States, Brown became a champion of Canadian writing. The old poet became a friend and mentor to Brown who especially admired Scott's treatment of northern themes. When he reflected on Scott's contribution to Canadian letters a few years after the poet's death, Brown opined that Scott's poetic output was directly inspired by journeys that the Indian Department underwrote, particularly the Treaty 9 expedition:

> The journey of 1905 was to be echoed and re-echoed through much of Scott's admirable poetry. For the finest, strongest, the deepest outcome, he had to wait ten years. It was in November 1915 that he wrote "The Height of Land" in which he has worked out with every resource of his art the illumination that comes to a person of imaginative insight in the heart of the north.[49]

The Height of Land is a lengthy, elaborate reflection on the artist in the material world. Its natural setting is the land that rises from the shore of Lake Superior. At the height of land, waters part, some flowing north to James Bay and, on the southern slopes, down to Lake Superior. Scott and the Treaty 9 team ascended the Pic River back to the rail line after visiting the Indigenous community at Heron Bay. Lake Superior held a fascination for Scott; his short story *Spirit River* is about an isolated community of settlers and Métis on its shores. *The Height of Land* relies directly on the poet's experience in the summer of 1906:

> Now the Indian guides are dead asleep;
> There is no sound unless the soul can hear
> The gathering of the waters in their sources.

As the contemplation of the spiritual and material worlds continues, Scott makes one of the few direct poetic references to a tension between a love of the natural world and the duties of life in modern, industrialized society:

> Upon one hand
> The lonely north enlaced with lakes and streams,
> And the enormous targe of Hudson Bay,
> Glimmering all night
> In the cold arctic light;
> On the other hand
> The crowded southern land
> With all the welter of the lives of men.[50]

The Height of Land has impacted Canadian letters (Canadian production of literature). Many of Scott's literary critics dwell upon it and some of the poets who emerged after him found its explicit depiction of the boreal Canadian landscape and its depiction of the lot of the artist in Canada, a source of inspiration.[51] One of those poets was E.K. Pratt, a professor of English at the University of Toronto.[52] Twenty years younger than Scott, and once a student of Pelham Edgar, Pratt reached out to the established poet as his own career was beginning:

> I am taking the liberty of sending you a little message of appreciation, although unknown to you personally. I had the pleasure last week of spending an evening at the home of Dr. Edgar, an esteemed friend of yours and no less beloved of mine. In the course of the evening by the fire he read some selections from "Lundy's Lane," particularly that magnificent "The Height of Land." I had known the poem for a considerable time, but its growing beauty was so vividly impressed upon me as he read that I asked him if you would not think it presumptuous of me to write you and express my appreciation directly…
>
> I should dearly love to submit a few of my poems under separate cover for your examination. I wanted to send some last year, but could not summon sufficient courage. Dr. Edgar, however, gave me new faith. Most of the verse springs out of the sea-craving life of Newfoundland, my native home.
>
> And could you once in a while send me a poem of your own – a new one? I should indeed be proud.
>
> Sincerely yours,
>
> E.J. Pratt[53]

Scott was an active member of the Royal Society of Canada – an organization that promotes and recognizes Canadian intellectual achievement – and served as its president in 1922. That year, he made a presidential address entitled *Poetry and Progress*. Scott reviewed Canadian achievements in the humanities and social sciences and proffered a report card on Canada approximately 50 years following Confederation. In this speech, as in some of his correspondence with Brown, Scott defended the poetic tradition which influenced him as a young man. In his own work, he was a practitioner of a classic British tradition and did not venture into the newer poetic forms that emerged in Britain and in the United States by the 1920s. In his keynote speech, however, Scott issued a challenge to younger writers in Canada to experiment and seek out newer forms:

> It is the mission of new theories in the arts, and particularly of new theories that come to us illustrated by practice, to force us to re-examine the grounds of our preferences, and to retest our accepted dogmas. Sometimes the preferences are found to be prejudices and the dogmas hollow formulae. There is even a negative use in ugliness that throws into relief upon a dark and inchoate background the shining lines and melting curves of true beauty. The latest mission of revolt has been performed inadequately, but it has served to show us that our poetic utterance was becoming formalized. We require more rage of our poets. We should like them to put to the proof that saying of William Blake: "The tigers of wrath are wiser than the horses of instruction."[54]

As an artist and spokesperson for Canada's learned society, Scott called for change, renovation and challenge within the arts, even in the realm of poetry. Scott wanted poets to behave as bold revolutionaries, precisely as he hoped Indians would not. In 2021, Indigenous rights and child welfare activist Dr. Cindy Blackstock is campaigning to have the Royal Society of Canada acknowledge Scott's now nefarious civil service activities especially in regard to residential schools for Indigenous children.[55]

In his *Poetry and Progress* presidential address to the Royal Society, Scott noted the beginnings of the national archives of Canada and the establishment of an ethnological institute in Ottawa. He also commended the development of the profession of history in Canada with the establishment of professional faculties of history at universities and the emergence of a more "scientific treatment" of the discipline:

> The former story-telling function of History and the endless reweaving of that tissue of tradition which surrounded and obscured the life of a people has given place to a higher conception of duty of the Historian and the obligation to accept no statement without the support of documentary evidence. The exploration and study of archives and the collation of original contemporaneous documents are now held to be essential, and the partisan historian fortified with bigotry and blind to all evidence uncongenial to his preconceptions is an extinct being.[56]

Perhaps Scott was correct in his assessment that the writing of Canadian history was steadily improving after Confederation. He eventually became the focus of that enhanced scrutiny. As the Indigenous rights movement gained momentum in Canada in the last half of the 20th century, a number of Canadian historians began to challenge the assessment of Scott and the policies of the Indian Department.[57] Ironically, Scott himself had played his own role in the development of a Canadian historiography. In 1910, he produced a biography of colonial governor John Graves Simcoe as part of a series of biographical works that he co-edited.[58] The Simcoe biography was regarded as one of the best in the series. However, its Canadian nation building intent is transparent. In its hagiographical portrait of Simcoe, it exemplifies the less-than-rigorous "story-telling function of history and the endless reweaving of tradition" that Scott himself warned of in his Royal Society address.

The sheer breadth of Scott's "uneven" output, to use Frye's adjective phrase, is remarkable. The poetry veers from excellence to craven sentimentality. Scott's "Indian poems" are perplexing in the tension between their racist assumptions juxtaposed with a rich evocation of the natural world and an occasionally sublime expression of universal human values. Scott was trapped as an artist between his great ability to reflect truths and the hateful, imperial values of racial superiority and rank paternalism that were the foundation of the civil service career at which he proved so adept. For theorist and poet Dennis Lee, it is a matter of finding the scholarly means to disentangle artists such as Scott from their imperially skewed perceptions of subjects who are also "victims":

> The colonial writer does not have words of his own. Is it not possible that he projects his own condition of voicelessness into whatever he creates? That he articulates his own powerlessness in the face of alien words, by seeking out fresh tales of victims?[59]

Scott was not only a poet; he produced collections of short stories; for a time, he was a newspaper columnist with *The Globe*; he was an active musician who met his first wife, the violinist Belle Botsford, when he was asked to accompany her on the piano at an Ottawa recital; he was active in theatre both as a director of Ottawa's Little Theatre and as a playwright with works produced in Ottawa and at Hart House at the University of Toronto.[60] Scott had a significant relationship with the University of Toronto, which awarded him an honourary doctorate in literature in 1922. The same year, he also participated along with an actor in a reading of his poetry organized by academic, Pelham Edar. The year prior, Scott read publicly during a centenary commemoration for the British poet John Keats.[61] In 1927, Scott combined his civil service connections with his musical sensibilities when he collaborated with the folklorist Marius Barbeau and the composer

Ernest MacMillan on the English transcription of three Nisga'a songs from the Nass Valley that had originally been recorded by Barbeau.[62] At the time MacMillan was both principal of the Royal Conservatory of Music and head of the Faculty of Music at the University of Toronto.[63]

When Frye reflected on the emergence of Canadian letters, he argued that Canada's unique position as a former colony of Great Britain which soon after came under American cultural and economic dominance created, "a frostbite at the roots of the Canadian imagination."[64] Perhaps Scott's overall output is a singular manifestation of such a "frostbite." Scott emerged in a literary and political environment at a time when Canadian nationalists felt an existential threat to the developing country's survival against the odds of geography and American Manifest Destiny. At the same time, such Canadians felt a deep attachment to Great Britain. As Frye argued, these conditions created a conceptual "garrison." A Canadian artist/mandarin such as Scott, a poet at the centre of Frye's stinging analysis of Canada's intellectual lot, was an archetypical resident within such a "garrison":

> Small and isolated communities surrounded with a physical or psychological "frontier," separated from one another and from their American and British cultural sources: communities that provide all that their members have in the way of distinctively human values, and that are compelled to feel a great respect for law and order that holds them together, yet confronted with a huge, unthinking, menacing and formidable physical setting – such communities are bound to develop what we may provisionally call a garrison mentality...
>
> A garrison is a closely knit and beleaguered society, and its moral and social values are unquestionable. In a perilous enterprise one does not discuss causes or motives: one is either a fighter or a deserter.[65]

In poetry, fictional prose, journalism and music, Scott was a foundational figure in Canadian culture. Esteemed by his contemporaries, he articulated an artistic vision for the new nation state. As a bureaucrat, he also exemplified the values and priorities that were prevalent in Canada during his lifetime.

Jacques Soustelle and the vulgarisation of French ethnology

Scott was a person of middle-class origins who rose to serve Canadian political elites and frequent the country's artistic establishment. Soustelle, born of the working class, was at the forefront of a move to popularize French ethnology in the 1930s. Having begun his graduate studies as a prodigy from Lyon in philosophy, Soustelle quickly developed a passion for the hands-on, field ethnology championed by Paul Rivet. As a student of Rivet's, Soustelle was among a small group of ethnological neophytes who moved away from the "arm chair" efforts of a Marcel Mauss and others professors associated with l'École normale supérieure in developing a participant-observer model of ethnology that was given a home at l'Institut d'ethnologie where Soustelle studied.

As French archaeology and anthropology spun off a new ethnographic form, Rivet and his students promulgated a set of ideas that encouraged acceptance and observation of Indigenous societies co-existing, however uneasily, with the modern industrialized world. The youthful, academic Soustelle, freshly imbued with the *indigenista* ideology of the Mexican Revolution, proclaimed his new faith in his first book *Mexique Terre Indienne*:

> *Considérer les Indiens comme constituent des nationalités, leur reconnaitre des droits culturels et*

linguistiques, leur donner l'espagnol comme langue de relations, mais leur garantir le respect des leurs (j'ajouterai même: leur apprendre à écrire), bref, respecter la substance des sociétés indigènes pour qu'elles entrent de plain-pied dans l'unité du Mexique, avec leurs particularités, leurs fierté, bannières déployés, en pleine conscience d'elles-mêmes. Car c'est tous ensemble, comme l'histoire de leurs races et de leurs terres les a formés, tous ensemble et tous entiers, sans renier aucun d'entre eux ni rien en eux-mêmes, que ceux d'en bas sortiront de leur humiliation et gagneront leur place au soleil. Rien ne doit être perdu des richesses de civilisation dont ils sont porteurs. Elles sont, ces richesses, comme des pierres précieuses formées dans les profondeurs noirs, qui n'ont même pas conscience de les contenir; la tâche d'aujourd'hui est de les découvrir et les dégager, afin qu'elles soient vues de tous. Ainsi le passage dans le monde des générations oubliées n'aura pas été tout à fait vain.[66]

To consider Indians as constituting nationalities, to acknowledge their cultural and linguistic rights, to give them Spanish as a language of business, but to guarantee respect for their own (I will also add teach them to write), in sum, to respect the substance of Indigenous societies so that they can enter Mexican society on equal terms, with their particularities and their pride fully displayed in full possession of their identity. Because it is only all together, like the history of their races and their lands have shaped them, all together without renouncing anyone among them or in them, that those at the bottom will emerge from their humiliation and take their place in the sun. Nothing should be lost of the riches of the civilization that they carry forward. These riches are like the precious stones formed in the deepest darkness, that they are not even aware of possessing; today's task is to discover and release them, so that they can be seen by all. In that way the path through this world of forgotten generations will have not been in vain.

Soustelle put his ideas into practice back home in the 1930s. Rivet and Soustelle were directors of *le Musée de l'Homme* which opened its doors in the Trocadero Palace (an ethnological museum in Paris) in 1938 at a time when the Popular Front, a left-of-centre coalition, gained political power in France.[67] This popularizing effort, or *vulgarisation* as it was called *en français*, developed in a threatening European political context. Rivet and his young associates, such as Soustelle, were alarmed by the growing strength of Nazism in Germany, of Italian fascism under Mussolini and the assault by General Francisco Franco against Spanish republicanism. In 1934, Soustelle, under his own name rather than the pseudonym Jean Duriez, wrote a highly polemical article raising the spectre of fascism gaining a foothold in France.[68] His alarm appeared prophetic considering the easy alliance in the name of the family and traditional French values that Général Maréchal Philippe Pétain would strike with Hitler's government in 1940:

Le grand art de fascisme (et ce par quoi il diffère de n'importe quel régime d'autorité), c'est de faire passer les opprimés du côté des oppresseurs. À la répression physique s'ajoute la pression morale, l'hypocrite et menteuse déclamation qui retourne contre leur propre classe des travailleurs aveuglés.[69]

The great art of fascism (and in this respect it differs from all other forms of authority) is to turn the oppressed into oppressors. To physical repression one adds moral pressure, the hypocritical and lying declamation that turns the blinded workers against their own class.

Soustelle's impolitic assertions about the dangers of a blinded working class and of the social toxicity provoked when the oppressed find common cause with their oppressors, foreshadowed his analysis of the rise of the FLN in Algeria 20 years later. As with his embrace of the pedagogy of the rural education campaigns of *indigenismo* in Mexico, Soustelle stubbornly applied his anti-fascism of the 1930s Europe to the Algerian conflict. In his energetic efforts to launch *le Musée de l'Homme* at the side of his mentor Rivet, Soustelle fancied himself a servant of the popular classes, determined to open a previously rarefied world of academic exoticism to everyday French people. Twenty years later, Soustelle saw himself as an advocate for the popular masses of Algeria in the teeth of the armed appeals of the FLN.

The leaders of *le Musée de l'Homme* were determined to find means to popularize the dissemination of information about the "forgotten" societies in the colonized world. Soustelle proudly explained how the new museum would bring ordinary French people and their families into contact with a rich ethnographic vision of the past and present. He appeared on radio and contributed articles about the mission of the new museum in the popular press.[70] Soustelle's desire to open wide the doors of the new museum was influenced by political concerns. He saw museums and public culture as essential means of public education in perilous times. In an interview with a Parisian magazine published in 1938 to coincide with the opening of *le Musée*, Soustelle emphasized the universal qualities of human achievement that ethnological museums exposed while warning of the lethal racial theories which were very popular among German scholars:

> *Je vous parlerai du point de vue de l'ethnographie, en ce qui concerne les théories sur les races humaines mises en vogue dans certains pays par des « autorités » qui ne pas savantes. Nous, ethnologues, nous voyons qu'il n'y a pas de race qui n'ait contribué au patrimoine commune de la civilisation par des inventions souvent capitales. Aussi bien, si on fait l'inventaire du « matériel » de la civilisation européenne, on y trouve des apports extrêmement importants de populations de toutes origines et notamment d'Asie Mineure, ou sémitiques, tel le christianisme. D'autre part, le monopole de là haute civilisation n'appartient nullement à l'Europe. Cet été, j'étais à Copenhague, à un congrès international de savants. On n'y pouvait voir personne, sauf les allemands, qui prît au sérieux le racisme, et pas même eux quand on les prenait à part.*[71]

> I will speak to you from the perspective of ethnography, about matters concerning theories about human races currently in vogue in certain countries by "authorities" who are not knowledgeable. We ethnologists see that there is no race that has not contributed to the common patrimony of civilisation with important inventions. As well, if one does an inventory of the "material" of European civilization, one finds important contributions from all origins, especially that of Asia Minor, or Semitic societies, such as Christianity. In addition, Europe does not have a monopoly on high civilization. This summer, I was in Copenhagen, at an international congress of academics. One could not find anyone, except for the Germans, who took racism seriously, and not even them when you spoke to them individually.

Efforts of popular education by the leading lights of *le Musée de l'Homme* were not restricted to the print media. Even before the museum opened its doors, both Jacques and Georgette Soustelle, as well as their colleague Germaine Tillion, made radio broadcasts about their journeys and scientific findings in Mexico and Algeria. The scripts reveal the presenters' efforts to popularize their scientific work; Tillion, for example, dedicated one program to the simple re-telling of a Berber fable she had translated; Georgette and Jacques Soustelle collaborated on a program about Mexico in which they discussed an Otomí festival they had witnessed.[72] Some of Jacques Soustelle's Mexican lectures are preserved in the digital audio division of the *Bibliothèque Nationale–Mitterrand*. While Soustelle spoke in everyday language for his radio public, he did not entirely shed his professorial skin. His perorations are punctuated by the sharp sound of chalk striking slate as Soustelle would emphasize and repeat a point while writing a keyword on a blackboard for the benefit of a live audience.[73] In his embrace of radio, Soustelle was no doubt influenced by popular education radio of revolutionary Mexico that was prevalent in the 1930s and served to promote nationalism, the folk arts and tourism.[74]

The new impulse in French social sciences often reflected a pronounced commitment to social justice, to the recognition of Indigenous peoples and the desire to open a diverse world of civilizations to ordinary citizens through public education. Writer Michel Leiris expressed the new thinking in *Spartacus*, one of the left-leaning journals to which Soustelle contributed from Mexico:

> *Considérant toutes chose comme liés, n'étudiant jamais un élément d'une société envisagé isolément, mais l'examinant au contraire en fonction de tous les autres, observant les mœurs, les coutumes les langues, non comme des choses figées, comme des curiosités seulement intéressantes par leur exotisme ou leur archaïsme, mais comme des choses vivantes qu'il s'agit de saisir dans leur mouvement, dans leur actualité, l'ethnographie apparaît une science éminemment dialectique.*[75]

> By considering all things linked together, not studying an isolated element of a society, but rather examining things in relation to others, observing the mores, the customs, the languages, not as fixed things, not as curiosities only of interest for their exoticism or archaic value, but as living things which need to be understood in their movement and currency, ethnography becomes an eminently dialectic science.

Soustelle himself continued a conversation about the practical application of ethnographical study as a lever to redeem and elevate oppressed peoples in his relationship with Germaine Tillion. Soustelle relied on fellow ethnologist Tillion's expertise of Indigenous Algerians in developing the social reform program built on Soustelle's perception of Mexican *indigenista* principles in 1955-56. Such efforts belie the negative and reductive perception of Soustelle as a "fascist" sympathizer, a fellow traveller with *l'Organisation de l'armée secrète* (OAS) which became a widely shared misperception following his notorious falling out with de Gaulle over Algerian independence. Soustelle adamantly maintained until his death that as governor general of Algeria he attempted to invoke sound, scientific methods that had been formed by his experiences and observations in Mexico as a young ethnologist.[76]

His Mexican research fuelled Soustelle's meteoric rise in the French academy prior to the Second World War. Further, it was a fascination with Mexico and Latin America that soldered the relationship with Paul Rivet as doctoral supervisor and intellectual mentor. As war clouds gathered in Europe, the *Musée de l'Homme* traded on the strengths of its leadership, specifically the *americanistas* who founded it: Rivet and his academic prodigy Soustelle. Rivet believed that the ongoing discovery and display of Mesoamerican cultures would help popularize interest in ethnology and bring new audiences to the *Musée*. Rivet and Soustelle vaunted the richness of Mexico in the mainstream press. Soustelle trumpeted the significance of discoveries at Monte Alban in the state of Oaxaca that were uncovered in part by Mexican archaeologist Alfonso Caso, who would remain a critical Mexican scientific contact for the French researchers:[77]

> I believe that Mexico possesses the richest ethnological treasures in the world. After viewing the excavations being made at Ohaca [sic] near Montalban I must say I believe the discoveries made there can be compared with the finding of Tutankaman's tomb.[78]

Rivet and Soustelle emphasized Mesoamerica in the heady days surrounding the opening of the new museum. A press release from the division run by Georgette Soustelle invited reporters to a preview of a major exhibition in 1939:

Département d'Amérique communique de presse Musée de l'Homme
INAUGURATION DE LA NOUVELLE SALLE D'AMERIQUE – PRÉSENTATION À LA PRESSE
Le moulage d'une grande stèle de Copan annonce le monde maya et mexicain. Céramique,
masques, statues, révèlent la civilisation raffinée de ces peuples…
L'ouverture au public de cette riche section constitue une nouvelle étape dans la réorganisation totale
du musée d'ethnographie devenue, en 1938, le Musée de l'Homme.[79]

Press Release Museum of Man Department of the Americas
**INAUGURATION OF THE NEW HALL OF THE AMERICAS –
PRESENTATION TO THE PRESS**
The cast of a gigantic stele from Copan announces the Mayan and Mexican world. Ceramics,
masks, statues, reveal the refined civilization of these peoples…
The public opening of this rich section marks a step forward in the organization of the Museum of
Ethnography, which became, in 1938, the Museum of Man.

The exhibition of 1939 included a *soirée Mexicaine* featuring music and dance attended by Mexican diplomats.[80] This event dovetailed with contemporary Mexican campaigns to project its rich folklore to Europe and the United States. Such campaigns began under the modernizing dictatorship of Porfirio Díaz and were continued enthusiastically by post-revolutionary governments which had ties to the Soustelles and Rivet.[81]

Emphasizing the importance of Latin America also fit with Rivet's and the Soustelles' patriotism and sense of France's place in the world. If the French academy, and by extension, the French public, could shift its gaze to the Latin countries of the Americas, it would decrease the cultural dominance of the United States in the French imagination. It also opened a window on part of the world where American influence was often perceived negatively because of aggressive American foreign policies in much of Latin America. In 1938, Soustelle wrote a magazine article inviting academics and even tourists to consider the richness of Latin America as an alternative, and perhaps antidote, to Washington's heavy influence:

> *Nous vivons en un temps où un Etat américaine domine l'économie mondiale et même certaines*
> *formes de sentir; son cinéma envahit nos villes, comme ses crises affolent nos bourses… On sait aussi*
> *qu'en dehors des Etats-Unis, le continent découvert et colonisé depuis quatre siècles porte de vastes*
> *cités saxonnes ou Latines : Québec, Mexico, La Havane, Rio, Buenos-Aires… Que reste-t-il donc à*
> *découvrir en Amérique?*
>
> *…Au Mexique, au Pérou, dans toutes les Andes, dans les villages que l'on atteint sans peine par le*
> *rail ou la route, ou tout au plus à dos de mulet, vivent des Indiens à qui l'on a accordé le plus souvent*
> *qu'une attention distraite, comme à des choses trop habituelles. Or, jamais leur langage n'a fait l'objet*
> *d'une étude sérieuse, jamais on n'a recherché, derrière le mince écran du christianisme imposé, leurs*
> *véritables croyances, jamais on n'a entrepris une analyse approfondies de leurs caractères ethniques*
> *grâce aux méthodes les plus récentes de l'anthropologie. Le champ des recherches possibles est donc*
> *immense. Et il faut faire vite, car les populations perdent leur langages, oublient leurs traditions, dis-*
> *paraissent par le jeu des métissages.*[82]

We live at a time in which the American state dominates the world economy and even some ways of feeling; its cinema invades our cities, just as its crises afflicts our stock exchanges… One also knows that outside the United States, the continent discovered and colonised for four centuries holds important cities whether Anglo Saxon or Latin: Québec, Havana, Rio, Buenos Aires… What else remains to be discovered in America?

…In Mexico, in Peru, all over the Andes, in villages, that one reaches by difficulty by rail or road, or moreover on the back of a mule, live Indians to whom one has paid only a distracted attention, as if they were too familiar. However, their languages have not been seriously studied, we have not researched, under the thin veil of imposed Christianity, their true beliefs, never have we undertaken a deep analysis of their ethnic characteristics according to the most up-to-date anthropological methods. The field of possible research before us is therefore immense. And it needs to be done soon, because populations lose their languages, forget their traditions and disappear as Metis societies develop.

Soustelle made a significant contribution to modern Europe's comprehension and appreciation of Indigenous cultures in the Americas. The work is distinguished by the breadth of his curiosity and the elegance of his writing.[83]

Soustelle had a foot in a world of collections driven by imperial ambition and another in an emerging, more popular, accessible, *diffusionniste* (to use Christine Lauriére's formulation) form of ethnology.[84] The new museum boasted its ability to stage exhibitions of material that Soustelle and his 19th century scientific predecessors has wrenched from Mesoamerica from an assumed position of European cultural superiority. In his political journalism from the 1930s, Soustelle celebrated the capacity of contemporary Indigenous peoples, who crafted a syncretic faith from Indigenous and Christian roots of their own invention. He celebrated the capacity of Indigenous Mexican cultures to adapt new technologies in domains such as agriculture and music. On the other hand, as his 1938 article in *Science* demonstrated, sometimes he regretted the process of *mestizaje* through which supposedly purely Indigenous characteristics were subsumed in new regional and national identities. His proclivity to assume that he possessed special insight into the transition from Indigenousness to modernity would not serve him well in *l'Algérie française*.

Duncan Campbell Scott and Jacques Soustelle: The artists as mature men

The final stages of the careers and public lives of Scott and Soustelle bear little resemblance. Scott faded elegantly from the scene into a respectful, fruitful retirement which lasted 15 years; Soustelle never retired. He remained vitally active in France, Mexico and elsewhere until the end of his days. Scott stepped down from Canadian civil service in 1932 at age 70. As a newly re-married elder, Scott settled into a life of writing, editing, playing and listening to music and receiving vistors from the world of letters and the visual arts at his handsome home on Lisgar Street in Ottawa until his death in December 1947.

Scott was saved from a solitary retirement by romance late in his life. Belle Botsford, Scott's first wife, died in 1929.[85] The couple had lost their only child Elizabeth, when she died in 1907 of a fever while attending a Parisian convent school.[86] As a mature artist contemplating retirement from the civil service, Scott met Elise Aylen, a young poet from a well-to-do French Canadian Ottawa family. In 1929, she was 27 years old, the recently widowed Scott was 67. Aylen had approached the venerable Scott with samples of her poetry. Scott was soon smitten. He began to write tender letters to her as he travelled the country on department business:

> Friday morning and what a glorious day – the sun pouring down the Bow Valley – the mountains like great crystals brilliant with snow & flawed with dark ridges and circles of trees… How I wish you cld see it all with your clear eyes & your sensitivness to beauty – I have seen the Rockies and the Selkirks many times but never in March & I have an added interest this time something makes me look at them thro' a lens that gives a new aspect a fresh meaning would that I cld get it into words & say them.[87]

Scott wrote the forward to Aylen's *Roses of Shadow*, a collection of her poems. In that short essay, Scott expressed his dismay about much of modern poetry and, as he had done in his presidential address to The Royal Society of 1922, insisted that attentiveness to tradition was the only true means to advancement in the arts:

> You cannot dispense with art in poetry, and art is a hard mistress, but she is liberal with rewards. Much of the ugliness of current free verse arises from the lack of practice in the older forms and if my advice were to be sought, I should advise poets to invent even more difficult forms within which to exercise their powers of invention. Mastery is to be gained through severe discipline rather than through easy liberty.[88]

The introduction to Aylen's collection reveals an important element of Scott's assessment of poetry. He believed newer poetry should be rooted in classical forms. Here, as in his essay to the Royal Society of Canada, *Poetry and Progress*, Scott argued for a demanding intellectual standard for development of the arts in Canada.

Scott's enthusiasm for office life began to diminish, at least privately, as his relationship with Aylen blossomed. In their correspondence, the ageing Scott gave vent to dissatisfaction with his civil service career. As he travelled the country by train on department business in 1930, the love-struck sexagenarian Scott expressed frustration with his efforts to balance the demands of the department with his artistic pursuits. As he headed west in the late autumn of 1930, Scott composed a long letter to Aylen from Winnipeg and Regina. He wrote about the tensions between his artistic bent and his civil service job after meeting some ambitious prairie entrepreneurs, but steadied himself with more characteristic resolve:

> This business life would kill me, the men I meet all splendid fellows bent on making money seem so far away from me, I can only tolerate the Dept at home by forgetting it and living that other life, ineffective enough I suppose but more natural. I have had time to read your two dear letters they made me very homesick and dissatisfied which was not the effect you intended. The written words are sometimes as perverse & contrary as the spoken; not that the letters did not [illegible word] of you in every line, they did, but they made me weary of myself & what I am and what I ought to be. However, this is a weakness that must be overcome.[89]

Scott and Aylen were married in 1931, the year of Scott's retirement. They travelled extensively in Europe and throughout North America; and they settled into a highly cultured life in Ottawa. Scott made almost no further mention of his Indian Department career. The house on Lisgar Street became a salon for writers, painters and musicians.[90]

Aylen continued to write poetry, historical novels and, most remarkably, a play based on D.H. Lawrence's novel *The Plumed Serpent*.[91] Lawrence's work concerns the love affair between a British tourist and a charismatic Indigenous leader who leads a revolt rooted in Aboriginal Mexican spirituality. *The Plumed Serpent* depicts the 20th century Indigenous Mexican equivalent of political and religious practices which were illegal for Indigenous people in Canada during Scott's tenure at the department. The origins and inspiration of Aylen's unpublished manuscript for a play that was never produced, are murky. Aylen's adaptation of Lawrence's novel, although not precisely dated, was written while she was married to Scott and living on Lisgar Street. There is no record of a meeting or any correspondence between Aylen and Lawrence; and Lawrence died in 1930 before Aylen and Scott married.[92] In 1939, Scott and Aylen travelled together to the

Scott's first wife, Belle Warner Botsford, died n 1929. Two years *later Scott married the poet Elise Aylen (left), 40 years his junior.*

Chanie Wenjack School for Indigenous Studies,
Peter Gzowski College, Trent University,
Nogojiwanong-Peterborough, *October 2019*

I am attending and appearing on a panel of alumni at the 50th anniversary celebration of Indigenous Studies at Trent University in Nogojiwanong – Peterborough. At lunch, I approach a distinguished looking elderly man seated in a wheelchair who is one of the day's most honoured guests, praised by many speakers. He is Thomas H.B. Symons, founding president of Trent University. Along with Anishinaabe intellectual Waubegeshig Harvey McCue, Symons was one of the creative forces behind Canada's first Indigenous Studies program. Tom looks at me and says, "James, you have done a lot of fine work. You made a film about Duncan Campbell Scott. I knew him."

In that meeting and a subsequent lengthy telephone conversation, Tom was mildly dismayed by the present day depiction of Scott.[8] He remembered his father's friend who would stop by the Symons house when visiting Toronto. Tom and his siblings were especially fond of the visitor from Ottawa who played piano so well and often engaged the Symons children in sing-alongs. Tom expressed surprise at the acerbic tone some use in discussing Scott and said that he was aware of the "brickbats" thrown Scott's way, and that even given his personal support for reconciliation and social justice, Tom believed it is important to look at the whole individual and understand the historical context in which he lived.

Thomas Symons died in January 2021 at age 91. Tributes praised his role as an educator and his contribution to Indigenous education in Canada.[9]

American west. Lawrence had lived at a ranch near Taos, New Mexico for part of the 1920s while he made several extended trips to Mexico.[93]

The 15 years that Scott and Aylen had shared following his retirement were busy with dedication to writing, the arts in general and travel throughout Canada, the United States and Europe. Scott ascended to the role of elder statesman of Canadian arts and letters. As the Second World War ground to a close in Europe, Scott wrote to Brown, with whom he had collaborated on a Lampman collection, about Lawren Harris, a member of the Group of Seven, who had just passed by Lisgar Avenue:

> Lawren Harris was here yesterday just for a day, came in about half past four, had a cup of tea, smoked two cigarettes, cleaned his picture which needed it badly, had an animated talk, went into my bedroom at half after five, slept soundly for three quarters of an hour and then was off to dinner and a meeting and the night train to Toronto. Here is a man I admire greatly.[94]

Harris was but one of the painters who visited the Scott-Aylen home and whose work was hung there. Scott was one of the first Canadian establishment figures to embrace the work of Emily Carr. Carr had initially faced rejection for her effort to apply the sensibilities of impressionist painting she had studied in Paris to west coast Indigenous villages, and the rainforests and seascapes of the north-west. She had been ridiculed in stern Victoria, British Columbia, and initially rejected by the National Gallery in Ottawa. Finally in 1927, Carr gained acceptance at age 56 when her canvasses were included in a ground-breaking National Gallery of Canada exhibition, *West Coast Art: Native and Modern*.[95] Scott and painter Lawren Harris were among the influential Canadians who finally helped bring her work to attention. In 1941, she sent two of her paintings to the Scott's for their wedding anniversary, "and also as a tribute to the beauty and pleasure Dr. Scott has given to Canada through his poems."[96] The canvasses were eventually donated by Aylen to The National Gallery of Canada. In her correspondence with Scott, Carr expressed admiration for his poems and wrote of her struggle in writing stories on Indigenous themes.[97]

The warm relationship between Carr and Scott has been overlooked in the scholarship and works of popular culture about them as individuals. As a painter, Carr is generally regarded as an artist who synthesized Indigenous themes in a respectful and haunting manner. Mention is not made of her admiring attitude of Scott both as poet and Indian Department bureaucrat. *Klee Wyck*, Carr's 1941 book based on her observations of Indigenous communities in British Columbia, won the Governor General's Award for non-fiction in 1942.[98] Carr is today generally respected as an artist who possessed empathy for Indigenous peoples, while Scott is a vilified character because of his association with Canadian Indian policy. Both conducted salvage operations among Indigenous peoples to inspire their art and both were antimodernists who found in Indigenous ways an antidote to the conflicts of the modern world.[99]

Scott also befriended the renowned Québécois landscape artist Clarence Gagnon whose paintings Scott collected. The choice is fitting because Gagnon's pastoral work set in Québec mirrored the society that Scott described in his French-Canadian stories, which were among Scott's first published work.[100] Prior to joining the Canadian public service, the adolescent Scott had attended Stanstead College in the Eastern Townships of Québec and had childhood associations with Québec rural parishes that his father visited for his clerical work.

In 1919, Scott came to Gagnon's assistance in researching "native pigments" and was considering using in his paintings.[101] In 1921, Scott helped Gagnon determine the origins of a tomahawk that Gagnon had found in the Québec bush. In each case, Scott referred the matter to the anthropological branch of the Geological

Survey of Canada. In the case of the tomahawk, Scott reported back to Gagnon that folklorist Marius Barbeau had examined the tomahawk but could not provide a conclusive answer about its history.[102]

A few days later, Scott sought a return favour in eliciting information from Gagnon about accommodation in Paris, a city where Gagnon often lived:

> We have not been in Paris since 1907. Can you give me a few addresses for small hotels or pensions with reasonable rates? Don't imagine that we want anything extravagant because we don't, something on the left bank, comfortable and reasonable.[103]

Scott wrote six years later to Gagnon in Paris to congratulate the artist on his inclusion in a major exhibition which put Canadian artists on an equal footing with acclaimed French art of the 1920s.[104] Scott's keen interest in the world of visual art is further confirmed by a letter from Gagnon in 1931 commenting in detail on the effect the Great Depression was having on the prices of paintings.[105]

Despite their geographic differences, Carr was painting the northwest and Gagnon was representing Laurentian landscapes, there is a common factor in their work: both focused on landscape. Indigenous people generally viewed either as mythologized figures from the past or their present-day descendants in the process of acculturation, often figured in Scott's Indian poems. They were not present in the paintings he collected. Despite her fascination with Indigenous peoples, Carr's most celebrated British Columbian visual art is primarily of the natural world. Gagnon's villages and snow-covered vistas from Québec are similarly depopulated. Another of Scott's painter friends, Lawren Harris, like other Group of Seven members, often depicted regions of Ontario, such as the north shore of Lake Superior and Algonquin Park which are inhabited by Anishinaabe peoples who never appear in the paintings. Perhaps the selection of such paintings for his home reflected Scott's own apparent lack of interest in Indigenous peoples following his retirement.

As we have seen earlier, Scott lived through the beginning of mass media. He was frequently involved with radio broadcasts in the early days of the Canadian Broadcasting Corporation (CBC). He contributed scripts and poetry to the fledgling national broadcaster. He was the subject of a feature commemorating his 78th birthday in 1944.[106] Scott was also involved in the early days of Canadian documentary filmmaking when the National Film Board of Canada (NFB) emerged as a producer of film propaganda during the Second World War. During the First World War, Scott had written poems mourning a Canadian pilot and another for the mothers of deceased Canadian soldiers.[107] When the Second World War reached its end, the elderly Scott was invited to contribute a poem to the National Film Board as part of the narration for the production "Salute to a Victory." National Film Commissioner John Grierson wrote to acknowledge Scott's contribution, "We have been honoured in this association with a creative talent of which Canada has long had reason to be proud."[108] Grierson sent flowers along with his note. Scott graciously acknowledged Grierson's gesture.[109]

Scott even made a posthumous CBC appearance on air on January 16, 1948 as part of a "National School Broadcast on Canadian Poets." Scott had been recorded in late 1947 prior to his death that December. He was introduced to CBC listeners with the following script:

> In an old house in a quiet corner of Ottawa there lived, until within a few days of last Christmas, a man who was the last member of a group of four celebrated Canadian poets of a past generation. Duncan Campbell Scott, tall, grave-faced gentle-voiced – more like a Bishop than a Poet. A man of affairs who had yet found time to dream. A man rich in the experience of life, whose passing takes much from Canadian poetry; a Poet whose going will be mourned by all lovers of verse.

Two careers were his – that of poet and high office in the Department of Indian Affairs. His work took him into the wild north country, made him familiar with its woodland and sky, rivers and streams – and above all, its Red Man.[110]

Scott is heard briefly in the broadcast. It is the only recording of his voice extant. A frail, aged, thin-voiced poet reads a few lines billed as "a message for the children of Canada." Scott ended his brief performance with the following couplet:

If you be in search of Beauty,
Go where Beauty dwells.[111]

Aylen sold the house on Lisgar Street and left Canada forever within a year of Scott's death. Eventually she would settle at an ashram in India where she died in 1972.[112] In the weeks following Scott's death, the grieving Aylen wrote to family friend and Scott's co-editor of Lampman poetry, E.K. Brown:

Dear Edward,
Thank you and Peggy so much for your kind word of sympathy. I am sorry to have been so long in answering. I have written about fifty letters already, but all more or less formal ones. Somehow that seemed easier to me than the more personal ones. To write those who are our friends, and were close to us, costs one more. I still feel half dazed and wholly exhausted, and the dreadful pain and pity of his illness is still in possession of my mind. I wake up at night calling for the nurse, before I can realize the way things are. And when I look about the house and do not see him, I feel like a swimmer in deep water – I keep trying to find something solid to stand on and there seems to be nothing beneath me but an infinite depth. Perhaps it is as well that it is necessary for me to rent the house at once. I am already packing up and will leave as soon as I can find a tenant.[113]

The final days of Jacques Soustelle

Soustelle returned to France in 1968 from self-exile after his rupture with Charles de Gaulle. Following the student revolt in France of May 1968, Soustelle took advantage of a general amnesty offered by the de Gaulle government to return. While he had been pursued and carefully monitored by French intelligence because he was suspected of plotting against the French president, Soustelle was not apprehended, and even briefly returned clandestinely to France, during his seven years abroad.[114] Upon his permanent return in 1968, he resumed a very active public life engaged with academic, political and publishing activities although his reputation was tarnished in some quarters by his impolitic opposition to Algerian independence which had been achieved in the Evian Accords of 1962.[115]

In the last decades of his life, respect for Soustelle's writing and his broad connaissance of Mexico had a mitigating effect on the overwhelmingly negative assessment of his role in Algerian-French conflict. The fascination with Mexico that had inspired the graduate student prodigy endured. *Les quatre soleils*, his meditation on ethnological practice and the rise and fall of civilizations as seen through the prism of Mexico, was greeted with critical enthusiasm by academics and journalists.[116] Soustelle had written most of it in various libraries and apartments in Italy, Switzerland and Belgium during his self-imposed exile just prior to returning to France. The book's publication served as a reminder of Soustelle's preeminent status among European *savants* despite his controversial role in the Algerian-French conflict. The clarity and broad appeal of his storytelling approach made Soustelle a sought after authority on subjects concerning the Mexican past. He worked as a writer and presenter on documentary films about Mexico made for national French television audiences. His on-air style was energetic, as he strode through jungles in Chiapas, ascended the steps of temple ruins, or performed long, stand-ups in the exhibit rooms of the National Museum of Anthropology in Mexico City.[117]

Soustelle was also rehabilitated by the academy in this final career phase. With the election of centre-right president Valery Giscard d'Estaing, Soustelle was given the task of reviewing France's system of post-secondary education in the social sciences.[118] He proffered a ringing argument for funding of French research in disciplines including archaeology, anthropology and ethnology. As he and Paul Rivet had asserted in the 1930s with their writings and the establishment of le Musée de l'homme, Soustelle continued to believe that a lively milieu of French academic programs and public institutions dedicated to the social sciences should be national priorities. Re-established as a professor at l'Université de Paris, Soustelle supervised numerous doctoral candidates after his 1968 return.[119]

Although his standing as a Latin American expert was re-affirmed, Soustelle remained a political undesirable to many. He never escaped from the dark shadow of his thinking and actions about the Algerian question. Assumptions of his association with l'Organisation armée secrète (OAS) were reliably established in 1995 with the publication of Bernard Ullmann's biography.[120] Ullmann proved that Soustelle had participated in planning an assassination attempt against de Gaulle. He also established that there were no direct links between Soustelle and OAS's acts of violence against civilians. Soustelle's role in these matters is murky and contested. He was granted amnesty along with others by de Gaulle, but the shadow of his OAS association stuck with him.

As if the Algerian matter was insufficient to sully his name, Soustelle further complicated his reputation by taking unfashionable stands in defence of Israel and the South African government in the dying days of apartheid. As with l'Algérie française, Soustelle was adamant. Soustelle believed that a Zionist government could only reach an accommodation with Palestinian moderates should such a group emerge. As for South Africa, Soustelle argued that apartheid-era South Africa could achieve a democratic accommodation with the African National Congress (ANC) only when and if the ANC and its allies abandoned all violent activities.[121]

Soustelle's qualified redemption in the eyes of the French elite was complete in 1984 when he was named to l'Académie française despite the opposition of loyal Gaullists and the left.[122] Soustelle died in 1990 at 68 years of age.[123]

In the 21st century, Scott's poetry still provides a means to understand late and post-Victorian conceptions of Indigenousness that were prevalent among the elite of an emerging Canadian nation-state. Scott's profound interest in visual art, his involvement with the theatre both at Ottawa's Little Theatre and at Hart House in Toronto, as well as ongoing musical interests were perhaps not uncommon for a deeply cultured senior civil servant. In Scott's case, these pursuits, which bespeak an appreciation of a broad swath of the humanities, must be juxtaposed with his Indian Department activities which in the 1920s were an expression of Canadian coercive assimilation at its apogee, with Scott acting as its most powerful administrator and spokesperson.

Soustelle's ethnological oeuvre enjoys a higher reputation in its field today than Scott's poems and poetry do in Canadian letters.[124] Broadly speaking, Soustelle's social scientific work, and his reputation, survive due to his central role in the reformation of French ethnology in the 1930s and because his Mexican works remain eminently readable and accessible to a broad audience.

*Governor General Soustelle
(left) in southern Algeria.*

Chapter Five

POLITICS

Aujourd'hui la partie est jouée; l'humanité est nationale; le laïc a gagné. Mais son triomphe passe tout ce qu'il pouvait croire. Le clerc n'est pas seulement vaincu, il est assimilé. L'homme de science, l'artiste, le philosophe sont attachés à leur nation autant que le laboureur ou le marchand;...[1]

Today the game is over; humanity is national; the secularist has won. But his triumph surpasses his own expectations. The intellectual has not simply won, he has assimilated. The scientist, the artist, the philosopher are attached to their nation just as much as the worker or the shopkeeper.

IN 1927, FRENCH PHILOSOPHER Julien Benda skewered the spirit of his intellectual times in a slim work published in *La Trahison des clercs* (The Betrayal of The Intellectuals, or The Great Betrayal).[2] Benda produced his work in the aftermath of the horrors of the First World War. He predicted that nationalism, fuelled, in his view, by a *trahison* of artists, scientists, clergy and educators – the thinking class that Benda held accountable for popular attitudes – would inevitably lead to another global conflict. The rise of fascism and the outbreak of the Second World War gave Benda's masterwork the patina of prophecy.

Benda wrote at a time when Duncan Campbell Scott was at the height of his powers in the Canadian Indian Department and when Jacques Soustelle was beginning his meteoric rise in French academic life. Benda believed that in the modern era, the primary legacy of both Greek philosophy and of the enlightenment – independent and challenging free thinking – had been bent to the service of the nation. In different countries and separated by a few decades, Scott and Soustelle were instruments of national policies and of a hardened conception of the state that trumped ethical concerns and excluded entire communities from liberal principles. In their duty both Scott and Soustelle sometimes betrayed ideals of liberal, participatory, representative democracy that were the supposed foundation of the nations they were called to serve.

Scott's *trahison* [betrayal] was to repress what he otherwise considered universal principles of liberal political development and human rights to departmental policy. As a literary artist, Scott espoused widely held views of intellectual progress and the liberal political development of his young country.[3] As a clerc, Scott employed his intellect, ambition and skill to a "narrow vision" (to borrow author E. Brian Titley's turn of phrase) of Canadian Indian administration that undermined the human rights of Indigenous peoples.[4] Scott determined that Indian policy would help forge a national identity. That identity was constructed to overwhelmingly reflect British tradition despite the presence of Indigenous peoples, Francophones and the arrival of many non-British immigrant communities, languages and cultures in the new nation of Canada.

France's anguish over the Algerian question consumed Soustelle's energies for more than a decade; his role in the Algerian-French conflict continues to define him significantly in the 21st century. The drama of Algerian independence and the bitter struggle among the French over Algeria became personal in the battle between Charles de Gaulle and his one-time acolyte and political *dauphin* [mentee]. In the era following the Second World War as a global process of de-colonization began, Soustelle was placed on the frontlines of that struggle when named governor general of Algeria in early 1955. As an intellectual, Soustelle's appointment represented a last-ditch attempt by France to lever his academic background and specialized knowledge of Indigenous peoples to drive an ambitious, but belated set of reforms.[5] Ultimately, as his short tenure as governor general wound down, Soustelle chose to defend French militarization of the conflict and to oversee the implementation of repressive measures. Under extreme circumstances, testing the strength of democratic institutions in Republican France, Soustelle was fired from de Gaulle's cabinet and then embarked on a campaign in exile to reverse the course of history over Algerian independence.[6]

La trahison of Duncan Campbell Scott

As a senior civil servant, who worked for both Conservative and Liberal governments, Duncan Campbell Scott's actions are representative of a consensus about Indian policy shared by Canadian elites. Historian Ian McKay has characterized Scott as one of the "organic intellectuals" at the core of Canada's early 20th century civilizing thrust into the Canadian west and north.[7] McKay astutely positions Scott, whom he describes as "the brilliant *fin-de-siècle* poet-administrator," as an unavoidable candidate among Canadian cultural and political figures who merit reconsideration in aid of a reconnaissance of Canadian history.[8] McKay's instructive work on the Canadian liberal order framework challenges Canadian historians to look beyond the "inevitability and goodness" of Canada and to ponder alternative overarching models of Canadian history:

> ... this stance means taking much more seriously than is conventionally the case the Canadian liberals themselves – as coherent and rigorous proponents of a continent-wide transformation of society, inheritors of a great intellectual tradition which they then articulated to the vast heterogeneous terrain they sought to understand and to transform.[9]

In McKay's rejection of Canadian "inevitability and goodness," he targets Indian policy as a defining aspect of the project of Canadian nationhood in the critical period from the inception of the process that led to Confederation and the conclusion of the Second World War, roughly 1850 to 1945:

> That the country was (an in some respects still is) a "white settlers dominion," whose predominant political, legal and religious systems were imposed on its indigenous inhabitants, is an underlying assumption of the liberal order framework.[10]

Scott's role in Canadian Indian policy gives proof to McKay's assertion about Canadian Liberals, "The burden of responsibility for the most glaring offences against 'liberal democracy' must be born by Liberals themselves."[11]

In the emerging Canadian state, the relationship between a newly dominant national governing cohort dominated by non-Indigenous and the Indigenous groups residing in the wake and at the margins of a rapidly developing settler society was foundational and defining. Scott spent his bureaucratic career at the heart of the machinery of Canadian Indian policy during this crucial period. His legacy, and that of the explicitly assimilatory era of Canadian Indian policy, remain a matter of fundamental importance for Canadian historians and political theorists.[12]

La trahison of Jacques Soustelle

Soustelle's involvement in the Franco-Algerian drama coincided with the post-Second World War ascendancy of existential philosophy. In his intellectual combat over the future of French Algeria, Soustelle was engaged directly with two leaders of French existentialism, Albert Camus and Jean-Paul Sartre.

Camus was an Algerian of European background. The Franco-Algerian conflict caused him great political and personal anguish. His opposition to Algerian independence and his denunciation of terror tactics employed by both sides in the conflict made Camus an isolated figure among French intellectuals of the period.[13] His isolation was shared, to some extent, by Soustelle, and to an even greater extent, by Germaine Tillion, Soustelle's colleague in ethnology and politics.

Sartre stood on the other side of a bitter divide between French intellectuals.[14] Sartre advocated Algerian independence and embraced violent revolution and even terror tactics of the Algerian National Liberation Front (FLN) as a legitimate response to the violence of more than 125 years of French colonial rule in Algeria.[15] He embraced the combative views of psychiatrist Frantz Fanon, writing the introduction for Fanon's anticolonial classic work *Les damnés de la terre* [The Wretched of the Earth]. Fanon and Sartre believed Algeria would be freed only by anticolonial violence and that French reformers like Soustelle, Camus and Tillion were either naïve, hypocritical or both. In a shorter work specifically about Algeria, Fanon attacked Soustelle's criticism of FLN violence:

> *Les ministres français Lacoste et Soustelle ont publié des photos dans le souci de salir notre cause.*
> *Non, ce n'est pas vrai que la révolution soit allé aussi loin que le colonialisme.*[16]

French cabinet ministers Lacoste and Soustelle published photos with the aim of tarnishing our cause.
No, it is not true that the revolution has gone as far in that regard as colonialism.

The high stakes debate over the Algerian conflict among French intellectuals, and the sometimes extreme responses of Soustelle in that drama, provide a case study of the comportment of intellectuals caught in pressurized political situations and military conflicts. The complexity of Soustelle's role during the period he served as governor general has been smudged out to a significant degree by his notorious opposition to President de Gaulle's choice to surrender Algeria. I am fascinated by the widely shared observation that Soustelle's reformist zeal was squelched by the realities of war.[17] To what extent did Soustelle, while governor general, betray his own principles in defence of the French military position in Algeria?

The question of politics

Scott's role in Canadian Indian policy poses discomforting questions for the intellectual historian. Was Scott personally culpable for Canadian Indian policy during a period through which the Canadian state systematically violated the basic human rights of Indigenous peoples in Canada? Unlike Soustelle, who was clearly exceptional in so many regards, the problem of Scott unsettles the historical curiosity in no small part because, as political theorist Hannah Arendt famously observed of Adolf Eichmann (one of the major organizers of the Holocaust), Scott, although he became a government mandarin and leading cultural figure, was in some respects, "terribly and terrifyingly normal."[18] I am not equating Canadian Indian policy with Nazism, but in Arendt's journalistic account of the Eichmann trial and her highly articulated (and vigorously contested) portrayal of Eichmann's "banality," she raised broader questions about individual responsibility and accountability of bureaucrats serving governments of malevolent intent.[19] In that respect, Arendt's analysis is fundamental to a consideration of Scott, and others like him, the accomplished and, in some aspects of their lives, otherwise laudable, executors of Canadian Indian policy in the late 19th and early 20th centuries.

I examine Scott and Soustelle at moments of political exigency. My approach is deliberately selective, focussing on specific incidents and related archival evidence. These episodes reveal aspects of Scott's and

Soustelle's credo in contingent and contested political circumstances.

Canadian historiography about the Indian Department has developed greatly in the past 40 years.[20] I do not pretend to provide a comprehensive analysis of Scott's complicity in a wide range of department policies, but carefully try to observe his defence of specific initiatives he launched to enhance departmental control over Indian education and so-called enfranchisement, the policy by which Canadian Indians could surrender their "Aboriginal" and treaty rights in order to gain full Canadian citizenship.[21]

Many eminent historians and journalists have looked in great detail at the Franco-Algerian conflict in the period surrounding Soustelle's tenure as governor general from 1955-56.[22] I do not repeat that narrative. I focus on Soustelle's performance as governor general in light of his training and experience as an ethnologist and veteran *résistant* with formative experiences in Mexico of the 1930s and 1940s. This formation makes Soustelle a classic case of a *clerc*, leaping eagerly to the service of his nation in dubious circumstances to serve a poorly articulated cause.

Duncan Campbell Scott: Tightening the vice of Canadian Indian Policy

Scott's role in Indian Department business can be interpreted in many ways. Was Scott an artist simply too dulled by duty to sift through the implications of departmental policy? It is a plausible explanation. Was he merely "following orders" when it came to the grinding gears of the Canadian Indian policy mechanism? Or was he inspired by a keen ideological desire to see that the assimilation program could be made ever more effective?

E.K. Brown, professor and literary critic, elicited perhaps the most direct comment that Scott ever offered about his work at the Indian Department:

> Your remarks about the Indian poems are very good. I had for about 20 years oversight of their development and I was never unsympathetic to Aboriginal ideals, but there was the law which I did not originate and which I never tried to amend in the direction of severity. One can hardly be sympathetic to the contemporary sun-dance or Potlatch when one knows that the original spirit has departed and they are largely the opportunities for debauchery by low white men.[23]

Scott wrote the words above to Brown in 1941, some nine years after his retirement from the civil service and six years prior to his death. He was 71 years old. Scott was cooperating with Brown's efforts to compile his work for Canadian literary posterity. Brown admired many of the Indian poems. In the letter, Scott expresses a widely held late Victorian conviction that, sadly, much of the best of Indigenous cultures had vanished, and that a speedy, if sometimes rough transition to civilization was required; indeed, as Scott's letter suggests, in his mind even the best of Indigenous practice and belief had been tarnished, so what was the point of preserving anything? Scott expressed a view that continues as a pernicious element in Canadian settler ideology of Indigenous people by which they are deemed only to be authentic and worthy of respect in a romanticized pre-contact state.

Such attitudes of resignation about the moral decline of Indigenous tradition were widely shared. The question of personal responsibility is where the debate surrounding Scott is less settled. In the letter, Scott claims, "there was the law which I did not originate and which I never tried to amend in the direction of severity."[24] This defence is not tenable in light of the evidence. For example, E. Brian Titley's work proves that Scott, in his capacity as a senior civil servant, participated in making the Indian Act more stringent.[25] I will examine Scott's efforts to ratchet up coercive policies in the areas of enfranchisement, Indigenous spiritual practice, compulsory education, and the Indian Department's response to First Nations' political resistance.[26]

Scott, both as a literary artist and as a functionary of the Canadian state, is perhaps the clearest and most prolific spokesperson for Canadian liberalism's tortuous, often contradictory, efforts to deal with the "Indian question." That ideology fails the test of its own deluded logic. The massive project of social engineering directed at Indigenous peoples, that critical plank in the liberal order framework, was based on the twin principles of removal and integration. As cultural theorist and literary scholar Stan Dragland has asserted, these mutually exclusive aspirations do not dovetail in reality.[27]

One can ascribe to Scott his share of responsibility and intention in the broad pattern of Canadian Indian policy in its most determined social engineering phase. Some of his contemporaries took note of the artist's political bent. Brown proffered the following assessment:

> He was not a party-minded man – he preferred the Conservatives to the Liberals mainly because they were sounder in all that had to do with the British connection – but in his own round of activity he had an acute political sense. He knew how to defend the interests of the department when it came into conflict with others, and his own interest within the department. His conception of the national duty to the Indians was simple and sound. It was the result not of close ethnological study, but of immense experience and imaginative understanding. The poet in him and the civil servant agreed in believing that the future of the Indians, if it were not to be in extinction or degradation, depended on their being brought more and more nearly to the status of the white population. Special safeguards were a temporary necessity; but meanwhile by education and encouragement the Indians were to cease being interesting exotic relics and practise trying to hold their own in a society which could not be bent in their direction. Sometimes Duncan Scott felt that he should stress the special safeguards, the peculiar status, but it was to the end of bringing Indians into the national society that he strove with that mixture of guile and idealism that is the mark of the highest sort of civil servant.[28]

Brown presented Scott as a determined, individualistic, experienced civil servant of sufficient capacity to hone and firm up policies of the department to make them more effective. Similarly, the literary critic L.P. Weiss saw at least a striving for intellectual consistency in the policies that Scott was charged to implement:

> Like a significant number of his contemporaries in Canada, Scott accepted current Victorian concepts of history and change. Because he believed in the necessity and inevitability of change – what he and his fellow English Canadians called "progress" – he was able to view the death of Indian culture as beneficial to individual Indians.[29]

Rather than seeing Scott as a man of his time, others attribute to Scott individual culpability in malevolent Canadian Indian policy.[30] My purpose here is to weigh these possibilities in an "effort of reconnaissance" as prescribed by McKay. To my way of thinking, Scott did not violate Canadian values; he expressed and acted on the Canadian values of his time. As McKay explains, Scott was a comprehensible and intellectually consistent product of Canadian liberalism that put pride of place in individual property rights, limited forms of democratic practice, westward expansion and the supremacy of arrogated white-male-English-speaking Canadian mores in the first half century of nationhood. Ultimately that does not exculpate Scott, but it aids in contextualizing him.

Scott and Bill 14

> Our object is to continue until there is not a single Indian in Canada that has not been absorbed into the body politic, and there is no Indian question, and no Indian Department, that is the whole object of this Bill.[31]

> While the proposed legislation is radical, it gives the department control, removes from the Indian parent the responsibility for the care and education of his child, and the best interests of the Indians are promoted and protected. The clauses may apply to every Indian child over the age of 7 and under the age of 15.[32]

Scott wrote these words in support of a 1920 bill to amend the Indian Act, which emanated from the Union government of then Prime Minister Arthur Meighen. It was ardently championed by Scott who appeared before a parliamentary committee in its defence. This was a critical juncture in the most coercive phase of departmental policy and a defining moment in the tenure of Scott as deputy superintendent general.[33] The specific provisions regarding the toughening of compulsory enfranchisement were subsequently repealed by a government led by Liberal William Lyon Mackenzie King.[34] Notwithstanding that change, a rare defeat for a policy specifically advocated by Scott, other draconian measures regarding compulsory attendance at Indian schools survived. The department's obsession with enfranchisement endured until revisions of the Indian Act in 1951 and was further quieted by John Diefenbaker's Bill of Rights, which granted voting privileges to Indians residing on reserves in 1960. Ninety-three years after Confederation, a Canadian government decided that Indigenous citizens living on reserves deserved to vote. Whatever the ultimate legislative fate of draconian Indian Department policy on matters such as enfranchisement and compulsory attendance at residential schools, Scott's advocacy for Bill 14 at the mid-point of his administrative stewardship of the Indian Department provides a clear window on his comportment as a pro-active, ideologically-driven bureaucrat.

In Scott's own briefing notes in preparation for his various defences of the proposed changes to involuntary enfranchisement and education provisions in Bill 14, he correctly identified enfranchisement and compulsory school attendance as sources of potential controversy. Indian enfranchisement was a central intent of the liberal, "civilizing" Canadian policy. Enfranchisement in the department's view meant that Indians could gain full Canadian citizenship rights in return for surrendering their legal status as Indians. At various times since Confederation, enfranchisement was required of Indians in order to serve in the military, join certain professions or engage in some individual business practices.[35] The policy was applied haphazardly, but its underlying "civilizing" intent was clear. Scott's brief on enfranchisement underscores the fundamental role he envisaged for a more stringent policy in meeting the department's primary aim of assimilation:

> …we must come to the heart of the subject and provide legislation which will carry out the ultimate aims and objects of the policy which has governed the administration of this department since Confederation. It is illogical to develop a policy, spend money on it, and achieve results without possessing ourselves of the power to make a final disposition of the individuals who have been civilized and to despatch them into the ordinary life of the country with the knowledge they have every chance to succeed.[36]

In his appeal to the parliamentary committee set up to examine Bill 14, Scott revealed that the determination of the Canadian government to "enfranchise" Indians had met with overwhelming failure since Confederation. An Indian Department memo for the committee reveal that only 102 Indians had volunteered for enfranchisement in the 53 years since Confederation.[37] Earlier changes to the Indian Act in 1918 had sped the process up, but insufficiently. The departmental memo, as well as Scott in his testimony, declared that an additional 97 families totalling 258 individuals had applied for enfranchisement in the two years prior to the submission of Bill 14.[38] The rate of voluntary enfranchisement did not satisfy Scott. The 1920 amendments allowed the minister to identify Indians for enfranchisement without an application from the individuals concerned:

> …while the departure from the spirit of the existing Act is radical, it is in all respects desirable that we should have legislation enabling us to enfranchise Indians without the preliminary application from themselves and without the consent of the band.[39]

Scott had additional motivation in seeking provisions providing for mandatory enfranchisement. In a case concerning the Six Nations activist F.O. Loft, Scott wielded enfranchisement as a political weapon.[40] Loft was an Ontario civil servant who had served in the Canadian Forces as a lieutenant during the First World War. Following the war, he engaged in an effort to create a national political organization for Indian peoples across Canada. In 1919, he issued an invitation to Indian bands across Canada to join his League of Indians for a fee of $5:

> We as Indians from one end of the Dominion to the other, are sadly strangers to each other; we have not learned what it is to co-operate and work for each other as we should; the pity of it is greater because our needs, our drawbacks, handicaps and troubles are all similar. It is for us to do something to get out of these sad conditions. The day is past when one band or a few bands can successfully – if at all – free themselves from the domination of officialdom and from being ever the prey and victims of unscrupulous means of depriving us of our lands and homes, and even deny us our rights we are entitled to as free men under the British flag.[41]

In response, Scott directed his arguments for enfranchisement against Loft specifically:

> I am sending herewith a copy of a circular issued by an Indian of the Six Nations, F.O. Loft, who is earning his living outside the reserve. This may be a clever scheme to put him in funds, but it has the effect of disquieting the Indians and stirring up suspicion of the Department and the Government. Such a man should be enfranchised.[42]

Ultimately, Loft successfully resisted efforts for his compulsory enfranchisement. Loft, a Canadian military veteran, viewed enfranchisement as an end to achieve his denationalization as a Mohawk.[43]

Loft was one of several Six Nations activists who would attract Scott's ire following the First World War until his retirement in 1932.[44] Mohawk nationalists managed to take their claim for a "nation to nation" relationship with Canada to the League of Nations and to members of British parliament. In 1924, Scott enlisted the services of an Indian agent based in Brantford, Ontario to forcefully break up a traditional Iroquoian council with Royal Canadian Mounted Police officers to impose the elected band councillor system prescribed by the Indian Act.[45] With the introduction of Bill 14 in 1920 and with the First World War concluded, Scott was determined to spearhead this comprehensive effort to ramp up provisions aimed at assimilation. People such as Loft stood in his way. Scott attacked Loft's service in the Canadian military:

> He has some education, has a rather attractive personal appearance, but he is a shallow, talkative individual. He is one of the few Indians who are endeavouring to live off their brethren by organizing an Indian society, and collecting fees from them… I have proposed to him that he should

be enfranchised, which, I think, accounts for this sudden activity on his part. What he ought to get is a good snub. He volunteered for the war and looked very well in a uniform, but he was cunning enough to avoid any active service, and I do not think his record in that regard is a very good one.[46]

Loft was the same age as Scott. It is no wonder he did not engage in combat – he was 55 when he volunteered to serve. Loft was sent to France in a non-combat role.

Scott's activities in defence of Bill 14 bear the hallmark of an effective and determined senior civil servant, belying any notion of a detached artist simply following orders. Scott elicited support for the bill from likely supporters and he discouraged appearances by Indians who would be hostile to the measures. In the spring of 1920, there were 17 hearings in all. Despite Scott's efforts to stack the hearings in terms favourable to the department, most Indians who appeared opposed the measures.[47] Scott's displeasure was evident in his own testimony:

> Mr. Harold: A point has been brought up several times that the old method of enfranchisement was too hard, and that the new one is going to another extreme, and it has always appealed to me that if this were framed along lines so that the Indian had not to make the application, or take the initiative, and have it arranged so that he could automatically become a citizen, it would be better. Why do you approach it the way that you do instead of the other method?

> Mr. Scott: Because if you understood the Indian mind you would know. Surely we have had enough illustrations of it here. These gentlemen are perfectly able to address the Committee – far better than I am – as far as the form goes. But those are the people who will never move.[48]

Scott engaged in a lobbying and propaganda campaign to elicit support for the proposed amendments. He asked for letters to be written and attempted to limit the negative influence of the many Indians who testified. He sent identical telegrams to at least five heads of residential schools seeking expressions of support for the compulsory attendance provisions: "Would appreciate a letter from you supporting our new measure now before Parliament of compulsory attendance at Indian Residential schools."[49] In a letter to Reverend T. Albert Moore, a Methodist Church leader, Scott argued for strengthening the powers of the department regarding both enfranchisement and compulsory attendance at residential or day schools:

> You will note our proposals with regard to compulsory education. These clauses will enable us to send children to residential schools and to have control over them while there, which we have never had in the past.
> The enfranchisement clauses will enable us to give the rights of citizenship to such Indians as are found to be competent without the consent of their respective bands, which at present is necessary, and which has been an obstacle to progress, and to give enfranchisement without a long and vexatious period of probation. It may interest you to know that while under the old Act, since Confederation up to a year ago, we had only succeeded in enfranchising one hundred and sixty Indians, under the amendment, which I recommended and which was passed in the session of 1918, we have already enfranchised nearly three hundred Indians.[50]

Scott also sought appearances by Indians who might support the measure, offering to pay for their travel and accommodation.[51] He responded vituperatively to an inquiry by committee chairperson W.A. Boys who had fielded complaints from some Indians about lack of notice prior to the hearings:

I hope that the Committee will not consider it necessary that notices should be sent, because if we send a notice to one band or tribe, it would go to all, and the result would be that the city would be flooded with Indians who would gladly take this opportunity of having a free trip to the capital. Their evidence should not really be needed because we know that those who would come would be opposed to the Bill or any government measure, unless they see some immediate profit, financial or otherwise, without any outlay on their part, and representations on this side will be fully aired by the Indians now here and the Counsel they have engaged…

In considering the Bill the Committee should, of course, give full weight to the Indian psychology.[52]

The transcript of Scott's testimony before the committee reveals the ethical traps and ideological inconsistencies of the department's civilizing mission. Bill 14 provided the government of Canada the right to enforce mandatory attendance at Indian day or residential schools even without parental consent. This provision contributed to the suffering many Indian students endured in schools run on behalf of the department by religious organizations.[53] Scott himself was aware of the dangers inherent in the residential school system. In 1914, he had recognized as much in an encyclopaedia:

It cannot be gainsaid that in the early days of school administration in the territories, while the problem was still a new one, the system was open to criticism. Insufficient care was exercised in the admission of children to the schools. The well-known predisposition of Indians to tuberculosis resulted in a very large percentage of deaths among the pupils. They were housed in buildings not carefully designed for school purposes, and these buildings became infected and dangerous to the inmates. It is quite within the mark to say that fifty per cent of the children who passed through these schools did not live to benefit from the education which they had received therein.[54]

Six years later in his testimony to a parliamentary committee, Scott presented a staunch defence of the very system he described in such dire terms in 1914. In a memorandum on Indian education that Scott wrote in preparation for the hearings, he insisted on the government's right and Indian parents' obligations in regard to compulsory aspects of Indian education in Canada:

As an answer to an argument which might be raised against the invasion of the rights of the parents over the children, it should be pointed out that all Indians are wards of the Crown, and the western treaties all provide for education as part of the compensation for the cession of the Indian title. As this provision was inserted at the request of the Indians, and altogether in their interests, it follows that they have certain responsibilities, and must produce their children to be educated.[55]

Indian leaders negotiated for access to quality education in some treaty negotiations. Such leaders did not foresee the coercion and the widespread psychological, physical and sexual abuse that was part of the residential school experience for many Indian children. Indian parents did not intend to "produce their children" for such treatment. Further, in 1920, large parts of the Canadian west (most significantly almost the entirety of British Columbia) were not under treaty. Nevertheless, Scott, in enunciating departmental policy, presumed that its educational policies must be enforced all the way to the Pacific Ocean.

In addition to the vocal opposition of some of the Indian leaders who appeared at the committee, Bill 14's dual intent to accelerate enfranchisement while making attendance mandatory at Indian day and residential schools attracted attention in the media. In its editorial pages, *The Globe* of Toronto expressed the view that the enfranchisement measures were unfair to returning Indigenous veterans (such as F.O. Loft) who had served Canada valiantly in the war:

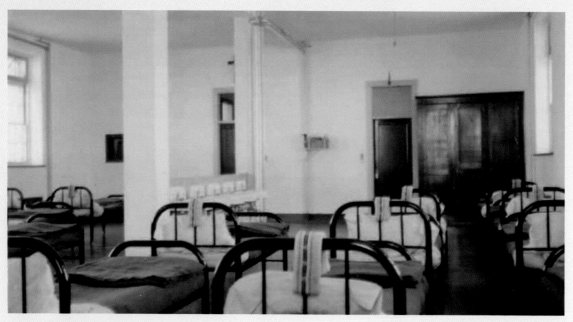

A boys' dormitory in Cross Lake
Indian Residential School, Cross
Lake, Manitoba, c.1940.

Nozhem Theatre, Peter Gzowski College, Trent University, *March 2011*

Brock Stonefish, a Delaware singer and guitar player settled into a chair on stage. To the right of Stonefish, Glen Caradus, a multi-instrumentalist and puppeteer, began his accompaniment with an Amerindian sounding line on a flute. Stonefish joined in with blues chords on his acoustic guitar and began singing his composition, *Residential Redemption...*

> I just want to go home
> Back to the place where I come from
> Instead, I lay here all alone with a sketchy blanket
> She said I'd make it,
> if I sang her song...
> The night came...
> took my brother and my little sister
> They took me from my mother,
> I never kissed her...

Stonefish's moving and warmly received performance followed a screening of my film *Duncan Campbell Scott – The Poet and The Indians* in which the residential school tragedy figures heavily. That evening's program, hosted by Trent University's Indigenous Studies program, also included a talk on reconciliation by a consultant to Canada's on-going Truth and Reconciliation Commission.

Following the film, lecture and musical performance, refreshments were served in a circular meeting room that often serves as a gathering place or informal classroom for Indigenous Studies students and faculty. On one side of the room, a large quilt featuring images of elementary school education and boreal and prairie nature scenes was displayed to admiring onlookers. The quilt honouring the work of the Truth and Reconciliation Commission was made by a group of women from around the Nogojiwanong-Peterborough area, all of whom are either residential school survivors or activists from Indigenous rights organizations.

Three thousand of them enlisted during the war, and the offer of the franchise might be taken as recognition of their services, but the bill appears to force this privilege upon them with consequences for which perhaps they are not yet prepared.[56]

In its conclusion, the same editorial expressed an understanding of Bill 14's ultimate intent, "The present bill contemplates the extinction of the system of reserves, and it is doubtful whether the country or the Indians themselves are prepared for this departure from traditional policy." *The Globe* foreshadowed a debate that would reverberate for decades.[57]

The discourse surrounding the issue in 1920 reflected the complicated challenges that Indian policy presented (and presents still) to the overall thrust of the Canadian liberal project. The *Ottawa Journal* also lauded Indian veterans, but supported the measures because, "THE JOURNAL has long advocated the extension of the franchise to Indians who are able to read and write. We do not think that a man's colour is ever a good reason to think of him as an inferior being, regardless of other considerations."[58] Newspaper readers also waded in. In a letter to the editor of *The Citizen* of Ottawa, R.N. Wilson, a justice of the peace in Alberta, characterized the measures regarding enfranchisement and compulsory attendance at residential schools as an assault of Canadian democratic values:

> The educational feature of Bill 14 is as bad as the rest of it, as it provides for arrest and imprisonment of children in sectarian boarding schools, the only schools in existence on most of the western reserves. In a country which boasts of religious freedom, it will be time enough to enforce compulsory education when we have provided the reserve with non-sectarian national day schools.[59]

Wilson also raised the matter of sexual abuse in the schools:

> Some of these schools are excellent and conducted by first class people, but all classes of girls necessarily attend them, the depraved and the good often occupying the same dormitory for years. In his capacity of justice of the peace in Alberta, the writer is frequently applied to by the authorities of Indian boarding schools in their efforts to check the practice of young men gaining access in the girls' dormitories in the night time, and in one case of the sort, involving four young men, two of whom were affected with loathsome disease. Would Mr. Meighen compel his daughter to take such risks? He certainly would not. Then let him withdraw his infamous legislation.
> – R.N. WILSON, Macleod, Alberta[60]

Most scholars who have specialized in Indigenous education agree that Scott's goal both as director of education and then as deputy superintendent general was to reduce risks of tuberculosis with cost efficient reforms while tamping down stories of predatory sexual behaviour by school personnel. Scott wanted the system to function better, while carefully managing costs. He was always concerned with the department's reputation in regards to the education program. There is no evidence that he challenged the fundamental assumptions on which the system rested.[61]

Scott's preparatory notes and his testimony in defence of Bill 14 reveal tenacity, occasional contentiousness and conviction of the fundamental righteousness of the department's cause. For example, Scott claimed he wanted more resources for the department's education efforts: "The appropriations are determined by Parliament; if I had my own way I would immediately double the appropriation for Indian education."[62] In sum, Scott wanted additional means to educate Indian children, even in a manner inconsistent with parental wishes if necessary, to accelerate the "civilization" and eventual assimilation of an otherwise doomed race:

I want to get rid of the Indian problem. I do not think as a matter of fact, that this country ought to have to continuously protect a class of people who are able to stand alone. That is my whole point. I do not want to pass into the citizens' class people who are paupers. That is not the intention of the Bill. But after one 100 years, after being in close contact with civilization it is enervating to the individual or to a band to continue in that state of tutelage, when he or they are able to take their position as British citizens, or Canadian citizens, to support themselves, and stand alone. That has been the whole purpose of Indian education and advancement from the earliest time.[63]

Scott and the (mis)use of ethnography

Scott, like Soustelle, enlisted ethnography in his defence of colonial policy. Scott's briefing notes on Bill 14 rely on a report commissioned by his department by Marius Barbeau about the "proposed disestablishment" of the Lorette Wendat reserve near Québec City:

> Last summer Mr. C.M Barbeau, of the Anthropological Division, Geological Survey, carried out an investigation at Lorette at our request, and his report will be in my hands in a few days. Mr. Barbeau tells me that the result of his investigation shows that these Indians are ready for enfranchisement.[64]

Barbeau's report reveals some of the achingly contradictory assumptions behind Canadian policies of assimilation and civilization for Indian peoples.[65] Barbeau describes the community as being very similar to other Canadian villages. His report proceeds to list a number of successful business activities in the community such as the manufacturing of moccasins, snowshoes and other items that reflect Wendat identity. These economic pursuits tied to the 20th century market economy on the outskirts of Québec City are cited as evidence of assimilation, rather than adaptation or, to use a phrase famously associated with Jacques Soustelle, integration. Historian Kathryn Magee Labelle argues that Barbeau participated in a "discourse of destruction" regarding the Wendat.[66] In addition to Labelle, Wendat historian Georges Sioui and filmmaker René Sioui Labelle also demonstrate that 21st century Wendat people are alive and actively self-identifying not only in Québec but also in Kansas, Ontario, Michigan and Oklahoma.[67]

Barbeau, in this particular ethnological assignment commissioned by the Indian Department, performed the same trick of liberal exclusion that underpins much of Scott's Indian poetry in which Indians are often portrayed as doomed vestiges of disappearing cultures. The Wendat imagined by Barbeau for the Canadian Indian Department are trapped, frozen, *figée* in the 17th century. Barbeau seems incapable of imagining a 20th century, French-speaking, self-described Wendat participating as such in the Canadian economy and polity. As with Scott in his attitudes about enfranchisement, Barbeau, in this instance at least, argues that the loss of a person's identity as an Indian is the appropriate price of joining Canada. Barbeau's ethnological efforts in Lorette suited Scott's purpose at the hearings to examine the proposed amendments to the Indian Act.

Scott and the department had a complex relationship with the nascent disciplines of ethnology and anthropology in Canada. In his 1922 address to the Royal Society of Canada, Scott lauded the creation of the National Museum of Ethnology, Archaeology and Natural History.[68] As in the case concerning Lorette, Scott sometimes marshalled ethnological evidence to substantiate his convictions about doomed races. In other instances, social scientists opposed departmental policy and Scott ran afoul of Canada's emerging social scientists.

Following a hardening of policy championed by Scott in 1918, Indian agents and prosecutors in British

Snake Rapids on the Albany River in 1905, travelled by Scott during Treaty 9 negotiations, The Albany is Ontario's second longest river, flowing through the ancestral lands of the Cree and Ojibwa. Today, with only one highway providing access, the Albany remains pristine.

Wendat man René Sioui Labelle prepares his diving gear and a 16mm film camera with underwater housing. We are at the headwaters of the Albany River with a small crew preparing to film a sequence of *Duncan Campbell Scott – The Poet and The Indians*. Sioui Labelle is a certified scuba diver in addition to being a superb documentary cinematographer and accomplished director/producer.

As we worked on the Scott film and on other projects in James Bay Cree Territory of northern Québec, Manitoba, Ottawa and South Africa, we often joked about the irony of a filmmaker from an Indigenous people that the Canadian state claimed had disappeared actively revising Wendat history and raising consciousness about other Indigenous peoples of Canada and other parts of the world.

Columbia in 1920 achieved the first convictions for potlatching since 1897. Scott maintained that the persistence of the potlatch in British Columbia (ceremonies to name chiefs), exchange gifts and affirm clan territories, as well as the sun dance on the prairies, undermined the department's civilizing efforts. However, the collective wisdom of Canadian social science did not follow the departmental line on the potlatch. Anthropologists Edward Sapir, Franz Boas and others had contributed to a report from the anthropological division of the Department of Mines, which contended that the potlatch was a positive manifestation of Indigenous culture and that its maintenance would facilitate a positive transition for Indigenous in British Columbia to modern Canada. Scott had this report suppressed.[69]

Le plan Soustelle

Many scholars have debated French liberalism, decolonization and the political application of the social sciences. Questions about Soustelle's role in the Algerian conflict are part of that discourse.[70] Soustelle's mission as governor general and its aftermath contributed to the demise of the fourth republic and the return of Charles de Gaulle as president. Between 1955 and 1968, Soustelle would engage many of France's leading political and intellectual figures in a tempestuous debate over the future of French Algeria. Raymond Aron, Albert Camus, Franz Fanon and Jean Paul Sartre were among the luminaries of French intellectual life who took sides in a debate in which Soustelle was never far from centre stage.[71] From his installation as governor general in early 1955 through the final demise of French rule in 1962 and in the bitter years of his self-exile following the Evian Accords, Soustelle was a marker of French stubbornness in his singular defence of *l'Algérie française*.

In her work on the colonial archive of Indonesia and the forms of knowledge that it stores in terms of both revelation and obfuscation, Ann Laura Stoler discusses the role of willful or culturally blind ignorance as part of the colonial experience. In simple terms, the colonizer who maintained loyalty to imperial power had to adopt a sort of ignorance about the world within the colony.[72] Some who refused to play ignorant simply left because of their incapacity to abide by the colonial conditions. Soustelle in his zeal to reform *l'Algérie française* in the name of integration seemed blind to the harsh legacy of 125 years of French rule. Soustelle also failed to identify the contradiction between his ramping up the corrosive power of French militarism while simultaneously imagining a rapid transition which would find French ruler and Algerian Muslim subaltern harmoniously co-existing.

When Soustelle arrived in Algeria as governor general in 1955 intent on putting his knowledge of Indigenousness from Mexico to practical application, he represented a peculiar instance in which a colonial regime turned to an intellectual bent on overcoming ignorance and on the production of new forms of knowledge to salvage and redeem colonial authority.[73] Stoler's admonition regarding the complexity of "colonial lives" serves as a useful frame in considering Soustelle's simultaneously enlightened, contradictory, vicious and doomed vision of *l'Algérie française*.

Soustelle's obdurate refusal to accept France's abandonment of Algeria and his illicit efforts to bring down de Gaulle following 1962 can obscure the nature of his efforts in Algeria as governor general when the French government and the majority of its citizens could not have imagined an outcome of Algerian independence.

Reaction among French political elites and the military to the unexpected *Tout Saint* [All Saints' Day] FLN assault was all the more acute because this Algerian revolt took place during the same year that France had suffered a calamitous defeat at Dien Bien Phu.[74] The government of Pierre Mendès France envisaged a two-pronged response: the crisis would be met by a powerful (in fact, disproportionate) military response and an overdue, comprehensive effort to reform French rule in Algeria.[75]

Soustelle had gained some familiarity with Algeria during the Second World War. He was intelligence chief for de Gaulle's administration in Alger prior to liberation.[76] After quitting London, the Free French forces of de Gaulle had set up a provisional government in Alger awaiting the liberation of mainland France in 1944. As the date of the liberation of mainland France neared, Soustelle travelled extensively in Algeria enhancing his understanding of the country and whetting a curiosity which would be given full vent in 1955.[77]

In the chaotic politics of the Fourth Republic, Mendès France's government was defeated in part because of opposition to the proposed installation of Soustelle whom the hard right, both in Paris and Alger, considered too left-wing.[78] Ultimately, in the aftermath of the debacle of *le Tout Saint*, Mendès France still turned to the social scientist with the background in Indigenous studies to help save Algeria. The subsequent centre-right government stuck by François Mitterrand's nomination of Soustelle.[79] The stakes would be extremely high for Soustelle. France's unequivocal insistence on crushing a revolt while at the same time advancing reforms would test the mettle of the full-time ethnologist and part-time, until then, politician. In the February 1955 debate over his installation, Adelmadjid Ourabah, a leftist member of the national assembly from Constantine, Algeria, reminded Soustelle of his academic roots when he demanded that Soustelle offer Muslim Algerians the same rights that Soustelle had championed for impoverished Mexicans in the 1930s.[80]

Soustelle was eager to respond to Mitterrand's challenge of delivering rapidly on a policy of integration. The economic and social lot of the Algerian majority had deteriorated in the decade following the defeat of Nazi Germany. Leading French and Algerian advocates for a more humane governance of *l'Algérie française* made the scope of the challenge confronting Soustelle abundantly clear. Soustelle's association with two such intellectuals reveals the complexities of Soustelle's fractious passage: Germaine Tillion and Albert Camus. His relationships with Tillion and Camus complicate any attempt to place Soustelle as an isolated, contrarian advocate for *l'Algérie française* and opponent of Algerian independence in the late 1950s and early 1960s.

Just prior to the Second World War, Camus had returned to his native land and delivered a devastating portrait of French colonialism in a series of articles originally published by the centre-left newspaper *Alger républicain*.[81] Camus was appalled that rural peoples in the land of his birth had been driven further into poverty by the expansion of settler colonialism. Training his acute journalistic eye on rural conditions in particular, Camus described the impact of deforestation caused by the French administration's depredation of oak forests to supply the wine industry with corks. Camus also described the desperate, environmentally disastrous attempts by residents to keep winter cooking and heating fires burning by denuding their lands of trees required to prevent soil erosion. Camus reported that conditions were desperate, poverty was rampant and that it was only a matter of time before grievous social and political unrest would erupt. His reportage also pointed to the special challenge that faced would be reformers and underscored by Tillion and Soustelle: the land could no longer support Algeria's Indigenous population. They argued that Algeria needed to be industrialized and urbanized for the benefit of all, not just the minority of European descent.[82]

Just prior to Soustelle's nomination as governor general, another leading French humanist returned to Algeria to survey conditions. Tillion, Soustelle's former colleague at *le Musée de l'Homme* and fellow *résistante* to the Nazi occupation of France, was engaged by Mitterrand to report on conditions of the people who she had studied as another of Paul Rivet's doctoral students in the 1930s. Tillion had lived among Berber peoples in the Aurès mountains of Algeria. Immediately following the outbreak of war, she returned to France and joined the resistance. Denounced by a collaborating priest, she and other members of the resistance she organized at *le Musée de l'Homme* were captured by the Nazi occupiers of Paris. Two of her male colleagues were summarily executed by the Germans. Tillion and her mother were sent to the concentration camp at Ravensbruck where her mother died. Tillion's almost complete doctoral thesis on Algeria was seized by the Gestapo, perhaps destroyed, and has never re-surfaced.[83]

Following the war, Tillion resumed her activities as an ethnologist, educator and social reformer. For the rest of her active working life, Tillion championed the poor of Algeria. Also, based on her personal experience as a concentration camp survivor, she became a highly esteemed advocate for political prisoners in many parts of the world, beginning with prisoners of the French military during the last phases of the Algerian conflict. Tillion was never an "ivory tower" academic. In the late 1940s, she looked back on her career with an activist bent:

> De mon cote je considérais les obligations de ma profession d'ethnologue comme comparable a celles des avocats, avec la différence qu'elle me contraignait a défendre une population au lieu d'une personne.[84]

> For my part I considered the obligations of my profession as ethnologist that like of lawyers, with the difference that my job forced me to defend a population rather than an individual.

During her mission to Algeria at the behest of Mitterrand in the autumn of 1954 and early 1955, Tillion, like Camus before her, was shocked by the degradation that had occurred since her doctoral research in the mid-1930s:

> Quand je les ai retrouvés, entre novembre 1954 et février 1955, j'ai été atterrée par le changement survenu chez eux en moins de quinze ans et que je ne puis exprimer que par ce mot: "clochardisation."[85]

> When I was among them again between November 1954 and February 1955, I was devastated by the change that had taken place in less than 15 years and that I can only express by this word: pauperization.

Tillion famously coined the phrase *clochardisation* to describe the social and economic collapse she reported to Mitterrand. *Clochard* means an extremely poor person, a pauper, even a "bum," or someone living on the streets. Travelling remote mountainous areas as Camus had done almost 20 years earlier, Tillion discovered that the Chaouii Berber tribes people already impoverished when she first lived among them in the 1930s had suffered a precipitous decline in living standards. Like Camus, Tillion reported that population growth and the expansion of agricultural businesses had severely diminished the land's capacity to support family-based sustainable forms of agriculture that had been in operation for centuries. The degradation of the small land holdings was compounded by a population explosion due to the success of French-introduced vaccination campaigns.[86] On the one hand, people were living longer and families were increasing in size; on the other, local resources necessary for rural survival were diminishing while there was no accompanying expansion of opportunity for the young in major cities such as Algiers, Oran and Constantine.

Tillion would eventually publish her findings in a dire report entitled *L'Algérie en 1957*.[87] The work was published under the auspices of an organization of resistance veterans. Tillion appealed to her colleagues, shocked as they were, like many in France, by the unexpected virulence of the Algerian revolt, to remember the sacrifice that thousands of soldiers from the Maghreb had made for France in the world wars. She pleaded for reconciliation and argued for maintaining the ties between *la métropole* and *l'Algérie française* that would become an obsession for Soustelle. As a trained ethnologist, Tillion was sufficiently horrified by what she saw happening in Algeria in 1954-55 that she described the overall effect as a process of inexorably driving untold thousands of Algerians into poverty with no viable economic means of rescue:

> *L'accroissement numérique brutal de la population, contraire a son expérience millénaire, la diminu-tion parallèle de ses ressources, l'effondrement de l'économie, le contact avec la supériorité décourag-eante des mécaniques étrangères, ont pour résultat de faire chavirer les civilisations archaïques qui subissent ces assauts. Tout, maintenant, s'effondre ou va s'effondrer: les arts, les techniques et toutes les ingénieuses coutumes qui permettaient a un groupe de vivre à peu près en paix.*[88]

> The staggering numeric growth of population, contrary to its millennial experience, the parallel loss of resources, the collapse of the economy, the discouraging contact with foreign technologies, resulted in the capsize of archaic civilizations undergoing these assaults. Now everything is collaps-ing or is going to: the arts, the technical skills and all the ingenious customs that allowed a group of people to live more or less in peace.

The economic and social situation outlined so vividly and persuasively by Camus and Tillion set the context for the reforms Soustelle promulgated when he began his tenure as governor general. Soustelle was also charged with acting on a series of measures aimed at enhancing the democratic participation of Muslim Algerians in a political process that was dominated by *colons*, the Algerians of European origin often referred to as *pied noirs*.[89] Such reforms had their origins in the Popular Front socialist government in 1936. In the intervening 20 years, nothing of substance had been achieved.[90]

After the war in 1947, the French yet again failed to move forward on significant reforms when another reform policy was undermined by electoral fraud perpetrated by *pied noir* extremists. In his own preliminary notes upon his arrival as governor general, Soustelle acknowledged that next to no progress had been made by 1955.[91]

In February 1955, Soustelle immediately enlisted the active participation of his ethnologist colleague. Rather than returning to France following her fact-finding mission, Tillion stayed in Algeria where she was invited by Soustelle to serve in his cabinet. Thus, the two ethnologists who had first met as students in in-ter-war Paris collaborated in the drama unfolding in Algeria in the 1950s. In Tillion's perception, the salva-tion of ordinary Algerians would demand a massive campaign of social engineering on the part of the French authorities:

> Une élévation rapide, générale et massive, a la fois du niveau de vie et de l'instruction, est une condition indispensable pour atteindre la mutation sociale qui peut seule sauver n'importe quelle population en cours de paupérisation.[92]

> A rapid, general and massive elevation at the same time of the standard of living and education is the indispensable condition to attain the social change that alone can save any population in the course of impoverishment.

In the early months of his administration with Tillion and other reform-minded ministers in his cabinet, Soustelle sought a major injection of French financing for education, health services and industrial training aimed at Algeria's Muslim majority. Soustelle's reform package also called for affirmative action in hiring Algerian Muslims in the civil service. Like the linguistic policies of some post-revolutionary Mexican *indi-*

genistas, Soustelle's plan called for universal public education in Arabic at all levels.[93]

Soustelle also immediately undertook a series of unprecedented fact-finding missions in remote parts of Algeria. As historians Bernard Droz and Evelyn Lever have noted, Soustelle's first actions showed the traces of his ethnological training and experience in the field.[94] Soustelle displayed extraordinary ambition in those early months. Soustelle's largesse as governor general included regular audiences with Muslim religious leaders and his attendance at events where foodstuffs were distributed to the needy.[95]

In a memoir of his experience as governor general, produced within months of his return to France, Soustelle emphasized that his Mexican experience was at the forefront of his attempted understanding of the Algerian situation:

> *J'ai retrouvé en fait, en Algérie, les mêmes problèmes qu'au Mexique; bien souvent, en voyant les gourbis de terre sèche et de chaume, entourés de haies de nopals, je me serais cru chez les Otomis du haut-plateau de l'Anahuac. On s'est aperçu là-bas, après avoir morcelé les latifundia par la réforme agraire, qu'il restait encore tout à faire, car la terre à elle seule ne nourrit personne.*[96]

> I found in fact, in Algeria, the same problems as that of Mexico; often, in seeing huts of dried earth and clay, surrounded by hedges of cacti, I believed I was back among the Otomí of the high plateau of Anhuac. One had perceived over there, after the dividing up into little plots of large land holdings by agrarian reform, that everything remained to be done, because the land on its own couldn't nourish anyone.

In a television appearance that coincided with that publication, Soustelle further argued the Mexican connection:

> *J'ai vu les choses un peu en ethnologue. C'est certain quand j'ai crée les SAS (sections administratives spéciales) je m'inspiré d'une chose très précise qui étaient les missions culturelles mexicaines qui étaient planté dans les villages mexicaines...*[97]

> I saw things through my ethnologist's lens. Certainly, when I created the SAS (special administrative sections) I was inspired precisely by the cultural missions that were planted in the Mexican villages...

The possibility of using Mexico as some sort of model for reform in North Africa had surfaced even prior to Soustelle's arrival. His mentor Paul Rivet, whose knowledge of *indigenismo* in post-revolutionary Mexico must have been influenced considerably by the observations of his then graduate student Jacques Soustelle, drew the link as early as 1936 in a Parisian leftist publication:

> *Au cours d'un récent voyage en Afrique du Nord, j'ai été frappé par l'étrange parallélisme qui existe au point de vue social et économique entre ce pays et un certain nombre de républiques du centre et du sud de l'Amérique.*
>
> *La révolution mexicaine qui a été si calomnié, n'a été en réalité qu'un immense effort pour concilier les intérêts des descendants des « conquistadores » et des Indiens asservis. Ce fut essentiellement une révolution agraire comme celle que nous avons réalisée au moment de la révolution, comme celle que tant de pays d'Europe centrale ont amorcée depuis la guerre.*
>
> *Écoles rurales: Bref, l'enseignement s'adapte étroitement au milieu et il est avant tout d'ordre technique et hygiénique; l'enseignement de la lecture, de l'écriture ne sont pas le but unique, ni même l'essentiel. Ce qui importe, c'est de créer dans les milieux indigènes des possibilités de développement matériel, d'améliorer leur niveau de vie et de faire ainsi apprécier les bienfaits de la civilisation.*[98]

During a recent visit to North Africa, I was struck by the strange parallelism that exists from the social and economic point of between this country and a number of republics of central and south America.

The Mexican Revolution which was so calamitous, was in effect only an effort to reconcile the interests of the descendants of the conquistadors and the oppressed Indians. It was essentially an agrarian revolution such as we experienced at the time of the (French) revolution, like those undertaken by some central European countries since the war.

Rural schools: To be brief, teaching adapts strictly to the milieu and concerns above all technique and hygiene; the teaching of reading, writing are not the only, not even the essential, goal. What's important is to create in the Indigenous areas possibilities of material development, to improve their standard of living and to encourage them to appreciate the benefits of civilization.

Some scholars have explored the connection between the Mexican example and Soustelle's efforts in Algeria.[99] Central to such research is a consideration of Soustelle's (and Mitterrand's) vaunted "integration." In the minds of its champions, "integration" meant a gradual switch from assimilation. Although Soustelle's vision of integration was lampoooned by the lives of Fanon and Sartre, his ideas have regained currency in recently published works.[100] What was clearly borrowed from the Mexican example in Soustelle's understanding was an ambitious attempt at social engineering to rapidly elevate a local, Indigenous population which could then, as the theory had it, participate as equals, with some cultural and linguistic traits intact, but with identities transformed, in a modern nation-state. Soustelle's perception of the Mexican experience was idealized. Perhaps the passage of 20 years since his preliminary field research in Mexico had dulled his memory and encouraged a somewhat naïve, selective view. Historians of the Mexican Revolution largely concur that the cluster of policies surrounding *indigenismo* were contested, inconsistent and often flawed.[101] In his preliminary work on Mexico published in 1936, Soustelle identified both the goal and the means by which such a transition might be effected through *indigenismo*:

> *Enfin ceux des Indiens qui sont déjà en marche, par l'agrarisme et par la diffusion de l'éducation, vers une autre destine que celles de leurs pères, de leurs aïeux et de cent générations dont l'incessant labeur est resté cache derrière le brillant décor du Mexique colonial, républicain et porfiriste. J'ai déjà rendu homage plusieurs fois, dans ces souvenirs, aux maîtres ruraux. Je les tiens pour le vrai ferment du Mexique d'aujourd'hui eux dont la peine et quelquefois le sang fondent peu à peu un people nouveau avec sept millions de paysans à peau brune opprimés et méprisés. Qu'on feuillette les rapports des missions culturelles et des écoles rurales publiées par le Sécretariat de l'Éducation; on y verra les marches épuisantes à travers les montagnes, l'hostilité des caciques et des prêtres, les rebuffades et les mauvais traitements.[102]*

Finally these Indians are on the march due to agrarianism and the spread of education towards another destiny than that of their fathers, of their elders and a hundred generations of which incessant labour remains hidden behind the brilliant décor of colonial Mexico, both republican and Porfirian. I have rendered homage many times, in these recollections, to the rural teachers. I hold them up as the true agents of change in today's Mexico, those of whom the effort and sometime blood creates bit by bit a new people out of seven million oppressed and castigated brown skinned peasants. Skim through the reports from the cultural missions and rural schools published by the Secretariat of Education; one finds there the exhausting hikes across mountains, the hostility of local leaders and priests, the snubs and the bad treatment.

With fellow ethnologist Tillion serving in his cabinet, Soustelle's journeys in the first months of his mandate reinforced his view that cultural missions, similar to what he had witneseed in Mexico in the 1930s, would be the catalyst of a massive educational and industrial training campaign. Members of the civil service remarked that wherever he travelled across the country, Soustelle insisted on visiting local schools.

Soustelle also wanted to link primary education with vocational training centres and workshops.[103] *Le plan Soustelle* called for the creation of *centres sociaux*, modelled on the cultural missions of Mexico, that would offer a cluster of educational, cultural and health services to assist both urban and rural populations to transition to an industrial economy. Cultural missions would also serve in a campaign against illiteracy and serve as adult education centres.[104] In their idealized form the centres were to be focal points of education, social work, health care and industrial training. Soustelle, Tillion and their eager reformist technicians felt their efforts could efface the bitter legacy of 125 years of French depredation of local populations in a matter of a few years.

Tillion was convinced that Soustelle's goals were correct, but she disagreed that social conditions in Algeria were necessarily similar to those of Mexico.[105] Tillion argued that rural Algeria could not possibly support the country's burgeoning population. She felt, therefore, that while Mexican *indigenismo* might well have a focus on rural peoples, the Soustelle administration should concentrate its efforts on training the surging youthful population with practical skills to work in French dominated industries.[106] While Soustelle derived his inspiration from rural outposts which reminded him of Mexico, Tillion did not merely rely only on her first-hand knowledge of rural Algeria garnered in the 1930s. Her growing awareness of the urban slums around Alger, Constantine and Oran led her to believe that the emphasis of social reform should be urban so that young Algerians could make a transition to an industrialized economy.[107] Tillion was aware of campaigns already underway in other parts of French Africa in which rural peoples were being integrated to larger industrial centres of the French colonial world.[108]

A government report on the establishment of "*le Service des centres sociaux*" described the program through the lens of social reform, literacy and various education initiatives at the local level without reference to the gathering storm of war in which the initiatives were launched:

> *Dans le principe, de qui s'agit-il? Tout d'abord, de créer une institution assez humble pour qu'elle soit de niveau avec la collectivité la moins évoluée et d'insérer cette institution dans la collectivité au point qu'elle en fasse partie intégrante.*[109]

> So basically, what are we talking about? First of all, to create an institution that's humble enough that it is level with a community that's not highly developed and then to insert this institution into the community in a way that makes it an integral part of it.

While in Soustelle's cabinet, Tillion engaged in an analysis of the education of young Algerians. She established that just 230,000 out of 1.1 million Muslim boys were receiving proper primary education; and that only 85,000 of one million school-age Muslim girls were receiving anything approaching adequate elementary education. Conversely, according to Tillion's data, 14 of 15 children of European origin, regardless of gender, had the benefit of a good education.[110] Tillion's briefing notes for her colleagues painted a grim picture of the challenge that the zealous reformers faced:

> *Mesure provisoires d'urgence Il n'est pas question de renoncer a faire l'effort nécessaire de pour donner a l'Algérie une scolarisation primaire normale, mais, en attendant d'y être parvenu, nous nous trouvons actuellement devant un état de fait: quatre garçons musulmans sur cinq qui ne pourront pas*

gagner leur vie; quinze garçons musulmans sur seize dont l'équilibre familial est compris d'avance. Ce sont les responsabilités que nous avons vis-à-vis de ces enfants qui doivent actuellement primer toutes les autres considérations.

En un mot nous devons viser d'abord à une scolarisation totale et ensuite a une scolarisation totalement alignée sur celle de la métropole. C'est seulement par une politiques de masses (et non plu de prototypes) que nous pouvons sauver l'Algérie.[111]

Urgent provisional measures It is not a question of renouncing the necessary effort to provide Algeria primary education, but, in waiting to get there, we find ourselves in the following state of affairs: four out of five Muslim boys cannot earn a living; fifteen Muslim boys out of sixteen for whom the family role is pre-ordained. There are the responsibilities we have for these children that must take priority over other considerations.

To be blunt we must aim at education for all and then on an education system that's in synch with that in France. It is only by policies for the masses (and not just prototypes) that we can save Algeria.

One effect of the reform proposals to "save Algeria" was the arrival of idealistic teachers, public health personnel, social workers and industrial trainers to staff the education system and the vaunted *centres sociaux*. As the conflict between France and Algerian rebels intensified in the late 1950s, these people became targets for *le Front de Libération National*.[112]

The escalating military conflict led to a political rupture between Soustelle and Tillion. Soustelle's instructions from Paris were clear: defeat the rebellion through an intensification of the military effort and win "hearts and minds" by finally acting on a series of long-promised reforms to better integrate Algeria with mainland France. On the same day, a state of urgency was declared by the government which undermined "universal" principles of French liberty; the government re-affirmed the broad outlines of its reform package, *le plan Soustelle*:

Dans cette œuvre de reprise en mains des populations qui nécessité une atmosphère de confiance, une attention particulière sera apportée au développement de l'action scolaire et sociale, des services médicaux et a l'ouverture de chantiers de travaux d'utilité publique permettant de lutter contre le chômage, la misère et le sous emploi.[113]

In this effort to put power in the hands of populations who require an atmosphere of confidence, particular attention will be paid to educational and social action, medical services and in opening of public works centres to combat unemployment, poverty and underemployment.

The pervasive doublethink of the French elite in its response to the developing crisis seeps through Soustelle's writings even in the early reformist stage of his governorship. In notes he prepared for a speech, Soustelle revealed fervently held convictions that appear to be at cross purposes – social reform and military force could somehow, together, quell the rebellion:

Pour le combattre il faut – et je m'y suis énergiquement employé – une action répressive qui prenne parfois la forme opérationnelle de caractère militaire; mais il faut aussi panser les plaies si douloureuses, les cicatriser et recréer les conditions d'une vigueur morale et matérielle nécessaires a la renaissance de la vie la ou elle est si cruellement meurtrie.[114]

To combat (the rebellion) requires – and I am energetically committed to it – repressive action that takes both operational and military form; but one also has to heal painful wounds, tend to the scars and recreate moral and material conditions necessary to the rebirth of life where it has been so cruelly devastated.

Tillion saw the contradiction in these policies. The schizophrenic policy posture became too much for her to bear as a cabinet member. While she respected Soustelle's sincerity in his struggle with the entrenched anti-Muslim attitudes of his European subjects, she was convinced that the enhanced militarization in the early months of Soustelle's administration would only drive more and more Indigenous Algerians into the arms of the FLN. In May 1955, she quit Soustelle's cabinet.[115] However, she carried on with her civil service responsibilities for development of *les centres sociaux*.

Like Albert Camus, Tillion is associated with the valiant, minority attempts to salvage France's honour and build a peace of co-existence in Algeria. Less than two months following her death, Paris celebrated Tillion with a major exhibition on her life and times, as well as conferences and screenings of films dedicated to her Second World War experience and her ethnological and political work in Algeria.[116] Like Camus and her former colleague Soustelle, Tillion was both a stalwart resister to Nazism and out of step with the French intellectual elite over Algeria. In death, she has achieved a deserved and rarified status as a model of engaged intellectualism.

The remarkable Tillion responded to her concentration camp internment with a musical that survives her. The operetta « *Le Verfugbar aux enfers* » [Inmates in Hell] was conceived in the autumn of 1944 to rally the spirits of Tillion's fellow Ravensbruck Nazi concentration camp detainees then hoping to survive until the camp's liberation. The work was performed outside Ravensbruck for the first time during the last year of Tillion's life on June 2 and 3, 2007 at *Théâtre du Chatelet*, Paris. After her death at 100 years of age on April 19, 2008, the operetta was also performed at Ravensbruck itself on the occasion of the 65th anniversary of the concentration camp's liberation.[117]

Soustelle's ambitious reform plans were undermined and contradicted by the expanded military effort that Tillion opposed. Following Soustelle's departure, a socialist government ramped up the military assault and granted extraordinary civil powers to the army in *l'Algérie française*.[118]

In the spring of 1955, on Soustelle's watch, France declared a "state of urgency" in Algeria. The designation was carefully chosen to grant the government extraordinary powers of detention without explicitly declaring martial law. With the state of urgency and creation of *centres d'hébergement* [detention centres], Soustelle adopted policies which vitiated the "universal" rights of freedom which he claimed were France's legacy to Algerians and the world. With the invocation of a state of urgency, the governor general authorized the detention without trial for those community activists, intellectuals and nationalists deemed capable of rallying ordinary Algerians to the cause of independence.[119]

Soustelle was directly responsible for the creation of these *centres d'hébergement*, which were established to remove anti-French subversive elements from the general population. Soustelle's distinctive handwritten notes on draft documents relating to the centres sometimes demanded a tightening of the regulatory system. For example, in a draft version of general instructions on the functioning of the centres, an article which would have permitted an administrative review by lawyers of detainees on individual cases was crossed out by Soustelle with instructions to omit the provision from the final version.[120]

The administrative conception and shadowy legal standing were part of a pre-approved plan devised by Soustelle and vetted by the minister of the interior in Paris, the month prior to the implementation of the state of urgency.[121] Muslim opponents protested the camps' legality as soon as they were established. Some

▲ *Germaine Tillion, hiking in Algeria c.1935.*

◀ *Nelly Forget, Paris, 2010.*

Paris, France, *June 21, 2010*

In a middle-class neighbourhood of Paris, an elderly woman energetically preserves an alternate vision of France's legacy in Algeria. Nelly Forget first served Germaine Tillion as a community organizer in various *bidonvilles*, the squalid urban ghettos of Alger, in the late 1950s. Following Algerian independence, Forget would go on to work as Tillion's secretary in both political and academic spheres.

Forget is director of *l'Association Germaine Tillion*. She maintains an archive in her apartment replete with textual and photographic evidence of the work a handful of Algerian and French social workers, health professionals, teachers and community organizers undertook under Tillion's leadership in the *centres sociaux*, conceived under the governorship of Jacques Soustelle. Carefully preserved pamphlets and newspaper articles contradict and complicate widely transmitted views of the conflict. An in-depth economic and cultural assessment of the challenges in one urban slum features an introduction by Georgette Soustelle, ethnologist and wife of the then governor general.[118] Newspaper clippings during the most tempestuous period of the Algerian-French conflict in the years immediately following the Soustelles' departure present a portrait of the courageous, diverse teams of women and men at work in the *centres sociaux*.[119]

civil servants expressed similar legal concerns. The Soustelle administration's legal department responded with a brief that justified the creation of the camps.[122] The centres were set up through a legal sleight of hand. A combination of euphemistic language and a skilful deployment of existing law provided a front of respectability for the creation of *centres d'hébergement* that were, in fact, concentration camps. In the battle for hearts and minds among French Algerians, in France and in the court of world opinion, the government of France carefully crafted a narrative about the "centres" that sought to obviate any association with Nazi prisoner of war or death camps. In his official announcement about the state of urgency, Soustelle reminded prefects that the law would prohibit creation of internment camps, while telegraphing just how the extraordinary powers of the state of urgency would allow for the same thing, albeit described differently:

> *L'Etat d'urgence est un instrument temporaire pour faire cesser toute forme de trouble et apaiser l'inquiétude des esprits. Il doit contribuer à la mission de pacification, entendu au sens large du mot, et préparer des lendemains sans amertume.*
>
> *J'entend que les restrictions de liberté, autorisées par la loi, soient limitées aux justes nécessités et qu'elles ne revêtent jamais un caractère de sanction collective.*
>
> *En aucun cas, comme souligne la texte de la loi, ne devront être créés des camps d'internement. Les individus assignes a résidence pourront logé par tous moyens (habitations en dur disponible, baraquements, tentes, etc...) a proximité de chantiers de travail...*[123]

> The state of urgency is a temporary instrument to put an end to trouble and calm worried spirits. It has to contribute to our pacification policy, understood in the broadest terms, and prepare for a future without bitterness.
>
> I expect that restrictions on liberty, authorized by law, to be limited to what is justified and not used as a form of collective punishment.
>
> In no case, as the law requires, should internment camps be created. Individuals assigned for residence can be lodged by all means (roofed houses where available, barracks, tents, etc...) near work sites...

Soustelle was engaging in double speak. In one phrase, detention centres are proscribed, in the next Soustelle envisages assigning individuals under house arrest to various types of structures in the proximity of work camps. This legalese allowed for the creation of *centres d'hébergement* under a law established to requisition labour dating from 1938. It gave Soustelle's administration power to place suspects under house arrest or to remove them to a *centre d'hébergement* to prevent their contact with the general population. At this juncture, with departure of Tillion and other champions of the reformist approach over a hardening military stance, it would appear that Soustelle was persuaded by the hardliners who believed that the suspected rebels deserved a stern hand. One of the advocates for the camps, Henri-Paul Eydoux, proposed dispensing with any presumption of innocence, "*Il faut être extrêmement sévère avec les suspects qui sont pour la plupart des combattants camouflé.*"[124] [Trans: "We have to be extremely tough on the suspects who are for the most part camouflaged combatants."]

The centres required continual monitoring by Soustelle's administration. An inspector general by the name of Ciosi assessed conditions in the camps and alerted the government as to their dubious legality. Ciosi did not advocate closing the centres; he viewed them as a useful tool in preventing "contamination" of the general population by renegade thinkers. He argued that given their dubious legal standing it was all the more necessary to see that they were well run. He often reported abuse, as in the following warning regarding the behaviour of French camp guards:

… il signale des brutalités excessives, des vols, des viols. Leur attitude, délibérément hostile, sans ménagement et sans nuance, sans souci de respecter les moeurs des autochtones, se traduit chez ceux-ci par une animosité qui, a travers eux, atteint la cause française.[125]

… there are reports of excessive brutality, of thefts, of rapes. Their deliberately hostile attitude, without grace and without nuance, with no thought given to the mores of the Indigenes, becomes an animosity, that because of them, undermines the French cause.

Ciosi drew his colleagues' attention to the delicacy and potential political embarrassment surrounding the loophole the government had utilized to allow for internment without resorting to martial law and an explicit suspension of French republican legal norms:

La loi nous interdi [sic] de donner aux « localités » ou sont assignes a résidence les individus que nous considérons comme dangereux ou suspects, l'allure de camp d'internement.
   L'absence de barbelés ne peut faire illusion et il serait assez puéril de vouloir jouer sur les mots. Nous sommes donc en infraction avec la loi.[126]

The law prohibits us from giving these "locations" where we assign individuals we consider dangerous or suspect, the appearance of an internment camp.
   The absence of barbed wire should not fool anyone and it would be childish to want to play with words. We are therefore in violation of the law.

Ciosi's reports from June 1955 bespeak the moral decay of the French administration as the conflict intensified and fundamental republican virtues espoused by the reformist governor general were abandoned. Ciosi described a detention network of scarce provisions, overcrowded conditions, poor medical treatment and even of a plague of scorpions. He wrote about the random dumping of ordinary Algerians guilty of nothing more than circulating without their identity papers and he exposed the waste caused by exorbitant prices paid to contractors who constructed the centres.[127]

By November 1955, some six months following the establishment of the centres, an administrative review requested by Soustelle raised questions about their efficacy in the battle for loyalty to the French cause that such measures were designed to buttress. The report suggested that the emergent leaders in each camp be removed to another specific camp so as to quell their influence over other inmates. Such a move, the author of the document argued, would allow for the moral re-education of those remaining in order to bring them back to the French cause by means of propaganda, meetings and film screenings in French and Arabic.[128]

Torture by French military officials began in the camps as early as 1955. These abuses were not as widespread at this stage as they were surrounding the events of the "Battle of Algiers" in 1958. The moderate journalist Henri Alleg was arrested for the first time during Soustelle's governorship.[129] In 1958, Alleg produced *La Question*, a literary classic about his harrowing experience of torture. Alleg's work, a sensation which produced line-ups outside its Parisian publisher's offices before it was banned, marked a turning point in shifting French opinion against the war.[130] In the latter stages of Soustelle's governorship, the malodorous reputation of the camps crossed the Mediterranean and undermined French credibility. A group of North African *émigrés* wrote to Soustelle from Lyon, illustrating that pockets of sympathy for independence existed in metropolitan France already. The letter respectfully called for a solution similar to Tunisia – a devolution to national independence, but denounced Soustelle for his internship policies, "*Votre nom restera lié à l'installation des 'centres d'hébergement' qui sont en réalité des camps de concentration.*"[131] [Your name will be forever linked with the establishment of 'detention centres' which are in reality concentration camps].

News of the camps served to rally international support for the FLN and turn the tide of opinion among French leftists against France's military campaign to squash the rebellion. A few years following Soutelle's tenure as governor general, Tillion participated in an international effort to investigate conditions and possible human rights abuses in the camps. Tillion drew on her experience as a Nazi concentration camp survivor to advocate for all prisoners on both sides of the conflict.[132] In 1957, she undertook a dangerous mission to meet FLN leaders in hopes of averting attacks on civilians and promote a ceasefire. Tillion insisted on the universal application of human rights that she understood as the legacy of the French revolution and the emergence of democratic forms of government.[133] She steadfastly adhered to universal values of liberty and human dignity. In an interview conducted in 2000, Tillion maintained that she was unaware of any torture being conducted by French forces during the period she served under Soustelle, but acknowledged understanding in hindsight that such activities were already underway at that time.[134] Under pressure of a widespread insurrection and acting in accordance with directions from Paris, Soustelle abandoned the fundamental principles of human rights that were the supposed touchstones of *la mission civilisatrice* in Algeria. Author Julian Jackson explores such contradictions in his biography of Charles de Gaulle:

> The irony was that the logic of Soustelle's progressive republicanism led him to defend by any means – including torture – to keep Algeria French while de Gaulle's pragmatic conservatism led him to ultimately accept Algerian independence.[135]

Hearts and minds

Soustelle relied on his wartime experience as a journalist and propagandist in Mexico serving General Charles de Gaulle in the battle for public opinion through the press.[136] The governor general wrote a quarterly overview of the status of the reform program, identifying difficulties in controlling the message delivered by the press at home and in the Arab world as a major area of concern.[137] By late fall 1955, the written summary of a meeting regarding *"Propagande et contre propagande"* expressed the Soustelle administration's frustration with controlling the press without resorting to *"une censure véritable."* Nevertheless, the Soustelle administration did engage in the suppression of opposition newspapers.[138] In the summary, Soustelle planned to meet with newspaper editors to encourage a more *"attitude raisonnable"* on their part. The summary states that the most practical method of obtaining favourable press would be to submit prepared articles to the press for publication.[139] Soustelle perfected this method in Mexico City during the Second World War with the creation of an ersatz press agency to disseminate pro-Free French and anti-Nazi articles in the Mexican and Latin American press.[140]

Soustelle also relied on his knowledge of and keen interest in cinema as part of the propaganda effort.[141] Soustelle, the movie buff and wartime propaganda master, established *La Service de Diffusion cinématographique* on February 15, 1955, under the direct command of his own office. Its administrator accepted that his team would serve more than a technical function. In a report to the governor general's office a Monsieur Murati wrote about the "varied and delicate tasks" his team would be asked to undertake and their key role in "information and propaganda in the Muslim milieu." Murati was pleased that the service would fulfil such a function but hoped the "agents" would get a civil service upgrade with their expanded tasks in order to, *"servir la cause française et l'éducation des masses en Algérie."*[142] Documentary films were used in the re-education effort of suspected FLN sympathizers in *les centres d'hébergement.* By the autumn of 1955, following startling setbacks in the war effort, Soustelle's government created a *Centre d'Action Psychologique* to train officers in their approach to the Muslim community by screening documentary films in training sessions.[143]

Following the departure of Tillion and other moderates from Soustelle's cabinet and inner circle of advisors, signs of deepening trouble spread throughout Algeria. By July, an official working for Soustelle's cabinet predicted a defection of previously loyal *interlocuteurs valables* in the Muslim community.[144] Even the Boy Scouts were for independence, as a letter to Soustelle from the head of the Muslim Scout association declared:

> ... *le jeune musulman a toujours souffert de l'équivoque du fait algérien. La personnalité de ce pays n'a jamais été définie d'une manière satisfaisante. Une telle équivoque est à l'origine d'une discrimination systématique qui hypothèque lourdement l'avenir de chaque musulman algérien.*[145]

> ... the young Muslim has always suffered from the equivocal nature of Algerian reality. The character of this country has never been defined in a satisfactory manner. This equivocality is at the root of systemic discrimination that puts a heavy mortgage on the future of every Algerian Muslim.

With the experience he had garnered by delivering radio lectures about Mexico from *le Musée de l'homme* in an effort to popularize ethnography in the 1930s, Soustelle employed his oratorical skills in the French propaganda campaign. In an effort to explain his policies and rally morale, Soustelle made a number of radio broadcasts to the people of Algeria. The language deployed in these radio scripts is official, almost regal in its tone but also expresses the urgent, somewhat panicked tone of an imperial power intent on diminishing the threat of the rising conflagration. In mid-August 1955, Soustelle lay claim to progress in the struggle for loyalty to his aims in Algeria:

> *Pour qui a connu l'AURES farouche et hostile de l'hiver dernier, et qui voit aujourd'hui les partisans Chaouïa le fusil en main veiller eux-mêmes a l'achèvement des moissons et défendre leurs mechtas contre les terroristes, il est évident qu'un profond changement est en train de s'espérer. La population de ces montagnes voit dans les postes lointain du bled, l'officier et le médecin se pencher fraternellement sur ces misères; elle voit monter les murs de nos bordj, progresser les pistes, culer l'eau. Le blé et l'orge rentrent pacifiquement aux villages et les paysans prennent part à leur propre défense. La confiance revient.*[146]

> For those who knew the ferocious and hostile Aures (mountain range area) of last winter and who today sees the Chaouiaa (Berber) partisans with rifle in hand bringing in their harvest and defending their lands against the terrorist, it's clear that a profound change is beginning to get underway. The mountain populations witness, in posts far from the village, the officer and the doctor tending to poverty; it sees the walls of our citadels and the progression of better roads and access to running water. Wheat and barley are brought back peacefully to the villages and the peasants are participating in their own defense. Confidence is returning.

In a bad situation spiraling toward outright disaster, Soustelle struck an oddly romantic tone invoking the heroic efforts of military and medical personnel in pacifying rural areas and strengthening loyalties to the French cause. In another radio speech, Soustelle praised the efforts of the newly formed rural police. He frequently paid homage to Muslim police and rural forces loyal to the French cause. He wanted his rhetoric to draw links between North African soldiers who had served France in both world wars and Muslim detachments serving in the battle against the FLN. Soustelle argued that all such loyalists were fighting for France against terrorism.[147] He seemed oblivious to the fact that a significant number of Muslim veterans of the French forces, which helped end the Second World War, went on to form the FLN.

In addition to his romantic evocation of heroic loyalties in the countryside, Soustelle's script for the broadcast of August 19, 1955 also demonstrated his awareness of Tillion's message about Algeria's economic future. He stated that his tour enabled him to witness the sort of changes that must occur in an industrialized, modern Algeria such as the development of a major iron deposit in development at Ouenza. Soustelle claimed that such progress would be the "salvation" of Algeria.

Soustelle delivered that broadcast on the eve of disaster. In districts surrounding the northern city of Philippeville, FLN militants attacked civilians of European origin and their Muslim allies. More than 100 died at the hands of the FLN, including some women and children. In the aftermath, most accounts concur that the French military and vigilante groups killed more than ten times that number in reprisal.[148] August 20, 1955 ended any hopes for success of *le plan Soustelle*. In the immediate aftermath, Soustelle frantically attempted to squelch vigilante campaigns, as the text of a telegram to Paris demonstrates:

> *Les évènements du 20 Août dans Nord-Constantinois font l'objet de relations déformées ou inexactes et d'interprétations tendancieuses – STOP.*
> *De violentes campagnes s'annoncent notamment de la part de certains élus – STOP.*[149]

> The events of the 20th of August in the north Constantine region are the subject of false or inexact relationships and tendentious interpretations – STOP.
> Violent campaigns are being announced especially by elected officials – STOP.

Soustelle understood that the FLN had calculated that a disproportionate, even lawless, French response would ultimately serve the cause of independence:

> *Il me revient de tout part ce matin que dans la région de Philippeville des éléments civils européens armées pourchassent indistinctement tous les musulmans. Les résultats sont la dispersion de la population, l'arrêt complet de la vie économique, la fuite des fallahs dans les maquis et l'anarchie totale. Cela doit cesser immédiatement. Je dis immédiatement…Seule les militaires et les forces de l'ordre ont qualité de repousser les attaques e poursuivre les assaillants selon les directives données par moi-même les 20 et 21 août. Ce qui précède constitue un ordre formel que vous voudrez bien porter sans délai à la connaissance de tous les intéresses.*[150]

> It has come to my attention this morning that in the Philippeville region armed European civilians are indiscriminately hunting down Muslims. The results are the dispersal of the population, the halting of all economic activity, the flight of peasants into the guerrilla groups and total anarchy. This must cease immediately… Only military personnel and other forces of order can bring attacks to an end and pursue the assailants in accordance with my orders of August 20 and 21. The preceding constitutes a formal order that you will want to impress on the awareness of all concerned without delay.

The calamity demanded a governor with front-line military experience. During the Second World War, Soustelle was primarily concerned with information, intelligence gathering and propaganda as he served the resistance in Mexico City, London and, finally, Alger. He had never been directly involved in armed combat. The crisis of late August 1955 overwhelmed his reform plans. Soustelle argued his case in the metropolitan press where he insisted that he was a force for the quelling of vigilante reprisals and the restoration of republican values in Algeria. In a letter to *Le Monde*, Soustelle denied French forces were engaged in brutality and complained that the paper was giving vent to excessively negative accounts of French policies.[151] Soustelle was simultaneously relaying complaints to the prefect of Constantine about the sacking of Muslim businesses by *pied noirs* and adding to the contingent of police officers under his direct command because he was convinced that some officials were turning a blind eye to, or even assisting, in the murderous vigilante campaigns.[152]

The horrendous spasm of violence surrounding August 1955 led to further deterioration in the political situation. Soustelle's reform plans were rejected by a group of Muslim moderates, the very *interlocuteurs* on which such plans depended. To Soustelle's dismay, a group of loyalist legislators defected. *Manifeste des 61* [Manifesto of the 61] declared that the policy of integration had been made irrelevant by the course of events and that the French had not been serious about it in any event. Some Muslim moderates asserted that *intégration* was insufficient and demanded that immediate steps be taken to create a federal relationship between Algeria and metropolitan France.[153]

Federalism, the wobbly but enduring bridge over differences in the Canadian polity, was a far off destination in Soustelle's thinking of 1955. Twenty years later, Soustelle would argue that federalism would have, could have and should have been the logical outcome of a gradual process of integration.[154] However, his thinking as governor general, and the policies of the metropolitan government he represented, echoed the sense of cultural and political superiority inherent in the liberal traditions of *la mission civilisatrice*. By the autumn of 1955, such thinking was a dangerous anachronism that cost would be reformers like Soustelle the support of hitherto loyal Muslim supporters in Algeria. Most notably, Ferhat Abbas, leader of a moderate political party whose nephew had been murdered by the FLN in the violence of August 20, 1955, resigned his legislative seat and rejected *le plan Soustelle*. Notes regarding Abbas' resignation and his public disavowal of Soustelle's proposed reforms, taken at a meeting between Abbas and members of the French cabinet in the fall of 1955, reveal the utter abandonment of Soustelle's reform package by the very political figures it was designed to mollify and integrate:

> *Vous, français, vous attendez toujours qu'il soit trop tard pur agir... Le fosse qui est en train de se creuser entre musulmans et français sera tel qu'il sera impossible de le combler...nous ne sommes pas chez nous en Algérie.*
>
> *Je ne demande pas qu'il y ait immédiatement une République Algérienne...mais il faut provoquer immédiatement, par les reformes hardies, un choc psychologique tel, que les musulmans puissent croire que quelque chose est enfin change en Algérie.*[155]

> You, the French, as always wait until it's too late to act... The chasm that is deepening between Muslims and the French will be such that it will be impossible to overcome... we are not at home in Algeria.
>
> I don't ask for the immediate creation of an Algerian republic... but one must immediately provoke, by means of fearless reforms, such a psychological shock that Muslims can believe that something finally is changing in Algeria.

Dr. Mohammed Benjelloul, who had promoted peaceful reform of Algeria's status since before the Second World War, suddenly denounced the French in his support of the fatal *Manifeste des 61*. To counteract the widening public desertion of reputable and recognizable loyalists, Soustelle's cabinet prepared documents of allegiance for the *imprimatur* of local leaders from the Muslim community.[156] This harks back to Duncan Campbell Scott's efforts to elicit Indigenous and Christian church leadership support for his Indian education schemes.

An increasingly exasperated Soustelle took his case to the metropolitan press and undertook a rhetorical combat with *Le Monde* defending his course of action following the events of August 20 and decrying the betrayal of erstwhile allies such as Abbas and Mohammed Benjelloul.[157] An exchange of private letters with the editor-in-chief of *Le Monde* is especially revelatory. Soustelle complained about the lack of support his policies were receiving in the paper and the sympathies he felt the paper was expressing for Benjelloul in his abandonment of *intégration*. In a riposte to Soustelle, editor Hubert Beuve-Méry complained of delays and the suppression of legitimate news by Soustelle's administration:

> *Cette recherche de la vérité est toujours une entreprise difficile et, dans certaines situations la publications peut poser, elle aussi, des problèmes délicats. Mais en ce qui concerne l'Algérie notamment, nos rédacteurs et nos chefs de service sont amenés à se plaindre trop souvent des difficultés supplémentaires qu'ils rencontrent dans le sens de la politique gouvernementale... Quand il s'agit non d'échauffourées ou de combats mais de textes en provenance d'Alger, ces retards ou ces silences pariassent encore plus inadmissibles. La motion que les 61 ont adoptée à Alger le 14 Décembre contre la politique « d'intégration » pouvait être rédigée en termes excessifs ou injustes. Elle émanait en tout cas de représentants du peuple algérien. Le 15 Décembre au soir elle n'avait pas encore été transmise aux journaux de la métropole.*[158]

> This search for the truth is always a difficult business and in certain cases publications themselves can pose delicate problems. But concerning Algeria notably, our editors and heads of departments have been led to complain too often of the additional difficulties that they are encountering because of government policy. When it is a matter not of clashes or battle but of articles coming from Algiers, these delays and silences are still more inadmissible. The motion that the group of 61 adopted on December 14 against the policy of integration could (not) be drafted in an excessive or unfair manner. It emanated after all from the representatives of the Algerian people. On the evening of the 15th of December it still had not been transmitted to newspapers in the capital.

By late autumn 1955, Soustelle's ambitious plans had collapsed. He had been transformed in the course of a year into the beleaguered chief of a desperate military regime.

The assassination of Ferhat Abbas' nephew was but one of a series of FLN targeted assaults on anyone suspected of collaborating with the French. The vigilantism of French civilians and municipal officials in the aftermath of *le 20 Août* spiraled into a pattern of reprisals that would end in the murderous campaigns of the *Organisation Armée Secrète* (OAS) in Algeria and in France itself. Late in 1955, Soustelle was relaying intercepted death threats directed against Muslim leaders from a *Comité Révolutionnaire des Patriotes Français d'Algérie*. This militant organization comprised of settlers and hardline members of the French military was a harbinger of the OAS. These "death sentences" were handed out to Muslim professionals stating that they would be killed within eight days of the death of any French (European) citizen in their town or district.[159] In December 1955, Soustelle sent a secret cable to Paris reminding his political masters that his request for 60,000 additional troops in October had been met by a contingent one tenth that size. In the same cable, Soustelle named 15 Muslim officials with ties to the French administration who had been assassinated in less than two months that autumn.[160]

What became of the reformer? Some speculate that Soustelle's reformist agenda was simply overwhelmed by military contingencies. Others argue that the departure of Tillion and other leftists from his cabinet and administrative entourage was a reaction to the metamorphosis of Soustelle's own reformist zeal into the posture of a war governor. Other observers have argued that Soustelle's conversion into a man of the sword was soldered firmly by the trauma he experienced with the civilian casualties of the FLN attacks of August 1955.[161] Soustelle rejected that point of view for the rest of his life. He first fulminated against in an anti de Gaulle screed produced early in his self-exile from France in 1962:

> *... je saisirai cette occasion répéter une dernière fois que ma propre position sur le problème algérien, contrairement a tant de déformations et de calomnies répandues, était et demeure fondamentalement rationnelle et en concordance avec la réalité historique, ethnique, religieuse, économique, de l'Algérie. Il est devenu courant de raconter que j'aurais trouvé à Aïn-Abid a El-Alia mon chemin de Damas, et que la vue des pauvres corps mutilés de femmes et d'enfants le 20 août 1955, m'aurait fait abandonner une politique « libérale ».., Une fois encore, je proteste contre ces mensonges. C'est ca, raison, fondée sur la connaissance, qui m'a dicté mes opinions et ma conduite.*[162]

> ... I shall take advantage of this situation to repeat for a final time that my own position on the Algerian problem, contrary to so many widely spread distortions and calumnies, was and remains fundamentally rational and in accordance with the historical, ethnic, religious and economic reality of Algeria. It has become fashionable to say that I discovered at Aïn-Abid a El-Alia, my road to Damascus, and that the sight of the poor mutilated bodies of women and children on the 20th of August 1955, led me to abandon my "liberal" policies. Once again, I protest against these lies. It is reason, rooted in knowledge, that dictated my opinions and conduct.

Other witnesses to Soustelle's final days as governor general disagree with that self-assessment. On January 22, 1956, Albert Camus held a public forum in support of a "civil truce" in Algeria. Greeted by death threats from the French colonial right, Camus gathered a cross section of intellectuals and public figures from all Algerian communities to join him in a call for both sides to stop killing civilians. It was to be Camus' last public appearance on the issue in Algeria in his lifetime. Tillion attended the meeting:

> *La guerre algéro-française devint cependant vite féroce mais au tout début de 1956 (exactement le 22 janvier a 17 heures, selon mon agenda) je me suis cependant trouvée dans la salle dite « du Progrès » ou Albert Camus plaidait passionnément pour la trêve civile; Ferhat Abbas le rejoignait sur l'estrade, et le service d'ordre fut assure par des étudiants musulmans dont beaucoup étaient peut-être inscrits au FLN. Dans la rue, on entendait des voix français criant « a mort Camus »...*[163]

> The Algerian-French war became even more ferocious but even so at the beginning of 1956 (exactly 5 p.m. on January 22 according to my agenda) I found myself in a room called "Progress" where Albert Camus pleaded passionately for a civil truce; Ferhat Abbas joined him on stage, and order was maintained by Muslim students many of whom belonged to the FLN. On the street, one heard French voices yelling, "death to Camus"...

After the brave, but largely futile, public meeting, Camus met privately with Soustelle. Camus hoped Soustelle would accept the sort of understanding and forgiveness a civil truce would require. Neither of the principals left a detailed account of this encounter, but Camus' close friend Emmanuel Roblès, who was with Camus in Algeria at the time, recalled that Camus found Soustelle somewhat welcoming, but sceptically wary of trusting the other side:

> *Le mardi après nombre d'entrevues et de démarches, notre comite se réunit au complet dans un salon du Cercle. Camus nous rend compte de ses entrevues, et surtout, de sa conversation avec Soustelle. Celui-ci s'est déclaré intéressé de notre action, mais la notion de l'innocence est a préciser. Et puis, il y a les « demi-pensionnaires », travailleurs le jour, combattants la nuit.*[164]

> On Tuesday after many interviews and comings and goings, our entire committee met in a lounge at The Circle. Camus brought us up to date on his interviews, and above all, of his conversation

with Soustelle. That one claims he is interested in our action, but that the concept of innocence is yet to be determined. And yes there are "day students" workers by day, combatants by night.

Soustelle suspected that some of Camus' Muslim allies might have been more sympathetic to the FLN than Camus presumed. It was only a few months after the governor general's abandonment by his presumed Muslim allies in the Committee of 61. The tensions surrounding Camus' troubled, final return to Alger are dramatized in a 2012 Italian film *Il Primo Uomo* based on his posthumous novel *Le Premier Homme*, the manuscript for which was found in the wreckage of the car in which Camus died in 1960 (two years prior to the French loss of Algeria). There is no reference to the meeting with Soustelle in either the novel or film adaptation.[165]

Camus was among those who believed that Soustelle transformed into a hard line militarist in response to FLN terrorism. In a letter to his friend Andre Rosfelder, written after his return from Algeria in pursuit of the civil truce, Camus expressed great frustration with Soustelle who had just stepped down as governor general, suggesting that Soustelle's turn of mind signified a devastating lost opportunity for the sort of federalism that Camus imagined as a way out of the conflict. Camus hoped for a quick political integration which could lead inevitably, he thought, to a federal arrangement between France and Algeria. Camus thought Soustelle arrived with the right idea but stalled in response to the military situation:

> *Après réflexion je n'ai aucune confiance (en Soustelle). Vous pouvez faire état auprès de vos amis de ce que je vous dis. Qu'ils essaient seulement de comprendre qu'un homme comme moi, qui n'a jamais connu le découragement, et qui a horreur de toute complaisance, ne vous écrit ceci sans raison. Je suis déchiré, voilà la vérité.*[166]

> Upon reflection, I have no confidence (in Soustelle.) You can let your friends know what I'm telling you. I trust they will understand that a man such as myself who has never been discouraged, and who is horrified by any convenience, does not write that without cause. I'm torn apart, that's the truth.

Camus was not the only French intellectual "torn apart" by Algeria. In the years following his departure as governor general, Soustelle's convictions about Algeria would lead him, for a time, toward anti-democratic, even murderous opposition to Algerian independence. After de Gaulle's abrupt about face on keeping Algeria, Soustelle, the product of liberal, democratic, republican values, insisted that his plan could have saved the day if only he had been given sufficient time and the French had held their nerve.[167] Soustelle defied overwhelming democratic evidence that the majority of French citizens, exhausted by eight years of warfare, approved independence: the public ratified de Gaulle's plan in a national referendum in April 1962. We don't know if FLN terrorism turned Soustelle the reformer into a hardened advocate of a military solution. His biographer Bernard Ullmann shows that the betrayal that Soustelle felt at the hands of his former chief and father figure Charles de Gaulle over the abandonment of *l'Algérie française* launched Soustelle along a dark path of association with outlaws in plotting an assassination attempt on de Gaulle in 1961.[168] With that association and with Soustelle's refusal to accept the verdict of the French majority, Jacques Soustelle, an intellectual descendant of *les lumières* would, at least temporarily, refute and tarnish the values he claimed to uphold as both a political figure and social scientist. He never grasped the corrosive impact of 125 years of French colonial depredation and oppression and had an inflated view of the power of his reform package. French sociologist Pierre Bourdieu described French Algerians' own kind of garrison mentality, the psychological and cultural face of colonialism that Soustelle did not effectively confront:

> ... *l'Européen crée un environnement qui lui renvoie son image qui est la négation de l'univers ancien, un univers où il ne se sent plus étranger, où par un renversement naturel, l'Algérien finit par apparaître comme l'étranger.*[169]

> ... the European creates an environment that reflects his own image that is the negation of the old order, a universe in which he no longer feels himself to be a foreigner, but by natural reversal, the Algerian ends up appearing to be the foreigner.

In leaving Algeria in February 1956 with his term as governor general complete, Soustelle was accompanied to his ship by a crowd of thousands of *pied-noirs* who belatedly saw in Soustelle their figure of possible collective redemption. Newsreel footage and photojournalism reveal an extraordinary scene in a simultaneous outpouring of admiration and some sort of collective regret about what Soustelle's departure represented.[170] Scant months later, Soustelle emotionally recounted the moment in his memoir of his governorship. He foreshadowed his bitter response to subsequent events in *Algérie française* in a prosaic conflation of patriotism tied to Algier's place in the saga of French imperialism, its critical role in the Second World War as de Gaulle's final base before liberation and Soustelle's own hardening political convictions:

> *Bien des souvenirs d'une époque où l'on mourait beaucoup où la lutte signifiait quelque chose, me remontaient au coeur. Alger! Notre capitale dans la phase décisive de notre histoire récente! Qui pourrait consentir à y voir flotter aucun autre drapeau que le nôtre?*[171]

> Many memories of an era when many died in a meaningful struggle, came back to my heart. Algiers! Our capital in the decisive phase of our recent history! How could anyone consent to see any flag flutter there but our own!

Scott and Soustelle were unlikely candidates for the leading roles each would play in modern Canadian and French history. Scott, the son of a Protestant minister, seemingly more given to a love of nature, poetry and music than politics, became a central, galvanizing force of Canadian Indian policy for more than a quarter century. Soustelle, a working-class prodigy from southwestern France who was selected by age 17 for a brilliant academic future, became a dauphin and then a scourge of France's most significant military and political leader of the 20th century. Each life bears witness to the ideas expressed by Julien Benda in 1927 who declared that in an age of "the betrayal of the intellectuals" service to the nation-state trumps ethics.

A wall mural of General Charles de Gaulle, composed of photos of members of the French resistance during the Second World War. City Hall, Paris, 2010.

Chapter Six

PAST IS PRESENT

ON JUNE 11, 2008 a crowd gathered outside the House of Commons in Ottawa. A giant video screen on a flat-bed trailer hitched to a pick-up truck was in position for an overflow crowd of curious onlookers that gathered waiting to hear Prime Minister Stephen Harper speak to Parliament. Inside Parliament, Indigenous Elders, some accompanied by their grandchildren, filed into an upper lobby that leads to the public gallery overlooking the House floor. Harper was about to apologize to the Indigenous people of Canada on behalf of all Canadians for the abuses and injustices of the residential school system.

In the gallery where I stood, Indigenous Elders, their children and grandchildren looked down upon the prime minister. An elderly woman stood and looked directly at Harper while clutching an eagle feather in her fist. A young man in the same gallery section caressed a skin drum. On the floor of the House of Commons, members of Parliament and the leaders of Indigenous organizations turned their attention to the prime minister as he rose.[1] When Harper acknowledged the presence of Elders in the gallery all of Parliament erupted in loud applause. In his preamble, Harper thanked the leader of the New Democratic Party Jack Layton for influencing his thinking about the issue. In a strong, clear voice, Harper said in part:

> The government recognizes that the absence of an apology has been an impediment to healing and reconciliation. Therefore, on behalf of the government and all Canadians, I stand before you, in this chamber so central to our life as a country, to apologize to the Aboriginal peoples for Canada's role in the residential school system. To the approximately 80,000 living former students, and all family members and communities, the government now recognizes that it was wrong to forcibly remove children from their homes and we apologize for having done this. We now recognize that it was wrong to separate children from rich and vibrant cultures and traditions, that it created a void in many lives and communities, and we apologize for having done this… We now recognize that, far too often, these institutions gave rise to abuse or neglect and were inadequately controlled, and we apologize for failing to protect you…[2]

The prime minister apologized for one of the principal policies that Scott had implemented as a senior civil servant for the government of Canada.

At dawn on the morning of the apology, Indigenous spiritual leaders, Elders, residential school survivors and their supporters gathered on Victoria Island in the Ottawa River below Parliament Hill for a sunrise ceremony. They sought serenity and national reconciliation.

The previous evening a celebration of the apology was held in the ballroom of an Ottawa hotel. Assembly of First Nations National Chief Phil Fontaine and Minister for Indian Affairs and Northern Development Chuck Strahl were in attendance as the crowd of several hundred survivors, their families, Indigenous activists and supporters were treated to an evening of speeches, dancing and songs in honour of those who had suffered from the residential school experience; and also in celebration of a successful conclusion to a long struggle that had led to the prime minister's formal apology.

The evening reached an emotional apogee when singer/songwriter Willie Dunn performed his epic of Indigenous-Settler relations in Canada, "The Ballad of Crowfoot." The multiverse song features this chorus:

Crowfoot, Crowfoot, why the tears?
You've been a brave man, for many years.
Why the sadness? Why the sorrow?
Maybe there'll be a better tomorrow.[3]

In Paris on June 18, 2010, solemn commemorations marked the 70th anniversary of the 1940 *appel* that Charles de Gaulle transmitted from London letting *les français* and the world know that he had decided to lead the resistance to the Nazi occupation of France. Across the Atlantic Ocean, a military attaché to the French ambassador responded to that *appel*. Twenty-eight-year-old Jacques Soustelle soon sent word from the Mexican capital that he would serve de Gaulle. Soustelle joined Paul Rivet, Germaine Tillion, and others associated with *le Musée de l'Homme* in joining the resistance.

At the city hall of Paris, a huge photo of de Gaulle during the Second World World War framed against hundreds of smaller photos of those who had served the resistance towered over the square. Media was replete with anniversary coverage of de Gaulle's BBC broadcast, announcing the creation of the *France libre* movement.[4]

In 2008, French President Nicolas Sarkozy inaugurated *l'Historial Charles-de-Gaulle*, a multi-media digital museum at the *les Invalides* defence establishment in the centre of Paris.[5] Images of Soustelle appear in digital video displays by de Gaulle's side in Algeria when the general visited following his return to power in 1958. At that time, de Gaulle vowed to maintain *l'Algérie française*. Within two years, de Gaulle had changed his mind on Algeria and fired a disobedient Soustelle from his cabinet.[6] Soustelle's role in plotting an assassination attempt on de Gaulle is not referenced at *l'Historial Charles-de-Gaulle*.

In their biography of Pierre Trudeau, authors Stephen Clarkson and Christina McCall added a phrase to the lexicon of Canadian political history and journalism. Trudeau, they wrote, "haunts us still."[7] Clarkson and McCall argued that the highly atypical Canadian Trudeau, whose charisma, unapologetic intellectualism and sex appeal set him apart from "normal" political life in Canada, "haunted" a Canadian public which could never pin him down or figure him out.

Duncan Campbell Scott and Jacques Soustelle haunt me still. This work, which had its beginnings while floating in a canoe on Lake Superior waters off the mouth of the Pic River almost 30 years ago, has taken me on a wondrous journey of discovery. The overarching questions about these men linger and, yes, haunt.

How is that Scott could blithely, or not so blithely, ignore or remain detached from what, in the light of 21st century hindsight, are the worst human rights crimes in Canadian history? Revelations regarding hundreds of unmarked graves of Indigenous children near the sites of former residential schools dominated Canadian media and tarnished Canada's image abroad throughout the spring and summer of 2021.[8]

The inescapable truth is that Scott embodies, in stark cultural and policy terms, the fundamental disconnect between Canadian liberalism and a positive, meaningful expression of Indigenous economic, political and human rights in the settler state Canada. Scott was not merely an individual; he was a manifestation of a bad system made by humans and changeable by humans. The hell of the matter is that Scott, in my view, accomplished some great artistic works. The best of his poems and short stories deserve their place in the pantheon of Canadian literature.

What intellectual, or dare I say, neat ethical summation can be made of Jacques Soustelle? Soustelle plotted, but failed to kill his mentor Charles de Gaulle. A contrarian to the end of his days, some of Soustelle's late life opinions about South Africa and the Middle East seem outlandish to many.[10] French journalist and

Governor General Soustelle (centre) visiting a rural Algerian elementary school in 1955.

Soustelle biographer Bernard Ullmann labelled Soustelle, *le mal aimé*, "the unloved one," or perhaps more accurately still, "the black sheep."[11] Soustelle's unruly presence hovers still over both the discipline of French ethnology and memories of the French-Algerian conflict to the present day. As a social scientist, the ringing clarity, profound curiosity and bold, genre-busting multi-disciplinary ambition of his best works about Mexico remain relevant. As a political iconoclast, his unpopular predictions and denunciations of theocratic Islamist excesses and his premature advocacy of a proto-federal cohabitation between a European *métropole* such as France and the decolonizing nations of Africa, such as Algeria, seem now, at times, to have the ring of prophecy.

In concluding, I offer some personal and more speculative thoughts about aspects of Scott's work that perplex me still. I shall also reflect on Soustelle's continuing presence in discourse concerning the legacy of French policies in *l'Algérie française*.

Self-repudiation and shame in the writings of Duncan Campbell Scott

Scott's lesser-known literary work occasionally displays a more complex view of Indigenousness than might be presumed. Despite the self-assurance about Indian policy Scott expressed before parliamentary committees and in his departmental correspondence, a careful reading of some of his literary output and personal correspondence reveals a more ambivalent, even psychologically troubled perspective about his role.

It is understandable that many literary critics who have considered Duncan Campbell Scott focus primarily on his poetry. Poetry forms the bulk of his fictional creative output and the Indigenous poems present a complex shaft for exploration and interpretation given Scott's civil service duties and the historical (and current) tension in Canada over Indigenous rights and the dynamic of Indigenous-Settler relations. Scott's poems about Indigenous people often express a settler society's horror, fear and miscomprehension of Indigenous people in Canada. In addition, the poems generally share the certitude of Scott's civil service prose as to the ultimate fate of the "savage Indian," destined to be relegated to the memory (and art) of a dynamic, technologically superior Canadian master race.

Any self-examination that Scott undertook did not stem from religious ethics or a sense of formal Christian charity. His work required that he liaise with Christian denominations in the running of residential schools, but it seems Scott did so as a matter of public policy rather than personal religious conviction. Although he was a minister's son, Scott was not active in any form of organized religion in his adult life. Scott told the critic E.K. Brown that institutional Christianity was part of his past:

> I have left the religion of my youth behind me, so have all the other Methodists in the country, but I have not gone into the United Church, but into the wilderness, and I do not feel at all lost in it.[12]

Scott had faith in intellectual progress. As he argued in his "Poetry and Progress" address to the Royal Society of Canada in 1920, Scott imagined that in his idealized Canada, a nation borrowing from British tradition with an important French speaking minority, and therefore differentiated from the American republic, would advance in arts and science in a maturing, distinct national identity. His belief in progress was underscored in the essay by a dovetailing of scientific method with poetic expression:

> The mental process by which a poet develops the germ of his poem and perfects it is analogous to the process by which a mathematician develops his problem from vagueness to a complete demon-

stration, or to the mental process whereby the shadow of the truth apprehended by the biologist becomes proven fact.[13]

Having aligned himself, the poet, with the progressive aims of science, Scott then argued that the art of poetry in a modernizing Canada could achieve an artistic expression that could fuse material and spiritual growth. Scott argued that an accomplished poet possesses a power akin to divine creation:

> This spirit endeavours to interpret the world in new terms of beauty, to find unique symbols, images and analogies for the varied forms of life. It absorbs science and philosophy, and anticipates social progress in terms of ideality. It is rare, but it is ever present, for what is it but the flickering and pulsation of the force that created the world?[14]

The spiritual forces present in Scott's poems seldom bring comfort. Phantoms, ghosts and nightmarish figures often appear. As we have seen earlier, "Powassan's Drum," one of his most accomplished and confounding works, depicts the nightmarish state provoked by an intellectual incapacity to comprehend forms of Indigenous spirituality. The contradictory muddle of policies of removal and assimilation that riddled Canadian Indian policy also bedeviled Scott's poetics. His poetic themes are rarely scientific or materialistic.

Another contradiction occasionally crops up in Scott's *oeuvre*: the sense of alienation in a natural world inhabited and defined by the presence of Indigenous peoples, yet suffused by a degree of comfort. In Scott's *Untitled Novel*, ca. 1905, the hero Robin Garrabant, the illegitimate son of a prosperous logger, has achieved business and political success as a member of the Canadian Parliament. With the death of a young woman that he had loved, Garrabant takes leave of his parliamentary duties for a week to seek solace in the Gatineau Hills:

> Two days later he had pitched his tents on the shores of Lake Achigan, nine miles east of Maniwaki. He was literally in the wilderness, the lumbermen had cut and carried off the best pine, but there was no settlement near him, not even a squatter's cabin, for many miles.[15]

The rivers and lakes of the Gatineau were the sites for the canoe trips that Scott took with his friend, the poet Archibald Lampman. The unpublished novel reveals Scott's familiarity with the region:

> In a few hours he grew to be but an item in this tranquil life, the loons fished and startled the heights with their ecstatic laughter, the wild geese played before their nests in the cool of early night, the beaver worked confidently at his dams, the deer came down with the dew to drink of the cool water and stamped upon the hard sand, the lake, like a giant mirror, took every change of sky, every alteration in colour of rock and wood, and he, taking up his part in this wild life, paddled, swam, fished and walked for hours through the old roads that were paths of sleep and oblivion so deep were they covered with moss. One morning he stood in the midst of an Indian camp; long ago they had cured venison there and the rude cedar cleavers, the smoke-frames and rolls of birch-bark were still upon the ground. Here were the relics of savage life, and it came to him curiously as a fact illustrated simultaneously by a thousand incidents from his past life that he, like these people, had been successful where he accepted and used natural opportunities.[16]

On this occasion Scott's hero identified with an Indigenous past. There were no living Indigenous people present at the fictional campsite. Scott's depiction of Garrabant at an abandoned campsite evokes an Indigenousness that provided inspiration, comfort and guidance to those alive in a settler present. Scott, the novelist, conjured images of a vanishing race as inspirational while at the same time engaging in his "day job" of ridding Indigenous peoples from the body politic of the Canadian nation.

If the *Untitled Novel* hints at some familiarity with the surroundings and ways of life of Indigenous peoples, it offers no clues as to Scott's feelings about his responsibility in Indigenous-Settler relations of his day. It is in a short story where one can detect an expression of regret, remorse and even self-abnegation over the matter in Scott's fictional work. *Expiation* was first published in 1923.[17] In this short tale set in 1808, a Scottish trader named Forbes Macrimmon is engaged by the Hudson's Bay Company at Missanabie Post. At that time, the Hudson's Bay Company was pitted in competition with "the French company"– the North West Company, with its headquarters in Montreal.

Missanabie Post is located in a region that Scott knew having travelled in the James Bay territory of Ontario in 1905 and 1906 on the Treaty 9 expedition. The main Indigenous character in the story, Daniel Wascowin, takes his name from the cook who accompanied Scott and his fellow Treaty 9 commissioners in the summer of 1905. The real Daniel Wascowin was also the subject of one of Scott's photographic portraits taken that summer, shot in profile seated by the hull of an overturned birch bark freighter canoe.[18]

In *Expiation* the "great hunter," Daniel Wascowin is Macrimmon's ally and principal asset in the contest with the usurping French trader, Pierre Loudet:

> His chief hope lay in his servant Daniel Wascowin. Daniel was almost a pure Indian, but there was a little white blood in him. He was a great hunter, who always took thrice as many skins as any one else, and his prowess gave him a position of control over the other Indians.[19]

Macrimmon's short-lived advantage over Loudet is due to Wascowin's expertise and loyalty. The partnership between Macrimmon and Wascowin is tested one evening when Macrimmon drinks "deep in the French company's rum" in the company of Loudet. In a drunken state Macrimmon catches sight of a Hudson's Bay Company copper bottomed pail in Loudet's quarters. Such items were valuable trading goods coveted by the best Indigenous fur trappers. Macrimmon in an angry hung-over state then accuses Wascowin of trading with the enemy. In a macabre turn, Macrimmon fires a pistol shot on each side of Wascowin's head to teach him a painful lesson. The scarred and deafened Wascowin leaves Missanabie Post. Deprived by his own angry actions, and of Daniel Wascowin's guidance and his influence over Indigenous traders, Macrimmon's business founders. "His" Indians defect to the French and Macrimmon is shamefully demoted by the company.

Three springs later following his disgrace, Macrimmon hears that a weakened Wascowin and his wife have returned from their trapping grounds. Pathetically, the wife can only proffer three mink skins of very little value because her husband is ill and incapable of hunting successfully because he was deafened by Macrimmon's angry outburst. Macrimmon goes to find his old friend:

> Daniel had crawled out of his canoe, and lay at the landing-place, unable to move. There was just a spark of spirit left in the body of bone and skin. He tried to smile as Macrimmon bent over him. On his forehead he saw the mark he had put there – the two crescents made by the hot pistol-barrels, blackened by powder as if tattooed. Yielding up at that moment everything of self there was in him, Macrimmon lifted the Indian in his arms, carried him to the house, and put him in his own bed...
> In the morning light the two men could only look helplessly into each other's eyes; and in a little while two of the eyes were darkened.[20]

Following Wascowin's death, the story concludes hauntingly, as it begins, with the spectre of a grieving Macrimmon wandering alone in the community wearing the three tanned mink pelts, "like a fillet bound upon his brow." Scott writes that the meagre skins dangling bizarrely from Macrimmon's head, "seemed to him symbols of the grievous wrong."[21]

In *Expiation*, Scott created a character in a position of power over Indigenous people who greatly regrets a wrong he has committed. The story is almost singular in Scott's fictional work for its representation of friendship between white and Indigenous men. Macrimmon comes to the tragic, guilt-ridden realization that he has unjustly brutalized and mortally wounded his only ally and friend in the deep Canadian bush. This fictional relationship stands in stark contrast to the civil servant who haughtily dismissed Indigenous opponents of Canadian Indian policy.

Another hint of self-examination about Indian policy is found in the letters Scott wrote to the young Elise Aylen. Two years prior to his retirement from the civil service, Scott stayed at The Empress Hotel in Victoria on departmental business. At that time, Scott and the department were vigorously attacking the "potlatch" in British Columbia and actively resisting Indigenous claims to land in the province. In a page of tightly packed scrawl attached to a short letter on Empress Hotel letterhead with a circle marked "my room" playfully scrawled on the letterhead's illustration of the hotel, Scott delivered a *cri de coeur* to the young woman he was courting in Ottawa:

> The presence of the mystery of life & the universe is intense. It may become a solace. If the mystery were solved for an individual that life would have lost all flavour, if the solution became a possession of the race mankind would cease to exist – To search it out so eagerly & forcefully becomes a torment But without hope of knowing the secret of being, what joy to feel oneself in the flow & very essence of the mystery, content to have this unresolvable secret between oneself and the Master of Life This quiescence will result in greater receptivity and The soul with further messages, hints, intuitions from the fresh center of all feeling that will surpass any knowledge that it could gain by searching for positive knowledge. Then why suffer dear Elise? I ask a question I cannot answer. For a mind and a heart like yours there should be an equipoise and an agreement but the lack of physical strength comes between them. I feel foolish in writing this as I am not bringing help with full hands. My philosophy after a life of drift is no consolation to one who is young & who wants sweetness and activity – I know now that that I have never fought against anything nor worked for anything but just accepted & drifted from point to point. I have dimly felt that if I worked & protested & resisted I should be wrecked – so maybe you will understand why with some gifts I have done so little – this confession will not help you and I seem to be treating you like a restless child – 'Now be quiet Elise!' & that sort of admonition – I think – that somehow & likely sooner than we think you will achieve a greater happiness.[22]

The then almost 70-year-old Scott made his confession of moral impotence to his 27-year-old girlfriend. Was he writing about his role in Canadian Indian policy? What is the source of such anguish in a man writing two years prior to his civil service retirement about his "life of drift" during which he "never fought against anything or worked for anything but just accepted" because "I have dimly felt that if I worked & protested & resisted I should be wrecked?" He may have been trying to impress his young girlfriend or genuinely grieving over his career of attacking Indigenous peoples. The answer is unknowable. Yet, in both scenarios, Scott reveals a recognition that his actions were not honourable.

Jacques Soustelle and discourse over the Franco-Algerian conflict

Notre conviction est faite. Oui, le déploiement de la force française est juste: pour protéger les uns et les autres contre la Terreur. Il faut que cette force juste aille jusqu'à la vraie victoire : la pacification des cœurs. Cette victoire ne sera pas celle du passé: c'est dans l'élan hardi de larges reformes économiques, sociales et politiques que se réalisera en Algérie une véritable communauté.[23]

  - Jacques Soustelle

We have made our choice. Yes, the deployment of French force is justified: to protect everyone from the Terror. This force must continue until real victory is achieved: the pacification of hearts. This victory will not simply be of the past: it is only with the vigour of significant economic, social and political reforms that a veritable Algerian community will come into being.

Le terrorisme est aussi une erreur quant à ses conséquences. Son premier résultat, en effet, et de fermer la bouche aux Français libéraux de l'Algérie et par conséquent, de renforcer le parti de la réaction et de la répression. Ceux qui, sur les lieux-mêmes, pourraient faire entendre la voix de la raison (et le gouverneur général lui-même) se voient imposer silence au nom de l'instituteur assassiné, du médecin blessé, du passant égorgé et des écoles incendiées.[24]

  - Albert Camus

Terrorism is also in error because of the consequences it produces. Its first effect is to close the mouths of French liberals in Algeria, and by result reinforcing the party of reaction and repression. Those who, even those living there (and the governor general himself) who could make understandable the voice of reason see silence imposed about the assassinated teacher, the wounded doctor, the bystander with his throat slashed and burnt out schools.

Les gens qui parlent d'abandon sont des imbéciles: il n'y a pas à abandonner ce que nous n'avons jamais possédé. Il s'agit, tout au contraire, de construire avec les Algériens des relations nouvelles entre une France libre et une Algérie libérée. Mais n'allons pas, surtout, nous laisser détourner de notre tâche par la mystification réformiste. Le néo-colonialiste est un niais qui croit qu'on peut aménager le système coloniale – ou un malin qui propose des réformes parce qu'il sait qu'elles sont inefficaces.[25]

  - Jean-Paul Sartre

People who speak of abandonment (of *l'Algérie française*) are imbeciles: one can't abandon what one never possessed. It's a matter, on the contrary, to build new relationships with Algerians between a free France and a liberated Algeria. But above all we should not be distracted from our task by reformist mystification. The neo colonialist is a simpleton who thinks one can rearrange the colonial system – or he's a nasty sort who proposes reforms because he knows they will be ineffective.

On aurait pu abréger la guerre de plusieurs années, cela n'aurait rien change quant au résultât: quand un pays évolue vers l'indépendance, c'est comme une avalanche, vous ne l'arrêtez pas. L'Algérie serait donc allée quand même jusqu'au fond du val de l'indépendance.[26]

  - Germaine Tillion

We could have carried the war on for many years, it wouldn't have changed the result: when a country begins its evolution to independence, it's like an avalanche, you don't stop it. Algeria would have gone anyway to the bottom of the valley of independence.

Ceux qui prônent l'intégration ont une cervelle de colibri même si ils sont très savants. Essayez d'intégrer de l'huile et du vinaigre. Agitez la bouteille. Au bout d'un moment ils se sépareront de nouveau. Les Arabes sont des Arabes, les Français sont des Français. Vous croyez que le corps français peut absorber dix millions de musulamns, qui demain seront vingt millions et apès demain quarante?[27]
  - Charles de Gaulle

Those who propose integration have got hummingbird brains even though they are well educated. Try to integrate oil and vinegar. Shake the bottle. After a while the two separate again. Arabs are Arabs, The French are French. Do you believe the French polity could absorb ten million Moslems, that tomorrow will be twenty million and after that forty?

JACQUES SOUSTELLE is central to an ongoing conversation among historians and political scientists about the decline of French imperial power in the modern era.[28] In his lifetime, he engaged vociferously with the likes of Charles de Gaulle, Jean Paul Sartre, Simone de Beauvoir and Raymond Aron. Most recently, Soustelle is experiencing a moment of quasi rehabilitation. Author Alain Herbeth's biography puts a positive spin on *le plan Soustelle* in *l'Algérie française*.[29] Julian Jackson, an eminent British historian of France, describes a Soustelle betrayed and belittled over his efforts in Algeria by his one-time mentor de Gaulle.[30] Speaking about his book at the University of Toronto in April 2019, Jackson said that Soustelle was psychologically tortured by de Gaulle and was bitter after being spurned by a man Soustelle considered a father figure.

More controversially, in 2018, French journalist and broadcaster Éric Zemmour, a highly outspoken and visible political commentator of Algerian Jewish descent, offered his own lengthy analysis of Soustelle.[31] Zemmour faintly praised Soustelle for his high-minded, but naive integrationist approach. Zemmour in turn slammed de Gaulle for ultimately defending a reductive vision of French national identity in his policies towards Algeria and Islam. His revisiting the antagonism between de Gaulle and his one-time protégé is testament to the way in which Soustelle's agonizing over *intégration* echoes persistently in French society. A lightning rod for persistent racial tensions in France, Zemmour has been fined for his views about immigration, Islam and crime in France.[32] In late 2021, Zemmour announced his candidacy for the French presidency.

During Soustelle's career, the debate over Algeria became a nasty family feud among intellectuals in *la métropole*. It was a feud that Soustelle waded into with conviction and, at times, venom. Following his return to France in 1956 at the end of his administration, Soustelle did not pause. He quickly published a memoir of his year-long sojourn as governor general.[33] In *Aimée et souffrante Algérie*, Soustelle argued for a maintenance of *le plan Soustelle* by a new leftist government. When he appeared on television after the book was released, he drew explicit links between his impressions of the situation in Algeria with the expertise he had gained in the 1930s as a doctoral student in Mexico.[34] He argued passionately that *intégration* based on Mexican *indigenismo* would be vindicated.

Unlike Franco-Algerian writer Albert Camus, who believed that Soustelle squandered France's last chance at redemption in Algeria, Germaine Tillion believed the point of no return was reached following Soustelle's departure. Tillion pointed to the decision by President Guy Mollet and Soustelle's successor Robert Lacoste, both socialists, to grant full police powers to the French military in Algeria. In her final years, Tillion still despaired over that decision which marked for her an irrevocable end to France's hopes of a "civil truce" and peace along the lines championed by Camus.[35]

By 1956, erstwhile friends Camus and Jean-Paul Sartre had already famously parted company following a 1952 feud in print over the inhumane excesses of Soviet communism. Sartre clung to a belief that the inevitable correctness of Marxist thought meant the socialist project must be defended. Camus believed that terror itself was an inevitable result of Marxist ideology. Camus also believed, as Soustelle did, that Moscow's allies in the decolonizing world like Algeria's FLN were terrorists rather than freedom fighters. At the height of the Cold War, Camus linked Algerian liberation movements to the threat of Soviet tyranny:

> ..averti depuis longtemps des réalités Algériennes, je ne puis non plus approuver une politique de démission qui abdonnerait le people arabe à une plus grande misère, arracherait de ses racines séculaires le peuple français de l'Algérie et favoriseraient seulement, sans profit pour personne, le nouvel impérialisme qui menace la liberté de la France et de l'Occident.[36]

> Having long been aware of Algerian reality, I cannot approve a policy of flight which would abandon the Arab people to even greater misery, jerked from the secular roots of the French people of Algeria to be favoured exclusively, without benefit to anyone, to the new imperialism that threatens the liberty of France and the West.

As an enthusiasm for decolonization and sympathy with the FLN gained support among leftists like Sartre, Camus grew ever more uneasy:

> Après tout, Gandhi a prouvé qu'on pouvait lutter pour son people, et vaincre, sans cesser un seul jour de rester estimable. Quelle que soit la cause que l'on defend, elle restera toujours déshonorée par le massacre d'une foule innocente où le tueur sait d'avance qu'il atteindre la femme et l'enfant.[37]

> Above all, Gandhi proved that one can struggle for one's people, and win, without ceasing to be admirable for a single day. Whatever the case one defends may be, it will always be dishonoured by the massacre of an innocent crowd, or by the killer who knows in advance that he will harm women and children.

Sartre lambasted "*notre réaliste au coeur tendre*" [our tender-hearted realist] for ill-considered aspirations of reform in Algeria. Sartre was clearly taking aim at Camus, Soustelle and all other humanitarian liberals without explicitly naming them:

> Et pourtant il est impossible de commencer les transformations économiques parce que la misère et le désespoir des Algériens sont l'effet direct et nécessaire du colonialisme et qu'on ne les supprimer jamais tant que le colonialisme durera. C'est que savant tous les Algériens conscient. Et tous sont d'accord avec ce mot d'un Musulman; "Un pas en avant, deux pas en arrière. Voilà la réforme coloniale.[38]

> And however it is impossible to begin the economic transformations because the poverty and despair of Algerians are the direct and necessary result of colonialism and these will never diminish as long as colonialism lasts. This is what conscious Algerians know. And everyone agrees with this statement from a Muslim: "One step forward, two back. That's colonial reform."

Sartre the urbane, privileged Parisian intellectual fancied that he made common cause with the oppressed of the colonized world. His anti-colonial writings are a screed against French intervention in Africa and Asia. He argued that effective partnerships between *la métropole* and Algeria could only be forged following liberation.[39] Unlike Camus, who claimed he could never approve of violence against civilians by any party, Sartre came to embrace the violence of decolonization. Sartre and his companion Simone de Beauvoir ridiculed Camus' call for a civil truce because in their assessment French colonialism had been victimizing Algerian civilians for 126 years.[40]

Sartre's anti-colonial writings have a scintilla of secular religion about them. For a contemporary reader, his confidence in liberation movements amounts to blind faith. To his credit, he does not shy from the devastation of Indigenous economies and culture caused by the favouring of settler interests. In this regard, Sartre exposed French colonial depredations and cruelty in Algeria with a clarity that Soustelle and Camus lacked.

The polemic between Albert Camus and Jean-Paul Sartre was echoed in a highly publicized sparring match between Soustelle and the philosopher Raymond Aron. Aron's "abandonment" (to use Soustelle's phrase) of French Algeria, was particularly stinging to Soustelle. Aron, like Soustelle, was considered to be a man of the centre. It was one thing to have well known leftists such as Sartre and his partner Simone de Beauvoir embrace Frantz Fanon and the FLN, it was quite another for Soustelle to witness the unexpected defection of intellectuals of "*le juste milieu*" (those in the centre) such as Aron. In response to Aron's public declaration that he could no longer support the French government's policies in Algeria, Soustelle quickly published a denunciation of what he regarded as a suddenly fashionable "decadence" among French intellectuals in their retreat from democratic values and embrace of Marxist revolutionaries *outre mer*. With the fire and vitriol that would fuel Soustelle's declarations about Algeria well into the 1960s, he denounced Aron and his ilk for nothing less than treason:

> *J'imagine le mépris des chefs fellagha pour les Français qui les soutiennent, pour ces auxiliaires qui brandissent le stylo a Paris tandis que les guerriers tirent des coups de feu dans la montagne. Le conflit algérien est a 80% une guerre psychologique ou l'adversaire trouve son arsenal chez nous.*[41]

> I imagine the anger of peasant leaders at the French who they support, for these auxiliaries who brandish a pen in Paris while fighters exchange gunfire in the mountains. The Algerian conflict is 80% psychological and the adversary finds his weaponry at our place.

Soustelle was affronted by Aron's position on the "heroism" of abandoning Algeria and allowing for independence. Throughout his defence of *l'Algérie française*, Soustelle frequently invoked his *résistant* anti-Nazi past as credible evidence of the constancy of his patriotism.[42] Soustelle bridled at Aron's argument that he, Aron, came to support Algerian independence because that position was consistent with republican values of the resistance. This sort of split between former French opponents of the German occupation over the Algerian question was widespread. The hard and courageous choice in the 1950s and 1960s, according to Soustelle, was in defending *l'Algérie française*. As far as Soustelle was concerned, Aron chose correctly in 1940 to oppose Hitler, but he was dead wrong in 1957 to support a proto-fascist FLN.

In his pamphlet, Aron expressly condemned policy of *intégration* claiming that Soustelle's reforms were too little, too late. In response, Soustelle undertook a vigorous defence of his policy and accused Aron and likeminded French intellectuals of the sort of blindness that led *les clercs* of the 18th century such as Voltaire to dismiss the importance of French possessions like *la Nouvelle France*:

> *On est stupéfait de la désinvolture avec laquelle notre nouveau Voltaire règle dédaigneusement le cas des « sables brulants » comme son illustre prédécesseur sacrifiait les « arpents de neige » du Canada.*[43]

> One is gobsmacked by the casualness with which our new Voltaire judges with disdain the case of "burning sands" just as his illustrious predecessor sacrificed the snowy acres of Canada.

Twentieth century energy politics and the Cold War were also deployed in arguments made by the respective camps. Soustelle insisted that France had to maintain its energy projects in cooperation with North African states in the Sahara as a fulcrum against dependence on either the United States or Arab countries with ties to the Soviet Union. This is classic Gaullist positioning of France vis à vis the Cold War superpowers.[44] In due course, de Gaulle managed to protect French business interests in the southern Sahara through the Evian Accords. Before he was dismissed from de Gaulle's cabinet because of his recalcitrance over Algeria, Soustelle had appeared on the cover of European edition of *TIME Magazine* to vaunt the great energy future in France's African possessions.[45]

Through invoking the need for energy independence and raising the scare over the FLN's ties to Egyptian nationalist leader Gamal Abdel Nasser and to Soviet-ruled Moscow, Soustelle exemplified a certain kind of French nationalism. This was the kind Soustelle had once associated with de Gaulle, that strove to maintain some French wiggle room between camps in the Cold War.

In his *riposte* to Aron, Soustelle also resolutely denied that Algeria had colonial status under French rule, it had, he argued, the status of *"une symbiose... une création"* [a symbiosis... a creation] that could eventually, as the argument went, become integrated fully into France.[46] In this respect, Soustelle's arguments resembled those of Camus, a thinker with whom Soustelle is seldom linked. In the preface to a collection of his political writings about Algeria, Camus clearly stated his preference for French-styled civilization over what he regarded as Soviet backed alternatives of dubious national liberation.[47] And with perhaps an admission of weary fatalism, Camus conceded defeat for his kind of humanism in face of a new logic of liberation that was tilted, as he sought, toward the Soviet empire:

> *Le temps des colonialismes est fini, il faut le savoir seulement et en tirer les conséquences. Et l'Occident qui, en dix ans, a donné l'autonomie à une douzaine de colonies mérite a cet égard plus de respect, et surtout, de patience que la Russie, que dans le même temps, a colonisé ou place sous un protectorat implacable une douzaine de pays de grande et ancienne civilisation.*[48]

> The colonial era is over, we must recognize this and understand the consequences. And the West which in the space of 10 years has granted autonomy to a dozen colonies deserves in this regard more respect, and above all, patience than Russia which over the same period, has colonized or placed under its protection a dozen countries belonging to a great and ancient civilization.

While Camus, Soustelle and Tillion agonized over difficult Algerian choices, Aron, Sartre and others on their side saw the Algerian conflict as an opportunity for France to place itself, however belatedly, on the right side of history by embracing Marxist de-colonizing movements throughout the world.

In his response to Aron, Soustelle stood by his former colleague in ethnology, the resistance and in the government of French Algeria, Germaine Tillion, and deferred to her specialized knowledge. Soustelle credits her with explaining best how France had brought Algeria to the threshold of modernity and French republican duty of working with Algerians to advance the process of education, urbanization and industrialization:

> *Mais venons-en aux deuxième problème: qu'est-ce que la France représente, économiquement, pour l'Algérie? Elle représente simplement la différence entre la vie et la mort. Je voudrais que personne n'entreprenne de raisonner sur ce problème sans avoir lu la brochure mince mais combien substantielle de Germaine Tillion. On y voit décrit avec une véracité criante l'affreux processus de paupérisation, pire, de « clochardisation » comme dit Germaine Tillion, qui broie le peuple des fellahs. On y voit comment tout se métamorphose en cendres et en ruine entre les mains de ces malheureux arrachés par nous à leur monde archaïque et pas encore entres dans le monde moderne. Tout le drame de l'Algérie est là. Que l'indépendance puisée y mettre un terme est un mensonge dérisoire ; le fellagha qui croit lutter pour voir « la fin de notre misère » ne sait pas qu'il est cyniquement trompe par la Ligue Arabe et des néo-féodaux avides de pourvoir; il ne sait pas que son Etat arabe, si jamais il voyait le jour, le condamnerait a une misère vingt fois plus profonde.*[49]

But let's get to the second problem: what does France represent economically for Algeria? She quite simply represents the difference between life and death. I hope no one undertakes to understand this problem without having read the slim but substantial brochure of Germaine Tillion (Algeria 1957). One will find described with screaming truth the tragic process of pauperization, "clochardi-sation" as Germaine Tillion calls it, that afflicts the peasants. One sees in this work the metamorphosis into ashes and ruins of these unfortunates pulled from us from their archaic world but not yet entered into the modern one. All of the Algerian drama is there. It's a derisory illusion and lie to believe that independence will put an end to it; the peasant who believes he is fighting to "put an end to our poverty" does not know that he is being cynically tricked by the Arab League and that these neo-feudalists covet power. He doesn't know that his Arab state, if it ever sees the light of day, will condemn him to a poverty twenty times more severe.

Tillion wrote her most enduring analysis of Algeria just after serving in Soustelle's cabinet. Her now famous description of "*clochardisation*" was a sobering reality check on Soustelle's idealized trumpeting of Mexican *indigenismo* and it underscored the humanitarian social obligation Tillion believed was at the centre of ethnology:

> *Croyez-moi, ce n'est pas une situation enviable. Comme me disait un vieux Kabyle : « Vous nous avez emmenés au milieu du gué, et nous y avez laisses. »*
> *…Les autres – quatre à cinq d'êtres humains, tous appartenant a la majorité – ont progressivement perdu les biens matériels et les stabilités spirituelles des sociétés anciennes, sans avoir pu, faute d'instruction et de technicité, devenir des hommes modernes. Ils se trouvent à la charnière des deux mondes – au milieu du gué – hantés par le passé qu'ils connaissent un pue enfiévrés par l'avenir qu'ils ont palpé en migrant, mais les mains vides et le ventre creux, entre leurs fantômes et leurs fièvres.*[50]

> Believe me, it is not an enviable situation. Like an old man from the Kabylia told me: "You took us to the middle of the creek and left us there." The rest, four to five human beings, all belonging to the majority, have progressively lost their material well being, their spiritual stability of ancient societies, without having been able, because of a lack of technology and education, to become modern beings. They find themselves at the hinge of two worlds – in the middle of the creek – haunted by the past that they know and a bit feverish from a future that they have brushed in migrating, but with empty hands and hollow stomachs, between ghosts and fevers.

In concluding his response to Aron, Soustelle decried the fatalism of French elites and the collusion of a "New Left" and a "New Right" (represented, as Soustelle would have it, by the conservative Aron) over Algeria. Soustelle persisted in emphasizing hope and prospects for cooperation. Referencing his own social scientific background, Soustelle claimed to have met recently with Algerian and European colleagues about new archaeological work undertaken in the mountains of Algeria for the museum in Alger.[51] Soustelle asserted that the real issue was decadence. Like his speculations about the collapse of Mayan civilizations while roaming the Lacondón rainforest in the 1930s, which, he argued, had occurred because Mayan elites distanced themselves from the concerns of normal people, Soustelle feared that Algeria was a symptom of a broader French malaise – a lack of will on the part of intellectuals in government, the civil service and the academy – *les clercs*, to use Julien Benda's term – to truly champion democracy in the face of competing ideologies.[52] In Soustelle's view, French intellectuals might take the fashionable position of abandoning Algeria, but in doing so they were quitting on ordinary Algerians be they Muslims, Jews, Christians or secular Europeans, and on France itself. In his polemical excesses, Soustelle argued that French civilization itself

Buffy Sainte-Marie performing at the 2015 concert in Ottawa, Ontario.

City Hall, Ottawa, Ontario, Marion Dewar Plaza, *June 3 2015*

A performer in her 70s bursts energetically onto stage in a multi-coloured jacket holding her arms wide above her head and approaches a microphone at centre stage. Indigenous star Buffy Sainte-Marie is performing a concert in downtown Ottawa at the closing ceremonies of the Truth and Reconciliation Commission. Before she begins a raucous set with her band, Ms. Sainte-Marie utters an unpleasant truth in a calm, deliberate tone. She says that she doesn't accept the proposition that non-Indigenous Canadians did not know about the realities of residential schools. She says such citizens had abundant opportunity to be informed over several decades. As I glance about me at surrounding faces in the crowd, it appears her remarks have an unsettling effect.

was at stake. He harked again to his academic past, even in Latin America French culture and language, he argued, continued to have influence as an alternative to American or Soviet power. France, Soustelle insisted, in deserting Algeria would willingly turn its back on worthy achievements of *la mission civilisatrice* in northern Africa.[53]

The chasm between French intellectuals over Algeria has fascinated many commentators. The spectacle of public argument between Camus and Sartre that began over Soviet-style communism and continued over French actions in Algeria has spawned numerous articles and monographs.[54] Historians of latter-day French Algeria are often drawn to Camus' magisterially disturbing creation Meursault, the feckless, morose, seemingly unmotivated *pied noir* killer protagonist of *L'étranger*.[55] Blinded by the sun Meursault guns down an unnamed Arab on a beach. It is a pointless, careless act of which Meursault is inexplicably proud. *L'étranger* is a non-ideological, humane prism into the complicated nature of relations between European and Indigenous Algerians.

To my way of thinking, a lesser-known work by Camus best encapsulates his tortured view of the conflict in his native land. The short story *L'hôte* evokes a situation that dramatically humanizes Soustelle's failed mission as governor general. *L'hôte* is the story of a *pied noir* French *instituteur*, an elementary school teacher, named Daru in an Algerian mountain school in an arid region not far from the Mediterranean coast.[56] The story recounts how Daru becomes fatally caught between factions in the Algerian/French conflict while trying to save an Algerian prisoner of the French police. The character Daru is precisely the sort of Franco-Algerian idealist that first rallied to the side of Soustelle and Tillion when they embarked on the creation of *centres sociaux*. The real-life equivalent to the murderous absurdity experienced by the fictional Daru is what rendered Camus speechless about his native land in the final years of his life. Like Camus, and others of good faith such as Soustelle and Tillion, the character Daru attempted pathetically, in his way, to salvage French honour and decency in Algeria. As a fitting testament to its power and the enduring scars of Algero-Franco memory of their conflict, Camus' story was adapted for the screen in 2014 by French director David Oelhoffen in *Loin des hommes* (Far from Men). Actor Viggo Mortensen plays Daru in a subversive turn that focuses on Daru's close relationship with Muslim villagers whose children he teaches, and with his Arabic and Berber friends who served with him in the French army during the Second World War, but then joined the FLN.[57]

More than half a century after Algerian independence of 1962, legacies of the Algerian-French war burst into polemic flame on a regular basis on both sides of the Mediterranean. Since the 1990s, the question of torture committed by French troops has resurfaced regularly in academic research, the press and parliamentary debates.[58] The shoddy treatment of Algerian military veterans who helped liberate France from the Nazis was the subject of *Indigènes*, an internationally acclaimed feature film in 2006.[59] Such veterans would form the military core of the Algerian independence movement when their faith in France died in the decade following the Second World War.

In 2007-08, Algerian filmmaker Jean-Pierre Lledo released *Algérie, histoires à ne pas dire*, a documentary film that took the contrarian view that not all Algerians supported independence in 1962 and that many Algerians of Islamic descent suffered after independence for their loyalties to France. The film attracted national media attention in France.[60] In February 2008, the film screened for two weeks in a cinema close to the Sorbonne campus of the University of Paris. Following the screenings director Lledo, film critics, historians and audience members participated in lively, sometimes fractious debates.[61] In 2011, Safinez Bousbia, a

Franco-Algerian director, delivered *El Gusto* her musical documentary about the deep ties between Algerian and French musicians in clubs of 1940s and 1950s Alger.[62]

In 2008, a novel by a second generation Algerian emigrant was both *fêted* and decried for its description of the "*ratonade*" of 1961 when loyalists of *l'Algérie Française* drowned north Africans in the Seine in a day of lynching.[63] In October 2012, President François Hollande acknowledged the killings.[64] In an address to the Algerian parliament, Hollande recognized the suffering caused by "unjust and brutal" French colonial policies in the country.[65] In 2015, novelist Michel Houellebecq really put the cat among the pigeons with his incendiary *Soumission* about an unsavoury French academic ensnared in an Islamist undermining of the French Republic from within.[66] The book was published on January 7, 2015, the same day as the infamous terrorist attack by Islamic fundamentalists on the offices of the satiric magazine *Charlie Hebdo* in downtown Paris.

In 2013 in Canada, places with names like Attawapiskat and Kesatchewan became staples of media and political discourse.[67] These troubled James Bay region communities in northern Ontario sit in the James Bay area where Duncan Campbell Scott brought Treaty 9 in the summers of 1905 and 1906. A hunger strike by Attawapiskat Chief Theresa Spence in the shadow of Parliament Hill, rail blockades, pipeline construction delays and the Idle No More Indigenous rights movement rose to prominence on the Canadian national agenda.[68] The investigation of residential schools, violence against Indigenous women and girls, fatalities among students from remote communities in places like Thunder Bay, Ontario and debates about fossil fuel pipeline construction through Indigenous territories are constant 21st century reminders of Canada's unfinished business in Indigenous-Settler relations.[69] Since the final report in 2015 of The Truth and Reconciliation Commission, Canadians and the world have wondered whether The Fair Dominion is a genocidal state.[70] In 2019, the final report of the National Inquiry into the Murder and Disappearance of Indigenous Women and Girls concluded that Canada treated Indigenous females with genocidal intent.[71]

Duncan Campbell Scott remains inextricably bound up in one of Canada's most punishing dramas. Scott's role continues to be the subject of media attention.[72] In 2013, author Mark Abley published his book about Scott that imagines conversations with Scott's ghost.[73] In 2014, Abenaki filmmaker Alanis Obomsawin explored the Treaty 9 legacy in her documentary *Trick or Treaty*.[74] In 2015, New Democratic Party parliamentarian Charlie Angus wrote *Children of the Broken Treaty* about miserable education options, appalling youth suicide rates and ill health in Treaty 9 communities.[75] These works underscore enduring concern with Scott's legacy.

A crisis of opioid use and suicide alongside renewed interest in mineral exploration make resolution of Indigenous grievances in Treaty 9 territory a test case for Canada's vow of reconciliation. Activists, health workers and storytellers document the difficult path ahead.[76]

Over 100 years following the supposed conclusion of Treaty 9 negotiations, economic, health and social crises in the communities as well as prospects for "The Ring of Fire" mining development trigger reconsideration of the undertakings made by Scott's team.[77]

Twenty-first century historical and journalistic inquiries underscore the shaky terms of what Scott believed to be a done deal in 1905-06.[78] The discovery of Scott's fellow treaty commissioner George McMartin's personal diaries supports Indigenous accounts that Scott and the commissioners warranted that traditional economic practices would be unhindered throughout the ceded territory. Members of the present-day Mishkeegogomang First Nation, the descendants of Osnaburgh's blind Chief Missabay who debated Treaty

DUNCAN CAMPBELL SCOTT
1862 - 1947

SCOTT IS RECOGNIZED AS ONE OF CANADA'S CONFEDERATION POETS. HIS WORK, INCLUDING SEVERAL VOLUMES OF POETRY AND SHORT STORIES, WAS INSPIRED BY THE CANADIAN WILDERNESS. HE IS ALSO NOTORIOUS FOR HIS 52-YEAR CAREER IN THE DEPARTMENT OF INDIAN AFFAIRS. AS DEPUTY SUPERINTENDENT, SCOTT OVERSAW THE ASSIMILATIONIST INDIAN RESIDENTIAL SCHOOL SYSTEM FOR ABORIGINAL CHILDREN, STATING HIS GOAL WAS "TO GET RID OF THE INDIAN PROBLEM." IN ITS 2015 REPORT, CANADA'S TRUTH AND RECONCILIATION COMMISSION SAID THAT THE INDIAN RESIDENTIAL SCHOOL SYSTEM AMOUNTED TO CULTURAL GENOCIDE.

SCOTT EST RECONNU COMME UN DES POÈTES DE LA CONFÉDÉRATION DU CANADA. SON ŒUVRE, DONT PLUSIEURS VOLUMES DE POÉSIE ET DE NOUVELLES, A ÉTÉ INSPIRÉE PAR LA NATURE SAUVAGE CANADIENNE. IL EST AUSSI CÉLÈBRE POUR SES 52 ANS DE CARRIÈRE AU MINISTÈRE DES AFFAIRES INDIENNES. À TITRE DE SURINTENDANT ADJOINT, IL A OBSERVÉ LE CARACTÈRE ASSIMILATEUR DES PENSIONNATS INDIENS POUR LES ENFANTS AUTOCHTONES EN DÉCLARANT QU'IL VISAIT À « SE DÉBARRASSER DU PROBLÈME INDIEN ». DANS SON RAPPORT DE 2015, LA COMMISSION DE VÉRITÉ ET RÉCONCILIATION DU CANADA A MENTIONNÉ QUE LE RÉSEAU DES PENSIONNATS INDIENS ÉQUIVALAIT À UN GÉNOCIDE CULTUREL.

GREAT CANADIAN PROFILES
PORTRAITS D'ÉMINENTS CANADIENS
BY/PAR
CIMETIÈRE BEECHWOOD CEMETERY

Plaque installed in 2016 at the Beechwood Cemetery, Ottawa, site of Scott's grave.

9's provisions with Scott, are contesting damages to traditional lands and waters in their territory.[79] The discovery of McMartin's diary bolstered efforts by other communities in the Treaty 9 territory seeking recognition of Queen Victoria's 1868 pledge of protection to the Indigenous peoples of Rupert's Land which Canada purchased from Britain at the time of Confederation.[80] These issues are very much in play. In 2018, residents of Ontario elected a majority Progressive Conservative government which immediately vowed to "Open up The North" and support development of the Ring of Fire.[81]

From where I write in Nogojiwanong – Peterborough, Ontario it is clear that work remains to be done. The lack of clean drinking water at Curve Lake First Nation just north of this small city has been testament to governmental incompetence and neglect. In 2020, Curve Lake launched litigation against the federal government in its frustration.[82] In summer 2021 on the cusp of an expected election call, an agreement in principle was reached by the federal government in Ottawa and multiple First Nations including Curve Lake involved in a class-action suit over undrinkable water.[83] Even with this welcome agreement, Ottawa is tardy in its 2015 commitment to solve the problem. The government of self-described Indigenous advocate Justin Trudeau claimed it would act with alacrity on recommendations of the Missing and Murdered Indigenous Women and Girls Inquiry (MMIWG). Advocates claim too little has been done.[84] Here in Nogojiwanong – Peterborough activists are protesting the lack of a murder charge in the downtown killing of Cileana Taylor

Ensa-be-bezhig Binoojiinh Gchi-piitendaagozi
Every Child Matters

JOIN US FOR A
HEALING TALK CIRCLE
ALL ARE WELCOME

SHARING STORIES OF RESILIENCE
FROM SPANISH RESIDENTIAL SCHOOL

Barbara Nolan
Dr. Edna Manitowabi
Dr. Shirley Williams
Martina Osawamick

Thursday June 3rd 7PM
to register: **https://bit.ly/2S3GRCp**

June 3, 2021

Scores of people of various ages both Indigenous and non-Indigenous gather virtually to listen to Elders Barbara Nolan, Dr. Shirley Williams, Dr. Edna Manitowabi and Martina Osawamick tell their stories of survival at residential school. The event takes place in the immediate aftermath of revelations of the unmarked graves of children near the grounds of the former Kamlooops Residential School in British Columbia. In the group at large, the grief is palpable even as mediated by the virtual communication of a pandemic. The principal speakers are clearly shaken by the weight of news suddenly dominating Canadian newscasts. Dr. Manitowabi wonders aloud why for so many years Canadians failed to accept or take action about the well documented abuses of the residential school system. With a mix of anger, compassion and steely determination she urges mainstream Canada to finally wake up to its national crime.

a woman from Curve Lake.[85] A proposal to advance implementation of The United Nations Declaration on the Rights of Indigenous People (UNDRIP) supported by the Trudeau government is embraced by some Indigenous organizations, but seen as toothless window dressing by some Indigenous critics.[86]

Recent scholarship and journalism in Canada continues to examine Scott's legacy, the coercive, sometimes violent, application of Canadian settlement across the west, and raise new levels of concern about a department with a culture of routine coercion and detachment from moral considerations in its relationship with Indigenous peoples.[87] Such works broaden knowledge and understanding of the government department where Duncan Campbell Scott worked for half a century and the policies he helped implement.

The discovery of unmarked graves in 2021 was sadly inevitable. Canada's complicity in the deaths of thousands of Indigenous children under its care in residential schools during the period Scott served the Indian Department was revealed nationally by the Truth and Reconciliation Commission. In 2016, activists allied with Reconciliation Canada added an accusatory plaque about Scott's role near his Ottawa gravesite stating that he was complicit in an act of cultural genocide.

In France, Jacques Soustelle remains an important figure in historical and political considerations of Algeria and the development of the social sciences.[88] Under Presidents François Hollande and Nikolas Sarkoczy, the French government, military, and business have repeatedly asserted French influence in north Africa. These developments might suggest that Soustelle's vision of cooperation and even of federal arrangements between France, Algeria and the former French colonies in Africa was not pure fancy. While falling short of official apologies, Hollande and his successor Emmanual Macron have acknowledged French malfeasance in Algeria. Hollande labelled French policies in Algeria as "brutal." As a presidential candidate Macron controversially said France's policies were a "crime against humanity" and once in power he became the first French president to acknowledge the use of torture in Algeria by French troops as official policy in 1957.[89]

Scott and Soustelle are juxtaposed in this work in order to better understand the history and ideology of policies directed at Indigenous populations in Canada, Mexico and in Algeria. During their lifetimes, both Duncan Campbell Scott and Jacques Soustelle first emerged as exemplary cultural and political fixtures of liberal, ruling establishments. They then became prisms for the examination of darker national histories. As contemporary nation states, like Canada and France, struggle to re-define relationships with domestic Indigenous groups or the descendants of former colonial possessions both abroad and at home, the lives of Scott and Soustelle continue to reveal much about failed relations with Indigenous peoples.

No individual or social group lives strictly in the present. The past is haunting. Memory constitutes part of a human's "present" consciousness. As storytellers, we are imperfect witnesses of the present and past. History sometimes repeats itself. The lives and work of Duncan Campbell Scott and Jacques Soustelle are relevant and resonant today.

Afterword

Day school for Indigenous children, Bear Island, Temagami, Ontario c.1905-06.

Dr. John S. Milloy

Professor Emeritus, Trent University and author of "A National Crime: The Canadian Government and The Residential School System, 1879–1986."

James Cullingham set himself a task of considerable magnitude and potential value – being, in his words, an investigation of the "legacies of colonialism, imperialism and liberalism," in two different colonial contexts through the eyes, ideologies and careers of two imperial Indigenous affairs administrators – Canada's most influential, long term head of the Department of Indian Affairs, D.C. Scott, and Jacques Soustelle, France's last governor general of Algeria.

Each man struggled with the relationship between colonist and colonized, within the very ill-defined, and even contradictory, models of assimilation and integration. And, in Canada's case, no less than in that of other imperial powers, equally deaf to "clarion calls for justice," the nation was driven primarily by an overriding concern for the "advance of their civilization and economic development." As such, Canada, he asserts rightly, "belongs in an international conversation about the domestic colonization of Indigenous people." And for Cullingham that "conversation" ended with the recognition of one reality only: that both countries and both men, despite being amongst "the best and brightest," failed, "… they and the societies they represented [got] it so wrong." It is, he declares, his task, his "mission to look back at their lives while pondering that question." That is a considerable task for anyone; but he carries it out masterfully.

ACKNOWLEDGMENTS

Thanks to Tom Bartsiokas, Erin Dolmage and Michael Maynard for their steadfast dedication in preparing this book. Thanks also to Seneca student interns Tanecia Haynes-Mckenzie, Jason Ma, Madison Shaw, Janet Suek and Nhu Vo (Belle) for their fine work. Thank you Elizabeth Wilton for proofreading.

Thanks to my York University doctoral dissertation co-supervisors Carolyn Podruchny and Anne Rubenstein. Carolyn and our colleagues in The History of Indigenous Peoples Network (HIPN) informed me and commented on parts of this work as it progressed. The Latin American Research Group in Toronto aided my process and gave excellent potlucks. *Le Séminaire d'Histoire de France de Toronto* run jointly by the University of Toronto and York University was an enjoyable and positive stimulus.

Professors William H. Beezley, William E. French, William D. Irvine, Eric Jennings, Suzanne Langlois, Marcel Martel, Kenneth Mills, Donald B. Smith and Patricia Wood generously helped steer my adaptation from journalism.

Archivists and librarians in Aix-en-Provence, San Cristóbal de las Casas, Mexico City, Oaxaca, Paris, Querétaro and Kingston, Ottawa and Toronto in Ontario facilitated this work. Thank you. *Merci. Miigwetch. Grazie. Muchísimas gracias!*

Colleagues in the School of Media and the School of English and Liberal Studies at Seneca offered support and understanding.

The Temagami and Trent University communities have befriended, mentored and supported me over many years. Deepest thanks to Bruce and Carol Hodgins, Marlene Brant Castellano, Stephen Hill, Mary Laronde, Linda Mathias, Don McCaskill, Waubegeshig Harvey McCue, John Milloy, Marvyn Morrison, Rita O'Sullivan, Gary and Wayne Potts, John Wadland, Fred Wheatley and Bella White.

Members of my Trent University undergraduate cohort David Boulding, Russell Diabo, and Peter Di Gangi have informed and inspired my work since we met in a previous millennium.

Michael Allder, Hugh Brody, David Colin Burt, Rudy Buttignol, Gil Cardinal, Stan Dragland, Roy Kaminiwaish, Scot Kyle, Emily Larimer, Jani Lauzon, Robert L. McDougall, Ovide Mercredi, Deborah Palloway, René Sioui Labelle, Peter Raymont, R.H. Thomson, E. Brian Titley, Loretta Sarah Todd, Winona Wheeler and Elizabeth Wilton helped focus my thinking about Duncan Campbell Scott while making a film about him.

In France, the publisher Isabel Gautray offered accommodation, de la bonne bouffe and friendship in Paris while recounting her family's flight from Algeria in 1962 and providing access to her remarkable library. Merci, Isa! At various locations between Sisteron and Grenoble over many years, local historian, hiker, philatelist, shepherd and skier Gabriel Carnevalé introduced me to his beloved Southern Alps and opera while telling me tales of the Atlas and Aurès mountains of North Africa. *Merci mon pote!*

Above all, I am deeply grateful to my wonderful wife Li Robbins who has supported me through many years on this project. Thanks as well to our family.

NOTES

INTRODUCTION

1. James Cullingham, director/producer, *Duncan Campbell Scott – The Poet and The Indians*, documentary film, NFB producer Michael Allder (Tamarack Productions and National Film Board of Canada – Ontario Centre, 1995), distributed by VTape in Canada, Icarus Films in USA.

2. Nicholas Flood Davin, "Report on Industrial Schools for Indians and Half-Breeds," Ottawa, 1879, CIHM No. 03651, York University Library microforms; Olive Patricia Dickason, *Canada's First Nations*, 257-305; Robin Jarvis Brownlie, *A Fatherly Eye: Indian Agents, Government Power, and Aboriginal Resistance in Ontario, 1918-1939* (Toronto: Oxford University Press, 2003); J. R. Miller *Shingwauk's Vision: A History of Native Residential Schools* (Toronto: University of Toronto Press, 1996); J.R. Miller, *Skyscrapers Hide the Heavens: A History of Indian-White Relations in Canada. 3rd ed.* (Toronto: University of Toronto Press, 2000), 99-207; John Sheridan Milloy, *A National Crime: The Canadian Government and the Residential School System, 1879-1986* (Winnipeg: University of Manitoba Press, 1999), 51-186.

3. Todd Shepard, "How Ethnographic Research in 1930s Mexico shaped French efforts to fight Algerian nationalism in 1955," paper delivered at the UNESCO History Project conference in Cambridge (6-7 April 2009); *The Invention of Decolonization: The Algerian War and the Remaking of France* (Ithaca and London: Cornell University Press, 2006), 47, 65, 69-70, 178; Stephen Tyre, "From Algérie Française to France Musulmane: Jacques Soustelle and the Myths and Realities of 'Integration,' 1955-1962," *French History* (2006), 20(3): 276-296.

4. James Cullingham, "Now ain't the time for your tears," *Active History*, June 28, 2021, http://activehistory.ca/2021/06/now-aint-the-time-for-your-tears/; Crystal Fraser, Tricia Fraser and Neil Logan, "A doctor's century–old warning on residential schools can help find justice for Canada's crimes," *The Globe And Mail*, July 17, 2021 https://www.theglobeandmail.com/opinion/article-a-doctors-century-old-warning-on-residential-schools-can-help-find/.

5. John S. Milloy, "John A's 'Hostages:' state formation and residential school education for First Nations' children," unpublished paper provided to the author June 2021. Milloy is author of a breakthrough work *A National Crime – The Canadian Government and the Residential School System 1879-1986* (Winnipeg: University of Manitoba Press, 1999).

6. David Halberstam, *The Best and the Brightest* (New York: Random House, 1972). Journalist Halberstam coined the phrase "the best and the brightest" in his consideration of the liberals who contributed to a series of fateful decisions to ramp up the United States military presence in Vietnam.

7. Robert L. McDougall, "D.C. Scott: A Trace of Documents and a Touch of Life," *Totems: Essays in the Cultural History of Canada* (Ottawa: Tecumseh Press, 1990), 188.

8. John Flood, *The Land They Occupied* (Erin, ON: The Porcupine's Quill).

9. Garnet Armand Ruffo, "Poem for Duncan Campbell Scott," *Opening in the Sky* (Penticton, BC: Theytus Books, 1994).

10. Truth and Reconciliation Commission of Canada, *Honouring the Truth, Reconciling for the Future: Summary of the Final Report of the Truth and Reconciliation Commission*, 2015.

11. Government of Canada, "Statement of Apology to Former Students of Indian Residential Schools June 11, 2008," accessed March 31, 2021, https://www.rcaanc-cirnac.gc.ca/eng/1100100015644/1571589171655, https://www.youtube.com/watch?v=xCpn1erz1y8.

12. Mark Abley, *Conversations with a Dead Man – The Legacy of Duncan Campbell Scott* (Madeira, BC: Douglas & McIntyre, 2013), 142-3.

13. See Bernard Droz et Evelyne Lever, *Histoire de la Guerre d'Algérie 1954-1962* (Paris: Seuil, 1982); Shepard (6-7 April 2009); Tyre, (2006), 20(3): 276-296; Raoul Girardet, *L'Idée Coloniale en France De 1871 a 1962* (Paris: La Table Ronde, 1972); Alistair Horne, *A Savage War of Peace: Algeria 1954-1962* (New York: New York Review of Books, 2006 – originally published 1977), 105-7; Julian Jackson, *A Certain Idea of France – The Life of Charles de*

Gaulle (London: Allen Lane – Penguin, 2018, 509-545; Éric Zemmour, *Destin Français* (Paris: Albin Michel, 2018), 544-568.

14. Droz et Lever, *Histoire de la Guerre d'Algérie*, 67-68.

15. Olivier Le Cour Grandmaison, *Coloniser, Exterminer: Sur La Guerre Et l'État Colonial* (Paris: Fayard, 2005); Carole Reynaud Paligot, *La République Raciale: Paradigme Racial Et Idéologie Républicaine, 1860-1930* (Paris: Presses Universitaires de France, 2006); Benjamin Stora, *La Gangrène Et l'Oubli* (Paris: La Découverte, 1991).

16. For a recent comprehensive biography of Rivet and profiles of many of students including Jacques & Georgette Soustelle and Germaine Tillion see Christine Laurière, *Paul Rivet Le Savant Et Le Politique* (Paris: Publications Scientifiques du Muséum National d'Histoire Naturelle, 2008); Laurière, "Paul Rivet" (Thèse doctoral dirigée par M. Jean Jarmin directeur d'études à l'EHSS, Paris).

17. Jackson, *A Certain Idea.*

18. Alain Herbeth, *Jacques Soustelle – L'Homme de l'Intégration* (Paris: Harmattan, 2015).

19. Kamel Daoud, Meursault, *Contre-Enquête* (Alger: Barzakh, 2013).

CHAPTER ONE

1. E.K. Brown, "Memoir" in *Selected Poems*, xi-xiii.

2. John A. MacDonald, letter of November 14, 1879 to William Scott. As cited in Arthur S. Bourinot "The Poet's Scrapbooks," *The Canadian Bookman and Author*, Vol. 38, No. 1, Summer, Ottawa, 1962, 6; "Ottawa's Grand Old Poet Shows His Rare Gifts," *The Ottawa Journal*, June 21, 1947. In an interview six months prior to his death, Scott recounted the circumstances of his being hired by MacDonald more than sixty years earlier.

3. Reverend William Scott, "Report Relating to the Affairs of the Oka Indians Made to the Superintendent General of Indian Affairs," LAC-BAC G10a RG10 Vol. 725 William Scott, Oka Indian Report.

4. Olive Patricia Dickason, *Canada's First Nations: A History of Founding Peoples from Earliest Times* (Toronto: McLelland & Stewart, 1992), 247-56; J.R. Miller, *Compact, Contract, Covenant: Aboriginal Treaty-Making in Canada* (Toronto-Buffalo-London: University of Toronto Press, 2009), 66-122; E. Brian Titley, *A Narrow Vision: Duncan Campbell Scott and the Administration of Indian Affairs in Canada* (Vancouver: University of British Columbia Press, 1986), 1-22.

5. Royal Proclamation, October 7, 1763, accessed January 2013, http://www.johnco.com/nativel/pro1763.html.

6. Stan Dragland, *Duncan Campbell Scott: The Poet and the Indians*, documentary film directed by the author. Tamarack Productions in co-production with The National Film Board of Canada, 1995. Dragland is a literary critic, novelist and a former professor of English literature at the University of Western Ontario. Stan Dragland's *Floating Voice: Duncan Campbell Scott and the Literature of Treaty 9* (Concord, ON: Anansi, 1994) is an erudite, multidisciplinary contemplation of Scott as a poet and Treaty Commissioner.

7. Douglas Lochead, "Preface," in *Powassan's Drum: Poems of Duncan Campbell Scott* (Ottawa: Tecumseh Press, 1985), xii; Gordon Johnston, *Duncan Campbell Scott and His Works* (Downsview, ON: ECW Press, 1983), 10, 26.

8. Duncan Campbell Scott, "Indian Place Names," *Selected Poetry of Duncan Campbell Scott*, edited by Glenn Clever (Ottawa: Tecumseh Press, 1974), 36; originally published in Scott's *New World Lyrics and Ballads* (Toronto: Morang, 1905).

9. Madge Macbeth, *Over My Shoulder* (Toronto: Ryerson Press, 1953), 143; Macbeth, "Duncan Campbell Scott–A Few of My Memories," *Canadian Author and Bookman*, Vol. 38, No. 1, Summer 1962, 2.

10. Donald B. Smith, *Seen But Not Seen: Influential Canadians and the First Nations from the 1840s to Today* (Toronto, Buffalo & London: University of Toronto Press, 2021), 120.

11. Sandra Gwyn, *The Private Capital: Ambition and Love in the Age of Macdonald and Laurier* (Toronto: McClelland and Stewart, 1984), 455-57.

12. Margaret Atwood, *Survival: A Thematic Guide to Canadian Literature* (Toronto: House of Anansi Press, 1972), 60; Northrop Frye, *The Bush Garden: Essays on the Canadian Imagination* (Toronto: House of Anansi Press, 1971), 132, 145; John Ralston Saul, *A Fair Country: Telling Truths About Canada* (Toronto: Viking Canada, 2008), 84-5, 231-38, 257. See also Carl Berger, *The Sense of Power: Studies in the Ideas of Canadian Imperialism, 1867-1914* (Toronto: University of Toronto Press, 1970), 116-19; Carl Berger, "the true north strong and free," in Peter H.

Russell, *Nationalism in Canada* (Toronto: McGraw-Hill, 1966), 3-26.

13. Duncan Campbell Scott, letter to E.K. Brown, May 10-12, 1944. LAC-BAC, E.K. Brown correspondence MG30 D61 Vol. 3; Emily Carr letter to Scott and Elise Aylen, March 22, 1941. LAC-BAC, LMS-0204, Box 10, Folder 31; Scott letters to Clarence Gagnon, February 8, 1919, August 2 & 6, 1921 and December 1, 1927. LAC-BAC, LMS-0204, Box 11; Clarence Gagnon letter to Scott, June 6, 1931. LAC-BAC, LMS-0204, Box 11.

14. Leonard W. Brockington, "Duncan Campbell Scott's Eightieth Birthday," *Saturday Night*, Vol. 57, No 47, (August 1, 1942).

15. *Times of Ceylon*, December 29, 1948. LAC-BAC E. Aylen-DC Scott fonds, LMS – 0204 Box 9, Folder 8.

16. John Masefield, letter to DC Scott, November 8, 1905. LAC-BAC, LMS 0204 Box 11, Folder 26.

17. John Masefield, "Address," D.C. Scott Memorial, January 22, 1948, St. Martin-In-The-Fields, London. Aylen-DC Scott fonds, LMS – 0204 Box 10, Folder 4.

18. Duncan Campbell Scott, "Watkwenies", originally published in Scott's *Labor and the Angel*, (Boston: Copeland and Day, 1898), 15; cited in Scott, ed. Cleaver, *Selected Poetry*, 13.

19. Daniel Pick, *Faces of Degeneration: A European Disorder. c.1848-c.1918* (Cambridge: Cambridge University Press, 1989), 1-74.

20. T.J Jackson Lears, *No Place Of Grace: Antimodernism and the Transformation of American Culture 1880–1920* (New York: Pantheon Books, 1981), 5.

21. Duncan Campbell Scott, "The Last of The Indian Treaties" originally published 1906, *Scribner's 40* (1906); re-printed in DC Scott, *The Circle of Affection* (Toronto: McClelland and Stewart, 1947), 109-22; and in *Duncan Campbell Scott: Addresses, Essay and Reviews, Vol.1*, Leslie Ritchie, ed., Introduction by Stan Dragland (London, ON: Canadian Poetry Press, 2000), 82-93; Dragland, *Floating Voice: Duncan Campbell Scott and the Literature of Treaty 9* (Concord, ON: Anansi,1994).

22. Duncan Campbell Scott, "The Forsaken," originally published in *New World Lyrics and Ballads* (Toronto: Morang, 1905), 15; cited in Scott, ed. Cleaver, *Selected Poetry*, 37.

23. *Times of Ceylon*, December 29, 1948. LAC-BAC E. Aylen-DC Scott fonds, LMS – 0204 Box 9, Folder 8.

24. W.L. Mackenzie King, "Message" on the occasion of D.C Scott Memorial, Office Of The High Commissioner For Canada, London, Jan.2, 1948. LAC E. Aylen-DC Scott fonds, LMS–0204 Box 10, Folder 4.

25. *Times of Ceylon*, December 29, 1948. LAC E. Aylen-DC Scott fonds, LMS–0204 Box 9, Folder 8.

26. Duncan Campbell Scott, *The Poems of Duncan Campbell Scott* (Toronto: McClelland & Stewart, 1926), 11.

27. LAC-BAC, Elise Aylen – Duncan Campbell Scott fonds, LMS-0204.

28. James Cullingham, "The Queen Among The Mohawks," *Active History*, July 7, 2010. http://activehistory.ca/2010/07/the-queen-among-the-mohawks/

29. Macbeth, *Memories*, 2.

30. Souster, *Powassan's Drum*, x.

31. Lochead, *Powassan's Drum*, xii.

32. Lears, *No Place…*; Daniel Wickberg, "Antimodernism As Counter Culture," Society for US Intellectual History Blog, January 24, 2016, accessed March 6, 2021, https://s-usih.org/2016/01/antimodernism-as-counterculture/.

33. Winona Stevenson (now Wheeler) in *Duncan Campbell Scott: The Poet and The Indians*, documentary film, Tamarack Productions in Co-Production with The National Film Board of Canada, 1995. James Cullingham, director/producer. Stevenson has since changed her family name to Wheeler. She is a professor and head of Native Studies at the University of Saskatchewan.

34. Bernard Ullmann, *Jacques Soustelle–Le Mal Aimé* (Paris: Plon, 1995), 16-17. Bernard Ullmann was a feature reporter with *Agence France Presse* throughout the 1950s and 1960s. His non-academic biography of Soustelle is a journalistic account of Soustelle's life with particular emphasis on Soustelle's association with Charles de Gaulle and the loss of French Algeria; Nicole Racine, "Jacques Soustelle" in Jean Maitre, *Dictionnaire Biographique Du Mouvement Ouvrier Français–Quatrième partie 1914-1939 de la Première à la Seconde Guerre Mondiale, Tome 41 Rova à Szy* (Paris: Les Éditions Ouvrières, 1992), 390-91; Nicole Racine is a French intellectual historian who wrote a biography of

Paul Rivet, Soustelle's maître.

35. Racine, "Soustelle, Jacques," 391; Jacques Soustelle, *Mémoires, Apocryphes Sous la Forme d'une Dialogue Avec Georges Suffert* (unpublished manuscript provided to the author by Bernard Ullmann in 2008); Christine Lauriere, *Paul Rivet Le Savant Et Le Politique* (Paris: Publications Scientifiques du Museum national d'Histoire naturelle, 2008).

36. Jacques Soustelle, *Mexique Terre Indienne* (Paris: Plon, 1936), 7.

37. Jacques Soustelle, *Les Quatre Soleils Souvenirs et Réflexions d'un Ethnologue au Mexique* (Paris: CNRS Éditions, 2009) Originally published in Paris by LibrariePlon, 1967.

38. Soustelle, *Terre Indienne*, 18-33.

39. Ibid, 18.

40. Soustelle, *Envers et Contre tout* (Paris: Robert Laffont, 1947), 216.

41. Soustelle, *Terre Indienne*, 141-145, 185-253; Jacques Soustelle, *Les Quatre Soleils: L'Itinéraire Intellectuel de Jacques Soustelle, Ethnographe du Mexique Terre Indienne* (Paris: Plon, 1967), 185-253.

42. Soustelle writing as Jean Duriez. Multiple issues of *MASSES* and *Spartacus*, (1932-1936), Bibliothèque nationale de France–Mitterand. See *MASSES*, September, October, November, December 1933; Soustelle, *Spartacus*, 7 décembre, 1934; 28 février, 1935.

43. Cited in Jacques Soustelle, *Aimée et Souffrante Algérie* (Paris: Plon, 1956), 7.

44. Germaine Tillion, "L'Algérie en 1957" in *L'Afrique Bascule Vers l'Avenir*, by Germaine Tillion (Paris: Éditions Tirésias Michel Reynaud, Paris 1999), 85, 91, 94-5; Tillion, *La Traversée du Mal Entretien Avec Jean Lacouture* (Paris: Arléa, 2000), 97-8.

45. Alistair Horne, *A Savage War of Peace: Algeria, 1954-1962* (New York: Viking Press, 1978).

46. Ullmann, *Le Mal Aimé*. 332-48; James D. Le Sueur, "Before the Jackal," 183-246 in *Ben Abro, Assassination July 14: An Underground Thriller*, with a historical essay by James D. Le Sueur (Lincoln & London: University of Nebraska Press, 2001). 'Ben Abro' is a pseudonym chosen by a couple of British students in Paris in the 1960s. Their spy novel is a thinly veiled portrayal of a French social scientist clearly based on Soustelle who joins in a plot to assassinate Charles de Gaulle over France's loss of Algeria. The book's publication resulted in a lawsuit brought by Soustelle against the authors that was settled out of court. The charges and counter charges over the involvement of Soustelle with the OAS is highly contested in the French historiography. There is wide agreement, supported by Ullmann's path-breaking research, that Soustelle participated in meetings in which various assassination attempts were discussed.

47. Soustelle, *Les Quatre Soleils*.

48. Claudio Lomnitz-Adler, *Deep Mexico, Silent Mexico: An Anthropology of Nationalism* (Minneapolis: University of Minnesota, 2001), 242-57.

49. Jacques Soustelle, *Discours de Réception de M. Jacques Soustelle à L'Académie Française et Réponse de M. Jean Dutourd* (Paris: Éditions Flammarion, 1984), 109-113.

50. Faligot, Roger and Kauffer, Rémi "Jacques Soustelle: La Fin d'un Homme de Science et de Politique," *Libération*, August 8, 1990, 36.

51. Jean Planchais, "La Mort de Jacques Soustelle…" *Le Monde*, August 8, 1990, front page.

52. Christian Duverger, "De l'ethnologue de Terrain au Vulgarisateur de Haut Niveau," *Le Monde*, August 8, 1990, page 8.

53. *L'Humanité*, August 8, 1990.

54. Le Quotidien de Paris, August 8,1990, cited in Dominique Balvet, "Jacques Soustelle et l'Algérie Française: Gaullisme et Anti Gaullisme" (PhD diss., Université Charles de Gaulle Lille 3, 2003), 769, footnote 69.

55. Eduardo Matos Moctezuma, "Rembranzas" in *Mille ans de Civilisation Mésoaméricaine Vol 1 Hommages à Jacques Soustelle Réunis par Jacqueline de Durand-Forest et Georges Baudot* (Paris: l'Harmattan, 1995). Spanish original: "La primera vez que oí el nombre de Jacques Soustelle fue en la Escuela Nacional de Antropología de México. Corría el año de 1960 y yo cursaba el segundo año de la carrera de Arqueología. Leí con avidez un libro que me pareció fascinante: *La vida cotidiana de los Aztecas*. Su contenido me llevó a conocer una de las sociedades mesoamericanas para la que era necesario leer tanto de fuentes históricos como de arqueología… el libro de Soustelle me abrió la puerta a las sociedades mesoamericanas." Translation by James Cullingham.

Twenty-three-year old Duncan Campbell Scott (1862-1947).

56. Ibid, 3-4. Spanish original: "Nunca me convenció lo que escribió en relación a su posición que o llevó a romper con De Gaulle, de quien había sido cercano colaborador durante la segunda guerra mundial." Translation by James Cullingham.

57. Jacques Soustelle, "Ou veut-on venir à Pretoria?' *Le Monde*, Paris, December 3, 1977, 7; Ullmann, *Le Mal Aimé*, 398-9; Jacques Soustelle, *La Longue Marche d'Israël* (Paris: Librairie Arthème Fayard, 1968).

58. Honouring The Truth Reconciling for the Future - Summary of the Final Report of The Truth and Reconciliation Commission of Canada 2015 https://ehprnh2mwo3.exactdn.com/wp-content/uploads/2021/01/Executive_Summary_English_Web.pdf; the commissioners found that Canada practiced cultural genocide in its residential schools policy. Reclaiming Power and Place The Final Report of Inquiry Into Missing and Murdered Indigenous Women and Girls, Supplementary Report – Genocide 2019 https://www.mmiwg-ffada.ca/wp-content/uploads/2019/06/

Supplementary-Report_Genocide.pdf; the commissioners found that Canada is genocidal in its treatment of Indigenous women and girls.

59. Northrop Frye, "Conclusion to a Literary History of Canada" in *The Bush Garden: Essays On The Canadian Imagination* (Toronto: Anansi Press,1971), 219.

60. Margaret Atwood, *Survival: A Thematic Guide to Canadian Literature* (Toronto: Anansi Press, 1972), 62.

61. Margaret Atwood & Robert Weaver, eds., *The Oxford Book Of Canadian Short Stories In English* (Toronto-Oxford-New York: Oxford University Press, 1986), 24-8.

62. Knister, Raymond, *Canadian Short Stories* (Toronto: Macmillan, 1928), xix.

63. Jane Urquhart, ed., *The Penguin Book of Canadian Short Stories* (Toronto: Penguin Canada, 2007).

64. R.L. McDougall, "Duncan Campbell Scott" in *The Canadian Encyclopedia,* Second Edition, Volume III (Edmonton: Hurtig Publishers, 1988), 1960.

65. Cullingham, *Poet and the Indians.*

66. Stan Dragland, "Introduction," *Duncan Campbell Scott: Addresses, Essays and Reviews (edited by Leslie Ritchie)* (London, ON: Canadian Poetry Press, 2000), xii.

67. Harold Cardinal, *The Unjust Society: The Tragedy of Canada's Indians* (Edmonton: Hurtig, 1969); H.A. McCue, *The Only Good Indian: Essays by Canadian Indians* (Toronto: New Press, 1972); Sally M.Weaver, *Making Canadian Indian Policy: The Hidden Agenda 1968-70* (Toronto: University of Toronto Press, 1981). Mr. Chrétien caused controversy in the autumn of 2021 when he denied having knowledge of the history of residential school abuses during his tenure as Minister of Indian Affairs. https://ici.radio-canada.ca/nouvelle/1834525/pensionnats-jean-chretien-abus-mauvais-traitements?depuisRecherche=true.

68. Jean Chrétien interview by James Cullingham 1984– audio cassette recording stored at University of Toronto Media Commons Archives, Cullingham–Tamarack Productions collection.

69. E. Brian Titley, *A Narrow Vision: Duncan Campbell Scott and the Administration of Indian Affairs in Canada* (Vancouver: University of British Columbia Press, 1986).

70. Christopher Bracken, *The Potlatch Papers: A Post Colonial History* (Chicago: University of Chicago Press, 1997); Robin Brownlie, *A Fatherly Eye: Indian Agents,*

Government Power, and Aboriginal Resistance in Ontario, 1918-1939 (Don Mills, ON.); (New York: Oxford University Press, 2003); R. Cole Harris, *Making Native Space: Colonialism, Resistance, and Reserves in British Columbia* (Vancouver: UBC Press, 2002).

71. Ian McKay, "The Liberal Order Framework: A Prospectus for a Reconnaissance of Canadian History," *Canadian Historical Review* 81, no. 4 (Dec. 2000), 617, 636; Ian McKay, "Canada as a Long Liberal Revolution" in *Liberalism and Hegemony: Debating the Canadian Liberal Revolution*, Jean-François Constant and Michel Ducharme (Toronto-Buffalo-London: University of Toronto Press, 2009), 353, 361.

72. Robert Stillman, as quoted in interview conducted by James D. Le Sueur, April 16, 1994 in Abro, *Assassination*, 244-245.

73. Jacques Soustelle, letter to his lawyer Charles Benfredj, November 11, 1989. Provided to the author by M. Benfredj, March 2008.

74. Jacques Soustelle, letter to his lawyer Charles Benfredj, July 1, 1990. Provided to the author by M. Benfredj, March 2008.

75. Ullmann, *Le Mal Aimé*.

76. Jean-Francois Deniau, "Éloge de Jacques Soustelle," reprinted in *Le Monde*, December 14, 1992, 9.

77. Ullmann, *Le Mal Aimé*, 409-412.

CHAPTER TWO

1. James West Davidson and John Rugge, *Great Heart: The History of a Labrador Adventure* (Montreal: McGill-Queen's University Press, 1997, c1988); Natalie Zemon Davis, *Trickster Travels: A Sixteenth Century Muslim Between Worlds* (New York: Hill & Wang, 2006); Natalie Zemon Davis, *Women On The Margins: Three Seventeenth Century Lives* (Cambridge, MA: Harvard University Press, 1995); Margaret Laurence, *The Prophet's Camel Bell* (Toronto: McClelland and Stewart, 1963); Mary-Louise Pratt, *Imperial Eyes: Travel Writing and Transculturation* (London & New York: Routledge, 2008); Wendy Roy, *Maps of Difference: Canada, Women and Travel* (Montreal & Ithaca, NY: McGill-Queen's University Press, 2005).

2. Germaine Warkentin, *Canadian Exploration Literature: An Anthology* (Toronto, ON.: Oxford University Press, 1993).

3. Jacques Soustelle, "Souvenirs, Apocryphes en forme de Dialogue avec George Suffert," 1988, unpublished manuscript provided to the author by Bernard Ullmann in 2008, 4.

4. Désiré Charnay, *Voyage au Mexique 1858-1861* (Paris: Ginkgo, 2001); Keith F. Davis, *Désiré Charnay, Expeditionary Photographer* (Albuquerque: University of New Mexico Press, 1981).

5. E.K. Brown "Memoir" in *Selected Poems of Duncan Campbell Scott* (Toronto: Ryerson, 1951), xi – xlii; Titley, *Narrow Vision*, 23-36.

6. Christine Laurière, *Paul Rivet–le Savant et le Politique* (Paris: Muséum National d'Histoire Naturelle, 2008), 239, 519-20, 618-20; Ullmann, *Soustelle*, 21-2.

7. Jean-François Sirinelli, *Génération Intellectuelle. Khâgneux et Normaliens dans l'Entre-deux-guerres* (Paris, Fayard. 1988), 104; Ullmann, Soustelle, 24-5.

8. Marcel Mauss. *Essai Sur le Don: Forme et Raison d'Échange dans les Sociétés Archaïques; Préface de Florence Weber* (Paris: Presses Universitaires de France, 2007). First published in l'Année Sociologique, seconde série, 1923-1924; Marcel Mauss, *Sociologie et Anthropologie; Introduction par Claude Levy-Strauss* (Paris: Presses Universitaires de France, 1993). Near the end of Soustelle's career, some forty years after his first trip to Mexico, Soustelle was still vaunting the influence of Mauss' seminal work in a 1975 report commissioned by the government of then French president Valery Giscard d'Estaing–Soustelle, *La Recherché Francaise en Archéologie et Anthropologie* (Paris: La documentation Française, 1975), 13.

9. Jacques Soustelle. "l'Homme et le Surnaturel–Les Phénonèmes religieux," *L'Encyclopédie française*, VII (Paris: Société nouvelle de l'Encyclopédie française 1935).

10. Soustelle, *Souvenirs*, 12-22.

11. Jacques Soustelle, *Les quatres soleils, Souvenirs Et Réflexions d'Un Ethnologue Au Mexique Terre Indienne* (Paris: Plon, 1967), 32-5, 39-46.

12. Jacques Soustelle, *Mexique Terre Indienne* (Paris: Grasset, 1936); various editions of *MASSES* and *Spartacus*, specific citations below. The dates of Soustelle's itinerary in Cuba and Mexico as well as the events that "Jean Duriez" reports on coincide with Soustelle's account in *Mexique Terre Indienne*. Perhaps already thinking of a prestigious academic future, Soustelle did not want to be associated

by name with overtly leftist publications. The French intellectual historian Nicole Racine as well as historical scholars Christian Desbordes and Dominique Balvet concur that Duriez was Soustelle's journalistic pseudonym. Christian Desbordes, "Jacques Soustelle et la defense de l'Occident," Thèse du Doctorat en science politique, Université d'Auvergne, 2000, 33; Nicole Racine, "Jacques Soustelle" in Jean Maitre, Dictionnaire Biographique Du Mouvement Ouvrier Français–Quatrième partie 1914-1939 de la Première à la Seconde Guerre Mondiale, Tome 41 Rova à Szy (Paris: Les Éditions Ouvrières, 1992), 390-1; Dominique Balvet, "Jacques Soustelle Et l'Algérie Française: Gaullisme Et Antigaullisme." Doctorat d'Histoire sous la direction de Jean-Francois Sirinelli, Université Charles de Gaulle Lille 3, 2003, 25.

13. J.R. Miller. "Compact, Contract, Covenant: The Evolution of Indian Treaty-Making" in Susan Neyland & Ted Binnema, eds., New Histories for Old: Changing Perspectives on Canada's Native Pasts (Vancouver: UBC Press, 2007), 66-91; J.R. Miller, Compact, Contract, Covenant: Aboriginal Treaty-Making in Canada (Toronto: University of Toronto Press, 2009), 207-14, 228-9, 297; for a useful discussion of the hardening tendencies in the transition from imperial to national concerns in North American "borderlands" and "national borders" see Jeremy Adelman and Stephen Aron, "From Borderlands to Borders: Empires, Nation-States, and the Peoples in between in North American History," The American Historical Review, Vol. 104, No. 3 (Jun., 1999) 814-841.

14. Government of Canada, "The James Bay Treaty – Treaty No. 9 (made in 1905 and 1906) and Adhesions Made in 1929 and 1930," LAC-BAC RG10 Vol. 3033, 235, 225 p.3.

15. John Flood, "The Duplicity of D.C. Scott and the James Bay Treaty," Black Moss Journal, Series 2, No. 2, (Fall 1976), 50-63.

16. Duncan Campbell Scott "The Last of The Indian Treaties," Scribner's 40 (1906); re-printed in DC Scott The Circle of Affection (Toronto: McClelland and Stewart, 1947), 109-22; and in Duncan Campbell Scott: Addresses, Essay and Reviews, Vol.1, Leslie Ritchie, ed, introduction by Stan Dragland (London, ON; Canadian Poetry Press, 2000), 82-93.

17. Olive Dickason, Canada's First Nations: A History of Founding Peoples from Earliest Times (Toronto: McClelland & Stewart Inc., 1992), 181-88; J.R. Miller,

Compact, Contract, Covenant: Aboriginal Treaty-Making in Canada (Toronto, Buffalo, London: University of Toronto Press, 2009), 66-70.

18. Canada, Department of Justice. The Constitution Act 1982, see sections 25 and 35 in The Canadian Charter of Rights and Freedoms, accessed August 2012, http://laws.justice.gc.ca/en/const/annex_e.html.

19. Scott, "Last of The Indian Treaties," in Ritchie, ed., Scott: Addresses, Essays, 82.

20. Bruce G. Trigger, "The Historian's Indian: Native Americans in Canadian Historical Writing from Charlevoix to the Present," Canadian Historical Review 67:3 (1986): 315-42.

21. Scott, "Last of The Indian Treaties," in Ritchie ed., 87.

22. March 10, 2020 Standing Committee on Indigenous and Northern Affairs https://www.rcaanc-cirnac.gc.ca/eng/1589898407928/1589898443385.

23. Ibid, 84.

24. Ibid, 84.

25. Ibid, 86-7.

26. Ibid, 84-5. Aboriginal guides from northwestern Ontario and Red River/Manitoba had extensive experience guiding British imperial and Canadian official parties. William Butler, intelligence officer to General Garnet Wolseley during the Red River Expedition of 1870 wrote extensively about his relationship with Aboriginal guides from the region in Canada at that time and in 1885 on the Nile River in Egypt when he accompanied Wolseley again – this time on a failed mission to rescue General Gordon in Khartoum. See William Francis Butler, The Campaign of the Cataracts: Being a Personal Narrative of the Great Nile Expedition of 1884-5 (London: S.Low, Morston, Searle & Rivington, 1887), esp. 142-44; Butler, The Great Lone Land: A Tale of Travel and Adventure in the North-West of America (Toronto: Musson Book Co., 1924); Roy MacLaren, Canadians on the Nile, 1882-1898: Being the Adventures of the Voyageurs on the Khartoum Relief Expedition and Other Exploits (Vancouver: University of British Columbia Press, 1978).

27. Dragland, Floating Voice, 3-5.

28. Translates literally as "valuable interlocutors." The term was used widely by Soustelle and other agents of French rule in Algeria to describe Algerian Muslim allies

Scott with his first wife, Belle Botsford, photographed by M.O. Hammond.

of the French cause. I employ it here to reference the local Indigenous individuals on which both Soustelle and Scott relied on first in their formative voyages discussed in this chapter.

29. Soustelle, *Terre Indienne*, 227.

30. Soustelle, *Quatres Soleils*, 57-61.

31. Ibid, 39-92.

32. Ibid, 12.

33. Soustelle, *Terre Indienne*, 253.

34. Fiddling became an intrinsic part of Métis culture in what became northwestern Ontario and parts of Manitoba, Saskatchwan and Alberta after contact. See Lynn Whidden, Audreen Hourie and Lawrence Barkwell, "Métis Music and Dance" and Oliver Boulette, "Red River Jig": A Fiddle Tune and Dance that Defines the Métis," in Barkwell, Leah Dorion and Hourie, eds, *Metis Legacy II: Michif Culture, Heritage, and Folkways*. Métis Legacy Series v. 2. (Saskatoon: Gabriel Dumont Institute, 2006), 161-172.

35. Scott "Last of the Indian Treaties," in *Addresses, Essays*, 85.

36. Gail Bederman, *Manliness and Civilization: a Cultural History of Gender and Race In the United States, 1880-1917* (Chicago: University of Chicago Press, 1995), 5-13.

37. Seneca College professor Erin Dolmage reflected in a conversation about this work that Scott as a poet and journalist "salvaged" Indigenous culture in a manner similar to activities of anthropologists, archaeologists and ethnologists like Soustelle. This matter will be picked up in Chapter 3.

38. Scott "Last of the Indian Treaties," in *Addresses, Essays*, 85.

39. In 2008, such recording devices were still on display at the Laboratoire de l'Ethnomusicologie at le Musée de l'Homme in Paris. There, in a cramped, high-ceilinged room off the main laboratory, hundreds and hundreds of boxes containing quarter-inch reel-to-reel audio tapes are filed on shelves. One such tape features the remaining recordings made by *la mission Soustelle 1932-4* and, fittingly enough, the recordings that the young Germaine Tillion made of Berber singers in the Aurès mountains of Algeria.

40. Jacques Soustelle, audio recording of Mazahua singers. Laboratoire de Ethnomusicologie, Musée de l'Homme,

Paris. Tape 76-11-37 Mission Germaine Tillion dans l'Aurès 1936 and Mission Jacques Soustelle 1932-4.

41. Soustelle, *Terre Indienne*, 73.

42. Soustelle, *Terre Indienne*, 66-67.

43. Musée du quai Branly, Paris. Fonds Soustelle–Documents. Dossier 5120. Dessin 71.1933.71.107 executé par le chef des danses de S Bartolo del Llano représentant J. Soustelle

44. Soustelle, *Terre Indienne*, 87.

45. Ibid.

46. Musée du Quai Branly, Paris. Fonds Soustelle–Objets. 71.1933.71.87 jupon; 71.1933.71.104 couronne de plumes.

47. Soustelle, *Terre Indienne*, 106-7, 126, 130. The phrase raza cósmica was coined by Mexican revolutionary philosopher, educator and politician José Vasconcelos in an essay originally published in 1925. See José Vasconcelos, *Obras Completas* (México: Libreros Mexicanos Unidos, 1957). Vasconcelos and Didier Tisdel Jaén, *The Cosmic Race: A Bilingual Edition* (Baltimore, Md: Johns Hopkins University Press, 1997; 1979).

48. Soustelle, *Terre Indienne*, 18; Soustelle letter to Paul Rivet from Toluca, Mexico November 30, 1932. MNHN.

49. Claudio Lomnitz-Adler, *Deep Mexico, Silent Mexico: an Anthropology of Nationalism* (Minneapolis: University of Minnesota Press, 2001), 250-7.

50. Duncan Campbell Scott "The Onondaga Madonna" in *Selected Poetry of Duncan Campbell Scott*, edited by Glenn Clever (Ottawa: Tecumseh Press, 1974), 14.

51. Brenda Macdougall, "The Myth of Metis Cultural Ambivalence," in Nicole St. Onge et al. *Contours of a People: Metis Family, Mobility, and History,* Nicole St-Onge, Maria Campbell, Brenda Macdougall and Carolyn Podruchny, (Norman: University of Oklahoma Press, 2012), 428.

52. Macdougall, "Myth…", 431.

53. Jonathan Franklin, "Book Illustration by Canadian Painters to 1916," accessed April 2012, National Gallery of Canada, Library, national.gallery.ca/pdf/exn16_e.pdf. "Howard was an example of a new breed of artist-designers in various media, including illuminations and wallpaper, and was an active exhibitor with the Toronto Art Students' League, which published distinctive calendars between 1893 and 1904."

54. Duncan Campbell Scott, *Via Borealis* (Toronto: Tyrell and Co. Toronto, 1906). First edition at Thomas Fisher rare Book Library, University of Toronto. Large reproductions of Howard's drawings in Lorne Pierce papers, Queen's University Archives.

55. Edgar Pelham, "Twelve Hundred Miles By Canoe. Among Indians in Northern Waters," *Canada: The Illustrated Weekly Journal for all Interested in The Dominion*, Vol. IV (November 24, 1906–March 16, 1907); Edgar, "Travelling With A Poet" chap. 5 in *Across My Path* (Toronto: Ryerson, 1952), 59-73.

56. Edgar, *Across My Path*, 60. In his chapter entitled "Travelling With A Poet," Edgar relies on expanded entries from the journal he kept in the summer of 1906. The journal entries were initially published in the magazine *Canada: The Illustrated Weekly Journal for all Interested in The Dominion* in 1906-7.

57. Edgar, *Across My Path*, 62.

58. Duncan Campbell Scott, "The Half-Breed Girl" excerpted from *Selected Poetry of Duncan Campbell Scott* edited by Glenn Clever (Ottawa: The Tecumseh Press, 1974), 43.

59. D.M.R. Bentley, "Shadows in the Soul: Racial Haunting in the Poetry of Duncan Campbell Scott," *University of Toronto Quarterly*, Volume 75, Number 2 (Spring 2006), 753-60; E.K. Brown, "Memoir" in *Selected Poems of Duncan Campbell Scott* (Toronto: The Ryerson Press, 1951), xix; Stan Dragland, *Floating Voice: Duncan Campbell Scott and the Literature of Treaty 9* (Concord, ON: Anansi, 1994), 18,48,50,52,76,189,190,191-2,197.

60. Macdougall, "Myth…", 424-43; Chris Andersen, Métis": *Race, Recognition, and the Struggle for Indigenous Peoplehood* (Vancouver: UBC Press, 2014), 5 -7.

61. Scott, "Last of the Indian Treaties," in *Essays, Addresses*, 92.

62. Scott's briefing notes and statement on enfranchisement LAC RG-10, Vol. 6810, file 470-2-3.

63. John S. Milloy, "Second Thoughts: The Great Civilization Debate 1836-1840," chap. 4. (Ph.D. diss., Oxford 1981), 227.

64. Scott, *Selected Poems*, Brown ed., 107.

65. Scott, "Last of the Indian Treaties," *Scribner's* 582-3.

66. Scott, *Selected Poetry*, 34.

67. Canadian Independent Filmmakers Cooperative, "Night Hymns on Lake Nipigon–poem by Duncan Campbell Scott with paintings by Norval Morrisseau," directed and produced by Trevor Davies and George Muncey, reading by John Arblaster, 1972. ISN#108498 VLTSLF#8903-5674 LAC-BAC.

68. Scott, *Selected Poetry*, 96. Anyone who has had the pleasure of listening to the musical sounds of fluent Anishnabemowin will attest to its lyrical qualities.

69. Jean Duriez (pseudonym for Jacques Soustelle), "La Question Religieuse au Mexique," Pt. 1 *MASSES* (Paris: No. 9, September 1933), 10-13.

70. As editorial consultant Erin Dolmage points out, some Canadian scholars of hybrid Indigenous and Christian religious formation make similar observations. See Allan Greer, *Mohawk Saint: Catherine Tekakwitha and the Jesuits* (Oxford: Oxford University Press., 2005).

71. Soustelle, *Terre Indienne*, 46-7.

72. Duriez (J. Soustelle), "Question Religieuse," 10-11.

73. Soustelle, "Question Religieuse," 10.

74. Nicole Racine, "Jacques Soustelle" in *Jean Maitre, Dictionnaire Biographique Du Mouvement Ouvrier Français–Quatrième partie 1914-1939 de la Première à la Seconde Guerre Mondiale, Tome 41 Rova à Szy* (Paris: Les Éditions Ouvrières, 1992), 390-1.

75. Scott, "Last of The Indian Treaties," in *Essays, Addresses*, ed., 93.

76. For valuable contributions to this theme, see Dragland, *Floating Voice*, 131-52; Elizabeth Waterston, "The Missing Face: Five Short Stories by Duncan Campbell Scott," *Studies in Canadian Literature*, Vol. 1, 2, (1976), 223-29, accessed July 2009, http://www.lib.unb.ca/Texts/SCL/bin/get.cgi?directory=vol1_2/&filename=waterston.htm.

77. Duncan Campbell Scott, *Selected Stories of Duncan Campbell Scott* (Ottawa: University of Ottawa Press, 1975), 11-26, 75-110.

78. Titley, *Narrow Vision*, 28.

79. Duncan Campbell Scott, "Lines In Memory of Edmund Morris," originally published in Scott's *Lundy's Lane and Other Poems* (Doran, New York, 1916); also Scott, *Selected Poetry*, 64.

80. Edward W. Said, *Culture and Imperialism* (New York, Vintage Books, 1994), xxi.

81. Personal communication, Kenneth Mills, Toronto.

82. Miller, *Compact, Contract*, 167-70.

83. D.M.R. Bentley, "Shadows in the Soul: Racial Haunting in the Poetry of Duncan Campbell Scott," *University of Toronto Quarterly* (Volume 75, Number 2, Spring 2006), 760-64; Dragland, *Floating Voice*, 22, 30, 155, 155-63, 171; for an overview of spiritual practices in the approximate area see Chistopher Vecsey, *Traditional Ojibwa Religion and its Historical Changes* (Philadelphia: American Philosophical Society, 1983); James Redsky and James R. Stevens, *Great Leader of the Ojibway: Mis-Quona-Queb* (Toronto: McClelland and Stewart, 1972); George Nelson, Jennifer S. H. Brown, and Robert Brightman, "The Orders of the Dreamed" in *George Nelson on Cree and Northern Ojibwa Religion and Myth, 1823*, edited by Jennifer S.H. Brown and Robert Brightman (Winnipeg: University of Manitoba Press, 1988); Edward S. Rogers, *The Round Lake Ojibwa* (Toronto: Published by the Ontario Department of Lands and Forests for the Royal Ontario Museum, 1962). Rogers spent ample time in the Round Lake area, north of Lac Seul, at a time that Ojibwa spiritual practices were widely remembered and practised by Elders. His work remains fundamental to the understanding of Indigenous peoples in that area. A white dog sacrifice is also part of traditional Iroquoian practice. See also Elisabeth Tooker, "The Iroquois White Dog Sacrifice in the latter part of the Eighteenth Century," *Ethnohistory* 12, no. 2 (Spring 1965), 129-140 as cited in Titley, *Narrow Vision*, 111, note 4.

84. Joseph L. Vanasse, "The White Dog Feast," *The Canadian Magazine* (Toronto: Vol. 30, No. 1, Nov. 1907), 62.

85. Jennifer S. H. Brown, "I Wish to Be as I See You": An Ojibwa-Methodist Encounter in Fur Trade Country, Rainy Lake, 1854-1855, *Arctic Anthropology* (1987), 19-31; Brown and Maureen Matthews, "Fair Wind: Medicine and Consolation on the Berens River," *Journal of the Canadian Historical Association* (1994), 55-74; Maureen Matthews and Roger Roulette, "Fair Wind's Drum: Maamiwan Obaajigewin," in Jennifer S. H. Brown and Elizabeth Viberts (eds.), *Reading Beyond Words* (Peterborough, ON: Broadview Press, 1996), 330-59; The author witnessed a spiritual sweat ceremony involving medicine people, political leaders, Elders and visitors from the Republic of South Africa in 1997 at the Sagkeeng First Nation on the Winnipeg River in Manitoba. See also Christopher Vecsey, *Traditional Ojibwa Religion and its Historical Changes* (Philadelphia: American Philosophical Society, 1983).

Soustelle talking to workers during construction of the Musée de l'Homme, c.1936–37.

86. Brittany Luby *Dammed: The Politics of Loss and Survival in Anishinaabe Territory* (Winnipeg, MB: University of Manitoba Press, 2020), 35-39.

87. Ibid, 15.

88. Ibid, 38.

89. Government of Canada, The James Bay Treaty–Treaty No. 9 (made in 1905 and 1906) and Adhesions Made in 1929 and 1930 LAC-BAC RG10 Vol.3033,235,225, P 4.

90. Katherine Pettipas, *Severing the Ties that Bind: Government Repression of Indigenous Religious Ceremonies on the Prairies* (Winnipeg: University of Manitoba Press, 1994), 123-4, 163-4; Titley, *Narrow Vision*, 67, 162-83.

91. Samuel Stewart, Treaty 9 Journal 1905. LAC-BAC, RG10 Vol 11399.

92. Vanasse, "The White Dog Feast," 62.

93. Pelham Edgar, "Travelling With A Poet," chap. 5 in *Along My Path* (Toronto: Ryerson, 1952), 60.

94. Scott, Treaty 9 Journal. LAC RG-10 Vol 11399.

95. Ibid, July 6, 1905.

96. Brown and Brightman (eds.), *Orders of the Dreamed*, 64-66.

97. "Bard of The Northland Stirs Hearers With Poems," *The Globe*, April 23, 1925, City News Section. "Mr. Scott further impressed his audience with the wealth of literary material available from the Indian whose Deputy Superintendent General he is in the Civil Service at Ottawa"; Bentley, "Shadows in the Soul," 760; Dragland, *Floating Voice*, 89, 161.

98. Scott, "Last of The Indian Treaties," 90.

99. Scott in *Clever*, ed., 83-86.

100. Dragland, *Floating Voice*, 166-171; Mathews and Roulette, "Fair Wind's Dream," in *Brown and Vibert*, eds., *Beyond Words*, 131.

101. Leonard W. Brockington, "Duncan Campbell Scott's 80th Birthday," *Saturday Night*, Vol. 57, No. 47, Toronto, August 1, 1942, 25; Madge Macbeth, "Duncan Campbell Scott: A Few of My Memories" in *The Canadian Author*

and Bookman (Ottawa: Volume 38, No. 1 Summer, 1962); Sandra Gwyn, *The Private Capital: Ambition and Love in the Age of Macdonald and Laurier* (Toronto: McClelland and Stewart, 1984), 455-7.

102. Titley, *Narrow Vision*, 67; Bentley, "Shadows in the Soul," 760-64.

103. Forms of spiritualism were popular among the Ottawa elite of Scott's civil service heyday including with Prime Minister William Lyon Mackenzie King. See Ramsay Cook, *The Regenerators: Social Criticism in Late Victorian English Canada* (Toronto, Buffalo, London: University of Toronto Press, 1985), 65-85, 167-168.

104. Gwyn, *Private Capital*, 466-70.

105. Duncan Campbell Scott letter to Elise Aylen September 8, 1929. Lord Nelson Hotel, Halifax NS, LMS-0204 Elise Aylen-DC Scott fonds LAC-BAC, Ottawa Box 1 Folder 4 "Personal correspondence DC Scott 1929."

106. Soustelle, *Terre Indienne*, 46-7, 52, 66-7, 199; Soustelle, "La Famille Otomi-pame du Mexique Central" (Paris: Institut d'ethnologie 1937); Soustelle, *Quatre Soleils*, 63, 80-2, 97, 103-6, 172-3, 188.

107. Soustelle, *Terre Indienne*, 149; Mariano Azuela, *Los De Abajo y Mala Yerba* (México, D.F.: Fondo de Cultura Económica, 2004), originally published 1915.

108. Soustelle, *Terre Indienne*, 29.

109. Ibid, 71, 227.

110. Soustelle, *Quatre Soleils*, 45-66. The American anthropologist Afred M. Tozzer, Danish archeologist Franz Blom and his wife the Swiss photographer Gertrude Darby were among those whose work among the Lacandóns influenced Soustelle.

111. Christine Barthe (sous la direction de), *le Yucatán est Ailleurs Expéditions Photographiques Désiré Charnay (1857-1886)* (Paris: Musée du quai Branly, Actes Sud, 2007); Alfred M. Tozzer, "A Comparative Study of the Maya and the Lacandónes," PhD dissertation, Harvard University, 1904; *Social Origins and Social Continuities* (New York: The Macmillan company, 1925); Ignacio Gutiérrez Ruvalcaba, *Teoberto Maler: Historia De Un Fotógrafo Vuelto Arqueólogo* (México, D.F.: Instituto Nacional de Antropolgía e Historia, 2008).

112. Soustelle, *Terre Indienne*, 155-160.

113. Ibid.

114. MNHN fonds Rivet 2 APIC Sous. Jacques Soustelle, letter to Paul Rivet. Mexico, March 20, 1934.

115. MNHN Soustelle letter of March 20, 1934 to Rivet.

116. Néstor García Canclini, *Culturas Híbridas: Estrategias Para Entrar y Salir De La Modernidad* (Buenos Aires: Paidós, 2001), 165-77; Quetzil E. Castañeda, *In the Museum of Maya Culture: Touring Chichén Itzá.* (Minneapolis: University of Minnesota Press, 1996), 5, 117-21; Alex Saragoza, "The Selling of Mexico: Tourism and the State, 1929-1952," in Gilbert Joseph, Anne Rubenstein, & Eric Zolov, *Fragments of a Golden Age–The Politics of Culture in Mexico Since 1940* (Durham, NC: Duke University Press, 2001), 91-115.

117. Soustelle, *Quatre Soleils*, 83.

118. Soustelle, *Terre Indienne*, 199.

119. Pick, *Faces…*, 37-73.

120. MNHN fonds Rivet 2 APIC Sous. Jacques Soustelle letter to Paul Rivet. Mexico, November 30, 1932. For a discussion of Gamio's multi-faceted role as anthropologist, activist and government employee, see Claudio Lomnitz, "Bordering on Anthropology: Dialectics of a National Tradition," in *Deep Mexico, Silent Mexico: An Anthropology of Nationalism* (Minneapolis and London: University of Minnesota Press, 2001), 250-4.

121. Titley, *Narrow Vision*, 76-7.

122. Alexander S Dawson, *Indian and Nation in Revolutionary Mexico* (Tucson: University of Arizona Press, 2004); Alexander S Dawson, "From Models for the Nation to Model Citizens," *Journal of Latin American Studies 17*, no. 2 (1998): 375-402.

123. Vasconcelos and Jaén, *The Cosmic Race*; Todd Shepard, "Algeria, France, Mexico, UNESCO: A Transnational History of Anti-Racism and Decolonization, 1932–1962," *Journal of Global History* (Cambridge, UK: Cambridge University Press, 2011), 6(2), 273–297.

124. Soustelle, *Terre Indienne*, 150.

125. Ibid, 151.

126. Soustelle, *Souvenirs*, 27-45.

127. Ullmann, *Le Mal Aimé*, 9-10.

128. Jean Duriez (Jacques Soustelle), "La Lutte Contre la Guerre et le Fascisme au Mexique" (Paris: *Spartacus* Décembre 14, 1934), 3.

129. Stephen Tyre, "From Algérie Française to France Musulmane: Jacques Soustelle and the Myths and Realities of 'Integration', 1955–1962." *French History* 20, no. 3 (09, 2006), 277-86.

130. Soustelle, *Terre Indienne*, 125-153.

131. Duriez (Soustelle), "La Question Religieuse au Mexique" (Paris: *MASSES*, editions of September, October, November and December 1933).

132. Duriez (Soustelle), "La Lutte Contre la Guerre et le Fascisme au Mexique" (Paris: *Spartacus*, Décembre 14, 1934), 3.

133. Jean Duriez (Jacques Soustelle), "Comment "ils" voient le Mexique" (*MASSES*, Juillet 1934), 12.

134. Jacques Soustelle, *Le drame algérien et la décadence française Réponse a Raymond Aron* (Paris: Plon–Tribune Libre 6, 1957), 2.

135. Duriez (Jacques Soustelle), (1934), 12.

136. MNHN fonds Rivet 2 APIC Jacques Soustelle from San Angel, Mexico to Paul Rivet, December 8, 1933. This folder of correspondence between Rivet and Soustelle contains many letters written by Soustelle to Rivet from Mexico between 1932 and 1940. Some touch upon Soustelle's doctoral research; some about his military service prior to June 1940; and some offer political commentary on the Cardenás and Camacho presidencies.

137. Duriez (Soustelle), "Comment 'ils' Voient le Mexique," 12.

138. MNHN fonds Rivet 2 APIC Soustelle letter to Rivet, Dec 8, 1935.

139. Soustelle, *Terre Indienne*, 1936; Soustelle, *La Famille Otomí-Pame Du Mexique Central*, Université De Paris. Travaux et Mémoires De l'Institut d'Ethnologie. Vol. 26 (Paris: Institut d'ethnologie, 1937).

140. Nicole Racine, "Soustelle, Jacques," in *Dictionnaire*, 390-1.

141. Robin Brownlie, *A Fatherly Eye: Indian Agents, Government Power and Aboriginal Resistance in Ontario, 1918-1939* (Don Mills, ON: Oxford University Press, 2003), 136-38; John S. Milloy, *A National Crime: The Canadian Government and the Residential School System, 1879-1986* (Winnipeg: University of Manitoba Press, 1999), 70-1; Pettipas, *Severing the Ties*, (1994), 149-51; Titley, *Narrow Vision*, 75-93, 162-183.

142. Duncan Campbell Scott, *The Circle of Affection* (Toronto: McClelland & Stewart, 1947), 109-22.

143. For example, *Les Quatre Soleils–Souvenirs et Reflexions d'un Ethnologue au Mexique* was re-published by CNRS of Paris in 2009. Soustelle's doctoral thesis of 1936 was published in Spanish as "La familia Otomí-Pame" in 1993 by Centro de los Estudios Mexicanos y Centroamericanos in Mexico City. As of July 2009, the book was available in bookstores in both Mexico City and Oaxaca. Soustelle's *The Daily Life of the Aztecs* originally published in French in 1955 was re-published by Dover Press of New York in 2002.

CHAPTER THREE

1. Aimé Césaire, *Discours Sur Le Colonialisme* (Paris: Présence Africaine, 1976; 1955); Frantz Fanon, *Les Damnes de la Terre Préface de Jean-Paul Sartre* (Paris: Maspero, 1961); Albert Camus, *Actuelles: Écrits Politiques* (Paris: Gallimard, 1977).

2. Ian Lustick, *State-Building Failure in British Ireland & French Algeria* (Berkeley: iiS Institute of States, International Studies, University of California, Berkeley, 1985), 72-3. See also Lustick, *Unsettled Disputed Lands: Britain and Ireland, France and Algeria, Israel and the West Bank-Gaza* (Ithaca, N.Y.: Cornell University Press, 1993), 239-301, 317; see also Lustick, "Two-State Illusion: The idea of a state for Palestinians and one for Israelis is a fantasy that blinds us and impedes progress," The New York Times, Sunday Review. Lustick argues that errors in judgement of French rulers in Algeria are being repeated in the Middle East.

3. The literature containing the narrative history of French history in Algeria is extensive. Two principal works are, Yves Courrière, *La Guerre d'Algérie* (Paris: Fayard, 2001); and Alistair Horne, *A Savage War of Peace: Algeria, 1954-1962* (New York: Viking Press, 1978).

4. Olive Dickason, *Canada's First Nations: A History Of Founding Peoples From Earliest Times* (Toronto: McClelland and Stewart, 1992), 257-72; J.R. Miller, *Skyscrapers Hide The Heavens: A History Of Indian-White Relations In Canada* (Toronto: University of Toronto Press, 1989), 83-98; E. Brian Titley, *A Narrow Vision: Duncan Campbell Scott And The Administration Of Indian Affairs In Canada* (Vancouver, UBC Press, 1986), 1-11.

5. Dickason, *Canada's First Nations*, 181-88; J.R. Miller,

Compact, Contract, Covenant: Aboriginal Treaty-Making in Canada (Toronto, Buffalo, London: University of Toronto Press, 2009), 66-70.

6. See for example Hugh Brody, *Maps and Dreams: Indians and the British Columbia Frontier* (Vancouver: Douglas & McIntyre, 1981); Colin Bundy, *The Rise & Fall of the South African Peasantry* (Cape Town and London: David Phillip-James Currey, 1979); Sarah Carter, *Lost Harvests* (McGill-Queen's Native and Northern Series. Vol. 3. Montreal QC: McGill-Queen's University Press, 1990); Cole R. Harris, *Making Native Space: Colonialism, Resistance, and Reserves in British Columbia* (Vancouver: UBC Press, 2002); John S. Milloy, "The Era Of Civilization–British Policy For The Indians of Canada, 1830-1860" (PhD dissertation, Oxford University, 1978); Noël Mostert, *Frontiers: The Epic of South Africa's Creation and the Tragedy of the Xhosa People* (New York: Knopf: Distributed by Random House, 1992); Adele Perry, *On The Edge of Empire: Gender, Race and the Making of British Columbia, 1849-1871* (Toronto, Buffalo, London: University of Toronto Press, 2001); Henry Reynolds, *The Other Side of the Frontier: Aboriginal Resistance to the European Invasion of Australia* (Harmondsworth: Penguin, 1982); E. Brian Titley, *A Narrow Vision: Duncan Campbell Scott and the Administration of Indian Affairs in Canada* (Vancouver: University of British Columbia Press, 1986). In 1995, I directed and produced the video documentary *We Have Such Things At Home*, a comparative examination of Native policy in Canada and South Africa. (Toronto: produced by Tamarack Productions–distribution www.vtape.org).

7. Herman Merivale, *Lectures on Colonization and Colonies* (London: Longman, Orme, Brown, Green, and Longmans, 1841); David McNab, "Herman Merivale and the Native Question, 1837-1861," *Albion: A Quarterly Journal Concerned with British Studies* 9, no. 4 (Winter, 1977), 359-384; Dickason, *First Nations*, 248, 264-5.

8. Keith D Smith, *Liberalism, Surveillance, and Resistance: Indigenous Communities in Western Canada* (Edmonton: AU Press, 2009), 8.

9. Uday Sing Mehta, "Liberal Strategies of Exclusion" in Frederic Cooper and Ann Stoler (eds.) *Tensions of Empire: Colonial Cultures in a Bourgeois World* (Berkeley/Los Angeles/London: University of California Press, 1997), 59-62; See also Mehta, *Liberalism and Empire: A Study in Nineteenth-Century British Liberal Thought* (Chicago: University of Chicago Press, 1999).

Soustelle's book "Loved and Suffering Algeria" was published in 1956.

10. See Ian McKay, "The Liberal Order Framework: A Prospectus for a Reconnaissance of Canadian History," *Canadian Historical Review* 81, no. 4 (Dec. 2000), 627-8, 640, 644; Jennifer Pitts, "Empire and Democracy: Tocqueville and the Algeria Question," *The Journal of Political Philosophy,* Volume 8, Number 3, 2000, 295-318; see also Pitts, *A Turn To Empire: The Rise of Imperial Liberalism in Britain and France* (Princeton, NJ: Princeton University Press, 2005), 138-147, 204-18; Lucien Sève, "Trois réflexions sur le libéralisme," *Le Monde Diplomatique,* June 2013 page 22; in this review essay, Sève looks at three recent publications in French that look at liberalism in the light of precepts of universal human rights. Of these works, Domenico Losurdo's is most pertinent to this dissertation; Domenico Losurdo, *Contre-Histoire du Libéralisme, traduit de l'Italien par Bernard Chamayou* (Paris: Découverte, 2013); Losurdo, *Liberalism: a counter history,* translated by Greg Elliott (London: Verso, 2011).

11. Patrick Deneen, *Why Liberalism Failed*, 50.

12. See Mehta, "Liberal Strategies"; Pitts, *A Turn to Empire,*

9, 63, 235, 248; Tzvetan Todorov, *Nous Et Les Autres: La Réflexion Française Sur La Diversité Humaine* (Paris: Éditions du Seuil, 1989), 262-79.

13. Mehta, "Liberal Strategies," 61. For a useful specific example in the northern Canadian context of the 1970s, in the midst of and gas exploration, see Mel Watkins and University League for Social Reform, *Dene Nation, The Colony Within* (Toronto; Buffalo: University of Toronto Press, 1977).

14. Sec. 91.42 The Constitution Act, Canada, accessed May 2010, http://laws.justice.gc.ca/en/const/3.html#anchorbo-ga:s_91-gb:s_91.

15. Sections 92.5 and 92a The Constitution Act, Canada, accessed May 2010, http://laws.justice.gc.ca/en/const/3.html#anchorbo-ga:s_91-gb:s_91. Such arrangements are part of the bedrock of Canada's constitutional existence. After a century of national life, Canadians attempted to revise the British North America Act on several occasions. Finally in 1982 the BNA Act was repatriated. Despite the inclusion of new recognition for "existing aboriginal and treaty rights," the crucial provincial-federal jurisdictional divide over resources was maintained. Such a division of powers was constitutionally entrenched in 1982 when the BNA Act became The Constitution Act.

16. Robin Brownlie, *A Fatherly Eye: Indian Agents, Government Power, and Aboriginal Resistance in Ontario, 1918-1939* (New York: Oxford University Press, 2003), 86, 156; Mari Heinrichs & Dianne Hiebert with the People of Mishkeegogamang, Mishkeegogamang: *The Land, The People & The Purpose* (Kelowna, BC: Rosetta Projects, 2003), 91-2, 119. See also Harris, Native Space and Paul Tennant, *Aboriginal Peoples and Politics: The Indian Land Question in British Columbia, 1849-1989* (Vancouver: University of British Columbia Press, 1990) for a discussion of these issues regarding British Columbia.

17. Duncan Campbell Scott, "The Last Of The Indian Treaties," *Scribner's Magazine*, Vol X.L. - 62 (1906), 577.

18. Government of Canada, The James Bay Treaty–Treaty No. 9 LAC RG10 Vol. 3033, 235, 225.

19. See J.R. Miller, *Compact, Contract, Covenant: Aboriginal Treaty Making in Canada* (Toronto, Buffalo, London: University of Toronto Press, 2009), 207-11; John Flood, "The Duplicity of D.C. Scott and the James Bay Treaty," *Black Moss* Sec. Series, No. 2 (Fall 1976), 50-63; John S. Long, *Treaty no. 9 Making the Agreement to Share the Land in Far Northern Ontario in 1905* (Montreal & Kingston, London, Ithaca: McGill-Queen's University Press, 2010), 3-9, 85; CBC Radio *Ideas*, "George MacMartin's Big Canoe Trip," first broadcast December 19, 2011. Radio documentary written and presented by Christopher Moore, produced by Sarah Wolch about Treaty 9 promises as recorded in diary of MacMartin, Treaty 9 Commissioner for Ontario. National English Language Radio Service of the Canadian Broadcasting Corporation, Toronto Broadcast Centre, accessed December 20, 2011, http://www.cbc.ca/ideas/episodes/2011/12/19/george-macmartins-big-canoe-trip/.

20. Scott, *Treaties*, 578.

21. Royal Proclamation, October 7, 1763, accessed May 2012, http://www.johnco.com/nativel/pro1763.html.

22. Miller, *Compact*.

23. McKay, "Canada as a Long Liberal Revolution: On Writing the History of Actually Existing Canadian Liberalisms," in Jean-Francois Constant and Michel Ducharme, eds, *Liberalism and Hegemony: Debating the Canadian Liberal Revolution* (Toronto, Buffalo, London: University of Toronto Press, 2009), 347-352.

24. Mckay, "Liberal Order Framework."

25. Dickason, *Canada's First Nations*, 400.

26. J. Arthur Lower, *Western Canada: An Outline History* (Vancouver and Toronto: Douglas & McIntyre, 1983), 96-7.

27. W.L. Morton, *Manitoba: A History* (Toronto: University of Toronto Press, 1967), 117; Gerald Friesen, *River Road: Essays on Manitoba and Prairie History* (Winnipeg: University of Manitoba Press, 1996), 58-64.

28. Jean Barman, *The West Beyond the West: A History of British Columbia*. 3rd ed. (Toronto: University of Toronto Press, 2007), 156.

29. Ibid, 339.

30. See George Manuel & Michael Posluns, *The Fourth World: An Indian Reality* (Don Mills, ON: Collier Macmillan Canada, 1974); H. A McCue, *The Only Good Indian: Essays by Canadian Indians* (Toronto: New Press. 1970).

31. Jeremy Adelman and Stephen Aron, "From Borderlands to Borders: Empires, Nation-States, and the Peoples in between in North American History," *The American Historical Review*, Vol. 104, No. 3 (Jun., 1999) 817-23.

32. Coulthard, Glen Sean, *Red Skin, White Masks* (Minneapolis: University of Minnesota Press, 2014); Betasamosake Simpson, Leanne, *This Accident of Being Lost* (Toronto: House of Anansi Press, 2017); *As We Have Always Done: Indigenous Freedom Through Radical Resistance* (Minneapolis: University of Minnesota Press, 2017); *Islands of Decolonial Love* (Winnipeg: ARP Books, 2015).

33. Betasamosake Simpson, …*Being Lost*, 5.

34. In addition to works already cited see Russell Diabo "First Nations Strategic Bulletin," available on-line, in libraries and on Diabo's Facebook page; Pamela Palmater, *Indigenous Nationhood: Empowering Grassroots Citizens* (Halifax, NS: Fernwood Publishing, 2015); Tanya Talaga, *Seven Fallen Feathers: Racism, Death, and Hard Truths in a Northern City* (Toronto: Anansi Nonfiction, 2017).

35. Pierre Elliot Trudeau, speech Vancouver, August 8, 1969.

36. Pierre Elliot Trudeau, "Les Séparatistes: Des Contre-Révolutionnaires," *Cite Libre*, Volume 15, No. 67, May 1964.

37. Ernest Renan, *Qu'est-ce qu'une Nation? Et Autres Écrits Politiques: Présentation Raoul Girardet* (Paris: Imprimerie Nationale Éditions, 1996), 227.

38. Alistair Horne, *A Savage War of Peace: Algeria 1954-1962* (New York: New York Review of Books, 2006–originally published 1977), 105-9; Bernard Ullmann, *Jacques Soustelle–Le Mal Aimé* (Paris: Plon, 1995), 190-5.

39. Philippe Baudorre and Centre d'études et de recherches sur François Mauriac, *La Plume Dans La Plaie: Les Écrivains Journalistes Et La Guerre d'Algérie* (Sémaphores Pessac: Presses Universitaires de Bordeaux, 2003); James D. Le Sueur, *Uncivil War: Intellectuals and Identity Politics During the Decolonization of Algeria* (Philadelphia: University of Pennsylvania Press, 2001); Le Sueur, "Decolonizing French Universalism': Reconsidering the impact of the Algerian War on French intellectuals," in *The Decolonization Reader* (New York; London: Routledge, 2003); Pascal Ory et Jean-François Sirinelli, *Les Intellectuels En France, De l'Affaire Dreyfus à Nos Jours* (Paris: A. Colin, 1986).

40. Horne, *Savage War*, 105-7.

41. Two of the best general histories on the Algerian-French war are: Yves Courrière, *La Guerre d'Algérie* (Paris: Fayard, 2001); Horne, *Savage War*.

42. Horne, *Savage War*, 83-104.

43. For a look back at Dien Bien Phu see *The Ghosts of War*, Michael Maclear, director, Memory Films 2004. Maclear, a Canadian, was the English-speaking world's preeminent broadcast journalist on the wars in Viet Nam for 30 years. *The Ghosts of War* is his essay-like documentary film reflecting on imperialism, war and lessons unlearned.

44. Horne, *Savage War*, 67-8, 99, 168-9; Alain-Gérard Slama, *La Guerre d'Algérie: Histoire d'Une Déchirure* (Paris: Gallimard, 1996), 46; Denise Bouche, *Histoire De La Colonisation Francaise, Tome Second, Flux Et Reflux (1815-1962)* (Paris: Fayard, 1991), 430, 434, 447-9.

45. Bouche, *Colonisation Francaise*, 430, 434, 447-9; Horne, *Savage War*, 78-9, 89, 98-9, 166, 268, 376, 434; Girardet, *l'Idée Coloniale*, 343-7.

46 Girardet, *l'Idée Coloniale*, 367-402.

47. Lustick, *State-Building Failures*, 72-6; Horne, *Savage War*, 99-100.

48. Horne, *Savage War*, 36-7, 41, 346; Slama, *Déchirure*, 22-9.

49. Charles-Robert Ageron, *Histoire De l'Algérie Contemporaine* (Paris: Presses Universitaires de France, 1979), 94-8; Bernard Droz et Évelyne Lever, *Histoire De La Guerre d'Algérie (1954-1962)* (Paris: Seuil, 1982), 33-6; Slama, *Déchirure*, 28-9; Horne, *Savage War*, 36-7, 41.

50. Ibid.

51. Horne, *Savage War*, 67-8, 175-6.

52. Girardet, *L'Idée Coloniale*, 340.

53. Horne, *Savage War*, 105-7; Ullmann, *Mal Aimé*, 186-90.

54. Horne, *Savage War*, 105-7.

55. Ullmann, (1995); Jacques Soustelle, *Souvenirs, Apocryphes en forme de dialogue avec George Suffert* (c.1986) (unpublished manuscript provided to the author by Bernard Ullmann); Odile Rudelle, Archives de l'Université Sciences-Po Fondation national des sciences politiques service des archives d'histoire contemporain–Témoignages sur la guerre d'Algérie Recueillis par Mme Odile Rudelle, M. Jacques Soustelle, 19 Février 1979.

56. Jacques Frémeaux, *France Et l'Algérie En Guerre 1830-1870, 1954-1962* (Paris: CFHM, Commission Française d'Histoire Militaire Institut de Stratégie Comparée Economica, 2002), 48-49.

57. See Jennifer Pitts, "Empire and Democracy: Tocqueville and the Algeria Question," *The Journal of Political Philosophy* (Vol. 8, Number 3, 2000), 299, 301; Pitts, *A Turn to Empire: The Rise of Imperial Liberalism in Britain and France* (Princeton, N.J.: Princeton Unversity Press, 2005), 204-26.

58. Pitts, "Tocqueville and the Algeria Question," 295-318; Pitts, *A Turn to Empire*, 2-6, 209, 222-4, 230, 233, 237; Tzvetan Todorov, *Nous et les Autres–La Réflexion Française Sure la Diversité Humaine* (Paris: Editions du Seuil, 1989), 262-79; Mehta, "Liberal Strategies," 75-7.

59. Alexis de Tocqueville, "Travail sur L'Algérie 1841," in *Tocqueville sur l'Algérie, Présentation par Seloua Luste Boulbina* (Paris: Flammarion, 2003), 112.

60. Germaine Tillion, "L'Algérie en 1956," in *L'Afrique Bascule Vers L'Avenir* (Paris: Editions Tirésias–Michel Reynaud, 1999), 67-74. Originally published in pamphlet form Tillion, *L'Algérie En 1957* (Paris: Association nationale des anciennes déportées et internées de la résistance, 1957), MqB.

61. Tocqueville, "Travail sur l'Algérie 1841," 74.

62.. BNF Mitterand, *De Coté de Chez Fred*. Feature interview in two parts with Jacques Soustelle, broadcast on French national television, 1989. In audio-visual subject headings for Jacques Soustelle and/or journalist Frédéric Mitterand.

63. Jacques Soustelle, *Lettre Ouverte aux Victimes de la Décolonisation* (Paris: Éditions Albin Michel, 1973), 123.

64. AOM 11CAB/38 Instructions April 4, 1955; minutes of meeting "TRES SECRET," État Major Mixte (June 29, 1955).

65. Pitts, "Tocqueville and the Algeria Question," 316. See also Olivier Le Cour Grandmaison, *Coloniser Exterminer Sur la Guerre de l'État colonial* (Paris: Fayard, 2005), 7-11.

66. Todorov, Nous et les Autres, 279.

67. Pitts, "Tocqueville and the Algeria Question," 303-4, 314-7; Pitts, Turn to Empire, 9, 248; Mehta, "Liberal Strategies," 67-8, 75-8.

68. Pitts, "Tocqueville and the Algeria Question," 308-9, 311.

69. Girardet, *L'Idée Coloniale*, 343-7.

70. Pitts, *Turn to Empire*, 300.

71. Le Sueur, "Decolonizing," 105.

Scott met Belle Botsford, a professional violinist from Boston, when she was performing in Ottawa.

72. Ibid, 106.

73. Ibid.

74. Ibid.

75. Albert Camus, *Actuelles III Chroniques Algériennes 1939-1958* (Paris: Gallimard, 1958), 11-25.

76. Christine Laurière, *Paul Rivet Le Savant Et Le Politique* (Paris: Publications Scientifiques du Muséum National d'Histoire Naturelle, 2008), 617-8.

77. Dickason, *Canada's First Nations*, 248, 264-5; Harris, Making Native Space, 6-9, 13-4; McNab, "Merivale and the Native Question," 365-9.

78. Merivale, *Lectures*, 490.

Elise Aylen Scott, a published poet, was born in Ottawa in 1904. She was married to Scott for 16 years. She died in India in 1972.

79. Ibid, 493.

80. Ibid.

81. Milloy, "Era," 177-92; Titley, *Narrow Vision*, 3.

82. Milloy, "Era," 192-5.

83. Merivale, *Lectures*, 494.

84. Titley, *Narrow Vision*, 1-9; Milloy, "Era," 324-32.

85. Merivale, *Lectures*, 26-27.

86. Ibid, 73-74.

87. Ibid, 549.

88. Ibid, 511-512.

89. Ibid.

90. Titley, *Narrow Vision*, 76-7.

91. Nicholas Flood Davin, "Report on Industrial Schools for Indians and Half-Breeds" submitted to the government of Canada, Ottawa, March 14, 1879. LAC, Microfilm reel C-1518.

92. Ibid, 1.

93. Ibid, 7.

94. Ibid, 14-15.

95. Ibid, 9.

96. Ibid, 11.

97. Milloy, *National Crime*, 31-2; Titley, *Narrow Vision*, 76-7.

98. J. R. Miller, *Shingwauk's Vision: A History of Native Residential Schools* (Toronto: University of Toronto Press, 1996), 101-3; John Sheridan Milloy, *A National Crime: The Canadian Government and the Residential School System, 1879-1986* (Winnipeg: University of Manitoba Press, 1999), xiv-xv, 7-8, 31-32; Maggie Siggins, *Bitter Embrace: White Society's Assault on the Woodland Cree* (Toronto: McClelland & Stewart, 2005), 145-7.

99. Titley, *Narrow Vision*, 94-109.

100. Duncan Campbell Scott briefing notes regarding compulsory education for appearance at Parliamentary Committee, (1920), LAC/BAC RG10 Vol 6810, file 470-2-3 Pt.7.

101. Miller, *Shingwauk's Vision*; Milloy, *National Crime*, 33, 70, 102-3; Titley, *Narrow Vision*, 76-93.

102. Milloy, "Era," 175-92; D. M. R. Bentley, "Shadows in the Soul: Racial Haunting in the Poetry of Duncan Campbell Scott." *University of Toronto Quarterly* 75, no. Number 2, Spring 2006, 754-6.

103. Pitts, "Tocqueville and the Algeria Question," 295-8.

104. Julien, Charles-André, *Histoire De l'Algérie Contemporaine: La Conquête Et Les Débuts De La Colonisation (1827-1871)* (Paris: Presses Universitaires de France, 1964), 425-6; Charles-Robert de Ageron, *Histoire de l'Algérie Contemporaine Tome II: De l'insurrection de 1871 au Déclenchement de la Guerre de Libération 1954* (Paris: Presses Universitaires de France, 1979), 32-9; Herbert Ingram Priestley, *France Overseas: A Study of Modern Imperialism* (New York: Octagon Books, 1966

originally published 1938), 76-86; Bouche, *Colonisation Francaise*, 112-3.

105. Lustick, *State-Building Failure*, 51-6.

106. Ageron, *Histoire de l'Algérie*, 9.

107. Jacques Soustelle, *La Vie Quotidienne des Aztèques à la Veille de la Conquête Espagnole* (Paris: Librairie Hachette, 1955), 128.

108. Soustelle, *Vie Quotidienne*, 59.

109. Soustelle, *Vie Quotidienne*, 143.

110. Ibid; Jacques Soustelle, "Souvenirs, Apocryphes en Forme de Dialogue avec George Suffert," unpublished manuscript provided to the author by Bernard Ullmann.

111. Horne, *Savage War*, 108; Stephen Tyre, "From Algérie Française to France Musulmane: Jacques Soustelle and the Myths and Realities of 'Integration', 1955–1962," *French History* 20, no. 3 (09, 2006): 276-296.

112. Rudelle, "Témoignages Soustelle," 282-4.

113. Jacques Soustelle, *Aimée et Souffrante Algérie* (Paris: Plon, 1956).

114. Ullmann, *Mal Aimé*, 235-40; Slama, *Déchirure*, 94-106; Horne, *Savage War*, 281, 368-70.

115. Ulllmann, *Mal Aimé*, 295-8.

116. Jacques Soustelle, *L'Ésperance Trahie, 1958-1961* (Paris: Editions de l'Alma, 1962); Jacques Soustelle, *Sur une Nouvelle Route* (Paris: Éditions du Fuseau, 1964); Jacques Soustelle, *La Page n'est pas Tournée* (Paris: La Table ronde, 1965).

117. Soustelle, *Nouvelle Route*, 33-35.

118. Ullmann, *Mal Aimé*, 359.

119. Jacques Soustelle, *Les Quatre Soleils* (Paris: Librairie Plon, 1967), 79; see A. L. Kroeber, *A Roster of Civilizations and Culture* (Chicago: Aldine Pub. Co., 1962).

120. Soustelle, *Quatre Soleils*, 103-4.

121. Ullmann, *Mal Aimé*, 359-363.

122. Jacques Soustelle, *La Pensée Cosmologique des Anciens Mexicains* (Représentation du Monde et de l'Espace) (Paris: Hermann & Cie, 1940), 10; Soustelle, *Quatre Soleils*, 120-22.

123. Soustelle, *Vie Quotidienne*, 143.

124. Jacques Soustelle, *Le Drame Algérien et la Décadence Française Réponse a Raymond Aron* (Paris: Plon–Tribune Libre 6, 1957), 2, 29-31, 37.

125. Titley, *Narrow Vision*, 75-109.

126. Queen's University Archives, Lorne Pierce Archives. Coll 2000.1 Box 80 Folder: DC Scott poems. Poem originally published in *The Montreal Star*, September, 1901.

127. LAC-BAC E.K. Brown correspondence MG30 D61 Vol. 3, letter from DC Scott to Brown, 19-23 November, 1943.

128. CBC Radio archives http://archives.cbc.ca/society/monarchy/clips/13518/, and http://archives.cbc.ca/society/monarchy/topics/2367/. Clips from Canadian Broadcasting Corporation's radio broadcasts of Royal tour arrival in Québec City on May 17, 1939 and on tour in Winnipeg May 24, 1939, accessed July 2012.

129. LAC-BAC LMS-0204, Folder 30 "A Farewell To Their Majesties" was commissioned from Scott at the request of CBC General Manager Gladstone Murray in a letter dated May 5, 1939. The poem was read on air by "Mr. Willis," almost certainly then CBC producer/announcer J. Frank Willis.

CHAPTER FOUR

1. Paul N. Edison, "Conquest Unrequited: French Expeditionary Science in Mexico, 1864-1867," *French Historical Studies* 26, no. 3 (2003), 459-495; Christine Lauriere, *Paul Rivet Le Savant Et Le Politique* (Paris: Publications Scientifiques du Muséum National d'Histoire Naturelle, 2008); see also Benedict Anderson, *Imagined Communities: Reflections on the Origin and Spread of Nationalism* (London: Verso, 1991); Alice L. Conklin, *In The Museum of Man: Race, Anthropology and Empire in France 1850-1950* (Ithaca: Cornell University Press, 2013).

2. Jacques Soustelle, *L'Art Du Mexique Ancien* (Paris: Arthaud, 1966); Pierre Verger; Introduction et Notes de Jacques Soustelle, *Mexique* (Paris: Paul Hartmann, 1955).

3. Wilfred Campbell, Archibald Lampman, and Duncan Campbell Scott, *At the Mermaid Inn: Wilfred Campbell, Archibald Lampman, Duncan Campbell Scott in the Globe 1892-93* (Toronto: University of Toronto Press, 1979).

4. Ullmann, *Mal Aimé*, 16-17.

5. Laboratoire de l'Éthnomusicologie, Musée de l'Homme,

Paris; Jacques Soustelle, "Profil du Gaullisme," *Hommes et Faits du XXe Siècle* (Paris: SERP, 1970); Marcel Boudo, dir. "La Splendeur du Mexique Ancien," Part 1: *Les Azteques*; Part 2: *Les Guerriers du Soleil* (Paris and Mexico City: France 3 Regions–Marseille and Televisa, Mexico: 1978). Digital copies available for screening at Inathèque, BNF Mitterand. Soustelle is credited as a producer and appears on screen as narrator. The documentary was re-broadcast on French television within weeks of Soustelle's death on September 24, 1990.

6. Stan Dragland, *Floating Voice: Duncan Campbell Scott and the Literature of Treaty 9* (Concord, ON: Anansi, 1994). The cover of Dragland's book features a photograph of Scott with his camera at a portage along the Treaty 9 route.

7. *Mexique Terre Indienne* and *Les Quatre Soleils* both feature Soustelle's ethnographic field photography from his first trips to Mexico.

8. Jacques Soustelle, *Aimée Et Souffrante Algérie* (Paris: Plon, 1956).

9. Conklin, *Museum* and Laurière, *Rivet*.

10. Lawrence Gustave Desmond, *Yucatán Through Her Eyes: Alice Dixon Le Plongeon, Writer & Expeditionary Photographer* (Albuquerque: University of New Mexico Press, 2009), 23-26.

11. Jacques Soustelle, *Mémoires, Apocryphes Sous la Forme d'Une Dialogue avec Georges Suffert*, unpublished manuscript provided to the author by Bernard Ullmann, 4.

12. Robert D. Aguirre, *Informal Empire: Mexico and Central America in Victorian Culture* (Minneapolis: University of Minnesota Press, 2005); Christine Barthe (sous la direction de), *Le Yucatán est Ailleurs Expéditions Photographiques Désiré Charnay (1857-1886)* (Paris: Musée du Quai Branly, Actes Sud, 2007); Lawrence Gustave Desmond, *Yucatán Through Her Eyes: Alice Dixon Le Plongeon, Writer & Expeditionary Photographer* (Albuquerque: University of New Mexico Press, 2009); Mary Louise Pratt, *Imperial Eyes: Travel Writing and Transculturation*, 2nd ed. (London & New York: Routledge, 2008); Alfred H. Siemens, *Between the Summit and the Sea: Central Veracruz in the Nineteenth Century* (Vancouver: University of British Columbia Press, 1990); Sebastián Van Doesburg, *Teobert Maler: Vistas de Oaxaca, 1874-1876* (Hamburg: Museum fur Volkerkunde, 2004).

13. Edison, "Conquest Unrequited," 463.

14. See Claudio Lomnitz-Adler, *Deep Mexico, Silent Mexico: An Anthropology of Nationalism* (Minneapolis: University of Minnesota Press, 2001), 150-7.

15. Alexander S. Dawson, *Indian and Nation in Revolutionary Mexico* (Tucson: University of Arizona Press, 2004), 1-29; Dawson, "From Models for the Nation to Model Citizens," *Journal of Latin American Studies* 30.2 (1998), 279-308; Mary K.Vaughan and Stephen E. Lewis, "Introduction" in *The Eagle and the Virgin: Nation and Cultural Revolution in Mexico, 1920-1940*, Vaughan and Lewis eds. (Durham N.C.: Duke University Press, 2006), 1-2, 4-5; Vaughan, "Nationalizing the Countryside: Schools and Rural Communities in the 1930s," in Vaughan and Lewis eds., *Eagle and the Virgin*, 173-4; Claudio Lomnitz, "Final Reflections: What Was Mexico's Cultural Revolution?," in Vaughan and Lewis eds., *Eagle and the Virgin*, 342-3; Lomnitz, *Deep Mexico*, 241-257; Lomnitz, "Bordering on Anthropology: Dialectics of a National Tradition," in *Deep Mexico, Silent Mexico: An Anthropology of Nationalism* (Minneapolis and London: University of Minnesota Press, 2011), 228-62; Adrian A. Bantjes, "Saints, Sinners, and State Formation: Local Religion and Cultural Revolution in Mexico," in Vaughan and Lewis eds., *Eagle and the Virgin*, 141.

16. The literature on the relationship between the social sciences and Mexican national identity is extensive, contested and fascinating. Some of the most useful and provocative works: Roger Bartra, *La Jaula de la Melancolía* (México: Debolsillo, 2005) first published in Spanish, 1987; Guillermo Bonfil Batalla, *México Profundo: Una Civilización Negada* (México, D.F.: *Secretaría de Educación Pública*: CIESAS, 1987); Claudio Lomnitz-Adler, *Deep Mexico, Silent Mexico: An Anthropology of Nationalism* (London: University of Minnesota Press, 2001); Lomnitz, *Exits from the Labyrinth: Culture and Ideology in the Mexican National Space* (Berkeley: University of California Press, 1992).

17. Laurière, *Paul Rivet*, 25-155.

18. Ibid; see also Thomas, D. H., *Skull Wars: Kennewick Man, Archaeology, and the Battle for Native Identity* (New York: Basic Books, 2000).

19. Laurière, *Paul Rivet*, 91; Pick, *Degeneration*, 51-52, 135.

20. Stephen Jay Gould, *The Mismeasure of Man* (New York: W.W. Norton, 2008), 106.

21. C. Laurière, "Paul Rivet (1876-1958), Le Savant et Le

Politique" (PhD dissertation, École des Hautes Études en Sciences Sociales, Paris, 2006), 133.

22. Gruber, Jacob, "Ethnographic Salvage and the Shaping of Anthropology," *American Anthropologist* 72, no. 6 (Dec., 1970), 1289-99.

23. Michel Leiris, "L'ethnographe devant le colonialisme" in *Brisées* (Paris: Mercure de France, 1966), 190-193. This essay was originally delivered as a paper at an Association of Scientific Workers congress in Stockholm on March 7, 1950.

24. Christopher Bracken, *The Potlatch Papers: A Colonial Case History* (Chicago: University of Chicago Press, 1997); Regna Darnell, *And Along Came Boas: Continuity and Revolution in Americanist Anthropology* (Philadelphia, Penn: J. Benjamins, 1998); Regna Darnell and Julia D. Harrison, *Historicizing Canadian Anthropology* (Vancouver: U.B.C. Press, 2006); Michelle A. Hamilton, *Collections and Objections: Aboriginal Material Culture in Southern Ontario, 1791-1914*. McGill-Queen's Native and Northern Series. Vol. 63 (Montreal: McGill-Queen's University Press, 2010); Laurière, *Paul Rivet*, 172-4; Carole Reynaud Paligot, *La République Raciale: Paradigme Racial Et Idéologie Républicaine, 1860-1930* (Paris: Presses Universitaires de France, 2006).

25. Sarah Carter, *Lost Harvests: Prairie Indian Reserve Farmers and Government Policy* (Second Edition). (Montreal: McGill-Queen's University Press, 2019), 15-49, 79-129; Titley, *Narrow Vision*, 17-19, 40, 168, 185.

26. Laurière, *Paul Rivet*, 211-286; Pascal Ory and Jean-François Sirinelli, *Les Intellectuels En France, De l'Affaire Dreyfus à Nos Jours* (Paris: A. Colin, 1986); Jean-François Sirinelli, *Génération Intellectuelle: Khâgneux Et Normaliens Dans l'Entre-Deux-Guerres* (Paris: Fayard, 1988), 53, 104; 488-89; Carole Reynaud Paligot, *La République Raciale: Paradigme Racial et Idéologie Républicaine (1860-1930)* (Paris: Presses Universitaires de France, 2006), 305-10.

27. Jacques Soustelle, "Paul Rivet, Sabio y Ciudadano," *Cielo Abierto* (Lima: Volumen X, No.29, Lima, Perú. Julio-Setiembre 1984). English translation by author.

28. Gruber, "Ethnographic Salvage," 1,297.

29. Mary Louise Pratt, *Imperial Eyes: Travel Writing and Transculturation* (London & New York: Routledge, 2008 2nd edition. Originally published 1992), 132.

30. Soustelle, *Mexique Terre Indienne* (Paris: Plon, 1936), 34-54, 124-153.

31. Soustelle, *Terre Indienne*, 153, 264; Laurière, Paul Rivet, 369.

32. MqB, objets–fonds Soustelle 71.1933.71; 71.1936.

33. Soustelle, *Terre Indienne*, 216.

34. Desmond Pacey, "The Poetry of Duncan Campbell Scott," in *Duncan Campbell Scott: A Book of Criticism*, edited and introduction by S.L. Dragland (Ottawa: The Tecumseh Press, 1974), 102. First published in *The Canadian Forum*, XXVIII, 1948-9, 107.

35. See Sandra Gwyn, *The Private Capital: Ambition and Love in the Age of MacDonald and Laurier* (Toronto: McClelland and Stewart, 1984), 293-5.

36. Duncan Campbell Scott, *Duncan Campbell Scott: Addresses, Essays and Reviews* edited by Leslie Ritchie with an introduction by Stan Dragland (London, ON: *Canadian Poetry Press*, 2000), Vol 2, 332. The editor reports that she found this previously unpublished essay at the Queen's University archive in the Lorne Pierce Collection. It is a more ample version of other Scott essays on Lampman including the introduction to the Lampman collection *Lyrics of Earth, Sonnets and Ballads, 1925.*

37. Letter from Rupert Brooke to Wilfred Gibson, July 1913, cited in Sandra Martin and Roger Hall, *Rupert Brooke in Canada* (Toronto: PMA Books, 1978), 19-20, also similar letter from Brooke to his mother, 45; see also Gwyn, *Private Capital*, 465.

38. Duncan Campbell Scott letter to Lorne Pierce, July 15, 1925. QUA, Lorne Pierce archives.

39. Scott, *Addresses, Essays and Reviews*, Vol 2, 334.

40. Northrop Frye, "Letters in Canada" originally published in *University of Toronto Quarterly* (1951), re-published in *The Bush Garden: Essays on the Canadian Imagination* (Toronto: Anansi, 1971), 245.

41. Frye, *Bush Garden*, 9.

42. Lears, *No Place*.

43. DC Scott to EK Brown, Jan. 1944 EK Brown correspondence LAC-BAC Mg 30 D61 Vol. 3

44. Northrop Frye, review of *The Book of Canadian Poetry* by A.J.M. Smith, *The Canadian Forum*, December 1943; Frye, *Bush Garden*, 245.

45. Pelham Edgar. "Travelling With A Poet," chap. 5 in *Along My Path* (Toronto: Ryerson, 1952), 60; see also Edgar, "Duncan Campbell Scott," *Dalhousie Review* 7,

(April, 1927). This article is taken from Edgar's speech about Scott at the time Scott was awarded the Lorne Pierce gold medal for 1927 by The Royal Society of Canada. Edgar, "Twelve Hundred Miles by Canoe among the Indians in Northern Waters," in *Canada: An Illustrated Weekly Journal for all Interested in the Dominion*, November 24 and December 22, 1906; January 5 &19, February 2 & 16; March 16, 1907.

46. Pelham Edgar, "Travelling With A Poet," chap. 5 in *Along My Path* (Toronto: Ryerson, 1952), 60.

47. Duncan Campbell Scott, letter to EK Brown, November 12, 1943. EK Brown correspondence LAC-BAC Mg 30 D61 Vol. 3.

48. Duncan Campbell Scott, *Selected Poems of Duncan Campbell Scott with a Memoir by E.K. Brown* (Toronto, Ryerson Press, 1951); Scott, E. K. Brown, and Robert L. McDougall, *The Poet and the Critic: A Literary Correspondence between D.C. Scott and E.K. Brown* (Ottawa; Don Mills, Ont.: Carleton University Press; distributed by Oxford University Press Canada, 1983).

49. EK Brown, *Winnipeg Free Press,* June 24, 1950, EK Brown correspondence LAC-BAC Mg 30 D61 Vol. 3.

50. Scott, "The Height of Land," in *Duncan Campbell Scott: Selected Poetry, Edited by Glenn Clever* (Ottawa: The Tecumseh Press, 1971), 52-5.

51. Stan Dragland, *Floating Voice: Duncan Campbell Scott and the Literature of Treaty 9* (Concord, ON: Anansi, 1994), 229-253; Gordon Johnston, *Duncan Campbell Scott and His Works* (Downsview, ON, ECW Press, 1983), 32.

52. Frye, *Bush Garden*, 181-197.

53. E. J. Pratt, letter to Duncan Campbell Scott, January 18, 1918. LAC-BAC, LMS-0204, Box 12

54. Scott, "Poetry and Progress," 315. Also in Stan Dragland, *Duncan Campbell Scott: A Book of Criticism* (Ottawa: The Tecumseh Press 1974), 23. From William Blake's "Proverbs of Hell," in Blake's "The Marriage of Heaven and Hell," *The Poems of William Blake* edited by W.B. Yeats (London, Boston, Melbourne and Henley: Routledge & Kegan Paul, 1983–originally published 1905).

55. Personal communication with Brittany Mathews, Reconciliation and Research Coordinator, First Nations Child & Family Caring Society of Canada, May-June 2020.

56. Scott, "Poetry and Progress," 301-302.

57. Robin Brownlie, *A Fatherly Eye: Indian Agents, Government Power, and Aboriginal Resistance in Ontario, 1918-1939* (Don Mills, ON.; New York: Oxford University Press, 2003); Sarah Carter, *Lost Harvests* (Montreal: McGill-Queen's University Press, 1990); Olive Patricia Dickason, *Canada's First Nations: A History of Founding Peoples from Earliest Times* (Toronto: McLelland & Stewart, 1992); Miller, J. R., *Compact, Contract, Covenant: Aboriginal Treaty-Making in Canada* (Toronto: University of Toronto Press, 2009); Miller, *Skyscrapers Hide the Heavens: A History of Indian-White Relations in Canada*, 3rd ed (Toronto; Buffalo: University of Toronto Press, 2000); Miller, *Shingwauk's Vision: A History of Native Residential Schools* (Toronto: University of Toronto Press, 1996); John Sheridan Milloy, *A National Crime: The Canadian Government and the Residential School System, 1879-1986* (Winnipeg: University of Manitoba Press, 1999); Adele Perry, *On the Edge of Empire: Gender, Race, and the Making of British Columbia, 1849-1871* (Toronto: University of Toronto Press, 2001); Titley, *Narrow Vision.*

58. Duncan Campbell Scott and Matilda Ridout Edgar, *John Graves Simcoe. The Makers of Canada Series.* Vol. 4 (London; Toronto: Oxford University Press, 1926); Winona Wheeler (along with Titley) appears in the author's 1995 documentary. Her family name was Stephenson at that time.

59. Dennis Lee, "Cadence, Country, Silence: Writing in Colonial Space," in *Boundary 2* 3, no. 1, A Canadian Issue (Autumn, 1974), 162-3, as cited in Ashcroft, Griffiths and Tiffin, *The Empire Writes Back*, 142.

60. LAC-BAC, LMS-0204, Box 10, Folder 5. This folder contains Botsford ephemera. Belle Botsford was from Boston. She studied violin in Paris for 5 years; Sandra Gwyn, *The Private Capital: Ambition and Love in the Age of MacDonald and Laurier* (Toronto: McClelland and Stewart, 1984), 447-470. Scott's one act play "Pierre" was produced at Hart House Theatre in the 1920-21 season, his "Joy! Joy! Joy!" was performed by the same company in 1925-6. Thomas Fisher rare Book Library-Hart House Archives. A78-0023 Box 002 1928 Hart House Theatre.

61. Titley, *A Narrow Vision*, 28; program Hart House Theatre, University of Toronto, June 23, 1921. Lorne Pierce archives COLL 200.1 Box 80 File DCS poems QUA. Scott read "Ode for the Keats Centenary;" "Bard of The Northland Stirs Hearers With Poems," *The Globe*, April 23, 1925, City News Section; D.M.R. Bentley "Shadows in the

Soul: Racial Haunting in the Poetry of Duncan Campbell Scott," *University of Toronto Quarterly*, Volume 75, Number 2, Spring 2006, "Shadows in the Soul," 760; Stan Dragland, *Floating Voice: Duncan Campbell Scott and the Literature of Treaty 9* (Toronto: Anansi, 1994), 89, 161.

62. Marius Barbeau, English version by Duncan Campbell Scott, transcribed and arranged by Ernest MacMillan, *Three Songs of the West Coast: Recorded from singers of the Nass River Tribes, Canada* (London: The Frederick Harris Co., 1927) Edward Johnson Music Library, University of Toronto.

63. Ernest Macmillan in *The Canadian Encyclopedia*, accessed May 2012, http://www.thecanadianencyclopedia.com/articles/sir-ernest-macmillan,.

64. Northrop Frye, review of *The Book of Canadian Poetry* by A.J.M. Smith, *The Canadian Forum*, December 1943.

65. Frye, *Bush Garden*, 225-6.

66. Soustelle, *Terre Indienne*, 153.

67. Nicole Racine, "Jacques Soustelle" in Jean Maitre, *Dictionnaire Biographique Du Mouvement Ouvrier Français–Quatrième partie 1914-1939 de la Première à la Seconde Guerre Mondiale, Tome 41 Rova à Szy* (Paris: Les Éditions Ouvrières, 1992), 391; Laurière, *Paul Rivet*, 385-427; Conklin, *Musée*.

68. Jacques Soustelle, "Répétition Générale du Fascisme: a Ceux Qui Dissent le Fascisme n'est pas Possible en France," *Spartacus* (December 7, 1934), 7.

69. Ibid.

70. Nicole Racine, "Soustelle, Jacques," 391; Laurière, *Paul Rivet*; Correspondance Havas, January 28, 1936, *Lettres Du Mexique* featuring an unattributed report on Soustelle's research in Mexico, including several quotes from Soustelle. MNHN, clippings file.

71. Jacques Soustelle interview in *L'Oeuvre sur Louis Le Grand* November 20, 1938. "1/4 d'Heure avec un Jeune–Jacques Soustelle Sous–Directeur du Musée de l'Homme" by Georges Schneeberger. MNHN 2 AM 1B11a.

72. Jacques Soustelle, Radio Conférence 85 "Une Fête dans un Village Indien du Mexique," December 20, 1937. MqB Document (15058) id Dossier 1611 DA000312; Radio Conférence 50 "A Travers les Montagnes du Mexique" June 23, 1936. Document (15058) id Dossier 1604 DA000316; "Chez les Indiens Lacandóns" June 2, 1935, Document (15027) Dossier 1604 DA000319; Germaine

Tillion, Radio Conférence 77 "Un Conte Chaouïa," July 19, 1937. MNHN 2am 1 C9 a.

73. Jacques Soustelle, Radio Conférence 85 "Une Fête dans un Village Indien du Mexique," December 20, 1937. MqB Document (15058) id Dossier 1611 DA000312; Radio Conference 50 "A travers les montagnes du Mexique" June 23, 1936. Document (15058) id Dossier 1604 DA000316; "Chez les Indiens Lacandóns" June 2, 1935, Document (15027) Dossier 1604 DA000319.

74. See Joy E. Hayes, "National Imaginings On the Air: Radio in Mexico, 1920-1940," *The Eagle and the Virgin: Nation and Cultural Revolution in Mexico, 1920-1940*. Ed. Mary Kay Vaughn and Stephen E. Lewis (Durham, NC: Duke University Press, 2006), 243-258.

75. Michel Leiris, "La Jeune Ethnographe," *SPARTACUS*, No.3, March 1933, 10.

76. Jacques Soustelle, "*Souvenirs, Apocryphes dans la Forme d'une Conversation avec Georges Suffert*," unpublished memoir provided to the author by Bernard Ullmann, 1988; Odile Rudelle, Témoignages sur la Guerre d'Algérie, Fondation nationale des services politiques, Service des Archives d'Histoire Contemporain, Archives de Université Science-Po, Paris. Interview with Jacques Soustelle, February 19, 1979.

77. Jacques Soustelle correspondence with Alfonso Caso 1938-40, May 23, 1939: Soustelle enlists Caso's assistance on behalf of French doctoral candidate Roger Labrouusse; January 1, 1940: Soustelle writes of ending scientific exchanges because of the war while declaring that the musée will remain open. MNHN Archives Musée l'Homme Dossier Mexico (I) 2 AM 1K65e.

78. Paul Rivet as quoted in Peter C. Rhodes, United Press wire service, November 4, 1938, dateline: Paris. MNHN 2 AM 1K66a Mexico (11).

79. Press release inviting media to an information session to be held on January 18, 1939. MNHN 2 AM 1 11.

80. Correspondence concerning *Soirée Mexicaine*. Soustelle to Gilberto Bosques, Consul General of Mexico, February 25, 1939. MNHN Archives Musée l'Homme Dossier Mexico (I) 2 AM 1K65e.

81. See Alex Saragoza, "The Selling of Mexico: Tourism and the State, 1929-1960," in *Fragments of a Golden Age: The Politics of Culture in Mexico Since 1940* edited by Gilbert Joseph, Anne Rubenstein & Eric Zolov with a

forward by Elena Poniatowska (Durham: Duke University Press, 2001), 91-115.

82. Jacques Soustelle. "Amérique inconnue," *SCIENCE*, May 1938, 3-4. MNHN 2 AM 1B11a.

83. For an assessment of Soustelle's contribution see the papers presented and published in 1995 in his honour. Jacqueline de Durand, Forest, Georges Baudot, and Jacques Soustelle, *Mille Ans De Civilisations Mésoaméricaines: Des Mayas Aux Aztèques: Mélanges En l'Honneur De Jacques Soustelle* (Paris: L'Harmattan, 1995).

84. Laurière, *Paul Rivet*, 211-278.

85. Titley, *Narrow Vision*, 28-9.

86. Ibid, 29.

87. Duncan Campbell Scott, letter to Elise Aylen, CPR train March 6, 1929. LAC-BAC LMS-0204.

88. Duncan Campbell Scott forward to *Roses of Shadow*, Elise Aylen (London: Macmillan at St. Martin's House, 1930), iv.

89. Duncan Campbell Scott, letter to Elise Aylen, posted at Regina November 16, 1930. LAC-BAC, LMS-0204, Box 1, Folder 4.

90. Gwyn, *Private Capital*; Titley, *Narrow Vision*, 28.

91. Elise Aylen, *The Plumed Serpent, A Play in Three Acts. From the Novel by D.H. Lawrence*, LAC-BAC, LMS-0204, Box 7, Folder 8. The manuscript is undated, but the cover address is "Mrs. A.E. Scott, 108 Lisgar St." Aylen lived in the house from her marriage to Scott in 1932 until his death in 1947.

92. Oxford Dictionary of National Biography, accessed June 2013, http://www.oxforddnb.com.ezproxy.library.yorku.ca/view/article/34435.

93. A very useful "Biographical Note" including a timeline of Scott's life and times appears in Scott, *Selected Poetry*, v-viii.

94. Duncan Campbell Scott, letter to E.K. Brown, May 10-12, 1944. LAC-BAC, E.K. Brown correspondence MG30 D61 Vol. 3.

95. Michael Ostroff, director, *Winds of Heaven: Emily Carr, Carvers and The Spirits of The Forest* (documentary film) (Toronto, Cine Metu in Co-production with White Pine Pictures, 2010); Maria Tippett, *Emily Carr, a biography* (Toronto: Oxford University Press, 1979), 139-146.

96. Emily Carr letter to Duncan Campbell Scott and Elise Aylen, March 22, 1941. LAC-BAC, LMS-0204, Box 10, Folder 31.

97. Emily Carr, letters to Duncan Campbell Scott, July 2 and August 24, 1941. LAC-BAC, LMS-0204, Box 10, Folder 31.

98. *The Canadian Encyclopedia*, accessed June 2013, http://thecanadianencyclopedia.com.ezproxy.library.yorku.ca/articles/emily-carr.

99. I am indebted to Seneca College professor and editorial consultant Erin Dolmage for remarking on these similarities between Carr and Scott.

100. Duncan Campbell Scott, *In the Village of Viger and Other Stories*, New Canadian Library, no. 92. (Toronto: McClelland and Stewart, 1973). Original publication (Boston: Copeland and Day, 1896).

101. Duncan Campbell Scott letter to Clarence Gagnon, February 8, 1919 and August 2, 1921. LAC-BAC, LMS-0204, Box 11.

102. Duncan Campbell Scott letter to Clarence Gagnon, August 2, 1921. LAC-BAC, LMS-0204, Box 11.

103. Duncan Campbell Scott letter to Clarence Gagnon, August 6, 1921. LAC-BAC, LMS-0204, Box 11.

104. Duncan Campbell Scott letter to Clarence Gagnon, December 1, 1927. LAC-BAC, LMS-0204, Box 11.

105. Clarence Gagnon letter to Duncan Campbell Scott, June 6, 1931. LAC-BAC, LMS-0204, Box 11.

106. Emily Carr listened to the broadcast in Victoria, British Columbia. Emily Carr, letters to Duncan Campbell Scott, June 23, 1944. LAC-BAC, LMS-0204, Box 10, Folder 31.

107. Scott, "To A Canadian Aviator Who Died for His Country in France;" "To the Canadian Mothers, 1914-1918" both poems appear in Scott, *Selected Poems of Duncan Campbell Scott with a Memoir by E.K. Brown* (Toronto: The Ryerson Press, 1951), 169-71.

108. John Grierson, Government Film Commissioner, letter to Duncan Campbell Scott, May 10, 1945, LAC-BAC, LMS-0204, Box 11, Folder 37.

109. Duncan Campbell Scott letter to John Grierson, May 15, 1945. LAC-BAC, LMS – 0204, Box 11, Folder 37.

110. Letter from R.S. Lambert, Supervisor of Educational Broadcasts, CBC, to Mrs. Duncan Campbell Scott (Elise Aylen), December 31, 1947. Lambert sent Aylen a copy

of the script as a courtesy prior to broadcast. LAC-BAC Correspondence CBC May 5 1939-February 11, 1948. Recording of the National Schools Broadcast, January 16, 1948. LAC-BAC, V1 2000-02-0009 (ISN 108498) CD 8065 (1).

111. Letter from R.S. Lambert, Supervisor of Educational Broadcasts, CBC to Mrs. Duncan Campbell Scott (Elise Aylen), December 31, 1947. Lambert sent Aylen a copy of the script as a courtesy prior to broadcast. LAC-BAC Correspondence CBC May 5 1939–February 11, 1948.

112. Some of Aylen's works and ephemera about her life are stored in LAC-BAC, LMS-0204, Box 7, Folder 8; Box 9, Folders 5 and 8. The bulk of the correspondence between Aylen and Scott is in Box 1 in the same fonds.

113. Elise Aylen, letter to E.K. Brown, January 12, 1948. LAC-BAC, E.K. Brown correspondence, MG 30 D61 Vol 3, Folder: Scott, Elise Aylen.

114. Bernard Ullmann, *Jacques Soustelle–Le Mal Aimé* (Paris: Plon, 1995), 319-48.

115. Ibid, 363-89.

116. Jacques Soustelle, *Les Quatre Soleils: L'Itinéraire Intellectuel de Jacques Soustelle, Ethnographe du Mexique Terre Indienne* (Paris: Plon, 1967). Positive reviews included Charles Melchior-Bonnet, *Historia*, February, 1968; Lucien Guissard, "Les Quatre Soleils: un Voyage Philosophique," La Croix, October 22, 1967; L.L., "Un Livre Essentiel," *La Cité*, November 22-23 1969.

117. Soustelle, producer and commentary and Marcel Boudo, director, *La Splendeur Du Mexique Ancien–Les Azteques (3 Parties)* (Paris and Mexico City: France 3 and Televisa, 1978); other TV productions featuring Soustelle include *Chilam Balam*, commentary by Jacques Soustelle (Paris: France 2, 1981; *Les Mayas* (3 parts), commentary by Jacques Soustelle (Paris: TF1, 1976).

118. Jacques Soustelle, *Rapport Sur La Recherche Française En Archéologie Et Anthropologie* (Paris: La Documentation française, 1975).

119. Ullmann, *Mal Aimé*, 390-4.

120. Ibid.

121. Jacques Soustelle, "Ou Veut-on Venir à Pretoria?" *Le Monde*, December 3, 1977; Jacques Soustelle, *La Longue Marche d'Israel* (Paris: Librairie Arthème Fayard, 1968); Ullmann, *Mal Aimé*, 363-7.

122. Ullmann, *Mal Aimé*, 400-4.

123. Ibid, 408-9.

124. See Durand-Forest, Baudot and Soustelle, *Mille ans de Civilisation Mésoaméricaine.*

CHAPTER FIVE

1. Julien Benda, *La Trahison des Clercs* (Paris: Les Cahiers Verts, 1927), 222.

2. Benda, *The Treason of the Intellectuals*, translated by Richard Aldington (New York: W. Morrison, 1928 also New York: Norton, 1969); Benda, *The Great Betrayal* (London: G. Routledge & Sons Ltd., 1928).

3. The theme of progress is an undercurrent in much of Scott's poetic and prose work. He enunciated his own view on the subject most clearly in an address to the Royal Society of Canada in 1922. Duncan Campbell Scott, "Poetry and Progress" in Scott, Leslie Ritchie, ed. introduction by Stan Dragland, *Addresses, Essays, and Reviews Vol 1* (London, ON: Canadian Poetry Press, 2000). Also re-published in Dragland, *Duncan Campbell Scott: A Book of Criticism* (Ottawa: The Tecumseh Press, 1974), 7-30.

4. E. Brian Titley, *A Narrow Vision: Duncan Campbell Scott and the Administration of Indian Affairs in Canada* (Vancouver: UBC Press, 1986).

5. Jacques Soustelle, *Aimée et Souffrante Algérie* (Paris: Plon, 1956), 5-7; Alistair Horne, *A Savage War of Peace: Algeria, 1954-1962* (New York: Viking Press, 1978), 105-7; Todd Shepard, "How Ethnographic Research in 1930s Mexico Shaped French Efforts to Fight Algerian Nationalism in 1955." Paper delivered at UNESCO conference, Cambridge, April 6-7, 2009, 2-8.

6. Horne, *Savage War*, 341, 473; Bernard Ullmann, *Jacques Soustelle le Mal Aimé* (Paris: Plon, 1995), 292-8.

7. Ian McKay, "The Liberal Order Framework: A Prospectus for a Reconnaissance of Canadian History," *Canadian Historical Review* 81, no. 4 (Dec. 2000), 617-51; McKay, "Canada as a Long Liberal Revolution" in *Liberalism and Hegemony: Debating the Canadian Liberal Revolution*, Jean-François Constant and Michel Ducharme (Toronto-Buffalo-London: University of Toronto Press, 2009), 347-452.

8. McKay, "Long Liberal Revolution," 381.

9. McKay, "Long Liberal Revolution," 353.

10. McKay, "Long Liberal Revolution," 361.

11. McKay, *Rebels, Reds, Radicals: Rethinking Canada's Left History* (Toronto: Between the Lines, 2005), 89.

12. See as examples McKay, "Liberal Order," 626-7, 640, 644; John Ralston Saul, *A Fair Country: Telling Truths about Canada* (Toronto: Viking, 2008); Dale Turner, "Liberalism's Last Stand; Aboriginal Sovereignty and Minority Rights" in Curtis Cook and Juan David Lindau eds, *Aboriginal Rights and Self-Government: The Canadian and Mexican Experience in North American Perspective* (Montreal: McGill-Queen's University Press, 2000), 51-68.

13. See Albert Camus, *Actuelles III Chroniques Algériennes 1939-1958* (Paris: Gallimard, 1958). This is an essential compendium of Camus' journalism and political essays on the Algerian question.

14. See Raoul Girardet, *L'Idée Coloniale En France De 1871 à 1962* (Paris: La table ronde, 1972), 218-9; Roger Navarri, "Sartre et la Névrose Algérienne, Philippe Baudorre ed. in *La Plume Dans La Plaie: Les Écrivains Journalistes Et La Guerre d'Algérie* (Bordeaux: Presses Universitaires de Bordeaux, 2003), 137-48; Horne, *Savage War*, 237-8; see also James D. Le Sueur, "Decolonizing 'French Universalism' Reconsidering the impact of the Algerian War on French Intellectuals," Le Sueur, ed. in *The Decolonizing Reader* (London: Rutledge, 2003), 103-117; Le Sueur, *Uncivil War: Intellectuals and Identity Politics during the Decolonization of Algeria* (Philadelphia: University of Pennsylvania Press, 2001); Ronald Aronson, *Camus & Sartre: The Story of a Friendship and the Quarrel that Ended it* (Chicago: University of Chicago Press, 2004).

15. See Jean-Paul Sartre, *Situations V, Colonialisme et Néo-Colonialisme* (Paris: Gallimard, 1964). This collection includes a number of articles which outline Sartre's views on the Algerian question, perhaps most importantly his introduction to *Les Damnés de la Terre*, the eponymous 1961 text of Frantz Fanon.

16. Fanon, Frantz, *Sociologie d'une Révolution* (Paris: Maspero, 1959), 7.

17. Bernard Droz and Évelyne Lever, *Histoire De La Guerre d'Algérie (1954-1962)* (Paris: Seuil, 1982), 74-5; Alistair Horne, *A Savage War of Peace: Algeria, 1954-1962* (New York: Viking Press, 1978), 117.

18. Hannah Arendt, *Eichmann in Jerusalem* (New York: Penguin Group, 1963), 276.

19. Ibid, 252.

20. See bibliography for works including those by Robin Jarvis Brownlie, Sarah Carter, Olive Patricia Dickason, Kathryn Magee Labelle, Brittany Luby, J.R. Miller, John S. Milloy, Donald B. Smith and E. Brian Titley.

21. Titley, *Narrow Vision*, 4, 9, 12, 13, 34, 44, 48-51, 90, 104-7, 114-16, 203.

22. For respected and literate overviews of the Algerian conflict, see Charles-Robert Ageron, *Histoire De l'Algérie Contemporaine* (Paris: Presses universitaires de France, 1979); Yves Courrière, *La Guerre d'Algérie* (Paris: Fayard, 2001); Bernard Droz et Évelyne Lever, *Histoire De La Guerre d'Algérie (1954-1962)* (Paris: Seuil, 1982); Horne, *Savage War*; Alain-Gérard Slama, *La Guerre d'Algérie: Histoire d'Une Déchirure* (Paris: Gallimard, 1996).

23. Duncan Campbell Scott, letter to E.K. Brown July 2, 1941, in Duncan Campbell Scott, E. K. Brown, and Robert L. McDougall, *The Poet and the Critic: A Literary Correspondence between D.C. Scott and E.K. Brown* (Ottawa; Don Mills, ON.: Carleton University Press; distributed by Oxford University Press Canada, 1983), 25-26.

24. Ibid.

25. Titley, *Narrow Vision*, 104-7, 114-16, 156-59. Titley interview in Duncan Campbell Scott; *The Poet and the Indians*, documentary film, James Cullingham, producer/director (Toronto: Tamarack Productions and The National Film Board of Canada Ontario Centre, 1995).

26. J. R. Miller, *Shingwauk's Vision: A History of Native Residential Schools* (Toronto: University of Toronto Press, 1996); John Sheridan Milloy, *A National Crime: The Canadian Government and the Residential School System, 1879-1986* (Winnipeg: University of Manitoba Press, 1999); E. Brian Titley, *A Narrow Vision: Duncan Campbell Scott and the Administration of Indian Affairs in Canada* (Vancouver: University of British Columbia Press, 1986).

27. Stan Dragland interview in *The Poet and the Indians*, Cullingham, dir/prod.

28. Ibid.

29. E.K. Brown, "Duncan Campbell Scott: A Memoir," in E.K. Brown, *Responses and Evaluations: Essays on Canada*, edited by David Staines (Toronto: McClelland and Stewart, 1977), 127; also in Scott, *Selected Poems of Duncan Campbell Scott*, Brown ed. (Toronto: The Ryerson Press, 1951), xxv-vi.

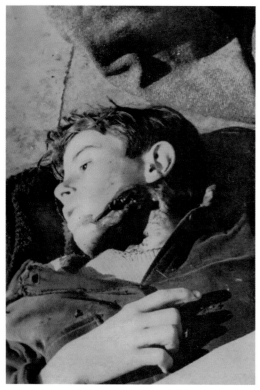

Many children were among the thousands of Algerian civilian casualties during the 1954-62 war of independence. Their deaths were often brutal.

35. Ibid, 118.

36. John Leslie and Ron MacGuire, eds., *The Historical Development of The Indian Act* (Ottawa: Indian and Northern Affairs Canada, 1978); *Indian Acts and Amendments* (Ottawa: Indian and Northern Affairs Canada, 1981); Wendy Moss and Elaine Gardner-O'Toole, "Aboriginal People: History of Discriminatory Laws," Ottawa, Library of Parliament: Law and Government Division, November 1987, Revised November 1991. See also John Leslie and Ron Maguire, eds., researched by Robert G. Moore, "The Historical Development of The Indian Act," Treaties and Historical Research Centre, Research Branch, Corporate Policy, Indian and Northern Affairs Canada, Government of Canada, 2nd edition, 1978. First Edition 1975 written by Kahn-Tineta Miller and George Lerchs.

37. Duncan Campbell Scott, notes on "Enfranchisement," 3. These notes were prepared in early 1920 in anticipation of Parliamentary Committee hearings on proposed changes to The Indian Act. These notes are in a file with a letter from Scott written on April 14, 1920 to Member of Parliament E.B. Devlin,. Scott wrote, "I have the pleasure in inclosing herewith a copy of the notes I used when before the Committee on Bill 14 a short time ago, and which I send you. I shall be glad to have them returned, as I require them for reference." LAC/BAC, RG10 Vol6810, file 470-2-3 Pt. 7 (also Microfiche reel C8533).

38. "Statement showing number of Indians enfranchised under section 122A.," Ottawa, January 9, 1920. LAC-BAC RG10 VOL 6810, file 470-2-3 (also Microfiche reel C8533).

39. Ibid; Scott, "transcript of testimony."

40. Scott, "Enfranchisement," 2.

41. Peter Kulchhyski, "'A Considerable Unrest' F.O. Loft and the League of Indians," in *Native Studies Review* 5 1&2 (1988), 95-117; Titley, 1986, 102-109.

42. F.O. Loft, open letter of November 14, 1919, LAC-BAC RG10, Vol. 6810 File 470-2-3 Pt. 7.

43. Scott, "Enfranchisement," LAC-BAC RG10 VOL 6810, file 470-2-3.

44. Ibid, 105. LAC/BAC Rg10, vol. 3211, file 527,781, Loft to Sir James Lougheed with memo by Scott attached, 9 February, 1921.

30. L.P. Weiss, "D.C. Scott's View of History & The Indians," *Canadian Literature* (Number 111, Winter 1986), 28.

31. Christopher Bracken, *The Potlatch Papers: A Post Colonial History* (Chicago: University of Chicago Press, 1997), 218-224.

32. Duncan Campbell Scott, transcript of testimony before Special Parliamentary Committee on Proposed Changes to Indian Act, April 1920. LAC/BAC RG10 Vol 6810, file 470-2-3 Pt.7, 63.

33. Duncan Campbell Scott briefing notes regarding compulsory education for appearance at Parliamentary Committee, 1920. LAC/BAC RG10 Vol 6810, file 470-2-3 Pt.7.

34. Titley, *Narrow Vision*, 104-117.

45. Donald B. Smith, *Seen*, 129, 132-137.

46. Titley, *Narrow Vision*, 1, 125-134.

47. As cited in Titley, *Narrow Vision*, 105; Scott to Sir James Lougheed, 21 February 1921, LAC-BAC Rg10, vol. 3211, file 527,781.

48. Titley, *Narrow Vision*, 48-51.

49. Transcript of committee proceedings, 57-58. LAC/BAC RG10, vol. 3211.

50. Scott, night lettergram to Rev. JT. McNally, Bishop of Calgary April 1, 1920. Night letter to Rev. R. Grandin, Oblate Fathers Provincial House, Edmonton, April 1, 1920. LAC-BAC RG10, Volume 6810, file 470-2-3) Pt. 7.

51. Scott to Rev. T. Albert Moore, general secretary Evangelism and Social Service, The Methodist Church, March 10, 1920. LAC-BAC RG10, Volume 6810, file 470-2-3.

52. Scott, letter to Chief Dan Whetung, Curve Lake, Ontario, April 1, 1920. LAC-BAC RG10, Volume 6810, file 470-2-3) Pt. 7.

53. Scott, letter to M.P. W.A. Boys, April 3, 1920. Response to Boys' letter of April 1, 1920. LAC-BAC RG10, Volume 6810, file 470-2-3) Pt. 7.

54. Miller, *Shingwauk's Vision*, 169-70; Milloy, *National Crime*, 70-1; Titley, *Narrow Vision*, 90-3.

55. Duncan Campbell Scott "Indian Affairs 1867-1912" from *Canada and its Provinces* Vol. 5, Section 3, "Upper Canada," Adam Shortt and Arthur G. Doughty, eds. (Toronto: Glasgow, Brook, 1914). Essay re-printed in Duncan Campbell Scott, *Addresses, Essays and Reviews*, edited by Leslie Ritchie, Introduction by Stan Dragland Vol. 1 (London, Canada: Canadian Poetry Press, 2000), 204-5.

56. Duncan Campbell Scott briefing notes regarding compulsory education for appearance at Parliamentary Committee, 1920. LAC/BAC RG10 Vol 6810, file 470-2-3 Pt.7.

57. "ENFRANCHISEMENT OF INDIANS," *The Globe*, (Toronto: March 20, 1920), editorial page. Press reports/letters to editor re. Indian Act Amendments LAC-BAC RG10 Vol. 6810.

58. For a discussion of reaction to related proposals by the government of Prime Minister Pierre Trudeau and Indian and Northern Affairs Minister Jean Chrétien in its 1969 White Paper proposal on Indian policy, see Sally M. Weaver, *Making Canadian Indian Policy: The Hidden Agenda 1968-70* (Toronto: University of Toronto Press, 1981), 3-11; see also Harold Cardinal, *The Unjust Society: The Tragedy of Canada's Indians* (Edmonton: Hurtig, 1969); H.A. McCue, *The Only Good Indian: Essays by Canadian Indians* (Toronto: New Press, 1972).

59. "THE INDIAN AND THE VOTE," *The Ottawa Journal*, March 23, 1920, editorial page. Press reports/letters to editor re. Indian Act Amendments LAC-BAC RG10 Vol. 6810.

60. R.N. Wilson, letter to the editor, *The Citizen* (Ottawa: June 25, 1920). Press reports/letters to editor re. Indian Act Amendments LAC-BAC RG10 Vol. 6810.

61. Ibid.

62. Titley, *Narrow Vision*, 75, 91-3; Milloy, *National Crime*, 70, 94-5, 181; Miller, *Shingwauk's Vision*, 140, 357.

63. Transcript of proceedings of special Parliamentary Committee, April 1920, 53-54. LAC-BAC RG10 VOL 6810, file 470-2-3 (also Microfiche reel C8533).

64. Ibid, 54-55.

65. Scott, "Enfranchisement," 3.

66. Marius Barbeau, "Lorette Reserve: A Report Concerning Its Proposed Disestablishment" for Indian Department–based on investigation conducted in August 1919. LAC/BAC RG10 Vol 6810, File 470; Donald B. Smith, *Seen*, 131.

67. Kathryn Magee Labelle, *Dispersed but Not Destroyed: a History of the Seventeenth-Century Wendat People* (Vancouver: UBC Press, 2013), 197-199, 207.

68. Georges E Sioui, *For an Amerindian Autohistory* (Montreal: McGill-Queen's Press, 1992); *Les Wendats: Une Civilisation Méconnue* (Sainte-Foy, Québec: Presses de l'Université Laval, 1994); *The Heritage of the Circle* (Vancouver: UBC Press, 1999); *Huron-Wendat: Histoires de Kanatha–Histories of Kanatha Vues et contées–Seen and Told* (Ottawa: Presses de l'Universite d'Ottawa, 2008); René Sioui Labelle, dir., *Kanata: L'héritage des enfants de Aataentsic*, Office nationale du film du Canada, 1998.

69. Re-printed in Scott, *Scott Addresses*, 302. Speech delivered on May 17, 1922 to the Royal Society of Canada. Originally published *Royal Society of Canada Proceedings and Transactions*, 3rd Series, 16 (1922), xlvii-lxvii. Also

re-printed in S.L. Dragland, ed., *Duncan Campbell Scott: A Book of Criticism* (Ottawa: Tecumseh, 1974), 7-30.

70. Bracken, *Potlatch Papers*, 218-224; Douglas Cole and Ira Chaikin, *An Iron Hand upon the People: The Law Against the Potlatch on the Northwest Coast* (Vancouver: Douglas & McIntyre, 1990), 101.

71. See Bernard Droz and Evelyne Lever, *Histoire de la Guerre d'Algérie 1954-1962* (Paris: Seuil, 1982), 67-8; Stephen Tyre, "From Algérie Française to France Musulmane: Jacques Soustelle and the Myths and Realities of 'Integration', 1955–1962," *French History* 20, no. 3 (09, 2006), 276-296; Todd Shepherd, "How Ethnographic Research in 1930s Mexico Shaped French Efforts to Fight Algerian Nationalism in 1955," UNESCO lecture, Cambridge, April 6-7, 2009.

72. See James D. Le Sueur, "De-Colonizing French Universalism' Reconsidering the Impact of the Algerian War on French Intellectuals" in *The Decolonization Reader*, Le Sueur ed. (New York; London: Routledge, 2003), 103-117; Le Sueur, *Uncivil War: Intellectuals and Identity Politics during the Decolonization of Algeria* (Philadelphia: University of Pennsylvania Press, 2001); Raoul Girardet, *L'Idée Coloniale En France De 1871 a 1962* (Paris: La table ronde, 1972), 193-235.

73. Ann Laura Stoler, *Along the Archival Grain: Epistemic Anxieties and Colonial Common Sense* (Princeton: Princeton University Press, 2009), 140, 247-8, 256, 278.

74. Jacques Soustelle, *Aimée et Souffrante Algérie* (Paris: Plon, 1956), 2-7; Jacques Soustelle, television interview "Lectures Pour Tous," French TV June 6, 1956. Soustelle described how his knowledge of Mexico informed his policies as Governor General of Algeria.

75. Horne, *Savage War*, 83-4.

76. Ibid, 98-9.

77. Denis Rolland, "Jacques Soustelle, De l'Ethnologie à La Politique," *Revue d'Histoire Moderne Et Contemporaine (1954-)* 43, no. 1, La vie politique en France, hommes et débats, 1930-1960 (Jan.-Mar., 1996), 137-150.

78. Jacques Soustelle, "Souvenirs, apocryphes sous la Forme d'une dialogue avec Georges Suffert," 122-6; Ullmann, *Mal Aimé*, 88-93.

79. Horne, *Savage War*, 105-8; Ullmann, *Mal Aimé*, 184-90.

80. Horne, *Savage War*, 107; Ullmann, *Mal Aimé*, 190.

81. As cited in *Jacques Soustelle, Aimée et Souffrante Algérie* (Paris: Plon, 1956), 7.

82. Albert Camus, *Actuelles, III Chroniques Algériennes 1939-1958* (Paris: Gallimard, 1958), 32-41. Camus' writings about Algeria were re-published in English in 2013. Camus, *Algerian Chronicles*, translated by Arthur Goldhammer. Edited by Alice Kaplan (Cambridge MA: Harvard University Press, 2013). Review essays appeared in major English language publications. James Campbell "Betwixt and Between Camus was a son of Algeria–the 'kingdom of poverty' that nourished all he wrote," *The Wall Street Journal*, May 4, 2013, page C5; Susan Rubin Suleiman, "The Postcolonial–Albert Camus' writings on Algeria reveal both hope and dread," *The New York Times*, Sunday May 12, 2013, Book Review section, 32.

83. Camus, *Chroniques Algériennes*, 32-41.

84. Nelly Forget and Nancy Wood, "Notice Biographique," in *Le Siècle de Germaine Tillion, Sous la Direction de Tzevtan Todorov* (Paris: Éditions de Seuil, 2007), 16-7.

85. Germaine Tillion, *L'Afrique Bascule Vers l'Avenir* (Paris: Editions Tirésias – Michel Reynaud, 1999), 18.

86. Germaine Tillion, *L'Afrique Bascule Vers l'Avenir* (Paris: Éditions Tirésias, 1999), 76. This is a re-publication of some of Tillion's most important writings about Algeria. This citation and those that immediately follow were originally published in the form of the pamphlet entitled *L'Algérie en 1957* (Paris: Association Nationale Des Anciennes Déportés Et Internées De La Resistance, 1957).

87. Tillion, *L'Afrique Bascule*, 78.

88. Ibid, 79.

89. Ibid, 79-80.

90. Horne, *Savage War* 30, 51-4.

91. Ibid, 36-7; Ageron, *l'Algérie Contemporaine*, 90-1; Ian Lustick, *State-Building Failure in British Ireland & French Algeria* (Berkeley: iiS Institute of International Studies, University of California, Berkeley, 1985), 71.

92. CAOM 11CAB/77 Soustelle March 21, 1955.

93. Tillion, *L'Afrique Bascule*, 94.

94. CAOM 11CAB/78 "Réformes," Annotated list of reforms with hand-written marginalia by Soustelle, June 6, 1955. List includes training of Muslim civil servants; land reform; creation of rural social centres; plans for

improved irrigation of Arab lands. On August 8, 1955 Soustelle received a MISE AU POINT, or update, on the state of his hurried reforms. The central points touch upon recruitment of Muslims for the civil service; school instruction in Arabic; and ensuring that Muslim faith would be separate from the state.

95. Droz and Lever, *La Guerre d'Algérie*, 67.

96. CAOM 11CAB/29 August 1, 1955 Office memo regarding "remise de denrées alimentaires" planned for an appearance by Soustelle in Tablat.

97. Soustelle, *Aimée et Souffrante*, 59.

98. Jacques Soustelle interviewed on "Lectures Pour Tous" by Pierre Desgroupes about Soustelle's book *Aimée et Souffrante Algérie*, December 19, 1956, Inathèque, BNF – Mitterand, Paris.

99. Paul Rivet,"Nous ne pourrons conserver l'Afrique du Nord que si nous y faisons une grande réforme agraire; ce que l'exemple du Mexique nous enseigne" (Paris: *L'oeuvre*, May 8 1937), 1-2. Thanks to Rivet biographer Christine Laurière for directing me to this article.

100. Todd Shepard, "Algeria, France, Mexico, UNESCO: a Transnational History of Anti-Racism and Decolonization, 1932–1962." Journal of global history, 6(2), 273–297 (Cambridge, UK: Cambridge University Press, 2011); "How Ethnographic Research in 1930s Mexico shaped French efforts to fight Algerian nationalism in 1955" (paper delivered at UNESCO History Conference, Cambridge, UK, April 6-7, 2009); Stephen Tyre, "From Algérie Française to France Musulmane: Jacques Soustelle and the Myths and Realities of 'Integration, 1955-1962," *French History* (2006) 20(3), 276-296.

101. See Herbeth, *L'Homme* and Zemmour, Éric, *Destin Français* (Paris: Albin Michel, 2018), 545-568.

102. Mary Kay Vaughan and Stephen E. Lewis, "Introduction–Utopia and Cultural Revolution," in *The Eagle and the Virgin: Nation and Cultural Revolution in Mexico, 1920-1940* (Durham: Duke University Press, 2006), 9-12.

103. Jacques Soustelle, *Mexique Terre Indienne* (Paris: Plon, 1936), 150.

104. CAOM 11CAB/77 Education nationale memo between members of Soustelle's office Eydoux to Juillet March 15, 1955.

105. CAOM 11CAB/77 minutes of meeting March 7, 1955.

106. Germaine Tillion, *À la Recherche du Vrai et du Juste*, (Paris: Éditions du Seuil, 2011), 249.

107. Ibid.

108. Tillion, *La Traversée du Mal*, 99-102; Tillion, *L'Afrique Bascule*, 72-4.

109. UNESCO Etudes et Documents d'Èducation, Sept 1954 No IX, Expérience Françaises d'Éducation de Base en Afrique Noire 1955 No XV, Etudes et Documents d'Éducation de base par H.W. Howes. From Nelly Forget's Centre Germaine Tillion archive.

110. AFGT "Le Service des Centres Sociaux," Direction Générale de l'Education Nationale en Algérie (Algiers: Baconnier Frères, 1957).

111. CAOM 11CAB/77 Germaine Tillion note "la Scolarisation des enfants de 6 a 14 ans," March 1955.

112. Ibid.

113. CAOM 11CAB/29 November 22, 1955 notes from education department to provide background for a Soustelle speech about the Centres Sociaux. These notes make reference to both the problem of recruiting qualified teachers from France and in providing adequate security for teachers in the countryside.

114. CAOM 11CAB/38 "Instructions," April 30, 1955 regarding application of the state of urgency.

115. CAOM 11CAB/29 Preparatory notes for Soustelle speech, delivered in August 1955 just prior to the FLN attacks on civilians around Philippeville on August 20, 1955.

116. Horne, *Savage War*, 114-117.

117. Muséum National D'Histoire Naturelle et Musée de l'Homme, "Germaine Tillion Ethnologue et Résistante," Dossier de Presse pour l'exposition à Musée de l'Homme, Palais de Chaillot, Paris, du 30 mai au 8 septembre 2008.

118. Cabinet du Gouverneur Général, service de Statistique du Gouvernement de l'Algérie et l'Agence du Plan de la Ville d'Alger avec introduction par Georgette Soustelle. Photographies, A. Garcia; dessin Erick de Saussure, "BOUBSILA Bidonville Algérois" (Alger: COMITEC, 1955-56).

119. Hossein Djebrane, "Les Centres Sociaux Contre L'ignorance et la Misère, Une Enquête de Hossein Djebrane," *Journal d'Alger*, July 7, 1959. Archives

Association Germaine Tillion.

120. Germaine Tillion, Mise en Scène Bérénice Collet, réalisation François Dubreuil, *"Le Verfügbar aux Enfers une Opèrette-Revue à Ravensbruck"* TMP Chatelet-Axesud-Association Germaine Tillion. DVD of performance recorded at 65th anniversary of the liberation of Ravensbruck, 16-19 April, 2010. Courtesy of Nelly Forget, Association Germaine Tillion.

121. Ibid, 147-64.

122. CAOM 11CAB/38 July 7, 1955 draft of "Instructions" with marginalia and approval signature of Soustelle.

123. Ibid.

124. CAOM 11CAB/41 Telegram marked SECRET VERY URGENT from Minister of Interior Bourges-Maunory to Soustelle March16, 1955.

125. CAOM 11CAB/41 Legal note from M. Passeron, directeur de législation May 21, 1955.

126. CAOM 11CAB/41 Letter from Soustelle to prefects explaining state of urgency April 8, 1955.

127. CAOM 11CAB/38 Memo from Eydoux to Soustelle December 2, 1955.

128. CAOM 11CAB/38 Undated note from Inspector General of Administration, M. Ciosi.

129. CAOM 11CAB/41 Inspector General Ciosi report June 6, 1955.

130. CAOM 11CAB/38 Minutes of meeting June 29, 1955. Reports on discussion about criticisms contained in a report from Inspector General Ciosi.

131. CAOM 11CAB/41 Memo from director Service Central des Centres d'Hébergement November 16, 1955.

132. CAOM 11CAB/38 July 8, 1955 Cabinet Soustelle to Minister of Interior Abel Thomas.

133. See Benjamin Stora, *La Gangrène et l'Oubli–La Mémoire de la Guerre d'Algérie* (Paris: La Découverte/Poche, 1998–originally published 1991), 56-57.

134. CAOM 11CAB/29 Open letter from Mouvement de Libération du Peuple November 19, 1955.

135. Germaine Tillion, *À la Recherché du Vrai et du Juste à Propos Rompus avec le Siècle Textes Réunis et Présentés par Tzvetan Todorov* (Paris: Seuil: 2001), 187-192.

136. Ibid; Forget and Wood, "Notice biographique," 25; Horne, *Savage Peace*, 214-7.

137. Germaine Tillion, "Entretien avec Jean Lacouture" in *La Traversée du Mal* (Paris: Aréa, 2000), 104.

138. Jackson, *A Certain Idea*, 512.

139. Denis Rolland, *Vichy et la France Libre au Mexique: Guerre, Culture et Propaganda Pendant la Deuxième Guerre Mondiale* (Paris: l'Harmattan, 1990), 74-85.

140. CAOM 11CAB/78 "Reformes" June 20, 1955 Bilan de L'Activité du cabinet.

141. CAOM 11CAB/46 "Le Libertaire" July 14, 1955. Page one articles about seizure of copies of paper in Alger. This edition also includes an article about launching a campaign in defense of political opponents sentenced to death in Algeria.

142. CAOM 11CAB/38 Summary of meeting held on November 3, 1955.

143. Rolland, *Vichy et la France Libre*, 74-5; CEMCA Centre d'Études Mexicaines et Centreaméricaines, Centre de Documentation, Ministère des Affaires Extérieures de France, Ciudad de México. This archive contains all copies of *Le Journal Français de Mexique.*

144. As a graduate student Soustelle reviewed films for leftist newspapers, evincing, for example, a particular admiration for the 'bad guy' Paul Muni in his portrayal of a rough Mexican-American character in the film *Bordertown* Soustelle's review emphasizes the anti-Mexican racism which Muni's character faced. Jacques Soustelle, "En regardant les Écrans," *Spartacus*, February 28, 1935. Muni also portrayed Mexican political hero Benito Juarez in the film *Juarez.*

145. CAOM 11CAB/101 February 24, 1955 memorandum from Murati to Governor General's office.

146. CAOM 11CAB/101 compte rendu conf. Stagiaires du CENTRE D'ACTION PSYCHOLOGIQUE November 3, 1955.

147. CAOM 11CAB/8 Unsigned note of July 9, 1955 to Governor General Jacques Soustelle.

148. CAOM 11CAB/7 "Affaires Musulmanes," July 7, 1955 letter to Soustelle from T. Tedjini, general commissioner, Boy Scouts Musulmans de l'Algérie.

149. CAOM 11CAB/29 Declaration of Governor General Jacques Soustelle Radio Algérie, August 19, 1955.

150. CAOM 11CAB/29 Text of Soustelle speech of August 17, 1955.

Protesting deaths of children in Indigenous residential schools, Toronto, 2010.

151. See Alain-Gérad Slama, *La Guerre d'Algérie – Histoire d'une Déchirure* (Paris : Gallimard, 1996), 53-54.

152. CAOM 11CAB/78 Teletype from Jacques Soustelle to Ministere Interieur – Cabinet – Paris August 27, 1955.

153. Jacques Soustelle, telegram Number 1486 to Prefect of Constantine August 25, 1955. From the papers of Henri-Paul Eydoux, cited in D. Balvet, "Jacques Soustelle Et l'Algérie Française: Gaullisme Et Antigaullisme." (PhD diss., Université Charles de Gaulle, Lille 3 2003), 201.

154. CAOM 11CAB/8 Soustelle letter in *Le Monde*, September 7, 1955.

155. CAOM 11CAB/14 Cabinet Militaire folder, November 1955. Complaint regarding sacking of Moslem businesses forwarded by Soustelle to Constantine prefecture; CAOM 11CAB/14 SECRET telegram to prefects of major cities September 20, 1955.

156. CAOM 11CAB/8 Secret note sent on to Minister of the Interior September 3, 1955 about moderate leaders such as Cheik Kerreoine calling for immediate federal status rather than "progressive integration" favoured by Soustelle.

157. Jacques Soustelle and Odile Rudelle, Jacques Soustelle Interviews, February 19 and April 23 1979. Paris: Université SciencesPo. Fondation Nationale des Sciences Politiques-Service des Archives d'Histoire Contemporaine, 8.

158. CAOM 11CAB/7 Report on Ferhat Abbas' meeting with French Ministers in Paris October 30, 1955. Marked SECRET.

159. CAOM 11CAB/8 Statement of support for government and policy of integration from municipal leaders of Tizi-Reniff. Most signed with fingerprints.

160. CAOM 11CAB/8 Soustelle, *Le Monde* letter,

September 7, 1955.

161. CAOM 11CAB/46 December 17, 1955 letter from Hubert Beuve-Méry, director *Le Monde* to Jacques Soustelle.

162. CAOM 11CAB/8 November 2, 1955 ARRET DE MORT with marginalia from Soustelle telling a deputy that the information had been handed over to police.

163. CAOM 11CAB/38 Telegram from Soustelle to Minister of Interior, December 19, 1955.

164. Horne, *Savage War*, 117, 120-4; Droz and Lever, *Guerre de l'Algérie*, 74.

165. Jacques Soustelle, *L'Espérance Trahie* (Paris: Editions de l'Alma, 1962), 255.

166. Tillion, *L'Afrique Bascule*, 60.

167. Emmanuel Roblès, *Les Rives du Fleuve Bleu* (Paris: Éditions du Seuil, 1990), 232.

168. Amelio, Gianni (director), *Il Primo Uomo* (film released 2012 Italy. Produced by Philippe Carcassonne, executive producer Richard Djoudi); Camus, Albert, (Catherine Camus ed), *Le Premier Homme* (Paris: Gallimard, 1994).

169. Albert Camus letter to André Rosfelder, February 26, 1956. As cited in Olivier Todd, *Albert Camus–Une Vie* (Paris: Gallimard, 1996), 634-5.

170. Soustelle and Rudelle, Soustelle Interviews, February 19 and April 23 1979 (Paris: Université SciencesPo. Fondation Nationale des Sciences Politiques-Service des Archives d'Histoire Contemporaine), 8-9; 28-40.

171. Ullmann, *Mal Aimé*, 332-9.

CHAPTER SIX

1. Leaders of Aboriginal organizations were granted unprecedented access to the floor of the House of Commons for the occasion by agreement of all parties in the House.

2. Prime Minister Stephen Harper, "Residential Schools Apology," transcript printed in *The National Post*, June 12 2008, page A25, accessed September 2009, http://www.youtube.com/watch?v=-ryC74bbrEE.

3. The song was also the centrepiece of Dunn's 1968 National Film Board of Canada film of the same title.

4. "De Gaulle crève l'écran–Radio, télévision, livres BD, iTunes… La commémoration du 18 Juin relance les produits éditoriaux sur le Général," *LE FIGARO*, 18 Juin, 2010, pages 32 et 38; "Comme en 40–Soixante-dix ans âpres l'appel du 18 Juin, 'Libération' refait les actualités du jour. Où grande et petite histoires se répondent," *Libération*, 18 Juin, 2010, supplément 'SPÉCIAL 18 JUIN'.

5. Grégoire Allix, "MUSÉES–Nicolas Sarkozy inaugure cet Historial multimédia ce vendredi Aux Invalides, un 'monument audiovisuel' est dédié à De Gaulle," *Le Monde*, 23 Février, 2008. Section Culture&vous, Page 23.

6. Ullmann, *Mal Aimé*, 297-8; Ian Lustick, *Unsettled States, Disputed Lands: Britain and Ireland, France and Algeria, Israel and the West Bank-Gaza* (Ithaca, NY: Cornell University Press, 1993), 286; Alistair Horne, *A Savage War of Peace: Algeria 1954-1962* (New York: New York Review of Books, 2006–originally published 1977), 366, 374.

7. Stephen Clarkson and Christina McCall, *Trudeau* (Montréal: Boréal, 1990).

8. See for example, "Remains of 215 children found at former Kamloops Residential School," *Vancouver Sun*, May 28, 2021, https://vancouversun.com/news/local-news/remains-of-215-children-found-at-former-kamloops-residential-school-first-nation; James Cullingham, "Now Ain't the Time for Your Tears," *Active History*, June 28, 2021 http://activehistory.ca/2021/06/now-aint-the-time-for-your-tears/; Holly Honderich, "Why Canada is Mourning the Deaths of Hundreds of Children," *BBC News*, July 15, 2021, https://www.bbc.com/news/world-us-canada-57325653.

9. Personal communication, author with Thomas H.B. Symons, October 2019 and May 23, 2020.

10. Don Tapscott, "Trent University's Founding President Thomas Henry Bull Symons was 'a Beacon of Intellectual Light,'" *The Globe And Mail Obituary*, January 4, 2021, updated January 5, 2021; Trent University, "Trent University mourns the Passing of Founding President Thomas H.B. Symons," Trent University website, January 2, 2021. https://www.trentu.ca/news/story/28869.

11. Bernard Ullmann, Jacques Soustelle, *le Mal Aimé* (Paris: Plon, 1995); see Jacques Soustelle, *La longue marche d'Israël* (Paris: Fayard, 1968).

12. Ullmann, 1995.

13. Personal communication between Duncan Campbell

Scott and E.K. Brown as cited in E.K. Brown, "Duncan Campbell Scott: A Memoir," in *Responses and Evaluations: Essays on Canada, edited by David Staines* (Toronto: McLelland and Stewart, 1977), 130-131; also in Duncan Campbell Scott, *Selected Poems of Duncan Campbell Scott* (Toronto: The Ryerson Press, 1951), xxviii.

14. Duncan Campbell Scott, "Poetry and Progress" in *The Circle of Affection* (Toronto: McClelland and Stewart, 1947), 124.

15. Ibid, 137.

16. Duncan Campbell Scott, *Untitled Novel, ca.1905* (Moonbeam, ON; Penumbra Press/Coach House Press, 1979), 297.

17. Ibid, 298.

18. Duncan Campbell Scott, *The Witching of Elspie: A Book of Stories* (New York: Doran, 1923), 101-11; also *Selected Stories of Duncan Campbell Scott, Edited and with an Introduction by Glenn Clever* (Ottawa: University of Ottawa Press: Ottawa, 1987), 103-110.

19. Dragland, *Floating Voice*, 140.

20. Scott, *Selected Stories*, 104.

21. Ibid, 109-110.

22. Ibid, 110.

23. Duncan Campbell Scott, letter to Elise Aylen, Empress Hotel, Victoria, BC, November 23, 1930. LAC-BAC, LMS-0204, Box 1, Folder 4.

24. Jacques Soustelle, excerpted from his "papier" enclosed in letter to Paul Rivet. March 30, 1956, MNHN, 2 APIC SOUS.

25. Albert Camus, "Terrorisme et Répression," *L'Express*, July 9, 1955, 4.

26. Jean-Paul Sartre, *Situations V: Colonialisme et Néo-Colonialisme* (Paris: Gallimard, 1964), pp.47-48. Originally published in *Les Temps Modernes*, No. 123, mars-avril 1956. Intervention dans un meeting "pour la paix en Algérie".

27. Germaine Tillion, *À la Recherché du Vrai et du Juste: À Propos Rompus avec le Siècle* (Paris: Seuil, 2001), 41.

28. Charles de Gaulle as cited by Zemmour, *Destin*, 564-5 from Peyferitte, Alain, *C'Était de Gaulle* (Paris: Éditions de Fallois–Fayard, 1994).

29. See Todd Shepard, *The Invention of Decolonization: The Algerian War and the Remaking of France* (Ithaca and London: Cornell University Press, 2006), 47, 65, 69-70, 178.

30. Herbeth, 2015.

31. Jackson, Julian, *A Certain Idea of France–The Life of Charles de Gaulle* (London: Allen Lane – Penguin Random House, 2018), 447, 460, 462, 484-6, 503, 510-13, 516, 520.

32. Zemmour, Éric, *Destin français* (Paris: Albin Michel, 2018), 545-568.

33. "Eric Zemmour condamné à 10 000 euros d'amende pour injure et provocation à la haine," *Le Monde/AFP*, September 25, 2020, accessed April 2, 2021, https://www.lemonde.fr/societe/article/2020/09/25/eric-zemmour-condamne-a-10-000-euros-d-amende-pour-injure-et-provocation-a-la-haine_6053635_3224.html.

34. Soustelle, *Aimée*.

35. Jacques Soustelle interviewed on "Lectures pour tous" by Pierre Desgroupes about Sosutelle's book *Aimée et Souffrante Algérie*, December 19, 1956, Inathèque, BNF – Mitterand, Paris.

36. Germaine Tillion, *L'Afrique Bascule Vers l'Avenir* (Paris: Tirésias, 1999), 61.

37. Camus, *Actuelles III* "Avant-propos", 11.

38. Camus, *Actuelles III* "Avant-propos", 17.

39. Jean-Paul Sartre, *Situations V*, 40.

40. Jean-Paul Sartre, *Situations V*, "Portrait du Colonisé Précédé du Portrait du Colonisateur de Albert Memmi," 52 (originally published in *Les Temps Modernes*, Nos 137-138, July-August 1957).

41. Sartre, *Situations V*, "Les Damnés de la Terre," (originally published as introduction to eponymous text of Frantz Fanon, 1961), 176.

42. Jacques Soustelle, *Le Drame Algérien et la Décadence Française Réponse a Raymond Aron* (Paris: Plon–Tribune Libre 6, 1957); Soustelle wrote this pamphlet in response to Aron's *la Tragédie algérienne* (Paris: Plon–Tribune Libre 2, 1957).

43. CAOM 11Cab/29 Script of declaration by Soustelle on Radio Algérie August 19, 1955 En dépit des difficultés et des souffrances, malgré même les échecs temporaires, envers et contre tout, une ALGÉRIE nouvelle est en train de se faire.

Indigenous childrens' moccasins on the steps of the Bata Library at Trent University, 2021. One of countless impromptu public memorials created following the discovery of hundreds of children's remains in unmarked graves adjacent to former Indigenous residential schools.

44. Soustelle, *Drame Algérien*, 31.

45. CAOM 11CAB/1 October 28, 1955 letter from Soustelle's secretary confirming meeting for Soustelle with M. Martin Directer de la compagnie dur Recherche et d'exploitation de Pétrole au Sahara.

46. Dominique Balvet, "Jacques Soustelle Et l'Algérie Française: Gaullisme Et Antigaullisme." Doctorat d'Histoire sous la direction de Jean-Francois Sirinelli, Université Charles de Gaulle Lille 3, 2003. Tome 3, 766. A photo of Soustelle appeared on the cover of *TIME Magazine*, August 17, 1959.

47. Soustelle, *Drame Algérien*, 37.

48. Camus, *Actuelles III* "Avant-propos," 11.

49. Ibid, 23.

50. Soustelle, *Drame Algérien*, 33-4.

51. Tillion, *l'Afrique Bascule*, 73.

52. Ibid, 51-60.

53. For Soustelle's argument about Mayan decadence see Jacques Soustelle, *Les Quatre Soleils* (Paris: Plon, 1967), 103-4; 121.

54. Soustelle, *Drame Algérien*, 1-6.

55. James D. Le Sueur, "Decolonizing 'French Universalism' Reconsidering the Impact of the Algerian

War on French Intellectuals," in Le Sueur, ed. *The Decolonizing Reader* (London: Rutledge, 2003), 103-117; Le Sueur, *Uncivil War: Intellectuals and Identity Politics during the Decolonization of Algeria* (Philadelphia: University of Pennsylvania Press, 2001); Ronald Aronson, *Camus & Sartre: The Story of a Friendship and the Quarrel that Ended it* (Chicago: University of Chicago Press, 2004); Shepard, *Invention*, 10, 63-64, 68-73, 94, 194.

56. Albert Camus, *L'Étranger* (Paris: Gallimard, 1957– originally published 1942); see Edward W. Said, *Culture and Imperialism* (London: Vintage, 1994), 67, 160, 161, 174-176, 178, 179-180, 181, 184-185.

57. Albert Camus, "L'Hôte" in *L'Exil et le Royaume* (Paris: Gallimard, 1957), 79-99.

58. David Oelhoffen (director), *Loin des Hommes* (Paris: One World Films, 2014).

59. Raphaëlle Branche, *Torture et l'Armée Pendant La Guerre d'Algérie* (Paris: Gallimard, 2001).

60. Rachid Bouchareb, dir. *Indigènes* (Alger/Paris: Mars Distribution, 2006). English title *Days of Glory*.

61. Jean-Pierre Lledo, dir. *Algérie, Histoires à ne pas Dire* (Paris: Colifilms Distribution, 2007).

62. Florence Beaugé, "Trois Historiens Face aux Tabous Algériens," *Le Monde* (Paris: February 27, 2008), 4.

63. Safinez Bousbia (director), *El Gusto* (Dublin: Quidam Productions, 2011).

64. Hamid Aït-Taleb, *De Grace* (Paris: Hachette, 2008).

65. Maia de la Baume, "Hollande Uses Softer Tone on Delicate Visit to Algeria," *The New York Times*, December 20, 2012, accessed December 12, 2012, www.nytimes.com.

66. Le Point.fr, "À Alger, Hollande Reconnaît les Souffrances de la Colonisation," Publié le 20/12/2012 à 17:03–Modifié le 20/12/2012 à 17:58; Harvey Morris, "Being French Means Never Having to Say…," *International Herald Tribune*, December 20, 2012, accessed December 29, 2012, http://rendezvous.blogs.nytimes.com. IHT Rendezvous cancelled June 28, 2013.

67. Michel Houellebecq, *Soumission* (Paris: Flammarion, 2015).

68. See Barrie McKenna, Ottawa, "First Nations Attawapiskat gets help with housing," *The Globe And Mail*, December 12, 2011, page A7; Gloria Galloway, "Aboriginal Affairs First Nations Unite to Support Attawapiskat Chiefs from Across Canada Blast Government for Sending Third Party to Troubled Community," *The Globe And Mail*, December 7, 2011, Page A5; David Ljungggren, "Natives have been betrayed, leader says," *Reuters*, December 6, 2011, 4:05pm; Alanis Obomsawin, dir., *The People of the Kattawapiskat River* (Montréal: National Film Board of Canada, 2012).

69. Myra Rutherdale, Erin Dolmage and Carolyn Podruchny, "Bodies of Water Not Bodies of Women, Canadian Media Images of the Idle No More Movement," *Active History*, May 22, 2015. http://activehistory.ca/papers/bodies-of-water-not-bodies-of-women-canadian-media-images-of-the-idle-no-more-movement.

70. Ghislain Picard and Terry Teegee, "No More Reports, No More Commissions: Indigenous People Want Immediate Action," *The Toronto Star*, June 18 2020, https://www.thestar.com/opinion/contributors/2020/06/18/no-more-reports-no-more-commissions-indigenous-people-want-immediate-action.html consulted July 21 2020; Talaga, *Fallen Feathers*.

71. Truth and Reconciliation Commission, *Honouring*, 2015.

72. National Inquiry into Missing and Murdered Indigenous Women and Girls, *Reclaiming Power and Place–The Final Report of the Inquiry into Missing and Murdered Indigenous Women and Girls*, Vancouver, 2019.

73. Bernie M. Farber, "The Troubling Legacy of Duncan Campbell Scott," *The Ottawa Citizen*, August 28, 2013, Op-Ed Section, accessed August 29, 2013, http://www.ottawacitizen.com/opinion/oped/troubling+legacy+Duncan+Campbell+Scott/8844210/story.html.

74. Abley, *Conversations*, 2013.

75. Alanis Obomsawin, dir, *Trick or Treaty?* (Montréal: National Film Board of Canada, 2014).

76. Charlie Angus, *Children of the Broken Treaty – Canada's Lost Promise and One Girl's Dream* (Regina: University of Regina Press, 2015).

77. Candida Paltiel, dir. *Canada's Rings of Fire* (Aljazeera– Witness, A Mining Stories Production for Al Jazeera, 2015), https://www.aljazeera.com/programmes/witness/2015/07/rings-fire-150729124056943.html; Tess Girard and Ryan Noth, dirs., *The Road to Webequie*, (Prince Edward County, ON: Fifth Town Films, 2016).

78. Doug Fischer, "The Grim Legacy of Treaty 9," *The Ottawa Citizen*, November 6, 2005,79. John S. Long, *Treaty No. 9–Making the Agreement to Share the Land in Far Northern Ontario in 1905* (Montreal and Kingston, London, Ithaca: McGill-Queen's University Press, 2010).

79. John S. Long, *Treaty No. 9 – Making the Agreement to Share the Land in Far Northern Ontario in 1905* (Montreal and Kingston, London, Ithaca: McGill-Queen's University Press, 2010).

80. Peter Edwards, "Lawsuit a Century in the Making Star Exclusive James Bay Native Band alleges 100 years of Neglect in Historic, Multi-Million suit," *The Toronto Star*, May 17, 2011, page A1; Christopher Moore, presenter, Sarah Wolch, producer, "George McMartin's Big Canoe Trip," *CBC Radio1 IDEAS*, December 19, 2011; Marj Heinrichs and Diane Hiebert with the People of Mishkeegogomang, *Mishkeegogamang: The Land, The People & The Purpose–The Story of Mishkeegogomang Ojibway Nation* (Canada: Rosetta Projects, 2003).

81. Debbie Mishibinijima, "Mushkegowuk Strengthen Rupert's Land case claim," *Wawatay News*, August 5, 2010, Volume 37, No. 16. Also http://wawataynews.ca/archive.

82. Cheryl Chetkiewicz, Justina Ray and Richard Lindgren, "A Sustainable Plan for Ontario's Ring of Fire," *Policy Options*, July 17, 2018; Dayna Scott, "Doug Ford's Repeal of the Far North Act won't Gain the Respect of Indigenous Communities," *The Globe And Mail*, March 25, 2019, Opinion page.

83. Joelle Kovach, "Curve Lake First Nation takes water crisis to court," *The Peterborough Examiner*, January 25, 2021, front page; The Examiner's View "No Excuse for Federal Inaction on First Nations Drinking Water," *The Peterborough Examiner*, editorial, March 3, 2021.

84. THE CANADIAN PRESS, "Feds, First Nations reach nearly $8B deal on drinking water suit," *The Peterborough Examiner*, July 31, 2021, A7.

85. Willow Fielder and Kristy Kirkup, "One Year After Landmark Report on Violence, Indigenous Women's Groups Slam Ottawa for Lack of Progress," *The Globe And Mail*, June 3, 2020; Pamela Palmater, "Genocide Against Indigenous Women and Girls Continues," *The Lawyer's Daily*, June 4, 2020, https://www.thelawyersdaily.ca/articles/19404/genocide-against-indigenous-women-and-girls-continues-pamela-palmate.

86. John Chidley-Hill The Canadian Press, "Police Urged to Pursue Homicide Charge," *The Peterborough Examiner*, March 24, 2021, front page.

87. Russ Diabo, "Federal UNDRIP Bill C-15 is an Attack on Indigenous Sovereignty and Self-Determination: Opinion," *APTN National News*, December 21, 2020, https://www.aptnnews.ca/national-news/undrip-bill-c-15-federal-government-soverignty-russ-diabo/. Consulted April 2, 2021.

88. See as examples Donald B. Smith, *Seen*; Luby, *DAMMED*; Sheldon Kraskowski forward by Winona Wheeler, *No Surrender: The Land Remains Indigenous* (Regina: University of Regina Press, 2019); James Daschuk, *Clearing the Plains: Disease, Politics of Starvation and the Loss of Aboriginal Life* (Regina: University of Regina Press, 2013); Ian Mosby, "Administering Colonial Science: Nutrition Research and Human Biomedical Experimentation in Aboriginal Communities and Residential Schools, 1942–1952," *Histoire Sociale/Social History* Volume 46, Number 91 (2013), 145-172; Candace Savage, *A Geography of Blood: Unearthing Memory from a Prairie Landscape* (Vancouver: Greystone Books and David Suzuki Foundation, 2012).

89. Of the French scholarship, see for example Laurière, *Rivet*; Raphaëlle Branche et Sylvie Thénault sous la direction de, *La France en guerre 1954-1962 Expériences Métropolitaines de la Guerre d'Indépendance Algérienne* (Paris: Autrement, 2008); Olivier Le Cour Grandmaison, *Coloniser Exterminer: Sur la Guerre et l'État Colonial* (Paris: Fayard, 2005); Raphaëlle Branche, *La guerre de l'Algérie: Une Histoire Apaisée?* (Paris: Seuil, 2005).

90. Maher Mezahi, "Viewpoint: France's President Macron Doesn't Get the Impact of Colonialism on Algeria," BBC, March 15, 2021 https://www.bbc.com/news/world-africa-56360817.

BIBLIOGRAPHY

ARCHIVES MUSEUM DU QUAI BRANLY, Paris, France

Fonds Soustelle (Jacques et Georgette); Paul Rivet; Germaine Tillion

Photography collection
Jacques Soustelle, Mexico 1932-1936

Physical archives
Georgette and Jacques Soustelle, Mexico
Unité patrimoniale Amériques
Numéro d'inventaire 71.1933; 71.1936
Appellation Arc

ARCHIVES MUSEUM NATIONAL D'HISTOIRE NAUTURELLE, Paris, France

(Salle des Valins et Bibliothèque de recherche)
Fonds Mexique, Musée de l'Homme, Paul Rivet, Georgette Soustelle, Jacques Soustelle et Germaine Tillion
Fonds Rivet 2 APIC Sous.

ARCHIVES MUSEUM L'HOMME DOSSIER MEXICO

(I) 2 AM 1K65e
2 AM 1B11a
2 AM 1K66a MEXICO (11)
MNHN 2am 1 C9 a
Germaine Tillion, Radio Conférence 77 « Un Conte Chaouïa », July 19, 1937. MNHN 2am 1 C9 a

ARCHIVES NATIONALES D'OUTRE-MER, Aix-en-Provence, France

GGA 11/CAB (archives concerning Soustelle Lorne Pierce archives COLL 2000.1 Boxes 46, 80, 81 administration 1955-56)

Boxes 7, 8, 12, 14, 20, 21, 28, 35, 38, 41, 57, 62, 77, 81, 82, 88, 96, 100

ARCHIVES ONTARIO

(See VISUAL CONTENT, page 240)

ARCHIVES DE PRESSES – MUSEUM DE L'HOMME

Bibliothèque nationale de France – Mitterand

Principal newspapers and magazines consulted 1930-1990:
L'Aurore
Combat
L'Humanité
L'Express
Le Figaro
Libération
Le Monde
Les Nouvelles littéraires
MASSES
Spartacus
Voici Pourquoi

INATHEQUE – ELECTRONIC MEDIA

Lectures pour tous, December 19, 1956 Interview with Jacques Soustelle about Aimée et souffrante Algérie.

Du côté de chez Fred, Frédéric Mitterand interview of Jacques Soustelle, 2 parts, Antenne 2, 1989.

JACQUES SOUSTELLE RADIO SCRIPTS

Radio Conférence 85 « Une fête dans un village indien du Mexique »December 20, 1937. Document (15058) id Dossier 1611 DA000312; Radio Conférence 50 « A travers les montagnes du Mexique » June 23, 1936. Document (15058) id Dossier 1604 DA000316; « Chez les Indiens Lacandóns » June 2, 1935, Document (15027) Dossier 1604 DA000319

LIBRARY ARCHIVES CANADA

Department of Indian Affairs

RG10a RG10
Vol. 725, William Scott, Oka Indian Report
RG10b RG10
Vol. 1028, D.C. Scott, Treaty 9 Journal (Jun 30-Sept 6, 1905)
Pelham Edgar, Treaty 9 Diary (May 22-Aug 16, 1906)

RG10d RG10
    Vol. 11, 399, Samuel Stewart, Treaty 9 Journal (Jun 30-
        Sept 6, 1905); (May 22-Aug 15, 1906)
RG10
    Vol 6810, File 470, Marius Barbeau, Lorette report
RG10
    Vol 6810, file 470-2-3 (also Microfiche reel C8533)
        Enfranchisement
RG10
    Vol 6810, file 470-2-3, Pt.7, Duncan Campbell
        Scott, testimony transcript and notes, Parliamentary
        hearings, Apr. 1920
RG10f RG10
    Vol. 6810, 473-12: Hearings Testimony, 1921-22

National Photography Collection

Acc. 1971-205, Box 3266 F1: Treaty No. 9 Photographs

Government Documents

Canada. Seasonal Papers. Department of Indian Affairs.
    Annual Reports 1862-1932

Literary Archives

LMS-0204
    Duncan Campbell Scott and Elise Aylen Boxes 1–14C
        Ephemera LMS-0204
    Duncan Campbell Scott, embroidered tobacco pouch,
        Box 14B
    Duncan Campbell Scott, embroidered moccasins, Box
        14C
MG 30 D 100
    Duncan Campbell Scott Papers
MG 30 D 276
    D.C. Scott – E. Aylen Papers
MG 30 D61
    Vol 3 E.K. Brown correspondence with DC Scott

Broadcast Archives

ISN 104533
    Title: National School Broadcasts. Part 2, Four
        Canadian Poets. Duncan Campbell Scott.
    Collection: CBC, Radio: Disc collection
    Collection number: 1978-0109
    Production: 1948-01-16.

ISN 129996
    Title: National School Broadcasts. Duncan Campbell
        Scott.

Collection: CBC, Radio: Special Disc collection
Collection number: 1989-0181
Production: 1947-09-16.
Consultation copy: C08478 (4)

ISN#108498 VLTSLF#8903-5674
    "Night Hymns on Lake Nipigon–poem by Duncan
        Campbell Scott with paintings by Norval
        Morrisseau," Canadian Independent Filmmakers
        Cooperative, video directed and produced by
        Trevor Davies and George Muncey, reading by John
        Arblaster, 1972.

MANUSCRIPTS OF INTERVIEWS / MEMOIRS OF JACQUES SOUSTELLE

Soustelle, Jacques et Odile Rudelle. "Jacques Soustelle Interviews, February 19 and April 23, 1979." Université SciencesPo. Fondation nationale des sciences politiques– Service des archives d'Histoire contemporaine, Paris.

Soustelle, Jacques et Georges Suffert, "Mémoires, Apocryphes Sous La Forme d'Une Dialogue Avec Georges Suffert." Unpublished manuscript, 1988.

THOMAS FISHER RARE BOOK LIBRARY, UNIVERSITY OF TORONTO

(See VISUAL CONTENT, page 240)

QUEEN'S UNIVERSITY ARCHIVES, Kingston, Ontario

Edmund Morris papers COLL 2140

BOOKS

Abley, Mark. *Conversations with a Dead Man: The Legacy of Duncan Campbell Scott.* Madeira Park BC: Douglas & McIntyre, 2013.

Abro, Ben. *Assassination July 14, an Underground Thriller, with a Historical Essay by James D. Le Sueur.* Lincoln and London: University of Nebraska Press, 2001.

Adas, Michael. *Prophets of Rebellion: Millenarian Protest Movements Against the European Colonial Order. Studies in Comparative World History.* Chapel Hill: University of North Carolina Press, 1979.

Ageron, Charles-Robert. *Histoire De l'Algérie Contemporaine*. Paris: Presses universitaires de France, 1979.

Aguirre, Robert D. *Informal Empire: Mexico and Central America in Victorian Culture*. Minneapolis: University of Minnesota Press, 2005.

Ait-Taleb, Hamid. *De Grace*. Paris: Hachette, 2008.

Arendt, Hannah. *Eichmann in Jerusalem: A Report on the Banality of Evil*. Penguin Classics. New York, NY: Penguin Books, 2006; 1963.

Andersen, Chris. *"Métis": Race, Recognition, and the Struggle for Indigenous Peoplehood*. Vancouver: UBC Press, 2014.

Anderson, Benedict. *Imagined Communities: Reflections on the Origin and Spread of Nationalism*. London: Verso, 1991.

Anderson, M. C., and Robertson, C. *Seeing Red: A History of Natives in Canadian Newspapers*. Winnipeg: University of Manitoba Press, 2011.

Aron, Raymond. *Mémoires*. Paris: Julliard, 1983.

Aronson, Ronald. *Camus & Sartre: The Story of a Friendship and the Quarrel that Ended it*. Chicago: University of Chicago Press, 2004.

Asch, M. *On Being Here to Stay: Treaties and Aboriginal Rights in Canada*. Toronto: University of Toronto Press, 2014.

Ashcroft, Bill, Gareth Griffiths, and Helen Tiffin. *The Empire Writes Back: Theory and Practice in Post-Colonial Literature*. New Accents. London; New York: Routledge, 1989.

Atwood, Margaret. *Survival: A Thematic Guide to Canadian Literature*. Toronto: Anansi, 1972.

Azuela, Mariano. *Los De Abajo; y, Mala Yerba*. México, DF: Fondo de Cultura Económica, 2004.

Ba Konare, Adame, ed. *Petit Précis De Remise a Niveau Sur l'Histoire Africaine a l'Usage Du Président Sarkozy*. Paris: Editions La Découverte, 2008.

Bantjes, Adrian A. *As if Jesus Walked on Earth: Cardenismo, Sonora, and the Mexican Revolution*. Latin American Silhouettes : Studies in History and Culture. Wilmington, DE: Scholarly Resources, 1998.

Barkwell, Lawrence J., Leah Dorion, Audreen Hourie, and Gabriel Dumont Institute of Native Studies and Applied Research. *Metis Legacy: Michif Culture, Heritage, and Folkways*. Metis Legacy Series; v. 2. Saskatoon: Gabriel Dumont Institute, 2006.

Barman, Jean. *The West Beyond the West: A History of British Columbia*. 3rd ed. Toronto: University of Toronto Press, 2007.

Bartra, Roger. *La Jaula De La Melancolia*. Mexico: Debosillo, 2005.

Baudorre, Philippe and Centre d'études et de recherches sur François Mauriac. *La Plume Dans La Plaie: Les Écrivains Journalistes Et La Guerre d'Algérie*. Sémaphores. Pessac: Presses universitaires de Bordeaux, 2003.

Berger, Carl. *The Sense of Power; Studies in the Ideas of Canadian Imperialism, 1867-1914*. Toronto: University of Toronto Press, 1970.

Blair, Peggy. *Lament for a First Nation: The Williams Treaties of Southern Ontario*. (Vancouver: UBC Press, 2008).

Borrows, John. *Canada's Indigenous Constitution*. Toronto: University of Toronto Press, 2010.

Bouche, Denise. *Histoire De La Colonisation Francaise, Tome Second, Flux Et Reflux (1815–1962)*. Paris: Fayard, 1991.

Bourdieu, Pierre. *Sociologie de l'Algérie*. Paris: Presses Universitaires de France, 1963.

Bourinot, Authur Stanley. *Five Canadian Poets: Duncan Campbell Scott, Archibald Lampman, William E. Marshall, Charles Sangster, George Frederick Cameron*. Montreal: Printed by Quality Press, 1956.

Boursier, Jean-Yves, sous la direction de. *Résistants Et Résistance*. Paris: Harmattan, 1997.

Bracken, Christopher. *The Potlatch Papers: A Colonial Case History*. Chicago: University of Chicago Press, 1997.

Branche, Raphaëlle. *La Guerre De l'Algérie: Une Histoire Apaisée?* Paris: Seuil, 2005.

———. *La Torture Et l'Armée Pendant La Guerre De l'Algérie*. Paris: Gallimard, 2001.

Branche, Raphaëlle et Sylvie Thénault sous la direction de. *La France en guerre 1954-1962 Expériences Métropolitaines de la Guerre d'Indépendance Algérienne*. Paris: Autrement, 2008.

Brown, Alison K. and Laura L. Peers. *Pictures Bring Us Messages–Sinaakssiiksi Aohtsimaahpihkookiyaawa:*

Photographs and Histories from the Kainai Nation. Toronto: University of Toronto Press, 2006.

Brown, Edward Killoran. *On Canadian Poetry.* Toronto: Ryerson, 1943.

Brown, Jennifer S. H. and Elizabeth Vibert. *Reading Beyond Words: Contexts for Native History.* Peterborough, ON: Broadview Press, 1996.

Brownlie, Robin. *A Fatherly Eye: Indian Agents, Government Power, and Aboriginal Resistance in Ontario, 1918-1939.* Canadian Social History Series. Don Mills, ON; New York: Oxford University Press, 2003.

Campbell, Wilfred, Archibald Lampman, and Duncan Campbell Scott. *At the Mermaid Inn: Wilfred Campbell, Archibald Lampman, Duncan Campbell Scott in the Globe 1892–93.* Literature of Canada, Poetry and Prose in Reprint. Vol. 21. Toronto: University of Toronto Press, 1979.

Camus, Albert. *Actuelles: Écrits Politiques. Collection Idées;* 375: Sciences Humaines. Paris: Gallimard, 1977.

——. *L'Étranger.* Paris: Gallimard, 1981. Originally published 1942.

——. *L'Exil Et Le Royaume.* Paris: Gallimard, 1972. Originally published 1957.

Carter, Sarah. *Lost Harvests.* Montreal QC: McGill-Queen's University Press, 1990.

Castellanos, María Bianet, Lourdes Gutiérrez Nájera, and Arturo J. Aldama. *Comparative Indigeneities of the Américas: Toward a Hemispheric Approach. Critical Issues in Indigenous Studies.* Tucson: University of Arizona Press, 2012.

Césaire, Aimé. *Discours Sur Le Colonialisme.* Paris: Présence Africaine, 1976; 1955.

Clarkson, Stephen and Christina McCall. *Trudeau.* Montréal: Boréal, 1990.

Cole, Douglas. *Captured Heritage: The Scramble for Northwest Coast Artifacts.* Seattle: University of Washington Press, 1985.

Cole, Douglas and Ira Chaikin. *An Iron Hand upon the People: The Law Against the Potlatch on the Northwest Coast.* Vancouver: Douglas & McIntyre, 1990.

Cook, Curtis and Juan David Lindau. *Aboriginal Rights and Self-Government: The Canadian and Mexican Experience in North American Perspective.* McGill-Queen's

Native and Northern Series. Vol. 21. Montreal: McGill-Queen's University Press, 2000.

Cooper, Frederick and Ann Laura Stoler. *Tensions of Empire.* Berkeley: University of California Press, 1997.

Conklin, Alice L. *In the Museum of Man: Race, Anthropology, and Empire in France, 1850–1950.* Ithaca: Cornell University Press, 2013.

Coulthard, Glen Sean. *Red Skins, White Masks: Rejecting the Politics of Liberal Recognition.* Minneapolis & London: University of Minnesota Press, 2014.

Courrière, Yves. *Les Fils De La Toussaint.* His La Guerre d'Algerie. Vol. 1. Paris: Fayard, 1968.

——. *La Guerre d'Algérie.* Paris: Fayard, 2001.

——. *La Guerre d'Algerie En Images.* Paris: Fayard, 1972.

——. *L'Heure Des Colonels.* His La Guerre d'Algerie. Vol. 3. Paris: Fayard, 1970.

——. *Le Temps Des Leopards.* His La Guerre d'Algerie. Vol. 2. Paris: Fayard, 1969.

Cunningham, Michele. *Mexico and the Foreign Policy of Napoleon III.* Basingstoke, Hampshire; New York: Palgrave, 2001.

Darnell, Regna. *And Along Came Boas: Continuity and Revolution in Americanist Anthropology.* Amsterdam Studies in the Theory and History of Linguistic Science. Vol. 86. Philadelphia, PA: J. Benjamins, 1998.

Darnell, Regna and Julia D. Harrison. *Historicizing Canadian Anthropology.* Vancouver: U.B.C. Press, 2006.

Daschuk, James. *Clearing the Plains: Disease, Politics of Starvation and the Loss of Aboriginal Life.* Regina: University of Regina Press, 2013.

Davidson, James West and John Rugge. *Great Heart: The History of a Labrador Adventure.* Montreal: McGill-Queen's University Press, 1997.

Daoud, Kamel. *Meursault, Contre-enquête.* Alger, Barzakh, 2013.

de Durand-Forest, Jacqueline, Georges Baudot, and Jacques Soustelle. *Mille Ans De Civilisations Mésoaméricaines: Des Mayas Aux Aztèques: Mélanges En l'Honneur De Jacques Soustelle.* Paris: L'Harmattan, 1995.

Deneen, Patrick J. *Why Liberalism Failed.* New Haven CT: Yale University Press, 2018.

Deniau, Jean-François, Alain Peyrefitte, Bertrand

Poirot-Delpech, Jean d' Ormesson, and 20 Académie française. *Discours De Réception De Jean François Deniau à l'Académiefrançaise Et Réponse d'Alain Peyrefitte: Précédé Des Allocutions Pour La Remise De l'Epée De Bertrand Poirot-Delpech, Jean d'Ormesson Et La Réponse De Jean François Deniau.* Paris: Plon, 1993.

Desmond, Lawrence Gustave. *Yucatan Through Her Eyes: Alice Dixon Le Plongeon, Writer & Expeditionary Photographer.* Albuquerque: University of New Mexico Press, 2009.

Desmond, Lawrence Gustave and Phyllis Mauch Messenger. *A Dream of Maya: Augustus and Alice Le Plongeon in Nineteenth-Century Yucatan.* 1st ed. Albuquerque: University of New Mexico Press, 1988.

Dickason, Olive Patricia. *The Myth of the Savage: And the Beginnings of French Colonialism in the Americas.* Edmonton, AB, Canada: University of Alberta Press, 1984.

Dickason, Olive Patricia and David McNab. *Canada's First Nations: A History of Founding Peoples from Earliest Times.* 4th ed. Don Mills, ON: Oxford University Press, 2009.

Dragland, S. L. *Duncan Campbell Scott: A Book of Criticism.* Ottawa: Tecumseh Press, 1974.

——. *Floating Voice: Duncan Campbell Scott and the Literature of Treaty 9.* Concord, ON: Anansi, 1994.

Droz, Bernard and Évelyne Lever. *Histoire De La Guerre d'Algérie (1954-62).* Points. Histoire. Vol. H60. Paris: Seuil, 1982.

Ducharme, Michel and Jean-François Constant. *Liberalism and Hegemony: Debating the Canadian Liberal Revolution.* Toronto: University of Toronto Press, 2009.

Edgar, Pelham. *Across My Path.* Toronto: Ryerson Press, 1952.

Fanon, Frantz. *Sociologie d'une Révolution–l'An V de la Révolution Algérienne.* Paris: Librairie François Maspero, 1959.

——. *Les Damnés de la Terre.* Paris: Librairie François Maspero, 1961.

Flanet, Véronique. *La Madre Muerte–Violencia En México, Prefacio De Jacques Soustelle.* Translated by Aurelio Garzón de Camino. México: Fonda de Cultura Económica, 1985.

Forsyth, Frederick. *The Day of the Jackal.* New York: Viking Press, 1971.

Frémeaux, Jacques. *Les Bureaux Arabes Dans l'Algérie De La Conquête. L'Aventure Coloniale De La France.* Destins Croisés. Paris: Denoël, 1993.

——. *France Et l'Algérie En Guerre. Hautes Études Militaires.* Vol. 22. Paris: CFHM, Commission Française d'Histoire Militaire Institut de Stratégie Comparée Economica, 2002.

Frye, Northrop. *The Bush Garden; Essays on the Canadian Imagination.* Toronto: Anansi, 1971.

García Canclini, Néstor. *Culturas Híbridas: Estrategias Para Entrar y Salir De La Modernidad. Estado y Sociedad.* Nueva ed. Vol. 87. Buenos Aires: Paidós, 2001.

Getty, Ian A. L. and Donald Smith. *One Century Later: Western Canadian Reserve Indians since Treaty 7.* Vancouver: University of British Columbia Press, 1978.

Girardet, Raoul. *L'Idée Coloniale En France De 1871 a 1962.* Paris: La Table Ronde, 1972.

Gould, Stephen Jay. *The Mismeasure of Man.* New York: W.W. Norton, 2008.

Greene, Graham. *The Power and the Glory.* London: Readers' Union, 1941.

Greer, Allan. *Mohawk Saint: Catherine Tekakwitha and the Jesuits.* Oxford: Oxford University Press, 2005.

Gwyn, Sandra. *The Private Capital: Ambition and Love in the Age of MacDonald and Laurier.* Toronto: McClelland and Stewart, 1984.

Haig-Brown, Celia and David Nock. *With Good Intentions: Euro-Canadian and Aboriginal Relations in Colonial Canada.* Vancouver: UBC Press, 2006.

Halberstam, David. *The Best and the Brightest.* 1st ed. New York: Random House, 1972.

Hall, Catherine. *Cultures of Empire: Colonizers in Britain and the Empire in Nineteenth and Twentieth Centuries: A Reader.* Manchester, UK; New York; NY: Manchester University Press; distributed exclusively in the USA by Routledge Inc., 2000.

Harris, R. Cole. *Making Native Space: Colonialism, Resistance, and Reserves in British Columbia.* Vancouver: UBC Press, 2002.

Herbeth, Alain. *Jacques Soustelle–L'Homme de l'Intégration.* Paris, Harmattan, 2015.

Horne, Alistair. *A Savage War of Peace: Algeria, 1954–62.* New York: Viking Press, 1978.

Jackson, Julian. *A Certain Idea of France–The Life of Charles de Gaulle*. London: Allen Lane, Penguin, 2018.

Johnston, Gordon. *Duncan Campbell Scott and His Works*. Downsview, ON: ECW Press, 1983.

Judt, Tony. *The Burden of Responsibility: Blum, Camus, Aron, and the French Twentieth Century*. Chicago: University of Chicago Press, 1998.

Julien, Charles-André. *Histoire De l'Algérie Contemporaine: La Conquête Et Les Débuts De La Colonisation (1827–1871)*. Paris: Presses Universitaires de France, 1964.

Kennedy, D., and Stevens, J. R. *Recollections of an Assiniboine Chief*. Toronto: McClelland and Stewart, 1972.

Kraskowski, Sheldon, foreword by Winona Wheeler. *No Surrender: The Land Remains Indigenous*. Regina: University of Regina Press, 2019.

Labelle, Kathryn Magee. *In collaboration with the Wendat/Wandat Women's Advisory Council. Daughters of Aataentsic: Life Stories from Seven Generations*. McGill-Queen's University Press, 2021.

——. *Dispersed but not destroyed : a history of the seventeenth-century Wendat people*. Vancouver: UBC Press, 2013.

Lafaye, Jacques. *Quetzalcóatl and Guadalupe: The Formation of Mexican National Consciousness, 1531–1813* [Quetzalcóatl et Guadalupe. English]. Chicago: University of Chicago Press, 1976.

Lampman, Archibald and Duncan Campbell Scott. *Lyrics of Earth: Sonnets and Ballads*. Toronto: Musson Book Co., 1925.

Laroui, Abdallah. *L'Histoire Du Maghreb: Un Essai De Synthese*, Vol. 1. Paris: Francois Maspero, 1982.

Laurière, Christine. *Paul Rivet Le Savant Et Le Politique*. Paris: Publications Scientifiques du Museum national d'Histoire Naturelle, 2008.

Lawrence, D. H. *The Plumed Serpent*. London: Secker, 1926.

Lears, T. J. Jackson. *No Place Of Grace: Antimodernism and the Transformation of American Culture 1880-1920*. New York: Pantheon Books, 1981.

Le Cour Grandmaison, Olivier. *Coloniser, Exterminer: Sur La Guerre Et l'État Colonial*. Paris: Fayard, 2005.

——. *De l'Indigénat: Anatomie d'Un Monstre Juridique: Le Droit Coloniale En Algérie Dans l'Empire Français*. Paris: Zone, 2010.

L'Estoile (de), Benoit, Federico G. Neiburg, and Lygia Sigaud. *Empires, Nations, and Natives: Anthropology and State-Making*. Durham: Duke University Press, 2005.

——. *La République Impériale : Politique Et Racisme d'État*. Paris: Fayard, 2009.

Le Sueur, James D. *"'De-Colonizing French Universalism' Reconsidering the Impact of the Algerian War on French Intellectuals."* In The Decolonization Reader, edited by James D. Le Sueur, 103. New York; London: Routledge, 2003.

——. *Uncivil War: Intellectuals and Identity Politics during the Decolonization of Algeria*. Philadelphia: University of Pennsylvania Press, 2001.

Legg, Charlotte Ann. *The New White Race – Settler Colonialism and the Press in French Algeria, 1860–1914*. Lincoln: University of Nebraska Press, 2021.

Leiris, Michel. *Cinq Études d'Ethnologie*. Collection Tel. Vol. 133. Paris: Denoël/Gonthier, 1988.

Lomnitz-Adler, Claudio. *Death and the Idea of Mexico*. Brooklyn, N.Y.; Cambridge, MA: Zone Books; Distributed by MIT Press, 2005.

——. *Deep Mexico, Silent Mexico: An Anthropology of Nationalism*. Public Worlds. Vol. 9. Minneapolis: University of Minnesota Press, 2001.

——. *Exits from the Labyrinth: Culture and Ideology in the Mexican National Space*. Berkeley: University of California Press, 1992.

Long, John. *Treaty No. 9 the Half-Breed Question 1902–1910*. Cobalt, ON: Highway Book Shop.

——. *Treaty No. 9 the Indian Petitions 1889–1927*. Cobalt, ON: Highway Book Shop, 1978.

——. *Treaty No.9 the Negotiations 1901–1928*. Cobalt, ON: Highway Book Shop, 1978.

Long, John S. *Treaty No. 9 Making the Agreement to Share the Land in Far Northern Ontario in 1905*. Montreal & Kingston, London, Ithaca: McGill-Queen's University Press, 2010.

Lorcin, P. M. E., & Shepard, T. edited and with an introduction by. *French Mediterraneans: Transnational and Imperial Histories*. Lincoln: University of Nebraska Press, 2016.

Losurdo, Domenico. Contre-Histoire Du Libéralisme [Controstoria del Liberalismo]. Translated by Bernard

Chamayou. Paris: Éditions de La découverte, 2013.

Luby, Brittany. *DAMMED: The Politics of Loss and Survival in Anishinaabe Territory*. Winnipeg: University of Manitoba Press, 2020.

Luis-Brown, David. *Waves of Decolonization: Discourses of Race and Hemispheric Citizenship in Cuba, Mexico, and the United States*. New Americanists. Durham, NC: Duke University Press, 2008.

Lustick, Ian. *State-Building Failure in British Ireland & French Algeria*. Berkeley: iiS Institute of International Studies, University of California, Berkeley, 1985.

——. *Unsettled States, Disputed Lands: Britain and Ireland, France and Algeria, Israel and the West Bank-Gaza*. The Wilder House Series in Politics, History, and Culture. Ithaca, NY: Cornell University Press, 1993.

Macbeth, Madge. *Over My Shoulder*. Toronto: Ryerson Press, 1953.

McCue, H. A. *The Only Good Indian: Essays by Canadian Indians*. Toronto: New Press, 1970.

Macfarlane, Heather and Armand Garnet Ruffo eds. *Introduction to Indigenous Literary Criticism*. Peterborough, ON: Broadview Press, 2016.

McClintock, Anne. *Imperial Leather: Race, Gender, and Sexuality in the Colonial Contest*. New York: Routledge, 1995.

McDougall, Robert L. *Totems: Essays on the Cultural History of Canada*. Ottawa: Tecumseh Press, 1990.

McKay, Ian. *Reasoning Otherwise: Leftists and the People's Enlightenment in Canada, 1890–1920*. Toronto: Between the Lines, 2008.

——. *Rebels, Reds, Radicals: Rethinking Canada's Left History*. Provocations. Toronto: Between the Lines, 2005.

Mallon, Florencia E. *Peasant and Nation: The Making of Postcolonial Mexico and Peru*. Berkeley: University of California Press, 1995.

Manuel, George and Michael Posluns, *The Fourth World: An Indian Reality*, Don Mills, ON: Collier Macmillan Canada, 1974.

Mehta, Uday Singh. *Liberalism and Empire: A Study in Nineteenth-Century British Liberal Thought*. Chicago: University of Chicago Press, 1999.

Merivale, Herman and Making of the Modern World–York University. *Lectures on Colonization and Colonies*. London: Longman, Orme, Brown, Green, and Longmans, 1841.

Miller, J. R. *Canada and the Aboriginal Peoples, 1867–1927*. Historical Booklet/Canadian Historical Association. Vol. 57. Ottawa: Canadian Historical Association, 1997.

——. *Compact, Contract, Covenant: Aboriginal Treaty-Making in Canada*. Toronto: University of Toronto Press, 2009.

——. *Skyscrapers Hide the Heavens: A History of Indian-White Relations in Canada*. 3rd ed. Toronto; Buffalo: University of Toronto Press, 2000.

——. *Lethal Legacy: Current Native Controversies in Canada*. Toronto: M&S, 2004.

Milloy, John Sheridan. *A National Crime: The Canadian Government and the Residential School System, 1879-1986*. Manitoba Studies in Native History. Vol. 11. Winnipeg: University of Manitoba Press, 1999.

Morton, W. L. *Manitoba: A History*. 2d-ed. Toronto: University of Toronto Press, 1967.

——. *Manitoba, the Birth of a Province*. Manitoba Record Society Publications. v. 1. Altona, MB: Printed by D.W. Friesen, 1965.

Nelson, George, Jennifer S. H. Brown, and Robert Brightman. *"The Orders of the Dreamed": George Nelson on Cree and Northern Ojibwa Religion and Myth, 1823*. Manitoba Studies in Native History. Vol. 3. Winnipeg: University of Manitoba Press, 1988.

Ondaatje, Michael. *From Ink Lake: Canadian Stories*. Toronto: Lester & Orpen Dennys, 1990.

Ory, Pascal and Jean-François Sirinelli. *Les Intellectuels En France, De l'Affaire Dreyfus à Nos Jours*. Collection U. Série Histoire Contemporaine. Paris: A. Colin, 1986.

Pelletier, W., & Poole, T. *No Foreign Land: The Biography of a North American Indian*. Toronto: McClelland, 1973.

Pettipas, Katherine. *Severing the Ties that Bind: Government Repression of Indigenous Religious Ceremonies on the Prairies*. Manitoba Studies in Native History. Vol. 7. Winnipeg: University of Manitoba Press, 1994.

Pick, Daniel. *Faces of Degeneration: A European Disorder c.1848–c.1918*. Cambridge: Cambridge University Press, 1989.

Pitts, Jennifer. *"Empire and Democracy: Tocqueville and the Algeria Question."* Journal of Political Philosophy 8, no. 3 (September 2000): 295-318.

Pitts, Jennifer. *A Turn to Empire: The Rise of Imperial Liberalism in Britain and France.* Princeton, NJ: Princeton Unversity Press, 2005.

Pratt, Mary Louise. *Imperial Eyes: Travel Writing and Transculturation.* 2nd ed. London; New York: Routledge, 2008.

Priestley, Herbert Ingram. *France Overseas: A Study of Modern Imperialism.* New York: Octagon Books, 1966 (originally published 1938).

Prochaska, David. *Making Algeria French: Colonialism in Bone, 1870–1920.* Cambridge: Cambridge University Press, 1990.

Redsky, James and James R. Stevens. *Great Leader of the Ojibway: Mis-Quona-Queb.* Toronto: McClelland and Stewart, 1972.

Reynaud Paligot, Carole. *Races, Racisme Et Antiracisme and Les Années 1930.* Paris: Presses Universitaires de France, 2007.

——. *La République Raciale: Paradigme Racial Et Idéologie Républicaine, 1860–1930.* Sciences, Histoire Et Société. 1re éd. Paris: Presses Universitaires de France, 2006.

Richardson, Boyce. *People of Terra Nullius: Betrayal and Rebirth in Aboriginal Canada.* Vancouver: Douglas & McIntyre, 1993.

——. *Strangers Devour the Land.* Vancouver: Douglas & McIntyre, 1991; 1975.

Roblès, Emmanuel. *Camus, Frère De Soleil.* Paris: Editions du Seuil, 1995.

——. *Les Rives Du Fleuve Bleu.* Paris: Seuil, 1990.

Rolland, Denis. *Vichy Et La France Libre Au Mexique.* Paris: L'Harmattan, 1990.

Ross, Malcolm Mackenzie. *Poets of the Confederation: Charles G.D. Roberts, Bliss Carman, Archibald Lampman, Duncan Campbell Scott.* New Canadian Library Original. Vol. 01. Toronto: McClelland and Stewart, 1960.

Roy, Wendy. *Maps of Difference: Canada, Women, and Travel.* Montreal; Ithaca: McGill-Queen's University Press, 2005.

Ruffo, Armand Garnet. *Opening in the Sky.* Penticton, BC: Theytus Books, 1994.

——. *Grey Owl: The Mystery of Archie Belaney.* Regina: Coteau Books, 1996.

——. *At Geronimo's Grave.* Regina: Coteau Books, 2001.

Said, Edward W. *Culture and Imperialism.* New York: Vintage Books, 1994.

——. *Orientalism.* 1st Vintage Books ed. New York: Vintage Books, 1979.

Sartre, Jean Paul. *Situations V: Colonialisme et Néo-Colonialisme.* Paris: Gallimard, 1964.

Saul, John Ralston. *The Birds of Prey.* New York: McGraw-Hill, 1977.

——. *A Fair Country: Telling Truths About Canada.* Toronto: Penguin Canada, 2008.

——. *The Comeback: How Aboriginals are Reconciling Canada.* Toronto: Penguin Canada, 2015.

Savage, Candace. *A Geography of Blood: Unearthing Memory from a Prairie Landscape.* Vancouver: Greystone Books and David Suzuki Foundation, 2012.

Schama, Simon. *Dead Certainties: Unwarranted Speculations.* 1st ed. New York: Knopf, 1991.

Scott, Duncan Campbell. *The Circle of Affection and Other Pieces in Prose and Verse.* Toronto: McClelland and Stewart, 1947.

——. *Selected Poems of Duncan Campbell Scott with a Memoir by E.K. Brown.* Ryerson Library of Canadian Poets. Toronto: Ryerson Press, 1951.

——. *Selected Stories of Duncan Campbell Scott.* Canadian Short Stories Series. 2nd ed. Vol. 1. Ottawa: University of Ottawa Press, 1975.

——. *Untitled Novel, Ca. 1905.* Moonbeam, ON: Penumbra Press, 1979.

——. *Beauty and Life.* Toronto: McClelland & Stewart, 1921.

——. *In the Village of Viger and Other Stories.* New Canadian Library; no. 92. Toronto: McClelland and Stewart, 1973.

——. *Via Borealis with Decorations by A.H. Howard.* Toronto: W. Tyrell, 1906.

——. *The Witching of Elspie: A Book of Stories.* Toronto: McClelland and Stewart, 1923.

Scott, Duncan Campbell and Arthur S. Bourinot. *More Letters of Duncan Campbell Scott*. 2nd series ed. Ottawa: The Editor, 1960.

Scott, Duncan Campbell and Matilda Ridout Edgar. *John Graves Simcoe. The Makers of Canada Series*. Vol. 4. London; Toronto: Oxford University Press, 1926.

Scott, Duncan Campbell, Archibald Lapman, and Arthur S. Bourinot. *Some Letters of Duncan Scott, Archibald Lampman & Others*. Ottawa: Published by the editor, 1959.

Scott, Duncan Campbell and Glenn Clever. *Selected Poetry*. Ottawa: Tecumseh Press, 1974.

Scott, Duncan Campbell, E. K. Brown, and Robert L. McDougall. *The Poet and the Critic: A Literary Correspondence between D.C. Scott and E.K. Brown*. Ottawa; Don Mills, ON: Carleton University Press; distributed by Oxford University Press Canada, 1983.

Scott, Duncan Campbell, Douglas Lochhead, and Raymond Souster. *Powassan's Drum: Poems of Duncan Campbell Scott*. Ottawa: Tecumseh Press, 1985.

Scott, Duncan Campbell and Leslie Ritchie. *Addresses, Essays, and Reviews*. 2 vols. London, ON: Canadian Poetry Press, 2000.

Scott, Duncan Campbell and Tracy Ware. *Uncollected Short Stories. Post-Confederation Poetry: Texts and Contexts*. London, ON: Canadian Poetry Press, 2001.

Scott, Duncan Campbell and Robert G. May. *In the Village of Viger: A Critical Edition*. Ottawa: Tecumseh Press, 2008.

Scott, James C. *Seeing Like a State: How Certain Schemes to Improve the Human Condition have Failed*. New Haven CT.; London: Yale University Press, 1998.

Shepard, Todd. *The Invention of Decolonization: The Algerian War and the Remaking of France*. Ithaca and London: Cornell University Press, 2006.

Siemens, Alfred H. *Between the Summit and the Sea: Central Veracruz in the Nineteenth Century*. Vancouver: University of British Columbia Press, 1990.

Simpson, Leanne Betasomosake. *As We Have Always Done*. Minneapolis: University of Minnesota Press, 2017.

——. *This Accident of Being Lost: Songs and Stories*. Toronto: House of Anansi, 2017.

——. *Islands of Decolonial Love*. Winnipeg: ARP Books, 2015.

——. *Dancing on Our Turtle's Back: Stories of Re-creation, Resurgence and a New Emergence*. Winnipeg: Arbeiter Ring Publishing, 2011.

Simpson, Leanne Betasomosake, ed. *Lighting The Eighth Fire: The Liberation, Resurgence and Protection of Indigenous Nations*. Winnipeg: Arbeiter Ring Publishing, 2008.

Sioui, Georges E. *For an Amerindian Autohistory*. Montreal: McGill-Queen's Press, 1992.

——. *Les Wendats: Une Civilisation Méconnue*. Sainte-Foy, QC: Presses de l'Université Laval, 1994.

——. *The Heritage of the Circle*. Vancouver: UBC Press, 1999.

——. *Huron-Wendat: Histoires de Kanatha Vues et Contées– Seen and Told*. Ottawa: Presses de l'Université d'Ottawa, 2008.

Sirinelli, Jean-François. *Deux Intellectuels Dans Le Siècle, Sartre Et Aron. Pour Une Histoire Du XXe Siècle*. Paris: Fayard, 1995.

——. *Génération Intellectuelle: Khâgneux Et Normaliens Dans l'Entre-Deux-Guerres*. Paris: Fayard, 1988.

Slama, Alain-Gérard. *La Guerre d'Algérie: Histoire d'Une Déchirure. Découvertes Gallimard*. Vol. 301. Paris: Gallimard, 1996.

Smith, Donald B. *Seen But Not Seen: Influential Canadians and the First Nations from the 1840s to Today*. Toronto, Buffalo, London: University of Toronto Press, 2021.

Smith, Keith D. *Liberalism, Surveillance, and Resistance. The West Unbound: Social and Cultural Studies Series*. Edmonton: AU Press, 2009.

Solberg, Carl E. *The Prairies and the Pampas: Agrarian Policy in Canada and Argentina, 1880-1930*. Stanford, CA: Stanford University Press, 1987.

Soustelle, Jacques. *Aimée Et Souffrante Algérie*. Paris: Plon, 1956.

——. *L'Anthropologie Française et Les Civilisations Autochtones De l'Amérique. The Zaharoff Lecture for 1988-9*. Oxford England; New York: Clarendon Press; Oxford University Press, 1989.

——. *L'Art Du Mexique Ancien. Et Civilisations*. Vol. 2. Paris: Arthaud, 1966.

——. *Les Azteques. Que Sais-Je?* Vol. No 1391. Paris: Presses

Universitaires de France, 1970.

——. *Deuxième Note Sur l'Ethnographie, La Préhistoire, l'Archéologie, l'Art Musulman, Les Beaux Arts En Algérie.* Alger: Imprimerie officielle, 1955.

——. *Le Drame Algérien Et La Décadence Française: Réponse a Raymond Aron.* Tribune Libre. Vol. 6. Paris: Plon, 1957.

——. *L'Esperance Trahie, 1958-1961.* Paris: Editions de l'Alma, 1962.

——. *Lettre Ouverte Aux Victimes De La Décolonisation.* Lettre Ouvert. Paris: A. Michel, 1973.

——. *Les Maya.* L'Odyssée. Paris: Flammarion, 1982.

——. *Mexique, Terre Indienne*; Orné De 16 Pages En héliogravure, De 2 Cartes Ed d'Une Planche En Couleurs. Paris: B. Grasset, 1936.

——. *Les Olmèques: La Plus Ancienne Civilisation Du Mexique.* Paris: Arthaud, 1979.

——. *La Page n'Est Pas Tournée.* Paris: La Table ronde, 1965.

——. *La Pensée Cosmologique Des Anciens Mexicains: (Représentation Du Monde Et De l'Espace).* Actualités Scientifiques Et Industrielles; 881. Ethnologie. Vol. 1. Paris: Hermann, 1939.

——. *Progrès Et Liberté: Discours Prononce a Lyon Le 12 Avril 1970.* Paris: La Table ronde, 1970.

——. *Les Quatre Soleils, Souvenirs Et Réflexions d'Un Ethnologue Au Mexique.* Terre Humaine. Paris: Plon, 1967.

——. *Rapport Sur La Recherche Française En Archéologie Et Anthropologie.* Paris: La Documentation française, 1975.

——. *La Vie Quotidienne Des Aztèques à La Veille De La Conquête Espagnole.* Vie Quotidienne. Paris: Hachette, littérature, 1982.

——. *La pensée Cosmologique Des Anciens Méxicains (représentation Du Monde Et De l'Espace) Conférences Prononcées Au Collège De France (Chaire d'Antiquités Américaines, Fondation Loubat), 1939.* Ethnologie. Vol. 1. Paris: Hermann & cie, 1940.

——. *La Longue Marche d'Israël.* Les Grandes Études Contemporaines. Paris: Fayard, 1968.

Soustelle, Jacques and Jean Dutourd. *Discours De Réception De M. Jacques Soustelle à l'Académie Française Et Réponse De M. Jean Dutourd*; [Suivis Des Allocutions Prononcées Lors De La Remise De l'Épée Par Alain Poher, Lévi-Strauss Et Jacques Soustelle]. Paris: Flammarion, 1984.

Snow, D. R., Harkin, M. E., Wurtzburg, S. J., and Campbell, L. *Skull Wars: Kennewick Man, Archaeology, and the Battle for Native American Identity.* Ethnohistory, 48(4), 713–722. United States: Duke University Press, 2001.

Spurr, David. *The Rhetoric of Empire: Colonial Discourse in Journalism, Travel Writing, and Imperial Administration.* Post-Contemporary Interventions. Durham: Duke University Press, 1993.

St-Onge, N., Campbell, M., Macdougall, B., and Podruchny, C. *Contours of a People: Metis Family, Mobility, and History.* Norman: University of Oklahoma Press, 2012.

Stich, K. Peter. *The Duncan Campbell Scott Symposium.* Re-Appraisals, Canadian Writers. Ottawa: University of Ottawa Press, 1980.

Stoler, Ann Laura. *Along the Archival Grain: Epistemic Anxieties and Colonial Common Sense.* Princeton: Princeton University Press, 2009.

Stoler, Ann Laura, Carole McGranahan, and Peter C. Perdue. *Imperial Formations.* School for Advanced Research Advanced Seminar Series. 1st ed. Santa Fe, NM; Oxford England: School for Advanced Research Press; James Currey, 2007.

Stora, Benjamin. *La Gangrène Et l'Oubli.* Paris: la Découverte, 1991.

Tennant, Paul. *Aboriginal Peoples and Politics: The Indian Land Question in British Columbia, 1849-1989.* Vancouver: University of British Columbia Press, 1990.

Talaga, Tanya. *Seven Fallen Feathers: Racism, Death, and Hard Truths in a Northern City.* Toronto: Anansi Nonfiction, 2017.

Tillion, Germaine. *L'Afrique Bascule Vers l'Avenir.* Collection "Regard Sur Notre Monde." Paris: Tirésias, 1999.

——. *L'Algérie En 1957.* Paris: Association Nationale Des Anciennes Déportés Et Internées De La Résistance, 1957.

——. *Il Était Une Fois l'Ethnographie.* Points. Vol. 513. Paris: Éd. du Seuil, 2004.

——. *Le Harem Et Les Cousins.* Points. Civilisation. Vol.

141. Paris: Éditions du Seuil, 1982; 1966.

——. *La Traversée Du mal entretien Avec Jean Lacouture.* Paris: Arléa, 2000.

Tilly, Charles. *Big Structures, Large Processes, Huge Comparisons.* New York: Russell Sage Foundation, 1984.

Tippett, Maria. *Emily Carr, A Biography.* (Toronto: Oxford University Press, 1979).

Titley, E. Brian. *A Narrow Vision – Duncan Campbell Scott and the Administration of Indian Affairs in Canada.* Vancouver: UBC Press, 1986.

Tocqueville, Alexis de. *Tocqueville Sur l'Algérie, Présentation Par Seloua Luste Boulbina.* Paris: GF Flammarion, 2003.

Todorov, Tzvetan. *Le siècle De Germaine Tillion.* Paris: Éditions du Seuil, 2007.

——. *Mémoire Du Mal, Tentation Du Bien.* Paris: R. Laffont, 2000.

——. *Nous Et Les Autres: La Réflexion Française Sur La Diversité Humaine.* Couleur Des Idées. Paris: Éditions du Seuil, 1989.

——. *La Conquête De l'Amérique: La Question De l'Autre.* Paris: Éditions du Seuil, 1982.

Trinh, T. Minh-Ha. *Woman, Native, Other: Writing Postcoloniality and Feminism.* Bloomington: Indiana University Press, 1989.

University League for Social Reform and Peter H. Russell. *Nationalism in Canada.* Toronto; New York: McGraw-Hill, 1966.

Urquhart, Jane. *The Penguin Book of Canadian Short Stories.* Toronto: Penguin Canada, 2007.

Vasconcelos, José. *Obras Completas.* México: Libreros Mexicanos Unidos, 1957.

Vaughan, Mary K. and Stephen E. Lewis. *The Eagle and the Virgin: Nation and Cultural Revolution in Mexico, 1920-1940.* Durham NC: Duke University Press, 2006.

Vecsey, Christopher. *Traditional Ojibwa Religion and its Historical Changes.* Memoirs Series. Vol. 152. Philadelphia: American Philosophical Society, 1983.

Vowel, Chelsea. *Indigenous Writes: A Guide To First Nations, Métis & Inuit Issues in Canada.* Winnipeg MB: Highwater Press, 2016.

Author E. Brian Titley, in Ottawa for the 2015 annual meeting of the Canadian Historical Association.

Warkentin, Germaine. *Canadian Exploration Literature: An Anthology.* Toronto, ON: Oxford University Press, 1993.

Watkins, Mel and University League for Social Reform. *Dene Nation, the Colony within.* Toronto; Buffalo: University of Toronto Press, 1977.

Weaver, Sally M. *Making Canadian Indian Policy: The Hidden Agenda 1968-70.* Studies in the Structure of Power, Decision-Making in Canada. Vol. 9. Toronto: University of Toronto Press, 1981.

Zemmour, Éric. *Destin Français.* Paris: Albin Michel, 2018.

ARTICLES

Adelman, Jeremy and Stephen Aron. "From Borderlands to Borders: Empires, Nation-States, and the Peoples in between in North American History." *The American Historical Review* 104, no. 3 (Jun., 1999): 814-841.

Alfred, Taiaiake. "From Noble Savage to Righteous

Warrior: Regenerating and Reinscribing Indigenous Presences." University of British Columbia, Vancouver, uploaded by UBC May 13, 2010, March 6, 2010, 2010.

Bantjes, Adrian A. "Saints, Sinners and State Formation: Local Religion and Cultural Revolution in Mexico." In *The Eagle and the Virgin: Nation and Cultural Revolution in Mexico, 1920-1940*, edited by Mary Kay Vaughan and Stephen E. Lewis. Durham: Duke University Press, 2006.

Bederman, Gail. *Manliness & Civilization: A Cultural History of Gender and Race In the United States, 1880-1917*. Chicago: University of Chicago Press, 1995.

Bentley, D. M. R. "Shadows in the Soul: Racial Haunting in the Poetry of Duncan Campbell Scott." *University of Toronto Quarterly* 75, No. 2, Spring 2006 (2006).

Borrows, John. "Drawing Out Law: Re-Imagining First Nation–Crown Relations through Indigenous Legal Traditions." Donald Creighton Lecture, University of Toronto, Department of History, March 18, 2010, 2010. Accessed on-line April, 2010 http://mediacast.ic.utoronto.ca/20100318-HIST/msl.htm.

Brading, David A. "Manuel Gamio and Official Indigenismo in Mexico." *Bulletin of Latin American Research* 7, no. 1 (1988): 75-89.

Campbell, James. "Betwixt and Between: Camus was a son of Algeria – the 'kingdom of poverty' that nourished all he wrote." *The Wall Street Journal*, May 4, 2013, C5.

Cullingham, James. "Now Ain't the Time for Your Tears." *Active History*, June 28, 2021. http://activehistory.ca/2021/06/now-aint-the-time-for-your-tears/.

Curry, Bill and Howlatt, Karen. "Natives Died in Droves as Ottawa Ignored Warnings." *The Globe and Mail*, April 24, 2007, 2007, sec. First.

——. "Ottawa Orders Panel to Probe TB Deaths." *The Globe and Mail*, April 25, 2007, 2007, sec. A.

Davin, Nicholas Flood. *The Demands of the North-West! [Microform]: A Speech Delivered in the House of Commons, Ottawa, on Wednesday, February 27th, 1889*. CIHM/ICMH Microfiche Series = CIHM/ICMH Collection De Microfiches; no. 30128.

Doremus, Anne. "Indigenismo, Mestizaje, and National Identity in Mexico." *Mexican Studies/Estudios Mexicanos* 17, no. 2 (2001): 375-402.

——. Twelve Hundred Miles by Canoe among the Indians in Northern Waters. *Canada: An Illustrated Weekly Journal for all Interested in the Dominion*, November 24 and December 22, 1906; January 5 &19, February 2 & 16; March 16, 1907.

Duffy, Andrew. "The policy battle that set the stage for a century of residential school death, misery, grief," *The Ottawa Citizen*, June 12, 2021. https://ottawacitizen.com/news/local-news/the-policy-battle-that-set-the-stage-for-a-century-of-residential-school-death-misery-grief.

Edgar, Pelham. "Duncan Campbell Scott." *Dalhousie Review* 7, (April, 1927).

Edison, Paul N. "Conquest Unrequited: French Expeditionary Science in Mexico, 1864-1867." *French Historical Studies* 26, no. 3 (2003): 459-495.

Fabre, Daniel. "L'Ethnologie Française à La Croisée Des Engagements (1940-1945)." In *Résistants Et Résistance*. Paris: Harmattan, 1997.

Farber, Bernie M. "The Troubling Legacy of Duncan Campbell Scott." *The Ottawa Citizen*, August 28, 2013, Op-Ed Section. Accessed on-line August 29, 2013. http://www.ottawacitizen.com/opinion/op-edtroubling+legacy+Duncan+Campbell+Scott/8844210/story.html.

Fischer, Doug. "The Grim Legacy of Treaty 9." *Ottawa Citizen*, 2005, sec. News.

Friedlander, Judith. "The National Indigenist Institute of Mexico Reinvents the Indian: The Pame Example." *American Ethnologist* 13, no. 2 (May, 1986): 363-367.

Gruber, Jacob W. "Ethnographic Salvage and the Shaping of Anthropology." *American Anthropologist* 72, no. 6 (Dec., 1970): 1289-1299.

Hayes, Joy Elizabeth. "National Imaginings on the Air: Radio in Mexico, 1920-1950." In *The Eagle and the Virgin: Nation and Cultural Revolution in Mexico, 1920-1940*, edited by Mary Kay Vaughan and Stephen E. Lewis, 243-258. Durham: Duke University Press, 2006.

Herskovits, Melville J. "Anthropology During the War." *American Anthropologist* 47, no. 4 (Oct.-Dec., 1945): 639-641.

Howlett, Karen and Curry, Bill. "Children Left 'Angry at the World.'" *The Globe and Mail*, April 25, 2007.

Hu-DeHart, Evelyn. "Globalization and its Discontents: Exposing the Underside." *Frontiers: A Journal of Women Studies* 24, no. 2 (2004): 244-260.

Hunter, Justine. "Is Growing Up in the Care of the State

any Better for Native Children Today?" *The Globe and Mail*, Jun 13, 2008.

Jenness, Diamond. *Canada's Indian Problems*. Washington: Smithsonian Institute, 1943.

Kaplan, Alice. "New Perspectives on Camus' Algerian Chronicles." In *Albert Camus Algerian Chronicles*. Translated by Arthur Goldhammer, 1-18. Cambridge, MA and London: The Belknap Press of Harvard University, 2013.

Lee, Dennis. "Cadence, Country, Silence: Writing in Colonial Space." *Boundary 2* 3, no. 1, A Canadian Issue (Autumn, 1974): 151-168.

Lomnitz, Claudio. "Final Reflections: What was Mexico's Cultural Revolution?" In *The Eagle and the Virgin: Nation and Cultural Revolution in Mexico, 1920-1940*, edited by Mary Kay Vaughan and Stephen E. Lewis, 334-349. Durham: Duke University Press, 2006.

Lustick, Ian S. "Two-State Illusion: The Idea of a State for Palestinians and One for Israelis is a Fantasy that Blinds Us and Impedes Progress." T*he New York Times, Sunday Review*, 1.

Lynch, Gerald. "An Endless Flow: D.C. Scott's Indian Poems." http://www.lib.unb.ca/Texts/SCL/bin/get.cgi?directory=vol7_1/&filename=Lynch.htm (accessed March, 2007).

Martin, Marc. ""Radio-Algerie," Un Acteur Méconnu De Mai 1958." *Vingtieme Siecle.Revue d'Histoire* no. 19, Numero special: Religion et politique aux etats-unis (Jul.-Sep., 1988): 97-99.

Martinière, Guy. "L'Expédition Mexicaine De Napoléon III Dans l'Historiographie Française." *Revue d'Histoire Moderne Et Contemporaine (1954-)* 21, no. 1, L'historiographie du Second Empire (Jan.-Mar., 1974): pp. 142-173.

McNab, David. "Herman Merivale and the Native Question, 1837-1861." *Albion: A Quarterly Journal Concerned with British Studies* 9, no. 4 (Winter, 1977): 359-384.

Milloy, John S. "John A's 'Hostages:' state formation and residential school education for First Nations' children," unpublished paper provided to the author, June 2021.

Mosby, Ian. "Administering Colonial Science: Nutrition Research and Human Biomedical Experimentation in Aboriginal Communities and Residential Schools,

1942–1952." *Histoire Sociale/Social History* 46, no. 91 (2013): 145-172.

Morton, W. L. "British North America and A Continent in Dissolution, 1861-1871." *History* no. NS 47 (1962).

Newhouse, David. "Indigenous Peoples, The Transformation of Canada and the Possibility of Reconciliation." Institute for Research on Public Policy, 2017.

"Remains of 215 Children Found at Former Kamloops Residential School: First Nation." *Vancouver Sun*, May 28, 2021. https://vancouversun.com/news/local-news/remains-of-215-children-found-at-former-kamloops-residential-school-first-nation.

Reparaz-Ruiz (de),G. and Harold E. Davis. "Hispanic and Hispanic-American Studies in France." *The Hispanic American Historical Review* 26, no. 3 (Aug., 1946): 425-436.

Rolland, Denis. "Jacques Soustelle, de l'Ethnologie à la Politique." *Guerres Mondiales Et Conflits Contemporains* 46, no. 180 (07, 1995): 171-185.

Rutherdale, Myra, Erin Dolmage and Carolyn Podruchny, "Bodies of Water Not Bodies of Women, Canadian Media Images of the Idle No More Movement," *Active History*, May 22, 2015. http://activehistory.ca/papers/bodies-of-water-not-bodies-of-women-canadian-media-images-of-the-idle-no-more-movement.

Rutherdale, Myra and J. R. Miller. "Lest we Forget." *The Globe and Mail*, June 13, 2008.

Sartre, Jean-Paul. "Préface." In Frantz Fanon, *Les Damnés de la Terre*. Paris: Librairie François Maspero, 1961.

Salutin, Rick. "Issues of Apology and Power." *The Globe and Mail*, Jun 13, 2008.

Shepard, Todd. "Algeria, France, Mexico, UNESCO: A Transnational History of Anti-Racism and Decolonization, 1932–1962." *Journal of Global History*, 6(2), 273–297. Cambridge, UK: Cambridge University Press, 2011.

——. "How Ethnographic Research in 1930s Mexico Shaped French Efforts to Fight Algerian Nationalism in 1955." Cambridge, April 6-7, 2009.

Duncan Campbell Scott. "The Last of the Indian Treaties." *Scribner's* 40, 1906.

——. "Indian Affairs 1763-1841," in *Canada and Its Provinces*, eds. Adam Shortt and A. G. Doughty (Toronto:

Edinburgh Univ. Press, 1913), Vol. 4, 695-725.

——. "Indian Affairs, 1840-1867," in Shortt and Doughty, eds. Vol. 7, 331-362.

——. "Indian Affairs, 1867-1912," in Shortt and Doughty, eds. Vol. 7, 594-626.

Tobias, John L. "Protection, Civilization, Assimilation: An Outline History of Canada's Indian Policy." *Protection, Civilization, Assimilation: An Outline History of Canada's Indian Policy* (1983): 39-55.

Trigger, Bruce. "The Historian's Indian: Native Americans in Canadian Historical Writing from Charlevoix to the Present." *Canadian Historical Review* LXVII, no. 3 (1986): 315-342.

Turner, Dale. "Liberalism's Last Stand: Aboriginal Sovereignty and Minority Rights." In *Aboriginal Rights and Self-Government: The Canadian and Mexican Experience in North American Perspective*, edited by Cook, Curtis and Juan D. Lindau. Montreal: McGill-Queen's University Press, 2000.

Tyre, Stephen. "From Algérie Française to France Musulmane: Jacques Soustelle and the Myths and Realities of 'Integration,' 1955–1962." *French History* 20, no. 3 (09, 2006): 276-296.

DISSERTATIONS / M.A. THESES

Balvet, Dominique. "Jacques Soustelle Et l'Algérie Française: Gaullisme Et Antigaullisme." Doctorat d'Histoire sous la direction de Jean-Francois Sirinelli, Université Charles de Gaulle Lille 3, 2003.

Crossley, John Edward. "The Making of Canadian Indian Policy to 1946." PhD, University of Toronto (Canada), 1987.

Desbordes, Christian. "Jacques Soustelle et la défense de l'occident." Thèse du Doctorat en Science Politique, Université d'Auvergne, 2000.

Fairweather, Joan G. "Is this Apartheid? Aboriginal Reserves and Self-Government in Canada 1960-1982." Université d'Ottawa/University of Ottawa, 1993. M.A. Thesis in History.

Laurière, Christine. "Paul Rivet (1876-1958), Le Savant Et Le Politique. Thèse dirigée Par M. Jean Jamin, Directeur d'Études à l'EHESS." Doctorat nouveau régime, École des Hautes Études en Sciences Sociales, 2006.

Leslie, John F. "Commissions of Inquiry into Indian Affairs in the Canadas, 1828-1858: Evolving Corporate Memory for the Indian Department." M.A. Institute of Canadian Studies, Carleton University, Ottawa, Ontario, 1984.

Milloy, John Sheridan. "The Era of Civilization: British Policy for the Indians of Canada, 1830-1860." Thesis for Doctor of Philosophy, University of Oxford, 1978.

Soustelle, Jacques. *La Famille Otomi-Pame Du Mexique Central*. Université de Paris. Travaux Et Mémoires De l'Institut d'Ethnologie. Vol. 26. Paris: Institut d'ethnologie, 1937.

GOVERNMENTAL REPORTS

Davin, Nicholas Flood. *Report on Industrial Schools for Indians and Half-Breeds*, Government of Canada, Ottawa, 1879. [Microform]. CIHM/ICMH Microfiche Series = CIHM/ICMH Collection De Microfiches; no. 03651; CIHM/ICMH Microfiche Series; no. 03651; CIHM/ICMH Microfiche Series; no. 03651.

Canada and edited by Leslie, John and Maguire, Ron. *The Historical Development of the Indian Act, 2nd Edition*, Ottawa: Indian and Northern Affairs Canada, 1978.

Canada and Donna Lea Hawley. *The Indian Act Annotated*. 2nd ed. Toronto: Carswell, 1986.

Government of Canada. "Statement of Apology to Former Students of Indian Residential Rchools June 11, 2008." https://www.rcaanc-cirnac.gc.ca/eng/1100100015644/157 1589171655.

Indian and Northern Affairs Canada, *People to People Nation to Nation: A Consultation Document Summarizing the Main Findings and Recommendations of the Royal Commission on Aboriginal Peoples*, Ottawa, 1997.

National Inquiry into Missing and Murdered Indigenous Women and Girls, *Reclaiming Power and Place – The Final Report of the Inquiry into Missing and Murdered Indigenous Women and Girls*, Vancouver, 2019.

Truth and Reconciliation Commission of Canada. *Honouring the Truth, reconciling for the future: Summary of the Final Report of the Truth and Reconciliation Commission*, 2015.

——. *Calls to Action*, National Centre for Truth and Reconciliation, University of Manitoba, Winnipeg, 2016.

AUDIO VISUAL MATERIALS / FILMS

Amelio, Gianni, dir. *Le premier homme*, (Rome and Paris, Cattleya and France 3 Cinema, 2011).

Bouchareb, Rachid, dir. *Indigènes* (2006) DVD distribution: Mars Distribution.

Boudo, Marcel. *La Splendeur De La Mexique–Les Mayas*, written by Jacques Soustelle. Vol. TV. Paris: TF1, 1976; *Les Aztèques*, written by Jacques Soustelle. Vol. TV. Paris and Mexico City: France 3 and Televisa, 1978. *Chilam Balam*, written by Jacques Soustelle. Paris: France 2, 1981.

Bousbia, Safinez, dir. *El Gusto* (2011) Ireland, Quidam Productions.

Brody, Hugh, dir. *Time Immemorial*. From the documentary series *As Long As The Rivers Flow*. (Toronto: Tamarack Productions in Association with The National Film Board of Canada, 1991) DVD distribution: Icarus Films, New York; Tamarack Productions, Toronto.

Campbell, Peter, dir. and Andy Bryce (prod.). *Finding Peter Bryce*, Moving Images Distribution, Vancouver, 2018.

Cullingham, James, dir. *Duncan Campbell Scott: The Poet and the Indians*. (Toronto: Tamarack Productions in co-production with the National Film Board of Canada, 1995) DVD distribution: VTape, Toronto.

——. *We Have Such Things At Home*. (Toronto, Tamarack Productions, 1997) DVD distribution VTape, Toronto.

Demy, Jacques, dir. *The Umbrellas of Cherbourg*. (1964) Beta Films, Madeleine Films and Parc Film. United States; Port Washington, NY: Koch Lorber; Distribution: Koch Vision.

Girard, Tess and Ryan Noth, dirs. *The Road to Webequie*, (2016) Fifth Town Films, Prince Edward County ON.

Godard, Jean-Luc, dir. *Le Petit Soldat* (1963) DVD distribution: Rialto Pictures.

Lledo, Jean-Pierre, dir. *Algérie, Histoires à ne pas Dire* (2007). DVD distribution: Albarès Collection Documentaire.

McLaren, Nadia, dir. *Muffins for Granny*, 2006.

Oelhoffen, David, dir. *Loin des Homes* (2014) Paris: One World Films.

Obomsawin, Alanis, dir. *The People of the Kattawapiskat River* (Montréal: National Film Board of Canada, 2012).

——. *Trick or Treaty?* (2014) (Montréal, National Film Board of Canada, 2014).

Ostroff, Michael, dir. *Winds of Heaven: Emily Carr, Carvers and the Spirits of the Forest*. (Toronto: White Pine Pictures, 2010) DVD distribution: McNabb Connolly.

Paltiel, Candida, dir. *Canada's Rings of Fire* (2015) ALJAZEERA-WITNESS, A Mining Stories Production for Al Jazeera.

Pontecorvo, Gillo, dir. *The Battle of Algiers*, (1966) Casbah Films and Igor Film. Irvington, NY: Distribution: Criterion.

Resnais, Alain, dir. *Muriel, ou, Le Temps d'Un Retour*, (1963) DVD Distribution: Koch Lorber Films.

Rial, Carmen, dir. *Germaine Tillion*. Nucleo de antropologia audiovisual e estudos da imagem. 2007.

Richardson, Boyce, dir. *Flooding Job's Garden*, from the documentary series *As Long As The Rivers Flow*, (Toronto: Tamarack Productions in association with National Film Board of Canada, 1991), dist. Tamarack Productions.

Simpson, Leanne, dir. *Sing Them Home,* short film accessed at RefRame Film Festival 2021, Nogojiwanong (Peterborough, ON).

Sioui Labelle, René, dir. *Kanata: L'héritage des Enfants de Aataentsic*. Office nationale du film du Canada, 1998.

Visconti, Luchino, dir. *Lo Straniero* (1967).

RADIO DOCUMENTARY

Moore, Christopher. *George MacMartin's Big Canoe Trip*. Christopher Moore. first broadcast December 19, 2011. Ideas, CBC Radio, Canadian Broadcasting Corporation.

PUBLIC PRESENTATION / CONFERENCE PAPER

Diabo, Russell, "Canada's War on First Nations," Temagami Trent Colloquium, Camp Wanapitei, Temagami, Ontario, September 21, 2012.

Jackson, Julian, "Interpreting de Gaulle," Centre for the Study of France and the Francophone World, Munk School, University of Toronto, April 24, 2019.

VISUAL CREDITS

Please note the author has exercised due diligence and undertaken an exhaustive search for copyright permissions of all images contained within this publication, to ensure fair dealing compliance. Please contact the author should you have any questions.

Archives of Ontario: p.9 Series C 275-1-0-5-S7614 At the Flying Post; p.21 Series C 275-1-0-6-S7612 Helen Sky – Flying Post; p.22 Series F 1075-18-0-75 D.C. Scott and Rupert Brooke, Ottawa; p.26 Series C 275-1-0-6-S7649 At Chapleau – Chief Cheesequimime; p.53 Series C 275-2-0-2-S7522. Jimmie Suaine – Guide; p.145 Series C 275-3-0-2-S7523 Snake Rapids – Albany River; p.186 Series C 275-1-0-6-S7670 Half breed school – Temagami; p.195 Series F 1075-18-0-57 D.C. Scott: portrait and portrait with wife

Courtesy John Aylen: p.127

James Cullingham: pp.13; 14; 16; 29; 42; 80; 155; 166; 180; 183; 219; 222; 235

Thomas Fisher Rare Book Library, University of Toronto: p.64 Duncan Campbell Scott Papers (MS Coll 13), Box 1B, Folder 2; p.204 Duncan Campbell Scott Papers (MS Coll 13), Box 1B, Folder 18; p.205 Duncan Campbell Scott Papers (MS Coll 13), Box 1B, Folder 19

Éditions Grasset – **Jacques Soustelle:**
p.61 Soustelle, Jacques. *Mexique, Terre Indienne*. Paris: B. Grasset, 1936, as seen on page 12

Scot Kyle: p.63

Library and Archives Canada: p.142 fonds/e011080269. Boys dormitory at Cross Lake Indian Residential School, Cross Lake, Manitoba, probably February 1940

Éditions Plon – **Jacques Soustelle:** pp.111 Soustelle, Jacques. *Aimée et souffrante Algérie*, Paris, Plon, 1956, as seen on page 32; p.132 *Aimée…* as seen on page 48; p.169 *Aimée…* as seen on page 136; p.201 *Aimée…* as seen on the front cover; p.214 *Aimée…* as seen on page 136

"TIME" magazine: p.106

Musée du quai Branly – **Jacques Chirac:** pp.35 *Numéro de gestion: PV0070333. Chef Lacandon et ses deux femmes. San Quentin, Chiapas*; p.53 PP0001821. *Jeune Lacandon portant une tunique en coton*; p.54 PV0071168. *Mexique. Lacandons de San Quentin avec les membres de l'expédition Soustelle*; p.70 Z796661. *Relevé d'une peinture sur un oratoire à San Bartolo del LLano, Ixtlahuaca, Mêx, Mexique (peuple mazahua) exécuté en 1933 par M. Mme J. Soustelle*; p.198 *Numéro de gestion: PP0001581. Jacques Soustelle parlant aux ouvriers travaillant à la construction du Palais de Chaillot en 1936-37*

Queen's University Archives: p.192 Locator 2001.1-08-7

Li Robbins: Outside back cover

Tracey Robinson: p.11

Association Germaine Tillion: p.155 Copyright *Association Germaine Tillion*

Nhu Vo (Belle): pp.47; 51; 77

Courtesy Chanie Wenjack School for Indigenous Studies, Trent University: p.184

Alex Williams: p.116

INDEX

DESIGN and PRODUCTION CREDITS

Book and cover design:

    Michael H. Maynard PhD, FGDC

Maps:

    Nhu Vo (Belle)

Copy editing:

    Tom Bartsiokas, with Tanecia Haynes-
    Mckenzie, Jason Ma and Cynthia Penman

Historical consultant:

    Erin Dolmage

Proofreading:

    Elizabeth Wilton

Photo rights management:

    Janet Suek

Photo technical support:

    Monica Shaw